National Park Guide

National Park Guide

By MICHAEL FROME

RAND McNALLY & COMPANY Chicago / New York / San Francisco

PHOTO CREDITS

Acknowledgment is made to the following sources for use of the photographs appearing in this book, on the pages listed: Independence Hall National Historical Park, viii; David Muench, xiv, 34-35, 61, 67, 86, 126, 139, 142, 171, 175, 178; M. Woodbridge Williams for National Park Service, 1, 14-15, 205; National Park Service, 2, 8, 10, 13, 70, 80, 90, 114, 137 (bottom), 150, 166, 167, 195, 196, 199, 201; Utah Travel Council, 4, 18; Jack E. Boucher for National Park Service, 6; Hans Wendler from FPG, 12; New Mexico Department of Development, 20, 138 (top); Dennis Hallinan from FPG, 24; J. S. Dixon for U.S. Fish and Wildlife Service, 25; Franke Keating, 26; Everglades National Park, 29; Ray Manley for Glacier Park, Inc., 30; Rex G. Schmidt for U.S. Fish and Wildlife Service, 39; Glen Fishback for Grand Teton Lodge Co., 40; S. J. Ovenshine from FPG, 45; Jack Zehrt, 49, 104-05, 122-23, 134 (left); Haleakala National Park, 51; Robert Wenkam, 52, 144 (left); Arkansas Publicity and Parks Commission, 56; Richard Frear for National Park Service, 58, 152; Kentucky Travel Division, 64; Ralph D. Churchill for National Park Service, 73; Ray Atkeson, 76-77, 82, 92, 98, 173, 174, 180, 183; Bob Haugen for National Park Service, 85; Fred Mang, Jr., for National Park Service, 89; Darwin Van Campen from DPI, 94; Michael Alexis for Caneel Bay Plantation, 108-09; Minnesota Department of Economic Development, 110; Ken Short, 116; William S. Keller for National Park Service, 120, 143, 202; Bruce Roberts, 133, 170; Washington Convention and Visitors Bureau, 134 (right), 135 (left); United Air Lines, 135 (right), 163; Dick Kent, 137 (top); American Airlines, 138 (bottom); Appomattox Court House National Historical Park, 141; 1607, Inc., Jamestown, 144 (right); Charleston (S.C.) Chamber of Commerce, 149; Stanford University Museum of Art, 151 (top); Abby Aldrich Rockefeller Folk Art Center, 151 (bottom); Nebraska Game Commission, 152 (left); Philadelphia Convention and Tourist Bureau, 153; Carol Bales, 154; Lexington Historical Society, 156; Grant Heilman, 157; New Hampshire Visitors Bureau, 158; Rhode Island Development Council, 162; Steve McCutcheon, 177; North Carolina Department of Conservation, 189; Neil Amerino, 209.

Preface to the Ninth Edition

Over the last twenty-five years, essentially the post-World War II era, I have not only been traveling continually to the national parks and trying to interpret these special places through books and magazine articles, but have also been searching for their meaning, their true place and purpose in the American scheme of things.

What is the central point of the national parks?

Because they are national parks are they, in fact, secure for the benefit of our generation and generations still unborn?

The first question may seem simple, but the answer is most elusive. In the course of time I've read volumes on park philosophy and practice. I've discussed all sides of the question with directors of the National Park Service, secretaries of the Interior, United States senators and representatives, park concessioners, outdoorsmen, well-versed conservationists, and with park superintendents, naturalists, and rangers out on the trail and around the campfire.

I've reviewed the history involved. When Congress in 1872 designated Yellowstone as the first national park—first anywhere in the world—it declared this wonderland would henceforth be "set apart as a public park or pleasuring ground for the benefit and enjoyment of the people."

The principle behind the law was that such treasures were too precious to belong to individuals to be exploited for profit, but should be held forever as a public trust.

The exact sort of pleasuring ground that Congress had in mind was not spelled out. If it had been, would the concepts of 1872 be as valid or hold the same meaning one century later?

In 1916, an Organic Act was adopted creating a new federal agency, the National Park Service. It declared the purpose of national parks, monuments, and reservations would be "to conserve the scenery and the natural and historic objects and the wild life therein, and to provide for the enjoyment of the same in such manner and by such means as will leave them unimpaired for the enjoyment of future generations."

Again, the definition of function poses questions. Which comes first, conservation or enjoyment? Satisfying the present generation or future generations? The rights of man to use the land for his enjoyment or the rights of wildlife to its own sanctuary?

John Muir, pioneer spokesman for the national parks, once wrote: "Thousands of tired, nerve-shaken, over-civilized people are beginning to find out that going to the mountains is going home; that wildness is a necessity, and that mountain parks and reservations are useful not only as fountains of timber and irrigating rivers, but as fountains of life."

Enos Mills, known as the "father of Rocky Mountain National Park," said it almost the same way: "A national park is a fountain of life. Without parks and outdoor life all that is best in civilization will be smothered. To save ourselves—to enable us to live at our best and happiest, parks are necessary. Within national parks there is room —glorious room—room in which to find ourselves, in which to think and hope, to dream and plan, to rest, and resolve."

Both were right, I'm sure; but it strikes me there is now something at least equally transcendent in assaying the role of national parks in our urbanized technological age.

This was brought home recently when I was reading *Faces of the Wilderness,* a book by Harvey Broome, the late president of the Wilderness Society. I knew Mr. Broome very well as a gentle spirit, sensitive to the needs of nature and his fellow man, always acting with tolerance and good humor. On my first hike with him in the Great Smoky Mountains, we ventured to the Chimney Tops—a steep climb, almost vertical for several hundred feet, hand over hand from one rocky perch to the next. It was raining and I dared to complain against the gods. Harvey answered with a laugh. "You don't complain about weather in the Smokies. You just learn to accept it!" I laughed, too, and learned.

In the book he wrote about the ever-present crowd scene in Yellowstone: "The atmosphere was holidayish but there was no wilderness. There was display without strong personal impact. People swarmed from their cars to see the buffalo, as though they were starved for the sight of something old and natural and primordial. And yet, so far have we moved from the past, several nearly grown boys referred to the bison as a deer."

When such events transpire in our national parks, one can be sure the nation is in trouble. Americans need to know the difference between bison and deer and to understand the role played by each in the interwoven web of life. We deeply need the humility to know ourselves as part of this great community which is much vaster than the community of man alone. "If we do not permit the earth to produce beauty and joy it will not, in the end, produce food either," the late Joseph Wood Krutch declared. "If we do not value it as beautiful as well as useful, it will ultimately cease to be even useful."

Thus a national park offers a uniquely equipped setting where Americans, starting in their tender years, can learn love and reverence for nature and, through nature, for one another. As I see it, this is the central point and purpose of national parks in our age. Let us make the most of them as such!

Now as to the second question concerning the fate and future of the national parks, it strikes me that laws of the past are not quite adequate of themselves. Threats against parklands are unending. I will cite only a few.

In the Everglades, for instance, a constant drying process as a result of South Florida drainage projects has caused depletion of native wildlife, damaging fires, and conditions favorable to invading exotic plants and animals. The most notorious recent invader is the Brazilian pepper, or *schinus,* which gains a foothold on dry hammocks and chokes out vegetation. The Park Service has found it very difficult to cope with either the water shortage or these invaders. The Everglades are also still threatened by the superjetport designed to be its neighbor. Will the airport be moved or will it in time be completed and destroy the park as it is now known?

In the West, the pristine air and quiet of Grand Teton National Park and of the valley known as Jackson Hole are endangered by persistent pressures to enlarge the local airport to accommodate jet aircraft. The Grand Canyon is in danger, too. Just a few years ago the canyon was the focus of a hard-fought battle over the proposed construction of two dams which would have damaged the very heart of the area. Current proposals to enlarge the Havasupai Indian Reservation at the expense of the national park would invite the strong possibility of commercial exploitation. Redwood National Park is in serious trouble because of extensive logging on high slopes around its borders. According to a government report, erosion caused by lumbering operations "could eventually cause the downfall of many of the park's largest redwoods."

Road building proposals are pending in Bighorn Canyon National Recreation Area and in many parks, including Canyonlands, Great Smoky Mountains, and Guadalupe Mountains. On the face of it, a new road may seem advantageous, but the injection of motor vehicles, together with noise, exhaust fumes, and large numbers of people, has predictable results: contamination, disturbance, refuse. And as visitation increases, the highway strip will need to be widened. The natural setting will change to an urban environment.

On many fronts, and without being recognized, the national park heritage shows signs of dissipation. The thoughtful visitor can help by studying the scene for himself, asking questions of park rangers and naturalists, joining conservation organizations (such as Friends of the Earth, National Parks and Conservation Association, Sierra Club, and Wilderness Society), writing letters to editors, and writing letters to congressmen.

The Rand McNally *NATIONAL PARK GUIDE* has been designed since the first edition in 1967 to give practical guidance—a clear picture of all the facilities in the parks and how to use and enjoy them fully—in the hope that appreciation will follow. I have tried to emphasize that enjoyment of the parks is not restricted to rugged outdoorsmen. Even invalids can thrill to the rare wonder and beauty of the wild precincts. If the book has made friends and supporters of the national parks' cause, nothing could be more gratifying.

I am ever grateful to the entire Rand McNally organization for its faith in this work, notably to two editors, Edwin Snyder and Sylvia McNair, for their patience and helpfulness, and to Don Eldredge and Donald Carey of the Trade Publishing Division.

I am also grateful to the National Park Service for its continuing cooperation, both at its Washington headquarters and throughout the field. It is a pleasure to be on the ground, where personnel have always been cooperative and friendly.

Finally, I abhor listing rules of conduct. The most valid counsel I can offer is to use the national parks as they were intended. Walk in the quiet places, unhurriedly. It isn't really how much distance one covers, but how much one absorbs. The slower pace expands the dimensions of time. It broadens appreciation of the meaning of earth to mankind.

Happy traveling, and welcome to the parks!

Michael Frome

Contents

A Bicentennial Preview

The nation is nearing the Bicentennial of the American Revolution. Advance interest is already high. Many Revolutionary focal points that travelers will want to visit are protected as part of the National Park System. Experiences that shaped the course of history can be relived at these places.

The most notable shrines are among them, including **Minute Man National Historical Park,** where the upstart colonials of Massachusetts defied the British regulars in April 1775 "and fired the shot heard round the world"; **Colonial National Historical Park,** embracing three famous Virginia sites, Jamestown, Williamsburg, and the final battleground of the American Revolution, at Yorktown, all within fourteen miles of each other; and **Independence National Historical Park,** Philadelphia, "the most historic square mile in America."

Since 1930 the National Park Service has preserved a number of major Revolutionary shrines. That year President Herbert Hoover established Colonial National Monument (later changed to Colonial National Historical Park). Then in 1933 many battlefields, memorials, and historic sites administered by the War Department and Agriculture Department were transferred to the National Park Service, a bureau of the Department of the Interior.

Prior to the 1930s some of the important Revolutionary sites had been in the hands of private historical societies. For example, the Ford Mansion, at Morristown, New Jersey, where General Washington and his ragged army spent two of the toughest winters of the war, had been owned by the Washington Association of New Jersey. In 1933 the mansion and other properties were presented to the federal government. These gifts soon led to others. In 1935 a donation of forty acres at Kings Mountain, South Carolina, was made by the Daughters of the American Revolution. This land became the nucleus of **Kings Mountain National Military Park,** commemorating a backwoods battle that proved to be a turning point on the road to independence.

These parks and more than a dozen others within the National Park System will play a vital role in the development of the story of the Revolution during the Bicentennial years. The Bicentennial, however, will be celebrated in one way or another at all the areas of the National Park Service throughout the fifty states. The service plans to reach as many visitors as possible, not just those in the East. For example, at **Fort Jefferson National Monument,** Florida, evening programs will focus on the 18th century role of the Dry Tortugas as a pirates' haven. At **Booker T. Washington National Monument,** Virginia, a cultural center will be dedicated near the birthplace of Booker T., the pioneer educator. At **City of Refuge National Historical Park,** Hawaii, a native cultural festival will include ceremonies, chants, and demonstrations in canoe carving and idol carving. Indian heritage programs will be presented at **Grand Canyon National Park, Glacier National Park,** and **Nez Perce National Historical Park.**

Historic sites associated with the American Revolution number in the hundreds. South Carolina alone has 168 skirmish and battle sites. New York has no less than 40 sites recognized as important landmarks, nearly 100 others preserved in one form or another. Thanks to state agencies, patriotic organizations, and other groups, students of the American Revolution and other travelers can visit and absorb historic substance at Jefferson's Monticello, the Boston "Massacre" site, Bunker Hill, Fort Ticonderoga, Brandywine Battlefield, Valley Forge, and the Lexington Green.

Then there is Newport, Rhode Island, where a visitor can walk narrow streets and see more than 300 little houses built before the American Revolution, and public buildings of that period still in use. Along the way one encounters the work of Peter Harrison, known as America's first professional architect. He began as a ship's steward and proceeded to a versatile career as a merchant captain, shipbuilder, wood-carver, and architect of great Boston churches. The most significant building in town, and Harrison's major work, is **Touro Synagogue,** oldest house of Jewish worship in the United States, founded by 15 families responding to Roger Williams's declaration of religious liberty. ("Forced worship," Williams wrote on fleeing Massachusetts, "stincks in God's nostrils.") When Washington appeared in this treasure house, in 1790, he pledged the government would yield "to bigotry no sanction, to persecution no assistance." His words were read anew in 1947, when the synagogue was designated a national historic site.

Restoration of such places began over a century ago with historic house museums associated with George Washington, such as Hasbrouck House, a stone structure at Newburgh, New York, where he had maintained headquarters during a trying period of the Revolution; and Mount Vernon, his great home on the Potomac River. In 1876, the national centennial, Independence Hall was opened as a monument to the principles of the Declaration of Independence and the Constitution. The Daughters of the American Revolution and the Colonial Dames began to save and furnish houses of signers of the Declaration, while state societies in Virginia and New England acquired sites of early English settlers. Veterans of the Civil War, highly organized and politically powerful, put the federal government in the field by lobbying successfully to establish parks at the battlefields where they had fought.

Meanwhile, under a new concept of land use, national parks were established. At first only natural areas were protected. Then the Antiquities Act of 1906 extended this coverage to Indian ruins designated as national monuments. The National Park Service was established by Congress in 1916, and finally, in 1935, the Historic Sites Act directed the National Park Service to preserve sites, buildings, and objects "for public use, inspiration and benefit."

Though our government still lags behind others in saving national treasures (the French began soon after their Revolution), the National Park Service maintains the Register of Historic Places, composed of structures and districts of exceptional value to American history or culture. This increases the chance of survival, but doesn't insure their future. Over half the 12,000 buildings in the survey of the thirties have been torn down.

If there is one lesson to be learned from the Bicentennial, it may be the need to save more. Many Americans these days are talking, worrying, and writing about endangered wildlife and open space. Relatively few have considered the equally important role of our historic and architectural heritage. Great stone and brick symbols of our civilization are being wiped out by freeways, subdivisions, and shopping centers faster than the bald eagle is disappearing—and there is no "breeding back." Every community needs to see and save its choice spots. Maybe it's not just "historic" neighborhoods that need saving, but also the neighborhoods where people live, that generate a sense of belonging. As we approach the nation's 200th anniversary in 1976, a review of such places is particularly timely. Seattle, as one example, has shown that it can be done. In 1968, an $85 million "development plan" was unveiled; the 60-year-old market, full of fruit and vegetable vendors, local craftsmen, and specialty shops was to be turned into an overpowering luxury hotel-apartment-commercial development. But a group called Friends of the Market rallied the signatures of 53,000 residents on a petition to place a save-the-market initiative on the next ballot. The measure passed overwhelmingly. In saving the market, Seattle salvaged an institution which is both a natural attraction for visitors and a source of necessary and low-cost urban services.

Historic shrines of the Revolution are the inspiration that proves this can be done. In Philadelphia, the city stepped in to rescue Independence Hall and Independence Square in 1818, when it was proposed to parcel out the land for building lots, and it continues to hold title to them. In the restoration of recent years, technicians of the National Park Service performed patient, minute work, taking apart brick walls and wood paneling, studying them piece by piece, scraping down the paints and plasters of many alterations to reach the originals. Historians examined four million manuscripts in this country and in the British Museum. The adventures of reclaiming this building are almost as exciting as its historic events, and worthy of them.

Three dramatic projects are being completed in the Philadelphia historical complex just in time for the Bicentennial. One is Franklin Court, a landscaped courtyard on the site of Benjamin Franklin's home, bordered by five homes restored to their appearance in the 1780s. One of the homes will contain a working printshop of the period. At the reconstructed City Tavern, which John Adams called "the most genteel tavern in America," visitors will be able to order meals and beverages, sampling the flavor of an 18th century inn. Then there is the Graff House, at the corner of 7th and Market streets, the three story brick house where Thomas Jefferson composed the first draft of the Declaration of Independence.

Nearby New Jersey was the "cockpit of the Revolution," with so many battles and skirmishes—more than 100—that you almost feel the whole war was fought in this little land. The visitor during the Bicentennial can relive many of these actions and retrace the steps of Washington and his troops. On Christmas night of 1777, the general and his ragamuffin army crossed the ice-clogged Delaware, paused at a little ferry house which still stands, and then, despite fears that the game was nearly up, plunged on through snow and sleet to attack the fates and the Hessians at Trenton. Next winter was little better, finding George and Martha at the Wallace House in Somerville, where she would huddle under quilts while guards rushed upstairs and pushed open the windows to aim their rifles into the frigid dark.

Then they went on to Morristown. It had been Washington's headquarters from January to May in 1777, and became his headquarters again, the main encampment of his ragged, beleaguered army during that deadly winter 1779–80. Now Americans of our time may enter **Morristown National Historical Park** and experience the greatest single site of the war. Here the Whippany River powered iron forges and furnaces, producing almost all the Revolutionary powder. It was both battleground and rest camp. Thomas Paine eyed the scene and wrote his immortal comment on the times that were trying men's souls.

The first decisive American victory in the Revolutionary War occurred at Fort Moultrie, in Charleston, South Carolina, presently a part of **Fort Sumter National Monument.** After this surprising event, South Carolinians, led by Francis Marion, the "Swamp Fox," and Thomas Sumter, "gamecock of the Revolution," harassed and bedeviled the British troops. Charleston, from whence they sprang, is sometimes described as a city lost in its past; yet it has beautifully restored streets, art galleries, a fine museum, and the Dock Street Theatre. Charleston indeed is endowed with a feeling of the past, in block after block of houses with piazzas and high ceilings, which are protected by the Charleston Ordinance, one of the modern advances in city planning, and by the activities of the Historic Charleston Foundation. Their charm demonstrates the adaptability of old buildings to new uses.

Many special events, such as demonstrations by interpreters in authentic costumes, will take place at these sites. You needn't wait till 1976 to see some of the best. For example, at the North Bridge Visitor Center, in Minute Man National Historical Park, musket firing displays are presented several times each Sunday afternoon during summer. Visitors can also hear talks, at North Bridge on the hour from 10 a.m. to 5 p.m., based on the events of April 19, 1775.

A great deal of restoration and construction is now under way: of historic structures, forts and battlefields, visitor centers, roads, and trails. The Park Service has two staff experts busy in casting, exactly as it was done 200 years ago, 150 Revolutionary War cannons—and they'll shoot, too. All are going to Bicentennial military parks. A major project involves conversion of Union Station in Washington, D.C., into the National Visitor Center, an orientation center for tourists.

Following are the areas to be highlighted by the National Park Service during the Bicentennial. For further information, consult the chapter on Historical Areas, starting on page 140.

Adams National Historic Site, Quincy, Massachusetts
Colonial National Historical Park,
    Jamestown-Williamsburg-Yorktown, Virginia
Cowpens National Battlefield Site,
    Gaffney, South Carolina
Federal Hall National Memorial, New York, New York
Fort McHenry National Monument, Baltimore, Maryland
Fort Necessity National Battlefield,
    near Uniontown, Pennsylvania
Fort Stanwix National Monument, Rome, New York
Fort Sumter National Monument,
    Charleston, South Carolina
George Rogers Clark National Historical Park,
    Vincennes, Indiana
George Washington Birthplace National Monument,
    near Fredericksburg, Virginia
Guilford Courthouse National Military Park,
    Greensboro, North Carolina
Hamilton Grange National Memorial,
    New York, New York
Hopewell Village National Historic Site,
    Elverson, Pennsylvania
Independence National Historical Park,
    Philadelphia, Pennsylvania
Kings Mountain National Military Park,
    Kings Mountain, South Carolina
Longfellow National Historic Site,
    Cambridge, Massachusetts
Minute Man National Historical Park,
    Concord-Lexington, Massachusetts
Moores Creek National Military Park,
    Currie, North Carolina
Morristown National Historical Park,
    Morristown, New Jersey
Mount Rushmore National Memorial,
    Keystone, South Dakota
National Capital Parks, Washington, D.C.
Salem Maritime National Historic Site,
    Salem, Massachusetts
Statue of Liberty National Monument,
    New York, New York

For reading matter on the Bicentennial, the Park Service has already prepared two fine publications. *Signers of the Declaration,* a beautifully illustrated 310-page hardcover book outlines the events leading to the Declaration, the principal buildings involved, and the lives of all 56 men who became signers ($5.65). *Guide to Historic Places,* a 135-page booklet provides a state-by-state descriptive listing of historical sites, and a chronology of political and military events of the American Revolution ($1.90). Both publications are available from the Superintendent of Documents, U.S. Government Printing Office, Washington, D.C. 20402, and at historical park visitor centers.

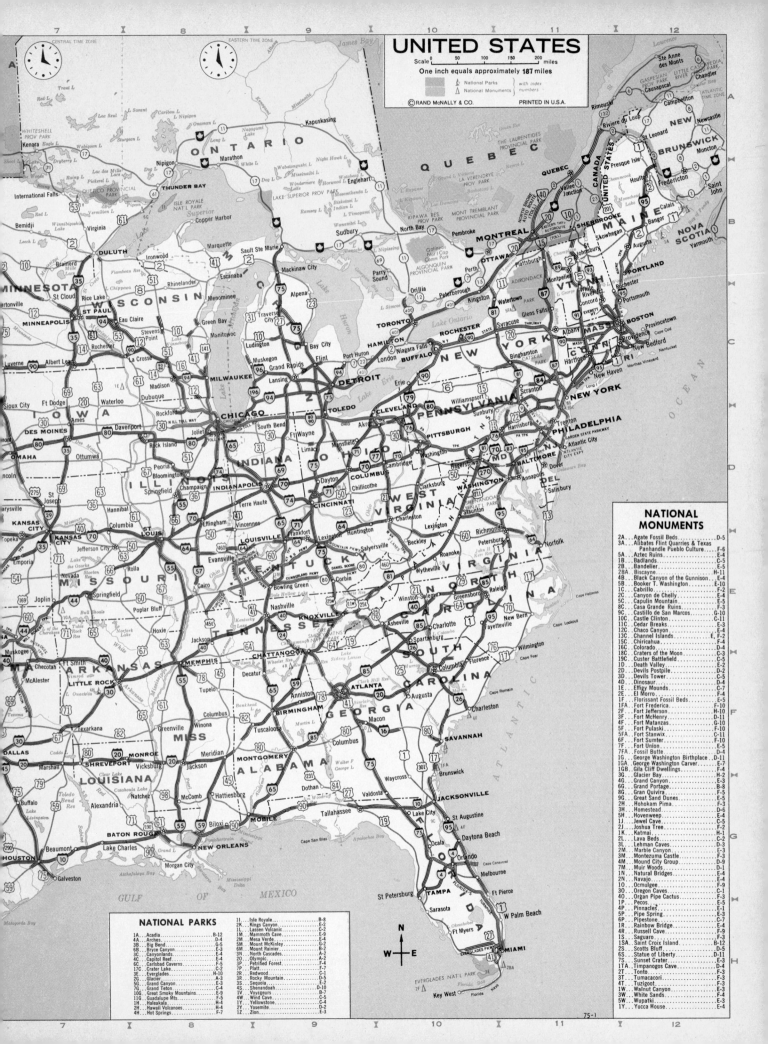

UNITED STATES

Scale 0 50 100 150 200 miles
One inch equals approximately 187 miles

△ National Parks *with index*
△ National Monuments *numbers*

© RAND McNALLY & CO.   PRINTED IN U.S.A.

CENTRAL TIME ZONE   EASTERN TIME ZONE

NATIONAL PARKS

1A...Acadia	B-12	1I...Isle Royale	B-8
1A...Arches	D-4	2K...Kings Canyon	C-2
3B...Big Bend	D-4	1L...Lassen Volcanic	C-2
6B...Bryce Canyon	E-3	1M...Mammoth Cave	E-9
3C...Canyonlands	D-4	2M...Mesa Verde	E-4
4C...Capitol Reef	E-4	5M...Mount McKinley	G-2
6C...Carlsbad Caverns	F-5	6M...Mount Rainier	B-2
1C...Crater Lake	C-2	3N...North Cascades	A-2
2G...Everglades	H-10	2O...Olympic	A-2
2G...Glacier	A-3	3P...Petrified Forest	F-4
5G...Grand Canyon	E-3	7P...Platt	F-5
7G...Grand Teton	D-3	2R...Redwood	C-1
10G...Great Smoky Mountains	E-9	3R...Rocky Mountain	D-5
11G...Guadalupe Mts.	F-5	3S...Shenandoah	D-10
1H...Haleakala	H-4	4S...Sequoia	C-2
2H...Hawaii Volcanoes	H-4	1V...Voyageurs	B-7
7G...Hot Springs	F-7	4W...Wind Cave	C-5
		1Y...Yellowstone	D-2
		1Z...Yosemite	C-2
		1Z...Zion	E-3

NATIONAL MONUMENTS

2A...Agate Fossil Beds	D-5
3A...Alibates Flint Quarries & Texas Panhandle Pueblo Culture	F-6
5A...Aztec Ruins	E-4
1B...Badlands	C-5
2B...Bandelier	E-5
2BA...Biscayne	H-11
4B...Black Canyon of the Gunnison	E-4
5B...Booker T. Washington	E-10
1C...Cabrillo	F-2
2C...Canyon de Chelly	E-4
5C...Capulin Mountain	E-5
8C...Casa Grande Ruins	F-3
9C...Castillo de San Marcos	G-10
10C...Castle Clinton	C-11
11C...Cedar Breaks	E-3
12C...Chaco Canyon	E-4
13C...Channel Islands	E, F-2
15C...Chiricahua	F-4
16C...Colorado	D-4
18C...Craters of the Moon	C-3
19C...Custer Battlefield	C-5
1D...Death Valley	D-2
2D...Devils Postpile	D-2
3D...Devils Tower	C-5
4D...Dinosaur	D-4
2E...Effigy Mounds	C-7
1E...El Morro	E-4
1F...Florissant Fossil Beds	E-5
1FA...Fort Frederica	F-10
2F...Fort Jefferson	H-10
3F...Fort McHenry	D-11
4F...Fort Matanzas	G-10
5F...Fort Pulaski	F-10
5FA...Fort Stanwix	C-11
6F...Fort Sumter	F-10
7F...Fort Union	D-4
7FA...Fossil Butte	D-4
1G...George Washington Birthplace	D-11
1GA...George Washington Carver	F-7
1GB...Gila Cliff Dwellings	F-4
3G...Glacier Bay	H-2
4G...Grand Canyon	E-3
6G...Grand Portage	B-8
8G...Gran Quivira	F-5
9G...Great Sand Dunes	E-5
2H...Hohokam Pima	F-3
3H...Homestead	D-6
5H...Hovenweep	E-4
1J...Jewel Cave	C-5
2J...Joshua Tree	F-3
1K...Katmai	H-1
1L...Lava Beds	C-2
3L...Lehman Caves	D-3
2M...Marble Canyon	E-3
3M...Montezuma Castle	F-3
1M...Mound City Group	D-9
7M...Muir Woods	D-1
1N...Natural Bridges	E-4
2N...Navajo	E-4
1O...Ocmulgee	F-9
3O...Oregon Caves	C-1
4O...Organ Pipe Cactus	F-3
1P...Pecos	E-5
4P...Pinnacles	E-1
5P...Pipe Spring	E-3
6P...Pipestone	C-7
1R...Rainbow Bridge	E-4
4R...Russell Cave	E-3
1S...Saguaro	F-3
1SA...Saint Croix Island	B-12
2S...Scotts Bluff	D-5
6S...Statue of Liberty	D-11
7S...Sunset Crater	E-3
1TA...Timpanogos Cave	D-4
2T...Tonto	F-3
3T...Tumacacori	F-3
4T...Tuzigoot	F-3
1W...Walnut Canyon	E-3
3W...White Sands	F-5
5W...Wupatki	E-3
1Y...Yucca House	E-4

N
W—E
S

75-1

ACADIA

Established as a national park, 1919

When Ralph Waldo Emerson wrote that "Nature is a mutable cloud, which is always and never the same," he could have been thinking of Acadia.

This is the finest surviving fragment of the New England coast that greeted the founders of this country, but is greatly altered from what they saw. Drive down along the shore, pounded by unending waters, and you will come to Anemone Cave, where you can see the continuing struggle among life forms for survival, with each feeding on the other, competing for nutrients of sea and air—and nature always, and never the same.

Acadia, 47 miles southeast of Bangor, Maine, became the first national park in the East (in 1919) and is the only one in New England. It was established as Sieur de Monts National Monument in 1916, changed to Lafayette National Park in 1919, and designated as Acadia National Park in 1929. It is small as national parks go, being only 36,981 acres, but is a treasure in a thousand and one ways, with surf-splashed cliffs rising to the highest point along the Atlantic coast and crowned with cool mountain forests.

In the interior, the landscape of deep-blue lakes shielded by steep slopes tells the story of ancient glacial action. Massive sheets of ice moved down from the frozen north, piling rock, gouging lakes, and shaving peaks to bare granite. Now this land remains under snow each year until April, when the delicate trailing arbutus signals the beginning of spring, first in a procession of 500 varieties of wildflowers. In the low wetlands ducks nest, persistent beavers build their dams, and migratory wading birds, like the magnificent great blue heron, poke their bills underwater searching ceaselessly for fish, frogs, or tadpoles.

Ours is a nation born of the sea, bred on salt spray, and nurtured with adventures of the deep, and here one feels it keenly. The waters of bays and harbors around Acadia are speckled in summer with sails of pleasure yachts, and in every direction the sea roars against the rocks. Champlain sailed this way on his 1604 exploration of the French province of Acadia, and the Jesuits established a short-lived settlement. In time, schooners and brigs were built in every cove, while offshore great fishing fleets would rendezvous and whiten the horizon with hundreds of sails.

Before the coming of the national park, this place of quiet beauty was well worked over with logging operations, a cog railroad, and a hotel atop Cadillac Mountain. It was a fashionable summer place of millionaires, but some, including John D. Rockefeller, Jr., saw the inspirational values and donated this land for the benefit of all people.

THE PRACTICAL GUIDE

If you are on a tour of New England, spend a day at Acadia, driving the Park Loop; but to really appreciate it, stay a week at a resort or camp in the park.

By car (bus and taxi tours available from nearby towns) follow the Park Loop on **Ocean Drive** for the sound and smell of the sea and the lick of the waves, and **Great Head,** a high promontory above the surf.

Anemone Cave is a key stop. Waves at work have tunneled 85 feet into granite cliffs. Pools glisten from a profusion of rockweed, algae, kelp, flowering anemone, and that brightly colored sea snail called dog whelk.

At **Otter Point,** a trail winds through spruce and fir to the shore, where wild roses meet salt spray. Many arctic plants grow in the cool ocean fringe. Offshore, cormorants and gulls congregate on a rocky shoal, while small lobster boats are seen hauling in their "pots"—a reminder that in America the delectable lobster grows only in the cold waters off northern New England. From the windswept summit of **Cadillac Mountain** magnificent vistas unfold, from the open sea to Mount Katahdin far inland.

Somesville, the site of Mount Desert Island's first permanent settlement (1761), lies on the loop road at the head of a steep-sided fjord called Somes Sound, in a setting reminiscent of the Norwegian or Icelandic fjords. **Beech Cliff,** several miles south, is reached on a five-minute walk through a spruce-fir forest. It overlooks Echo Lake for a breathtaking view of water, beach, mountains, and fir forests. Carry your camera to make panoramic pictures of the lake and beach area.

Nature walks are conducted by members of the park staff from July 1–Labor Day. Approximately 150 miles of footpaths reach every mountain summit and transverse every valley; they are designed for all types of walkers and hikers. The **Nature Center** at Sieur de Monts Spring contains displays on nature and history; the adjacent **Abbe Museum** contains Indian stone age relics. Evening campfire programs are held in summer.

Naturalist sea cruises are conducted among the islands of Frenchman Bay to Baker Island. The Isleford Historical Museum, on Little Cranberry Island (reached by boat from Northeast Harbor), is a treasury of mementos of early sailing and lobster fishing.

Isle au Haut, the least-known part of Acadia, is for those who want wilderness solitude. No public campsites, overnight accommodations, or transportation. This outlying island is reached by mail boat from Stonington, Maine.

Schoodic Peninsula, the only mainland section of the park (about an hour and a half by car from Bar Harbor), offers a good day-long side trip.

Photography. Excellent photo opportunities in the high surf pounding the rocky tip. It rises more than 400 feet, with a sweeping view east toward the Bay of Fundy and west toward the Mount Desert Mountains.

Swimming is popular from Sand Beach (among those who like their ocean water cold), and inland at Echo Lake Beach and Lakewood. **Fishing** is permitted inside the park, both freshwater (state license required) and saltwater from the rocks.

Accommodations. Motor courts and guest houses at once exclusive Bar Harbor, Northeast Harbor, Southwest Harbor, Winter Harbor. Reservations are advisable during July–August.

A meal to remember can be enjoyed at Jordan Pond House, in the park near Seal Harbor. Have the charcoal-broiled Maine lobster (which in this country is also served baked, boiled, stuffed, in chowder, salad, or as "lobster-burger") with popovers, and then fruit ice cream, on the porch or lawn, followed with a stroll along Jordan Pond through the beautiful forest of pine and hardwoods.

Campgrounds. Two campgrounds inside the park, Black Woods and Seawall, are usually filled by noon July–August. These are supplemented by private campgrounds in the towns. Anyway, the park is better for walking, cycling, and nature study than as a bedroom. Lamoine State Park lies less than 15 miles away, relatively uncrowded, with an outstanding view across Frenchman Bay, screened sites, a small beach, and boat landing.

Seasons. Most visitors come in summer, although campgrounds, picnic areas, and other facilities are open from about May 10 to October 15. June is a good month for wildflowers, birds, and fishing. September is marked by mild weather, autumn colors, and invigorating air. Snow and ice keep the park road system closed December through April. Be sure to bring warm clothing and a raincoat; evenings are cool even in summer and rainy days occur in any season.

Nearby. Bar Harbor is the starting point of the international motor ferry operating daily during summer to Yarmouth, Nova Scotia. An unusual point of interest is the Jackson Laboratory, center of biological research, open to visitors three times weekly. Bar Harbor and other towns offer deep sea fishing trips and boat rentals. They still retain the flavor of old fishing days around their docks, attractive to painters and photographers. At Southwest Harbor, one of the old fishing settlements from the days when schooners and brigs were built in every cave, shop for craft pieces, carved birds on driftwood bases. Bass Harbor, at the southernmost tip of the island, also recalls the tiny down-east boating villages. It is the setting of a photogenic white lighthouse.

Recommended reading. *The Story of Mount Desert Island,* by Samuel Eliot Morison.

For further information write Superintendent, Acadia National Park, Hulls Cove, Maine 04644.

ARCHES

Established as a national park, 1971

Erosion and weathering have produced more giant stone arches, windows, pinnacles, and pedestals in the red rock here than in any other section of the nation. More than 90 arches have been discovered and doubtless there are others tucked away in the more rugged, less easily penetrated portions of the park.

Exactly what forces fashioned these formations and the spectacular towers, sweeping coves, balanced rocks, and figures resembling men and animals in the red rock country? Geologists say the earth's crust first warped upward to form an anticline, an arch of stratified rock some 30 miles in length. Then the crest of the huge fold sank in, forming what are now known as Salt Valley and Cache Valley. Water entering cracks in the rock dissolved some of the cementing material, then running water and wind removed the loose sand, forming thin fins of soft sandstone. More rapid weathering of softer areas in vertical walls resulted in undercutting, while the carving by water and frost have persisted to this day.

Arches is part of a large area, one of the most spectacular and awesome on earth. The park should never be viewed, or considered, alone, but always within the context of the colorful canyonlands of Southern Utah and the upper Colorado River region, where the erosion of nature over aeons has dissected the anatomy of the earth and left it exposed in monumental grandeur.

It will prove especially interesting to compare the stone archways and fins of Arches with those of nearby Canyonlands National Park. At Arches, the rock in which the arches have formed was deposited as sand about 150 million years ago, during the Jurassic period.

This 300-foot layer, called the Entrada sandstone, lends itself to a cycle of erosion that results in a graceful, smoothly contoured natural arch. Canyonlands has some great arches, too, such as Druid Arch and Angel Arch, but they are found mostly in the Cutler Formation, which tends more toward the development of standing rocks (for which Canyonlands is famous) and apparently lacks the arch-forming capability of the Entrada.

Some arches, such as Delicate Arch, found in its impressive setting of precipitous cliffs and massive domes of "slickrock," have been left isolated by erosion of surrounding fins. In due course, the continued thinning by weather will eventually result in their collapse. The visitor can observe all stages in the process of development and decay.

Soil, grasses, and trees are scant in this setting. The sparse pinyon-juniper ecosystem prevails, though the land is by no means barren. The desert has a beauty all its own. The visitor will see a variety of birds as well as ground squirrels, rabbits, kangaroo rats, and other rodents. Deer, coyote, and foxes are present, too, but are most active at night.

Arches was proclaimed as a national monument in 1929 in order to preserve its great scenic and scientific values. It was enlarged and boundaries were changed several times until the park was established in 1971. The park now has a total of 73,389 acres. Unfortunately, not all the areas of geologic significance are within the park boundary. Conservationists hope to enlarge the park through addition of bordering public domain lands—or at least to achieve special wilderness designation for these key areas.

THE PRACTICAL GUIDE

The park lies only 5 miles north of Moab, a logical base of operations for both Arches and Canyonlands, unless you are camping. The park is divided into six distinct sections, with roads and hiking trails twisting through each area. You can't do justice to it by road, so try to allow at least one day for a good hike to see some of the most impressive features in each section.

Visitor Center. The center is just off US 160, and you'll find excellent pictures, displays, and explanations of the landscape. Even if you're driving through and have only an hour, it is worth a stop. The main park road starts from here. It winds to the top of the slick-rock plateau, then to **Courthouse Towers** for exciting views over the outlying mountains. Take the 1-mile hike from the parking area through **Park Avenue,** a narrow corridor where sandstone walls rise vertically 150 to 300 feet.

Continue over the paved road to **The Windows,** where you can see and photograph eight immense arches, as well as many smaller formations. After another 2.5 miles northeast you come to a junction with a graded road leading to viewpoints of **Delicate Arch,** the most famous landmark in the park, which derives its name from the precarious balance in which the arch is held atop its base. Early cowboys had their own name: "Schoolmarm's Bloomers." Take the 1.5-mile foot trail to the arch itself, for the view of the Colorado River gorge and the snow-peaked La Sal Mountains. This is also the site of the Wolfe Ranch Environmental Study Area.

Then drive past **Fiery Furnace,** a series of parallel fins that provide an interesting excursion for hikers. But this area can be a nightmare of passageways—only ranger-conducted tours are allowed. These leave each morning at hours noted at the Visitor Center. At **Devils Garden,** 9 miles north of Balanced Rock, the road ends. A 2-mile trail leads to beautifully sculptured arches—Pine Tree, Partition, Double O, and Dark Angel. **Landscape Arch,** the longest known natural stone arch in the world, is also along this trail. By turning off on the graded road at **Skyline Arch** and driving 8 miles across Salt Valley, you reach the **Klondike Bluffs,** a rugged section with a 1-mile hiking trail to **Tower Arch.** Before attempting to explore the bluffs, or any section of the backcountry, notify a park ranger. He will furnish latest road information plus briefing on backcountry travel.

Tour operators conduct a variety of trips from Moab. Best outfitters include: for river-running and day-river trips on paddlewheel riverboat, Tex's Tour Center (P.O. Box 67); jeep tours, Tag-a-Long Tours (P.O. Box 1206); horseback trips, Bob's Trail Riders (435 North Main). The zip code for Moab, Utah, is 84532.

Accommodations. A modern campground for tents and trailers is located at Devils Garden, an excellent base in the park interior. Campfire talks are given nightly during summer. There are no other services within the park, but good motels and restaurants are quite handy at Moab. For a different type of facility, consider Hoffman's Castle Valley Ranch (P.O. Box 81, Moab, Utah 84532), 30 miles from the park entrance in the La Sal Mountains; it provides cabins, campground, trail rides, and meals.

Seasons. It's dry desert here. See reference to weather on page 16, in Canyonlands section. From May to August, except in abnormally dry years, you can expect colorful displays of wildflowers in the moist places.

Nearby. The companion piece to Arches is **Canyonland** (see pages 14–16), a fantasy of red rock gorges, canyons, and sheer cliffs. This is the "standing up country," an explorer's delight on foot, horse, or jeep. **Behind the Rocks,** the red rock escarpment on the northern boundary of Moab, has only been penetrated in the past decade, but is becoming a high point for jeep tours.

Twenty-five miles southeast of Arches, **Fisher Towers,** a tall group of pinnacles, guard the entrance to **Castle Valley,** a beautiful area of meadows and pastures banked on one side by red rock and on the other by 12,000-foot peaks of the La Sal Mountains.

For further information write Superintendent, Canyonlands National Park, Moab, Utah 84532.

BIG BEND

Authorized as a national park, 1935

A Texan can claim almost anything about the mighty Big Bend and he will be speaking modestly. This wilderness park presents an opportunity for a desert experience unequaled in its region and perhaps in the nation.

The heart of the 709,088-acre park lies 410 miles west of San Antonio and 300 miles southeast of El Paso, but is worth all efforts to reach it, if only for the majesty of vastness, and the opportunity to absorb the adventurous, lonely frontier above the Rio Grande. It is not heavily visited—no more than 250,000 a year—so there is plenty of elbow room.

The nearest towns, Alpine and Marathon, are over 70 miles away, with a greater population of jackrabbits and antelopes than people in between, but Texas roads are smooth and well maintained. The approach through vast ranch country provides a fitting foreground to this masterpiece of southwest desert landscape, dominated by the upthrust of the massive Chisos Mountains. The Chisos may be snowless, but their crags, canyons, and rocky spires present a different color tone from every angle and at every hour, from the clear brightness of a sunfilled morning to the purple of twilight setting over the immense, varied wilderness.

Millions of years ago an inland sea covered the Big Bend. Sediments of mud, sand, and lime on the floor of the sea later hardened into rock; traces of shells and fossils are still found embedded over the area. During a later period dinosaurs and giant crocodiles (possibly 50 feet long) roamed through dark marshes and tropical forests. Then came a period of volcanic activity and mountain-building, followed by millions of years of erosion, and castles and cathedrals were carved in rock.

The waters of the Rio Grande have played their part in the carving process. The river extends for 107 miles along the boundary of the park—which also is the boundary between the United States and Mexico—on its great U-shaped bend, or *gran comba*, as neighbors on the opposite shore call it. Three times on its course the river cuts through massive, dramatic canyons: Santa Elena, Mariscal, and Boquillas, which provide sightseeing adventures for every visitor.

Human history is part of the treasure of the Big Bend. Bandits took refuge behind its rocky barricades. Comanche warriors passed through on their way into Mexico. Mexican revolutionaries invaded the United States into the Big Bend in 1916. Before the park was established, large livestock herds grazed where visitors now may enjoy wilderness camping.

Big Bend is a place to absorb the richness of the awesome desert. The park contains more than a thousand different plants, including rare species that grow only here.

At the beginning and end of the day, a wide range of animals are seen best. Among these are the coyote, ringtail, and possibly the rare kit fox in Tornillo Flats—sometimes the sleek pronghorn will be seen here, too. Mule deer and collared peccary, or javelina, are apt to be in the Grapevine Hills. Lizards and snakes are not uncommon, but they are anxious to give man a wide berth. You may see a tarantula on the hiking trail, but this giant spider is not unfriendly. Look him over respectfully, from a distance, and he will bother you far less than you can bother him. Travel with a good bird guide, for some 385 species dwell in the park. You may see the roadrunner streaking over the ground or the rare, lyric-voiced Colima warbler, whose only known nesting places are here and in Mexico.

THE PRACTICAL GUIDE

Allow at least three full days to explore the Big Bend, though a full week will occupy any visitor's time usefully, exploring by car, rafts, afoot, and on horseback.

Approaching from the west, El Paso lies 328 miles from Big Bend. You can reach the park by driving to Van Horn and Marfa, then south to Presidio and the Maverick Entrance—it's the long but scenic route, including the River Road along the Rio Grande. You can also head due east from Marfa to Alpine, then south to the Maverick entrance. Or from Alpine continue to Marathon, then south to the Persimmon Gap Entrance—the distance is longer but it takes less time. If traveling from and to the West, try to make a loop trip. Approaching from the east, Big Bend lies 405 miles from San Antonio, 251 miles from Del Rio, via Persimmon Gap.

After entering the park at Persimmon Gap, 39 miles south of Marathon, it is 29 miles to park headquarters at Panther Junction in the foothills of the Chisos. Use the giant relief map there to chart your course, and ask for current information on river and road conditions.

While in the park, divide your time. Allow the better part of a day for the trip to **Santa Elena Canyon,** a massive boxlike gorge carved through limestone cliffs. It lies 45 miles from the center of things at Chisos Basin. From the picnic area at the river shore a footpath leads along a rocky ledge into the heart of the canyon. On the way there or back, stop at **Castolon,** where adobe houses reflect pioneer settlement by rugged cattlemen and the U.S. Cavalry. You can purchase items of food or clothing at the historic Castolon Store, which has been in business since 1919. Nearby, the river is so narrow that you can cross by ferry (a rowboat) to the little Mexican farming village of **Santa Elena.**

Spend part of another day at **Boquillas Canyon,** the longest of Big Bend's famous gorges, where the floodplain of willows and cottonwoods is frequented by many birds, particularly spectacular with late afternoon sun on the canyon walls. It lies 35 miles from Chisos Basin. Be sure to take in the nature trail at Rio Grande Village, which covers this life community and opens views above the river. Then visit a village out of yesterday, **Boquillas,** across the "border without barricades." You will pay to ride across the river in a skiff, then on a burro for one mile to the village, but the modest fee is well worth it. However, do not encourage the Boquillas children seeking handouts.

If you are in good physical condition (not necessarily an expert rider), the day-long horseback trip to the **South Rim** is one of the finest experiences available in any national park. It reveals the full sweep of the nature community, upward through pinyon, oak, and juniper, through an "island forest in the sky" more like the north woods than southwest desert. The greatest reward is the view from the crest, over 7,200 feet, of the silvery Rio Grande, the tawny desert, and rugged Mexican Sierra del Carmen Mountains extending to the horizon. A shorter trip leads to the **Window,** a great gap in the mountains, ideal for picture-taking.

Lost Mine Trail from Panther Pass is the most popular hiking route; it takes three hours to make the 4-mile round trip to Lost Mine Peak, overlooking ridges and valleys, with a breathtaking vista from the top.

Old Ore Road, running north from Rio Grande Village to the yucca forest on Dagger Flats, is an interesting off-the-beaten-path primitive route. It parallels the old stage road to Boquillas across desert flats and arroyos. Hikers can use

it to reach the Telephone Canyon trailhead, intersecting the Strawhouse and Marufo Vega trails, the major network on the east side of the park. Remember that almost all roads in the park are primitive, little more than tracks across the desert. Be sure you're prepared for them; and allow plenty of time.

Hiking gear. Wear hiking shoes or boots, not sneakers, in this country to avoid painful contact with thorny mesquite, prickly pear, and catclaw. Wide-brimmed hats are most practical. Don't plan any longer hike across the harsh desert lowlands than you feel sure you can make. Carry a water bottle or canteen, but drink lightly. Nibble whole cucumbers to reduce thirst.

Boating is a choice experience on the Rio Grande—for experts. Inflatable rubber rafts, not canoes, are recommended for float trips. Some portaging may be necessary due to shallow water. Climate is best September to mid-November and in spring. Summers are definitely hot on the river. No boats or accessory equipment are available for rent or loan inside the park. Permit may be obtained at park headquarters or a ranger station.

Rubber raft trips are now offered by a local outfitter, covering one or two days. These offer the chance to camp overnight on a sand bar in Boquillas Canyon or Santa Elena Canyon. Mariscal Canyon is a good one-day trip. Ask at park headquarters or Chisos Basin, or write Glen Pepper, Box 47, Terlingua, Texas 79852.

Photography. Early morning is best at Santa Elena Canyon; by noon there is little or no sunlight on the walls. Boquillas Canyon, in shadow until noon, improves in the afternoon. Sunset through the Window makes a colorful study from almost any point. Shadows on the desert will give almost a third dimension to black-and-white pictures. You will get best results with long shadows early and late in the day.

Accommodations. Chisos Basin, at a 5,400-foot elevation, is the center of activity most of the year, with campground, modern concession-operated cottages and motel-type lodge, dining room, and supply store. Illustrated talks are given in the Basin most evenings from Easter through October, and at Rio Grande Village from November to Easter. Reservations are essential throughout the year. Write National Park Concessions, Inc., Big Bend National Park, Texas 79834.

Camping. When it grows cool at Chisos Basin in winter, it is still shirt-sleeve time in desert portions centered around Rio Grande Village, at 1,800 feet. Facilities there include trailer park, large

campground, and supply store. Ground fires are no longer allowed in Big Bend. Neither is wood collecting. Pick up white gas or charcoal at the supply store and be content with brazier or cookstove. Camping limit is 14 days. There also are primitive campsites (including a dozen on the Rio Grande) available with permit.

Seasons. Sunshine is abundant all year. Snow is light and rare in the mountains. Winter is nippy at higher elevations but pleasant in the lowlands (70 and 80 degrees even in January), and an ideal season here. Spring arrives early. The desert blooms from late February through April, when Dagger Flat, in the northeast part of the park, presents a rare spectacle of thousands of huge giant dagger yucca (Yucca carnerosana) unfolding massive clusters of creamy blossoms. Summer is hot (100 degrees) in desert and river valley, but pleasant at Chisos Basin and the best time of year for the mountains.

A good time to walk the desert is at twilight, the witching hour when deer feed on open hillsides and coyotes begin their nocturnal serenade. Be on the lookout for rattlesnakes out to feed on rodents. They won't strike if you keep your distance, so avoid sitting on rocks or logs they're likely to shelter under, and keep your eyes open. Don't worry about giant tarantulas you may meet; they're relatively harmless.

Nearby. Big Gap Wildlife Management Area, near the Persimmon Gap entrance, covers 100,000 acres, with fishing opportunities on a 20-mile stretch of the Rio Grande. Fort Davis National Historic Site, on the road down from Carlsbad Caverns, New Mexico, is a restoration of the most impressive old frontier fort in the Southwest. It adjoins Davis Mountains State Park, a combination of scenic peaks and canyons, with modern overnight lodge accommodations and recreation facilities. Motels are located in the towns of Alpine and Marathon, between Fort Davis and Big Bend. Leaving the park, County Route 170, the scenic **Camino del Rio,** leads northwest through the mining ghost towns of Terlingua, noted as the scene of the International Chili Cookoff in early November, and Study Butte to Presidio, a gateway into Mexico via Ojinaga and Chihuahua.

Recommended reading. *The North American Deserts,* by Edmund C. Jaeger should be reviewed before you arrive. Then pick up copies of the *Road Guide, Hikers Guide,* and *Guide to the Backcountry Roads and the River.*

For further information write Superintendent, Big Bend National Park, Texas 79834.

BRYCE CANYON

Authorized as a national park, 1924

Few, if any, places in the world provide better opportunity to realize the power and persistence of forces that have shaped the earth's surface than Bryce Canyon. Though displayed on an enormous scale within the 36,010-acre national park, the rock units show a simplicity of mass composition, form, and arrangement. Here is the geology of the last 60 million years laid bare. It began with layers of sediment being deposited by inland lakes and seas, followed by mountain building by powerful pressures from within the earth. Huge blocks were broken off, raised higher, until they formed distinct plateaus, or tablelands. Over the centuries rain, alternate frost and thaw, running water, plant roots forcing themselves deeper into the cracks, and chemicals in the air have exercised their influences through alternate layers of harder and softer rock.

This country was known to Indians and favored by the Paiutes, who described the formations as "red rocks standing like men in a bowl-shaped canyon." It was they who named the Paunsaugunt Plateau, which means "home of the beaver"; a reminder that many species of wildlife dwell in this high, cool plateau.

Adventurous trappers and prospectors may have visited the area during the period 1830–1850, and Mormon scouts searching for fields and pastures may have reached the south base of the Paunsaugunt Plateau between 1850 and 1866. It was the intrepid Major John Wesley Powell who initiated the scientific investigation of the valleys and plateaus of southern and central Utah, in 1871. His route began at Kanab, ascended Johnson Canyon, then crossed the many deeply trenched streams rising in the plateau walls of what is now the national park. One early Mormon settler, Ebenezer Bryce, pushed farther upstream than the others and tried raising cattle, but gave it up and departed, leaving only his name.

J. W. Humphrey, Forest Supervisor of the Sevier Forest, headquartered at Panguitch, was largely responsible for making the exquisitely scenic area of Bryce Canyon available to the public. He not only publicized its attractions in the local newspaper, but pressed for the development of primitive roads.

In 1919, Ruben C. Syrett began entertaining tourists at a homestead near the present Ruby's Inn and one year later built a small log lodge and a few cabins near Sunset Point.

The Bryce fever caught hold. In 1919, the Utah legislature memorialized Congress, urging the establishment of a national monument to be called "Temple of the Gods." The effort was rewarded in 1923 when Bryce Canyon National Monument was designated by presidential proclamation, and was given even greater recognition the following year when Congress raised the status of the area, naming it Utah National Park. In subsequent years the park was enlarged in size and its name changed once again.

The heart of the park is but a short, narrow strip along the jagged edge of the Paunsaugunt Plateau, one of the seven great "tables" dominating southern Utah. Below the plateau rim stand cathedrals, palaces, chessmen awaiting the next move, and entire miniature sculptured cities. Many formations are named, such as Thor's Hammer, Queen's Castle, Gulliver's Castle, Hindu Temples, and Wall Street, but you will find plenty of them that may suggest names of your own.

These are colored variously pink, iron-red, and orange, blended with white, gold, and cream, and here and there striped with lavender and blue. All of this spreads out from the amphitheaterlike rim as far as the eye can see until, far in the distance, it blends into the expansive Utah-Arizona landscape of plateaus dark with evergreen forests.

THE PRACTICAL GUIDE

The park is small enough so that you can cover the full drive along the high rim and back, a distance of 34 miles, in less than three hours. Scenic overlooks provide broad perspective before seeing the formations at close range from hiking and riding trails.

The approach roads to Bryce are deceptive: 4,000 feet in elevation are gained in the last 60 miles. This is high country, ranging from 8,000 to 9,000 feet above sea level, and demands a leisurely pace, particularly for anyone with a heart condition. Allow extra time for everything, including eating and hiking.

Visitor Center. Located at the entrance, it contains orientation exhibits on geology, biology, and archaeology. Illustrated talks are presented daily in summer.

Main Bryce Amphitheater, between **Boat Mesa** and **Bryce Point,** a distance of 4 airline miles, contains a concentration of sights. In this compact area are 21 miles of trail and spectacular vistas. You can see how the vegetation changes with elevation. Sagebrush claims the valley floors below. The slopes up to 7,000 feet are covered with pinyons and junipers. Above and below the rim, between 7,000 and 8,500 feet, are ponderosa, limber and bristlecone pine, and Douglas fir.

Navajo Loop, most popular hike (about 1½ miles and 1½ hours), starts from the inspiring setting of **Sunset Point.** During summer a naturalist leads the walk, starting at 9 a.m. It begins with a gradual 521-foot descent into the canyon, then winds among an outstanding array of formations, with time for rest and picture-taking en route. The last lap is an amazing series of stairlike switchbacks.

Under-the-Rim Trail, completed in 1965, offers 35 miles of hiking into quite wild country, with opportunities for solitude and exploration. Yet it parallels the main park road, so it can be taken conveniently in sections, and can be reached from three spur trails. Extending from Bryce Point to the south boundary at **Rainbow Point,** this trail opens the heart of the Pink Cliffs' scenery. The traveler who is concerned with preserving park features for the future will stay on the trails. The traveler who is concerned with his children's safety will be sure they do the same.

Horseback rides afford the least strenuous way of probing the canyon trails, on a morning or afternoon trip from Bryce Canyon Lodge. There is a lot of variety to enjoy, riding through cool and shadowed arches, switchbacks, over ridgetops, and along the base of cliffs.

Photography. Opportunities are limitless. Use your imagination to bring home more than a visual record of where you have been; shoot your own interpretation of what you have seen. In Bryce Canyon you can experiment with sidelighting and backlighting, using the brilliant landscape to your advantage. Be careful to shade your lens in shooting toward the sun. The deeper the blue of the sky, the more intense will be the coloring of the rocks. Telephoto and wide-angle lenses are helpful, but not essential. **Yovimpa Point** is the best place in the park to catch the setting sun's rays on the Pink Cliffs; it is unsurpassed for beauty.

Accommodations. Bryce Canyon Lodge consists of rather plain cottages, with and without bath. Dining room and coffee shop. For reservations, write TWA Services, Inc., Box 400, Cedar City, Utah 84720. Good motels are located in Panguitch, at Ruby's Inn outside the park, Hatch, and along US 89 and Utah 12.

Camping. Two campgrounds are located inside the park near the Visitor Center, with groceries available at the inn. Camping limit, 14 days.

Seasons. If you come in late spring or summer, wildflowers alone will make your trip worthwhile, including paintbrush, columbine, yarrow, and penstemon. Temperature, like vegetation, varies with altitude.

Between April and October, days are warm, with occasional thundershowers, followed by cool evenings.

The lodge is open from mid-June to mid-September only, but the park road is kept open throughout the winter, when white snow contrasts with the brilliant colors of the Pink Cliffs. Skies are deep blue and haze-free.

Nearby. Dixie National Forest encircles the park. The nearest recreation area is at **Pine Lake,** elevation 8,200 feet, 12 miles southeast of Widstoe; it has fishing, boating, camping. **Red Canyon** campground is located midway between Bryce and Panguitch, off Utah 12. **Panguitch Lake,** in addition to forest camping, has boat rentals, cabins, and fishing. Panguitch itself is an interesting ranching community, with access to spectacular wilderness country on the little-surveyed Kaiparowits Plateau.

If you are coming from the direction of Salt Lake City, consider a side trip to **Capitol Reef National Park,** a 20-mile uplift of sandstone cliffs, near Torrey. West of Cedar City, a short side trip will take you to **Cedar Breaks National Monument,** a huge natural amphitheater in the Pink Wasatch Cliffs.

Bryce Canyon, **Zion,** and **Grand Canyon** national parks are intimately related geologically. A visit to all three of these parks is like a tour through gigantic galleries of 600 million years of the geologic past—a magnificent opportunity unmatched anywhere else.

For further information write Superintendent, Bryce Canyon National Park, Bryce Canyon, Utah 84717.

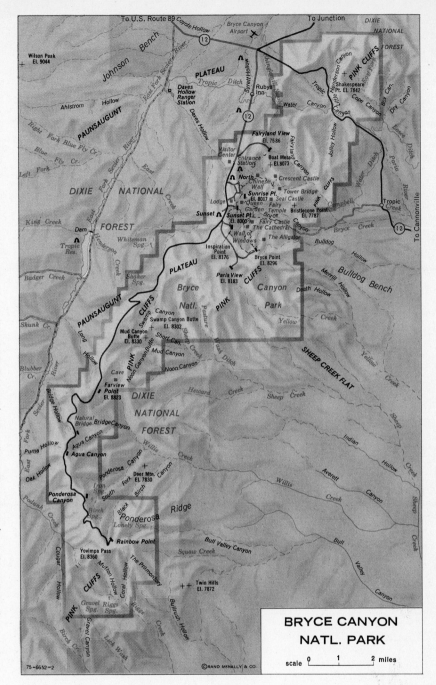

BRYCE CANYON NATL. PARK

scale 0   1   2 miles

CANYONLANDS

Established as a national park, 1964

Until recent years the Canyonlands region was little known outside of southern Utah. A few dirt roads penetrated the edges, but most of it was inaccessible. Since 1964, when it became the 32nd national park, the world has been learning of the flaming color and rocky landscape surrounding the confluence of the Green and Colorado rivers.

The two rivers are entrenched in deep, winding gorges, from which benches of land spread outward to meet cliffs of orange-red sandstone. And dramatizing this wild setting are the weird performers created by natural erosion—towering spires, arches, needles, bits of level bottomland, sandbars, and bold mesas.

The spectacle is exciting to the eye without any questions asked. What makes it important as a work of scientific study as well as art, however, is the geology of erosion. Here the rivers sliced through layers of rock and stripped them back to raveled ancient edges. Tributary streams, rain, and frost then carved the details. The puzzles of how and when these events happened are part of the enchantment of Canyonlands. They await scientists and laymen who seek to understand the wondrous ways in which nature shapes the land.

The elevations in the new park range from 3,600 feet in low-lying basinlands to plateaus and mesas of almost 7,000 feet.

Though portions of the 337,559-acre national park are still unexplored, evidences of prehistoric man have been located throughout the area in ruined villages and in petroglyphs chipped nearly a thousand years ago.

Native plants and animals are typical of the arid pinyon-and-juniper community, except for the cottonwoods and water-loving plants around the seeps and springs. Deer, coyotes, and foxes are among those present but rarely observed. From May to August, except in extra dry years, wildflowers carpet the moist locations, reflecting the ability of living creatures to adapt to a harsh environment. A local native population of desert bighorn inhabits a portion of the park.

THE PRACTICAL GUIDE

Travel is limited in the park. Paved roads are not yet developed (and will always be restricted to protect the wilderness character of the region). Portions of the backcountry can be seen only by four-wheel-drive vehicles, boat, horseback, or afoot. Yet, visitors can get a generous sampling of the area and should plan to spend three days.

Two approaches are available by passenger car to the Canyonlands frontier. The northern gateway is the old pioneer Mormon town of **Moab,** where Zane Grey set many of his novels—in the days before uranium, oil, and potash. A well-graded, dry-weather road off US 160 leads to the **Island in the Sky** section of the park. The tip of this mesa, dominating the land between the two rivers, **Grandview Point,** affords the first spectacular rimrock view of the park with its red-hued cliffs, buttes, and mesas. At the end of a short hiking trail, **Upheaval Dome,** a mysterious fragment of geology, is a deep, vertical-walled crater with a cream-colored mass of stone upthrust through surrounding red-tinged sandstone.

From the southeast gateway, **Monticello,** at the foot of the Abajo Mountains, US 160 travels north 15 miles to Church Rock, the turning place into the park, on a graded, unpaved road veering due west. This road (which can be slick when wet) leads first to the landmark known as **Newspaper Rock,** in Indian Creek State Park, where a series of petroglyphs were chipped into the cliffside by prehistoric Indians. The Ranger Station at **Cave Spring** is a good place to learn about road conditions farther ahead. Passenger cars find it passable to **Squaw Spring** and Squaw Flat Campground, about 3 miles beyond the Ranger Station and, over a graded dirt road, to **Elephant Hill,** at the brink of the spectacular **Needles Area.** Here the sandstone, broken into blocks by close-set joints, has eroded into a fantasy of thousands of red and white rounded pillars, spires, and balanced rocks, some rising as high as 30-story buildings. Just to the west, the same sandstone in the **Grabens** looks entirely different in parallel valleys.

Four-wheel drive vehicles afford op-portunities to explore more of the park. A challenging jeep trail heads west from Squaw Flat into the heart of the Needles and **Chester Park** along **Devil's Lane** to the confluence of the Green and Colorado.

Tour operators. Jeep tours of one day are conducted by local experts into the Needles, and also deeper into the backcountry to see such features as **Angel Arch,** a sandstone bridge guarded by an angel-like figure. Angel Arch and surroundings were only discovered and named as recently as 1955. Outfitters also run guided pack trips for hikers and horseback riders. Kent Frost, Canyonland Tours, 295 Blue Mountain Drive, Monticello, Utah 84535, is one of the best operators of land tours. Tex McClatchey, Box 67, Moab, Utah, runs interesting jet boat and float cruises by water.

Boating access into portions of the park is feasible from two directions. One is from the town of **Green River,** which is the starting point of the annual 196-mile Friendship Cruise and Motorboat Marathon to Moab every May and June. The other direction is from Moab on the Colorado River to the confluence of the two rivers. Boat tours are run frequently, giving a new dimension to the Canyonlands experience. Wild **Cataract Canyon,** below the junction, is known as "the explorers' nightmare and modern river-runner's challenge." Guided expeditions with proper boats and expert rivermen are the best way to view these large rapids.

Accommodations. The park has no overnight lodgings, food, or gasoline facilities. Motels are located in Moab, Monticello, and Blanding (22 miles south of Monticello). Camping supplies are available in these towns.

Camping. Inside the park, campgrounds at **Squaw Flats** are equipped with tables, drinking water, fireplaces, and pit toilets; 14-day limit. Firewood is not available, so bring your own fuel. Primitive camping is permitted at designated locations in the **Island in the Sky** section and in the backcountry. Plan to carry extra water at all times. State park campgrounds are located at **Indian Creek,** near the Needles area, and at **Dead Horse Point,** north of Moab. Good campgrounds are located in timbered settings of **Manti-La Sal National Forest.**

Seasons. This is desert country, where daily, as well as seasonal, temperature changes can be extreme: hot days in summer up to a maximum of 110 degrees, cooling rapidly after sundown to a low shortly before sunup, then rising rapidly again. The average annual temperature is from 50 to 55 degrees, but there are lows of 20 below zero. Some snow falls on the rims during winter. The spring and autumn are mild and pleasant. The average annual precipitation is five to nine inches, much of the moisture coming in late-summer thundershowers.

Nearby. The companion piece to Canyonlands, **Arches National Park,** outside of Moab, contains an overwhelming concentration of redrock arches, immense windows, and pinnacles.

Within 25 miles of the heart of Canyonlands, the Monticello and Moab districts of **Manti-La Sal National Forest** provide the contrast—high cool woodlands rising to summits of the La Sal and Blue mountains, over 11,000 and 12,000 feet, with fishing, camping, and scenic drives. Downstream on the Colorado lies **Glen Canyon National Recreation Area,** where Lake Powell, a major watersports center, is formed behind the third highest dam in the world. Near Blanding and Bluff, **Natural Bridges National Monument** contains three huge sandstone bridges, magnificent canyons, and ancient Indian ruins. **Hovenweep National Monument** embraces a chain of well-preserved but isolated prehistoric Indian towers in the famed "Four Corners" region of the Southwest, near the point where the boundary lines of Colorado, Utah, Arizona, and New Mexico converge. Southwest of Bluff, the town of **Mexican Hat** is gateway to fantastic **Monument Valley,** a land of buttes and mesas, where the Navajo Indians are developing visitor facilities astride the once-remote Utah-Arizona desert boundary.

Recommended reading. *Standing Up Country,* by Gregory Crampton.

For further information write Superintendent, Canyonlands National Park, Moab, Utah 84532.

CAPITOL REEF

Established as a national park, 1971

In 1880, American geologist Clarence E. Dutton recorded his impressions as he gazed upon the tilted cliffs and rainbow rock layers of a strange, little-known land in south-central Utah. "The colors are such as no pigments can portray," he wrote. "They are deep, rich and variegated; and so luminous are they that light seems to flow or shine out of the rock rather than to be reflected from it."

Capitol Reef itself is a 20-mile-long uplift rising 1,000 feet above the Fremont River (roughly midway between Canyonlands and Bryce Canyon national parks), embracing the beauty Mr. Dutton described; but this is only a portion of the new park. It now includes the most spectacular, readily understood monocline in the United States. Exposed and eroded rock layers laid down more than 125 million years ago stand on edge like pages of a gigantic geology book.

Due to its isolation and difficulty of access, the Capitol Reef country actually was undiscovered and unexplored until comparatively recent times. The earliest inhabitants apparently were prehistoric Indians who arrived during the Basketmaker III period, dating back to about A.D. 700, and who remained until not later than 1275 (when the great 25-year drought began). These people left reminders of their occupancy in the form of large, distinctive petroglyphs, some of which are found near Fruita and on Pleasant Creek.

The first white men of record to see any part of this area were members of the William Wolfskill party of 1829. They didn't enter the Capitol Reef, but saw it from a distance while passing over Thousand Lake Mountain on their way to extend the Old Spanish Trail from Santa Fe to Los Angeles. This trail was followed every year thereafter for 26 years by traders and explorers, including John Charles Fremont (in the winter of 1853). On his celebrated voyage down the Colorado River in 1869, John Wesley Powell discovered the Dirty Devil River, which he later renamed the Fremont and revisited on his expedition of 1871.

Soon afterward, Professor A. H. Thompson, Powell's geologist, explored and mapped the area, applying names to various features, which are still in use. Other geologists followed, including C. E. Dutton, who looked down on Capitol Reef and described the Waterpocket Fold.

Settlement, principally by stockmen, was light. Two residents of Torrey, Ephraim P. Pectol and Joseph Hickman, labored for 25 years to get some recognition for the area. Hickman Bridge and Pectol's Pyramid are named for them. They were aided by Dr. J. E. Broaddus, a well-known Salt Lake City photographer.

In 1937, a scenic spur of this huge monocline was proclaimed Capitol Reef National Monument. With the addition of 215,056 acres that take in the entire Waterpocket Fold running north to south and striking downward west to east, the area was made a national park in 1971. It presents a complete geological story. Cathedral Valley, included in the north end of the park, contains spectacular monoliths, 400 to 700 feet high, of reddish brown sandstone capped with grayish yellow strata—colorful "cathedrals," many freestanding on the valley floor.

THE PRACTICAL GUIDE

The main access to the park is via Utah 24, an all-weather road connecting with new I-70 on the east (near Green River) and on the west with US 89 (near Salina). Although the road cuts through the northern portion of the park, this area is best enjoyed by hikers and backpackers. A number of trails, ranging from easy to strenuous, provide opportunities for everyone. Serious distance hikers need to recognize problems of possible lack of water or too much of it. The arid climate makes the park susceptible to long droughts which dry up seeps, springs, and waterpockets. Then, a sudden shower may send tons of water hurtling down a narrow canyon. Always check with park rangers on water and weather conditions.

Entering from the west, the road passes a series of scenic viewpoints— **Chimney Rock, Panorama Point,** and **Goosenecks**—opening on footpaths of varying lengths. Goosenecks overlook faces the deep zigzag canyon carved by the Fremont River. You'll find others en route east, notably **Hickman Bridge** and **Behunin's Cabin.**

Visitor Center. Six miles inside the boundary, the modern headquarters features displays of the area's first inhabitants, pre-Columbian Indians of the Fremont culture, and of the 19th century Mormon settlers. The film on geological forces will help prepare you to tour the park on the scenic road leading south. Observe Park Service precautions about flash floods: never park in a shallow lowland area or enter a gorge while it's raining.

On this route **Grand Wash** affords a fairly easy hike of 2¼ miles along the bottom of the wash. You'll pass between sheer canyon walls displaying unusual rock formations, with several prehistoric pictographs in view. There is another trail, more strenuous, climbing steeply to the high cliffs and **Cassidy Arch,** named for Butch Cassidy, the outlaw who used the area as a hiding place. Four miles south of Grand Wash the road leads toward a dead end at **Capitol Gorge,** passing thousands of potholes carved by wind and water, and the start of a hiking trail to the **Golden Throne,** a massive butte providing spectacular views over the entire canyon. Inside the gorge you'll find Indian petroglyphs, names of pioneers carved into the rock, and enormous natural water tanks.

For years Grand Wash and Capitol Gorge were the most popular attractions of the national monument, but there are many more accessible now, particularly for those with four-wheel-drive vehicles. **Cathedral Valley** is one such section, a good day's trip from the Visitor Center. Rock formations bearing such names as Temple of the Sun, Queen of the Wash, Giant's Armchair, Walls of Jericho, and Gunsight Dike suggest the appearance of this new park addition. Going north into Cathedral Valley it is first necessary to pass through the **Valley of Decision,** a narrow gap where a driver must choose whether to proceed or, in the face of clouds and threatening skies, turn back. Once inside there is no way out during a flash flood; even with a moderate rain, if the driver gets across he may still be stranded at least a few hours. But it may well be worth it for the chance to see and photograph the sandstone buttes against the background of towering Thousand Lake Mountain.

Then there's the **Waterpocket Fold,** a strip of colorful rock layers almost 70 miles long. It derives the latter part of its name from a great folding over of the earth's crust, while the first part signifies the shallow depressions sometimes eroded in Southwest sandstone, which collect rainwater and hold it for long periods as a boon to man and animal alike. The best way to get to it is over the **Burr Trail,** an old cattle-drive route; actually, it's the only way to go east-west across the fold. From the west, approach through the town of Boulder, expecting switchbacks and steep grades on a road best for four-wheel-drives, suitable for auto traffic, and not recommended for heavy trailers. Before entering the park you'll pass through a 30-mile stretch of public domain land and find plenty of spectacular sandstone country, everything from near white buff to deep red. From the top of Burr Trail, you come to the junction with **Muley Twist Canyon,** running north and south. North are several arches, accessible by jeep or foot traffic, while to the south is choice backpacking country. Unless you've been this way before, you might do best to go in with a guide.

Tour operators. One-day trips in four-wheel-drive station wagons are conducted by Lurt and Alice Knee of Sleeping Rainbow Guest Ranch (P.O. Box 93, Torrey, Utah 84775). Peace and Quiet, Inc. (P.O. Box 163, Salt Lake City, Utah 84110) conducts longer trips of seven days, using jeeps and backpacking.

Accommodations. A park campground is located 1½ miles south of the Visitor Center near the Fremont River. Evening programs are conducted during the summer by park naturalists. Sleeping Rainbow Guest Ranch (see above) occupies a tract of private land ideally located inside the park at the end of the Scenic Drive. Another good spot is Rimrock Lodge, 2 miles west of the park boundary near Torrey. Closest accommodations on the east are 38 miles from the Visitor Center at Hanksville.

Seasons. Summer daytime temperatures at the Visitor Center (elevation 5,418 feet) are in the 80s and 90s; nights are generally cool. Spring and autumn are mild, with cold weather lasting from mid-December through February. An abundance of insects and birds brings new life to spring. In the lowlands of Cathedral Valley, desert plants turn glorious shades of red and gold in autumn.

Nearby. At Boulder, on the site of an Indian ruin dating back nearly 1,000 years, and currently under excavation, **Anasazi State Park** gives an introduction to the Anasazi—the Ancient Ones—who roamed the Southwest. **Calf Creek Recreation Area,** between Boulder and Escalante, run by the Bureau of Land Management, provides good camping facilities and a 2-mile scenic trail to Calf Creek Falls. **Escalante Canyon,** portions of which are accessible by car or jeep, is explored best on backpack trips of two to four days. Escalante country, wild and beautiful, combines deep, narrow canyons, rivercut cliffs, natural bridges, hanging gardens, and waterfalls—one of the finest unprotected wilderness areas in America. Best months for hiking the canyons are April, May, September, and October. In the **Henry Mountains,** rising to over 11,000 feet on the east side of the Waterpocket Fold, the Bureau of Land Management has established four developed recreation sites, with access to hiking.

For further information write Superintendent, Capitol Reef National Park, Torrey, Utah 84775.

CARLSBAD CAVERNS

Established as a national park, 1930

The chambers of Carlsbad Caverns National Park have been probed to a depth of more than 1,000 feet, but even today this magnificent network of caves (all part of the vast Carlsbad Cavern) has not been completely explored. Other cave systems are known to be deeper. A few have more miles of surveyed passageway. But it can truthfully be said that none surpasses Carlsbad in the immensity of its chambers. The famous Big Room is considered the largest underground room found anywhere in the world.

Immensity is not Carlsbad's only distinguishing quality. The formations of limestone are of endless variety and beauty. Some of the inverted spires known as stalactites are shaped like fragile chandeliers. Stalagmites grow from the floor like massive domes or frozen waterfalls of stone. In some cases, stalagmites and stalactites are joined, forming monumental columns and pillars. Yet alongside may be densely clustered growths called helictites, phenomenal for their delicate appearance.

The limestones in the caverns are very old. They began to form 200 million years ago, during the Permian period, from organic life on a barrier reef bordering an inland sea. In a process that began less than 60 million years ago, these caverns were hollowed out by underground water slowly dissolving its way through cracks in the earth. In more recent times, the inside water has drained away and another stage of formation has begun. Slowly and carefully, nature builds anew on drops of rain and snow seeping down from the surface. Each drop carries a tiny amount of dissolved limestone. The water evaporates, depositing its cargo. After centuries of evaporation and accumulation of deposits, the results are amazing.

During the 1880s ranchers and settlers of New Mexico referred to the part of the cavern that was visible as Bat Cave. They were content to let the bats have it as their special place. Soon after, however, the deposits of bat guano attracted attention. Within a few years thousands of tons were extracted by a mining company. Early in this century a local boy, James Larkin White, went exploring, armed only with a kerosine lamp. His reports on the marvels found in the cave attracted the interest of others, notably Robert Holley of the General Land Office, and Dr. Willis T. Lee of the United States Geological Survey. On October 25, 1923, President Calvin Coolidge proclaimed Carlsbad Cave a national monument, embracing 719 acres.

With national publicity, Carlsbad became famous. Visitors thronged to this remote attraction, even though (in those pre-elevator days) it meant entering the cave via a miner's bucket lowered by windlass several hundred feet to the cavern floor. Carlsbad remained a national monument for only seven years. In 1930, a bill to make it a national park passed Congress without opposition and was approved by President Herbert Hoover.

One would never expect, without warning, to find such a display beneath the foothills of the rugged Guadalupe Mountains in southern New Mexico, a few miles north of the Texas border. Above ground, desert-like flatlands and mountains sweep away to remote horizons. Below, a whole new world unfolds.

More than 35 caverns lie within the 46,753-acre park, but development has been limited to the largest and most easily accessible of these, the mighty Carlsbad Cavern, in which the famous Big Room alone has a ceiling as high as a 25-story building and a floor space large enough for 14 football fields.

THE PRACTICAL GUIDE

You can stop off to view the cave and above-ground environment in half a day with ease—unless spelunking is your special interest. In former years guided tours were conducted on a regular schedule, but now you may enter at any time during operating hours to spend as long, or as short, a period as you wish underground. Rangers are available to answer questions and provide assistance.

Two traditional trips are available plus a rugged new one opened in 1974. The long one requires approximately three hours with 3 miles of walking, starting with a relatively steep descent down switchback trails to a depth of 829 feet. The shorter tour requires about one hour and covers 1½ miles of mostly level trail in the Big Room, 750 feet below. It begins at the Visitor Center, descent is by elevator.

From early June through Labor Day, the caverns are open 7 a.m. to 6 p.m. During the rest of the year hours are from 8 a.m. to 3:15 p.m.

Visitor Center. The building lies at the end of the 7-mile drive from the park entrance. Stop here first to see the displays on the history of the caverns. Take a few minutes to prepare yourself before going below. Of special interest are plants and animals growing above and below ground.

The cave walk begins at the natural entrance, through an arch 90 feet wide and 40 feet high in its greatest dimensions. National Park Service guides are in charge. The caverns' temperature remains at 56 degrees throughout the year; carry a sweater or wrap. The trail extends a mile downward through the main corridor, with high ceilings and large passages, through the **Green Lake Room,** named for a small green pool, into the **King's Palace,** which many visitors consider the most ornate of all chambers. Electric illumination reveals the circular form of the Palace, and its curtains of glittering cave onyx. The trail leads through a series of brilliantly scenic rooms. The **Queen's Chamber** is adorned with formations so translucent that a light placed behind them brings out faint tints of pink and rose.

The **Papoose Room** is a beautiful little chamber, its low ceiling gleaming with stalactites. All of these are only a prelude to the **Big Room.** After a luncheon stop and rest the walk continues to the vast chamber where the ceiling arches 255 feet overhead. One formation poised over the path is aptly named Sword of Damocles. It is followed by totem poles, snowbanked forests, the celebrated Rock of Ages in a dark central alcove, and the Giant Dome. All trips end with a welcome elevator ride to the Visitor Center at the surface.

New Cave, a section previously not open to the public, is the target of wilderness tours over 1 mile long. New Cave is accessible only by walking up a steep 1¼-mile primitive trail from Slaughter Canyon. New Cave, discovered in 1937 by a goat herder, Tom Tucker, searching for lost animals, was used in 1950 for filming *King Solomon's Mines.*

Photography. You will probably do most of your shooting in the Big Room. It will be helpful to learn in advance the equipment and exposures to use below; also to identify the principal features, such as Hall of the Giants, Giant Dome, Temple of the Sun, and Rock of Ages. Don't overlook the four scenic rooms on the first part of the long trip. Photos may be taken at will, the only restriction being that visitors are not permitted to leave the paved trails.

Bat flights can be observed every evening from late May through October, as bats spiral outward for night-long feeding on insects in the surrounding valleys. Despite age-old superstitions, the bats of Carlsbad Caverns reveal themselves to be fascinating creatures: alert, great divers and flyers, and useful to man by feeding on destructive insects. More than a quarter-million of them may spend the day hanging head-downward in dense clusters from the walls and ceilings. At night they zoom out, 5,000 a minute, on the trail of beetles and moths. A park naturalist explains the bat flight each evening just before the flight begins.

The famous bat population, as well as Carlsbad's general environment, is now seriously impacted by warming and drying of the air inside the cave. This has been caused, in part, by using cave air to air-condition the Visitor Center sited over the entrance.

Aboveground the surface of the national park conserves an attractive display of semiarid vegetation and wildlife. The fleet pronghorn is sometimes seen in valley flats and lower canyons. Fawns of the mule deer arrive into the world in late June and early July. Lizards of many kinds perch on top of rocks while sunning themselves and watching for food or enemies. Stroll along the self-guiding nature trails, if only to learn the identifying names of cactuses and other plants that clothe the desert of the Southwest.

Guided trips are conducted several times daily over the **Oak Springs Trail.** An observation tower atop the Visitor Center provides the best view of the vast Delaware Basin. On a clear day you can see Guadalupe Peak, highest point in Texas.

If you want to hike the backcountry, register first at the Visitor Center. Trails are poorly defined but can be followed with a topographic map. There is no water available in the backcountry, so don't plan an extensive trip without adequate preparation.

Accommodations. Families traveling with pets will be pleased to find kennels available at the park. There is also a nursery for children too young to undertake the cavern tour. However, there are no overnight facilities in the park. Motels, hotels, and campgrounds are located in Carlsbad, 29 miles from the park, and in between.

Seasons. The park is open every day of the year. Winter temperatures are mild, snow and ice rare. Spring is an excellent time to visit, when desert flowers bloom. Summer days are hot, but the cool caverns provide welcome relief, and evening temperatures drop.

Nearby. Carlsbad Caverns, though isolated, can be included on an itinerary into Mexico through El Paso, Texas; or on a visit to Guadalupe Mountains National Park, 34 miles south.

For further information write Superintendent, Carlsbad Caverns National Park, 3225 National Parks Highway, Carlsbad, New Mexico 88220.

CRATER LAKE

Established as a national park, 1902

It was only yesterday, as time is measured, 10,000 years ago, when Mount Mazama, a 12,000-foot volcanic peak, rose above the green crest of the Cascades, along with her neighbors, Mount Shasta, Mount Adams, Mount Hood, Mount Rainier, Mount Baker—all mighty sentinels of the northwestern range. Then about 6,600 years ago Mazama erupted with violence.

The mountaintop collapsed, forming an immense basin 20 square miles in area, surrounded by towering walls. This masterpiece of nature's creation is known as a *caldera*. The entire lake, cradled in the extinct volcano, can be taken in by the eye at one time from the rim of lava cliffs, a spectacle hard to match anywhere.

The color of the lake in southern Oregon is the deepest, most brilliant blue; this is no accident, but is related to its depth of 1,932 feet, returning blue rays of sunlight from its depths. Around it is a sharply contrasting Cascadian world of pines, firs, and hemlock.

This scenic wonder apparently was discovered in 1853 by John Wesley Hillman, one of a party of miners searching for the Lost Cabin Mine near the headwaters of the Rogue River. He and his friends voted to name it "Deep Blue Lake," but the discovery was not made public for 31 years. Prospectors and soldiers followed at intermittent intervals. The first official exploration was conducted in 1873 by Dr. J. S. Diller, a geologist, who conducted a sounding of the lake and recorded its depth at 2,008 feet.

William Gladstone Steel, a transplanted Kansan, who first saw Crater Lake in 1885, is credited as "Father of the Park." His determined crusade began with a petition to President Grover Cleveland that all lands around Crater Lake be withdrawn from homesteading and other claims; this was granted February 1, 1886. From then on he fought an uphill battle until Congress voted to establish the national park, with an act which President Theodore Roosevelt approved on May 22, 1902. Steel was appointed the second superintendent in 1913.

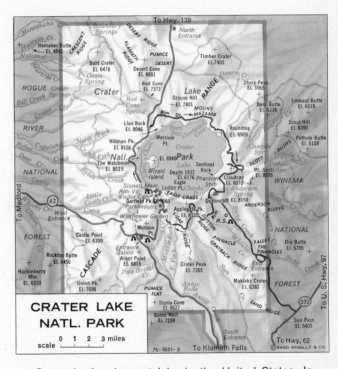

CRATER LAKE NATL. PARK

scale 0 1 2 3 miles

Crater is the deepest lake in the United States. In the Western Hemisphere only Great Slave Lake in Canada is deeper. While the lake is the focal point, the 160,290 acres of green meadows and forests inside the park serve as a sanctuary for species of wildlife under harsh attack elsewhere. The badger, coyote, bobcat, and mountain lion are rare, but do exist; more common is the beautiful red fox. The yellow-bellied marmot usually can be found in the rock slides. Golden-mantled ground squirrels make their appearance at every parking turnout. The bald eagle, golden eagle, and California gull are seen frequently over the lake. The raven and peregrine falcon are in the area between Devils Backbone and Llao Rock. Numbers of jays and nutcrackers accompany the traveler along the rim. Less conspicuous songbirds can be heard, and sometimes seen, along the hiking trails.

THE PRACTICAL GUIDE

If you're on a tour trying to see as much as possible of the Pacific Northwest, Crater Lake can be covered in the better part of a day. But pick that part thoughtfully, perhaps at sunrise, when the calm, mirrorlike water reflects the high peaks; or late afternoon, when deer are best seen in the meadows.

Approaching from Klamath Falls (46 miles away) via the south entrance, or from Medford (69 miles) via the west entrance, note the action of Annie Creek, Castle Creek, and other streams carving their vertical-wall canyons ever deeper in the channels where glaciers flowed.

Visitor Center. Interpretive displays will answer many questions about how Mazama was built and then destroyed. The broad terrace of **Sinnott Memorial,** outside the exhibit building, is an excellent orientation point, where talks on the origin of the lake are given several times daily. A coffee shop is open weekends and holidays.

The Visitor Center may be reached by taking **Rim Drive,** one way clockwise, 35 miles around the lake. Buses operate from Klamath Falls in summer, and scenic bus tours around the drive are

scheduled daily. **Cloudcap,** among the snowbanks and whitebark pines, provides a sweeping vista that complements the one at Sinnott Memorial. Hikers may want to follow the 2½-mile trail to the fire tower at the summit of Mount Scott. **The Pinnacles,** 6 miles off the Rim Drive (from Kerr Notch), are spires and fluted columns formed when loose volcanic fragments solidified around gas and steam vents.

A number of trails lead from the drive to other views. The end of **Discovery Point Trail** is near the spot where the young miner Hillman and his friends first spotted the incredible sight of what he called the "Deep Blue Lake." **Garfield Peak** is one of the best vantage points, with a clear view of **Wizard Island,** actually a small volcanic cone produced by seething fire within the caldera after destruction of Mazama.

Tour operator. A 2½-hour launch trip around the lake, accompanied by a park naturalist, from the boat landing at the foot of Cleetwood Trail, affords an intimate perspective of the inside of a volcano and its multicolored lava cliffs. The concession-operated launches run from mid-June through Labor Day, 9 a.m. to 4:30 p.m. The trail is the only access to the water. It is only 1.1 miles, but allow plenty of time, and don't carry any more gear than you need; it is steep going down, steeper on the return. It is well worth the effort and price for the unusual vistas of Wizard Island and Phantom Ship.

Hiking trails of varied types provide the chance for exercise and intimate contact with nature. Eighty-nine miles of trail through evergreen forest are open to walkers. The leisurely trail through **Castle Crest Wildflower Garden** presents orchids, violets, columbine, asters, and a host of others, identified by plant labels. A 2½-mile trail from the Rim Drive, on a fairly gentle grade, leads to the fire tower at the summit of **Mount Scott,** above Cloudcap—this is the highest point in the park, 8,926 feet, almost 2,800 feet above the lake.

Pumice Desert, produced by ancient volcanic action, lies along the north entrance road leading to Diamond Lake (4 miles north) and Bend (92 miles north). The lodgepole pine, a slender tree, is striving for a foothold and to fulfill a mission in clothing old devastation with a new forest.

Campfire programs are held every evening at Mazama Campground. Indoor campfire programs are conducted at Rim Village and Crater Lake Lodge. The programs change nightly and each naturalist interprets them in his own manner.

Rowboats are available for rental. If you have fishing gear, try for kokanee, the little land-locked salmon, and for rainbow trout. No license required.

Accommodations. Crater Lake Lodge and cabins at Rim Village offer plain accommodations. Advance reservations advisable. Write Crater Lake Lodge, Inc., Crater Lake, Oregon. Many motels are located in Klamath Falls, Medford, and other nearby communities.

Camping. Three campgrounds in the park operate first-come, first-served. Trailers welcome, but no hookups. Other

campgrounds are located in surrounding national forests. Also, become acquainted with Bureau of Land Management recreation sites. Two of the largest in Oregon border Gerber Reservoir, with facilities for fishing, boating, swimming, hiking, and trailer sites. From the banks of Fishermen's Bend, spectators on Memorial Day get a fine view of the White Water Challenge, featuring boaters braving the rapids of the North Santiam River.

Seasons. Lodge and cabins are open from about June 15 to September 10, and campgrounds from July through September. Weather of the short two-month summer is unpredictable, with warm days and chilly nights. The north entrance is usually closed by snow until mid-June, and the Rim Drive till early July; but the south and west entrances are open all year. From late October through May heavy snowfalls create a glistening attraction, with reflections of high peaks in the mirrorlike water.

Nearby. The Cascade Mountains surrounding Crater Lake comprise one of the finest recreation areas of the Northwest. Four miles north of the park, **Diamond Lake** lies within **Umpqua National Forest,** with campgrounds on the east

shore and miles of forest trails to **Mount Bailey** and **Mount Thielsen,** and along the Oregon Skyline Trail. To the south, the **Wildlife Refuges** are a major stopover on the Pacific Flyway for ducks and geese, and a favored resting place of thousands of sandhill crane and the famous Klamath white pelican. **Lake of the Woods** is one of the most attractive areas of Winema National Forest, with good fishing for rainbow trout and camping near the base of Mount McLoughlin. The **Ashland Loop Drive** passes through stands of Douglas fir and ponderosa pine within **Rogue River National Forest.** So does the Skyline Trail, running from Washington to the California border. **Ashland** is the scene of the Oregon Shakespearean Festival, mid-July to early September. If driving up from the west coast of California, be sure to stop at **Oregon Caves National Monument,** a limestone and marble cavern with formations of unusual beauty, and if coming from the east, at **Lava Beds National Monument,** a scene of ancient volcanic activity which became a battleground in the Modoc Indian War of 1873.

For further information write Superintendent, Crater Lake National Park, Box 7, Crater Lake, Oregon 97604.

EVERGLADES

Authorized as a national park, 1934

At the southern tip of the Florida peninsula there lies an expanse of tall, swaying grasses; tropical plants and trees; and dozens of low islands, or keys, rising from the sheltered waters of Florida Bay. This is the Everglades, a refuge for beautiful tropical birdlife in variety and abundance found hardly anywhere else on earth.

The Everglades constitute a refuge for man, too—a place at booming Miami's doorstep where he can find inspiration from the unimproved works of nature. This great biological exhibit in an aquatic setting presents a living drama of nature. Some habitats, such as the Everglades themselves, and some of the birds, reptiles, and mammals, are either rare or cannot be seen elsewhere in the nation. Here are the storks (the only ones in the United States) called wood ibis, huge birds whose pure white feathers contrast with their jet-black wing tips. Along the palm-fringed shoreline, brown pelicans may be seen gliding or flapping their wings while flying in formation to a distant rendezvous. Over the mangrove swamp inland, yellow-crowned and black-crowned night herons soar over the trees. Elsewhere are the roseate spoonbills, big pink birds with crimson splashes, and the great white herons spreading their immense wings seven feet from tip to tip.

These birds and others, colored blue, green, black, yellow, red, and several shades in between, gather by the thousands to build their nests and bring their young into the world. Their refuge in the Everglades, covering 1,400,533 acres, is larger than the state of Delaware, and is the third largest of our national parks.

Long before the European explorers arrived aboriginal Indians, the Calusas and Tequestas, were attracted to this region by its abundant resources—the great beds of conchs, oysters, and clams. They made their homes on the islands or on the river banks and hammocks nearby, utilizing the fish, game, and plant foods around them. The modern Indians—Miccosukees and Seminoles—arrived in Spanish Florida after the American Revolution. Many Creeks of Georgia and Alabama,

crowded by the invading white settlers, fled to the Florida peninsula. They were forced continually southward, finally retreating to the Everglades, where deer, fish, and fruit were plentiful. They traded alligator hides, otter skins, and egret plumes with the white settlers. The white men were few, primarily hunters and fishermen, though some came to cut cypress and mahogany trees, or to remove royal palms to beautify budding urban communities, or to farm on the limited land available.

At the turn of this century the Everglades area was known as the home of many varieties of birds of striking beauty; some, like the egrets, were prized for plumes on women's hats. They were shot on a large scale and even then threatened with extinction. The National Committee of Audubon Societies raised funds in 1902 to engage a warden, Guy Bradley, but he was murdered in 1905. It was a tragedy that gave impetus to both the bird conservation movement and to the preservation of the area.

Proposals to safeguard the Everglades were advanced when Theodore Roosevelt was president, and continually thereafter. "It has its place among the country's native wonders, like the Mammoth Cave and Niagara Falls," wrote Edwin A. Dix and John M. McGonigle in an article in *Century Magazine* of February 1905. "After all, it is rather a good thing to have a little of wonderland left." Interest in Paradise Key was particularly strong. Sparked by the Florida Federation of Women's Clubs, Royal Palm State Park was established in 1916. Five years later, in 1923, Stephen T. Mather, director of the National Park Service, declared in a report, "There should be an untouched example of the Everglades of Florida established as a national park." The Tropical Everglades National Park Association, headed by Dr. Harold Bailey and Ernest F. Coe, was founded to lead the citizen movement to achieve that goal. Through their efforts, Congress in 1929 authorized a study on the desirability of a national park. Action, however, was slow, even though in 1934 Congress actually voted to establish an Everglades National Park, for opponents in the House tacked on a provision that no money be appropriated to purchase land for five years.

Over the next ten years, unfortunately, little progress had been made. But Governor Spessard Holland was very interested in the project and worked with citizen groups to get the money needed for Florida's share of the land purchase. In 1946 the State legislature provided $2 million for the purchase of private lands in the area. This action cleared the way for the park's establishment. Everglades National Park was dedicated December 6, 1947, by President Harry S. Truman. Leaders in the effort, besides Coe and Bailey, had been Spessard Holland, who had gone from the governor's chair to the United States Senate, and John D. Pennekamp of the *Miami Herald*. The largest single donation of private lands was made by the family of Barron G. Collier, who gave 32,000 acres, including important parts of the Ten Thousand Islands and the mangrove coast.

Since then the Everglades have been increasingly damaged by civilization's inroads. Dikes and drainage canals constructed between Lake Okeechobee and the park have deprived the Everglades of much of the natural flow of fresh water. A partially completed jetport at its border is another grave threat, to the park and to those who find it a source of peace and inspiration.

The true everglades were called by the Indians *Pa-hay-okee,* the "grassy waters" or "river of grass,"

but the park is a many-sided spectacle of unusual plant communities and wildlife. Clusters of trees and dense vegetation in the open glades form islands called hammocks, with hardwood trees more typical of the West Indies, including the mahogany, strangler fig, and coppery-barked gumbo-limbo. In other sections are bald cypress and pine forests of the Southern swamps. Hundreds of interesting plants grow from the edge of Florida Bay and the Gulf of Mexico into the wilderness, ranging from the graceful, towering royal palms to delicate lilies and ferns.

The Everglades teem with life—from fish, crustaceans, and shellfish to snakes, deer, raccoon, and possum, right up to cougar and black bear. The lagoons provide a pasture for Florida's strange, air-breathing, vegetarian "sea cow," the manatee. The most celebrated swamp dwellers are the blunt-nosed alligator, who sticks to fresh water, and the rare long-snouted crocodile, who prefers his water salty. The great diversity of water habitats produces a limitless variety of aquatic life. Salt waters extend from the clear depths of the Gulf on the west to the supersaline shallows of most of Florida Bay. Clear fresh waters of the glades and brown-stained waters of the mangrove rivers produce microscopic life that serves as food for fish, which in turn feed the rich birdlife. This explains why conservationists have pressed for establishment of the Big Cypress National Preserve in order to safeguard the last natural flow of fresh water. It is a struggle for survival of the Everglades.

THE PRACTICAL GUIDE

It is possible to get a peek of the Everglades in a couple of hours. If you are driving down to Key West, or staying in Miami on a quickie vacation, go through Homestead into the park at least for a little while. You may like it enough to return another time for a week.

This is a park of wonderful watery boulevards and byroads for boaters. In fact, the Western Water Gateway at Everglades, southeast of Naples, provides access *only* by boat. Visitors traveling by boat are well advised to obtain a set of navigational charts; an expert guide may add to enjoyment of the park, and to better fishing.

Visitor Center. Approaching from Homestead, the Visitor Center on Florida 27 features an excellent slide program. Two miles beyond, the **Royal Palm Area** presents a good Everglades cross section. Here the **Anhinga Trail,** an elevated boardwalk across the slough, features a dependable wildlife show, with alligators, water snakes, and a variety of

wading birds. The **Gumbo-Limbo Trail,** an easy 1/3-mile loop, will introduce you to airplants, ferns, orchids, and tropical hardwood trees.

Flamingo, 39 miles from the park entrance, at the subtropical tip of the mainland, is the main center, converted from an old fishing village. This is your base for exploratory trips into the wilderness of Whitewater Bay and hundreds of miles of winding mangrove rivers, the channels and keys of Florida Bay, the gulf area, the mangrove coast, and tropical beaches of Cape Sable. Flamingo has a fine marina, the gateway to sport fishing, birdwatching, and photography. Canoe trails afford excellent means of observing native fauna; campsites are along the trails.

Tour operators. Boat tours are offered from Everglades City by a National Park concessioner, Sammy Hamilton, a native of the area. His trips are among the finest anywhere in the national parks.

Mangrove wilderness trips are conducted by boat from Everglades up

Halfway Creek past Indian shell mounds built by the Calusa Indians some 2,000 years ago. The **Bird roost trip** runs in the evening, before twilight, past Chokoloskee Island to the Ten Thousand Island Area.

Boat-a-cades, a unique feature of this park, leave Flamingo and Everglades on Chokoloskee Bay most Saturdays during winter. Bring your own boat (or rent one) and follow a ranger on an all-day cruise through backcountry waterways. Boats must be able to maintain a speed of 15 m.p.h. Besides these maritime caravans, **sightseeing boat trips** of one to four hours are operated to Whitewater Bay and (a sunset cruise) to Florida Bay.

Wilderness tram tours of about two hours are designed to interpret plant and birdlife of the area. Early in this century, egrets and spoonbills were slain and whole rookeries destroyed in hunting for plumes for women's hats; at one period these beautiful birds almost disappeared, but now they display their plumage for admiration, not exploitation.

Shark Valley open-air tram bus tours provide a new opportunity to see an abundance of wildlife. The tours originate at a parking area just inside the park entrance, 30 miles west of Miami on the south side of the Tamiami Trail. The trail separates the park from the proposed Big Cypress Fresh Water Reserve. The trip parallels a canal to the Shark Valley Observation Tower, which affords an excellent view. Trams depart at half-hour intervals, 9:30 a.m. to 4 p.m. Allow one and one-half hours. Cost of the tour is included in the $2 daily entrance fee charged for each private car and its occupants.

Naturalist programs include daily talks and walks during the winter season. The visitor centers at Flamingo and Parachute Key house displays on natural and human history, from the era of the ancient Indian mound builders to the age of the modern bird conservers. Slide lectures every evening.

Fishing waters offshore are famous for sea trout, small tarpon, redfish, snapper, and other fish. Fully equipped charter boats run from Flamingo and Everglades. Freshwater fishing with rod and reel requires a Florida fishing license; none is needed for salt water.

Accommodations. Flamingo Lodge offers modern motel-type rooms. Housekeeping cottages are suited for family use. Swimming pool for lodge and cottage guests. Rates are lower May 1–December 15 than during the winter peak. The concessioner also operates houseboats which sleep a maximum of six and cruise 8 to 10 miles per hour in Florida Bay. Write Everglades Park Company, 18494 South Federal Highway, Perrine, Florida 33157, for current rates and reservations. Motel accommodations in Everglades, Homestead, the Keys, and many resorts of South Florida.

Camping. Campgrounds in the park are located at Long Pine Key (6 miles from park entrance) and Flamingo, with stay limited to 14 days. Camping is permitted in the backcountry, if you first obtain a permit at park headquarters or a ranger station. Camping facilities near the park are located at Collier-Seminole State Park, 19 miles north of Everglades, on the Tamiami Trail, and at private campgrounds north of Homestead.

Seasons. Winter and early spring are ideal for bird and wildlife watching—because animals concentrate around the few remaining water areas. The weather is usually mild enough for shirtsleeves. Mosquitoes can be a problem in late spring and are likely to become fierce by summer, when conditions are apt to range from uncomfortable to unbearable. From June until August giant loggerhead turtles crawl onto the beaches at Cape Sable to lay their eggs.

Nearby. Showpiece of the Seminole country is the **Dania Indian Reservation** at Hollywood, north of Miami, with an outstanding arts and crafts center and display of Seminole life. The **Seminole campground,** open to the public year-round (fee charged), is a base for airboat and swamp-buggy tours.

For a naturalist's tour south of Miami, start with the beautiful **Fairchild Tropical Garden** in Coral Gables, displaying palms, cycads, an amazing rain forest, and desert forest. Include a stop at **Redland Fruit and Spice Park,** a center of tropical plant culture, north of Homestead. Coming down the west side of Florida, start at the **Thomas A. Edison Botanical Gardens and Laboratory,** where the wizard of electricity maintained his summer home amid 14 acres of rare trees, ferns, and flowers. The **Everglades Nursery,** 6 miles southwest, one of the largest nurseries for palms and tropical plants, presents a bougainvillea exhibit every February. On the way south, **Everglades Wonder Gardens,** at Bonito Springs, display over 2,000 specimens of native wildlife. In Naples, the **Caribbean Gardens** contain an outstanding collection of orchids, bromeliads, and air plants—plus a large assortment of waterfowl—on its 30 subtropical and tropical acres. From mid-January to May 1, you can take an all-day combination tour of the Gardens and the National Audubon Society's **Corkscrew Swamp Sanctuary.** Corkscrew, a wildlife sanctuary of 6,000 acres, is truly the companion piece to the Everglades. Containing our country's largest remaining stand of virgin bald cypress, many towering 130 feet, it is 35 miles from Naples and is reached on station-wagon tours.

South from the park on the sparkling overwater road to Key West, **John Pennekamp Coral Reef State Park,** in the Atlantic Ocean off Key Largo, is the first underseas park in continental United States—a fantasyland of coral beauty, protected as the breeding ground of fish, shellfish, and turtles. You can explore the park by glass-bottom boat and see brilliantly colored fish swimming among old wrecks caught in the reef. On shore the park has a campground, nature trail, wading area, and marina (rental boats and diving gear available). Another state park, **Bahia Honda,** south of Marathon, has facilities for fishing, picnicking, boating, camping, and an excellent beach for swimming. In Key West, a visit to the **Audubon House** is appropriate, for it is restored to its appearance of 1832, when it was occupied by America's greatest nature painter; it was he who discovered the great white heron that now finds its refuge in the national park. Finally, the land runs out, but 70 miles west of Key West lies **Fort Jefferson National Monument,** a 19th century coastal fort in the reef islands called the Dry Tortugas, famous for their rich bird, plant, and undersea life.

For further information write Superintendent, Everglades National Park, Box 279, Homestead, Florida 33030.

GLACIER

Established as a national park, 1910

One million acres is a large parcel of real estate, even in Montana, but hardly any area of that size concentrates as much rugged mountain splendor as Glacier National Park. The scenery of its thousand waterfalls tumbling from glacial snow masses into sparkling lakes and streams, surrounded by lustrous primitive forests, is overwhelming to everyone who comes this way. Yet the experience here is an intimate one, for you can walk or ride a horse in the company of myriad wildflowers up to the frozen rivers themselves, and spend a cool summer's night in a chalet within easy walking (or riding) distance of a glacier.

This mighty place of scientific, scenic, and inspirational values is more than one nation's park. Its proper name is Waterton-Glacier International Peace Park, a reminder that it lies not only astride the Continental Divide, but spills over the border into southwest Alberta; through a sanctuary of nature two countries commemorate the universal spirit of good will.

The sharp, precipitous peaks and sheer knife-edged ridges tell a classic geological story dating from the dawn of earth's history, when most of the western states were covered by a shallow sea. Some of the oldest known sedimentary rocks, formed of mud, clay, and sand in that early sea, are on view, exposed by action of what is called the *Lewis overthrust,* representing a procession of change through millions of years during which one edge of the earth was thrust upward and over another. From this upland, glaciers and streams later shaped the peaks and valleys, gouged out the lakes, and sculptured rich land formations of the high Rockies—such as the amphitheater called a *glacial cirque;* the thin knife-edge of rock, an *arête;* and the towerlike sentinel gouged by two or more glaciers, a *horn.*

As a wilderness sanctuary totaling 1,013,598 acres, which the Indians of the adjacent plains regarded with awe, Glacier is one of the last strongholds of the proud grizzly bear. Bighorn sheep, mountain goat, mule deer, moose, and elk are other large American mammals to be seen and respected. The park's trails provide the sophisticated traveler his best wildlife viewpoints. Hawks and eagles wheel overhead, grouse are apt to skirt upward from the brush, the slate-gray water ouzel—shaped like a chunky wren with short tail—may be seen along swift-flowing streams, and thrushes are heard singing in the undergrowth. There are at least 57 species of mammals and 210 species of birds, and this is one place where they are holding their own.

Few areas in the West produce a more comprehensive show of trees, plants, and wildflowers. Glacier is a rendezvous of a thousand species of the south, east, west, and even the Arctic. In the valleys on the east side are stands of Engelmann spruce, subalpine fir, and lodgepole pine, but across the western slopes, where moisture is heavier, the forests are more luxuriant with groves of ponderosa pine, Douglas fir, larch, hemlock, and western red cedar. Beneath these trees and across the open meadows a colorful display of wildflowers stands out everywhere as one of the park's major attractions. The showiest is bear grass, a misnamed member of the lily family, while other flowering plants include the glacier lily along the edge of snowbanks, Indian paintbrush, fireweed, gentians, and asters.

THE PRACTICAL GUIDE

Before completion of the Going-to-the-Sun Road in 1933, visitors went on five- to seven-day loops around the park traveling by horseback (once there were 1,200 horses kept in the park for tourists), bus, when possible, and motor launch. Seven days, or even 14, are still not too much to spend in this park with its superb thousand-mile network of hiking and riding trails. John Muir, after a visit to Glacier, advised: "Give a month at least to this precious reserve. The time will not be taken from the sum of your life. Instead of shortening, it will definitely lengthen it and make you truly immortal."

If you are on a northwestern tour, Glacier deserves three full days and two nights. If you're crossing the country aboard Amtrak's Empire Builder, stop over a day and cross the park by bus—the railway has terminals at both the east and west entrances.

Visitor Center. From the Canadian side, an outstanding launch trip runs from Waterton townsite south on Waterton Lake, across the international boundary to the modern Waterton Visitor Center, a major national park project completed in 1966. Besides the exhibits and observation deck, a hikers' shelter and ranger station make this site a trailhead for spectacular backcountry.

The naturalist program is one of the most extensive in the park system, including conducted overnight trips to Sperry Glacier, Garden Wall, and Granite Park; accompanied boat and trail trips, evening campground programs, and slide talks in the hotels. Note that displays at each Visitor Center tell a different phase of the Glacier Park story. See them all.

Going-to-the-Sun Road, the 50-mile link between St. Mary Lake on the east side and Lake McDonald on the west side of the park, crosses the Continental Divide at Logan Pass (elevation 6,664 feet), where springtime prevails and alpine flowers reach their height of bloom as late as August. One of the outstanding scenic routes in the world, Going-to-the-Sun climbs gently above treeline while it unfolds vistas of lakes, waterfalls, and high cliffs. It provides access to walking trails and field trips.

A concession-operated shuttle service now supplements private auto transportation on Going-to-the-Sun Road from McDonald Lake Lodge to Logan Pass. Oversize vehicles are no longer permitted on the road because of physical limitations.

Tour operators. All-expense tours ranging from one to ten days may be arranged by travelers arriving by bus or train with Glacier Park, Inc., the principal concessioner; these include trips by bus, horse, and launch, plus meals and lodging.

Trail rides on saddle horses are tops in Glacier. A popular all-day trip leads from **Many Glacier Valley** through fields of wildflowers to **Iceberg Lake,** in a high glacial cirque, where chunks of snowbank slip into the lake and float like bergs. Other trips range from two hours and half-day tours for novices to energetic steep climbs for experts. Guided-pack trips of a week or more, with time for fishing, hiking, and photography, can be arranged with the park-approved outfitter, who ranks among the best in Montana. Hiking parties can also engage packer, cook, and pack horse. Write Rocky Mountain Outfitters, Inc., Ronan, Montana 59864. (After June 1, East Glacier Park, Montana 59434.)

Hiking trails fan out in all directions from hotels, chalets, and campgrounds. One popular easy walk, the **Avalanche Lake Trail,** leads from Avalanche Campground, in a wooded grove off the Going-to-the-Sun Road, along a stream filled with potholes scoured out by stones swirling in the torrent of milky glacial water from Sperry Glacier. The trail leads 2 miles to Avalanche Basin, where half-a-dozen waterfalls plunge over 2,000-foot-high rock walls. It is a good route on which to carry a picnic lunch and fishing gear.

For serious overnight hiking, obtain topographic or hiking maps and Ruhle's "Guide to Glacier," available throughout the park. Park officials advise against trying to cover too much country in a day, or crossing glaciers, which can be treacherous. Hikers should always register at a ranger station both before beginning and on reaching destination. Mountain climbing is ill advised because of fragile rock, unpredictable weather, and hidden glacial crevices. Though normally shy, grizzly bears can be a problem in the backcountry when approached without warning. Hikers do well to carry a cowbell, or rocks in a can, to make their presence known on the trail. Singing is also effective.

Sperry Chalets afford the opportunity to make an intriguing overnight hike without being burdened with camping gear. Cooking is done for you when you arrive and servings are plentiful; box lunches available. The chalets, reached only by trail from Lake McDonald or Sun Point, are in a high mountain cirque near the Continental Divide, with opportunity for exploring Sperry Glacier and fishing in nearby lakes. Mountain goats are often seen climbing the sheer rock

walls. **Granite Park Chalets** are located in one of the best hiking regions of the park and make a good target for the long-distance hiker on the trek south from Waterton or north from Logan Pass. There also are four shelter cabins in the park, equipped with cots and cookstoves, but without bedding or cooking utensils.

Chief Mountain International Road is an outstanding park-to-park highway on the eastern flank of the mountains, through the Blackfeet Indian Reservation, and around the base of Chief Mountain, with a view of the Great Plains bending eastward, then through a beautiful spruce and fir forest. It crosses the Canadian border with a clear view of Mount Cleveland, Glacier's highest peak (elevation 10,448 feet). **Waterton Lakes National Park,** on the Canadian side, receives half as many visitors as Glacier, but is a jewel in its own right.

Launch trips are operated on Lake McDonald, the largest lake in the park, on the west side; Two Medicine Lake, in the southeast corner; St. Mary Lake, surrounded by soaring peaks, waterfalls, and primitive forest; and on Swiftcurrent and Josephine lakes, in the Many Glacier region, to view spectacular glacier-carved scenery. Special cruises are scheduled for photographers only, usually in early morning. Small boats and fishing tackle are available for rental.

Fishing. No license required; general season extends from June 20 to October 15, though special season dates apply to some waters. Streams and lakes abound in fish. Seasonal migrations of native cutthroat, Dolly Varden, and kokanee on the west side provide much speculation, but mackinaw, or "lake trout" are taken in the larger lakes. The pygmy whitefish is the most unusual, found only in a few widely scattered localities in North America. Fly casting with artificial fly is generally used, live or dead fish for bait not permitted.

Accommodations. The best concentration of attractions is in the Many Glacier Region, the setting of Many Glacier Hotel, where bighorn sheep sometimes are seen on the lawn; the modern Swiftcurrent Motor Inn, and economy (cold water) Swiftcurrent Cabins. Rising Sun Cabins and modern Rising Sun Motor Inn are located inside the park near the St. Mary entrance. Glacier Park Lodge is at the southeast corner but outside the park. Across the park is Lake McDonald Lodge, originally built about 1914 as a hunting lodge; the Sunday smorgasbord is a specialty. All the above, plus the modern Village Inn, at the foot of Lake McDonald in Apgar (a tourist settlement inside the park), and Prince of Wales Hotel at Waterton Lake, are operated by Glacier Park, Inc., East Glacier Park, Montana 59434 (from October 16 through May 31, Box 4340, Tucson, Arizona 85717). Sperry and Granite Park chalets are run by B. Ross Luding, Martin City, Montana 59926. Reservations are usually necessary for hotels, motels, cabins. Other motels and cabins on the west side are located in Apgar and outside the park on US 2 in West Glacier, Hungry Horse, Whitefish, and Kalispell; on the east side, on US 2 around East Glacier Park, and along US 89 in the vicinity of Browning and St. Mary. Several new motels have been built in Waterton townsite on the Canadian side.

Camping. Major campgrounds are located around Lake McDonald, Swiftcurrent, St. Mary, Rising Sun, and Two Medicine. Smaller, less developed facilities should not be overlooked. **Kintla Lake** campground, for instance, is an isolated beauty spot in the North Fork Valley near the Canadian border, with wonderful hiking along the lake. Attractive campsites can be found along the North Fork of the Flathead River in **Flathead National Forest,** and southeast of the park in **Lewis and Clark National Forest.** Canadian campgrounds are different from those in the United States, being equipped with community kitchen shelters.

Seasons. Glacier is essentially a summer park. Going-to-the-Sun Road is usually closed by snow from mid-October until early June. Naturalist-conducted activities run from about June 15 to Labor Day. Accommodations inside the park are open mid-June to mid-September. Still, early June has its special appeal, with light crowds, freshness of spring, and wealth of flowers. So has September (even the end of the month). With the coming of autumn, scarlet berries and yellow and orange leaves make the park a colorful panorama. The golden-yellow needles of the larch, a strangely behaved conifer, stand out in bright contrast against a background of its green neighbors. During summer, days are warm, evenings chilly. Warm clothing is essential for hiking in the high country; so is a raincoat to cope with thundershowers.

Souvenirs worth saving. In Apgar village, **Montana House** is just what its name implies, a showcase of arts, crafts, and handmade clothing of the entire state—one of the best gift shops of the Northwest. The **Northern Plains Indian Crafts Association** has a trading center at St. Mary, just outside the park. Shops at Waterton sell English woolens, Es-

kimo sealskin slippers, and wildlife prints.

Nearby. Eight miles from Whitefish, near the west entrance, the 6,800-foot **chairlift at Big Mountain** provides a different perspective of the park, plus spacious **Flathead Valley.** From the Visitor Center at **Hungry Horse Dam,** 564 feet high, you can see the huge manmade lake in **Flathead National Forest;** campgrounds and boat landings are on the lakeshore. **Flathead Lake,** south of Kalispell, is the largest natural freshwater lake west of the Mississippi (28 miles long, 10 miles wide), bordered by

the mighty Mission Mountains and the forested foothills of the Salish Mountains. At Browning, 12 miles from East Glacier Park, the **Museum of the Plains Indian,** near the center of the millionacre Blackfeet Reservation, interprets ancient customs of Indians of the Great Plains. Wood carvings and frescoes alone make the visit worthwhile.

Recommended reading. *Roads and Trails of Waterton-Glacier,* by George C. Ruhle.

For further information write Superintendent, Glacier National Park, West Glacier, Montana 59936.

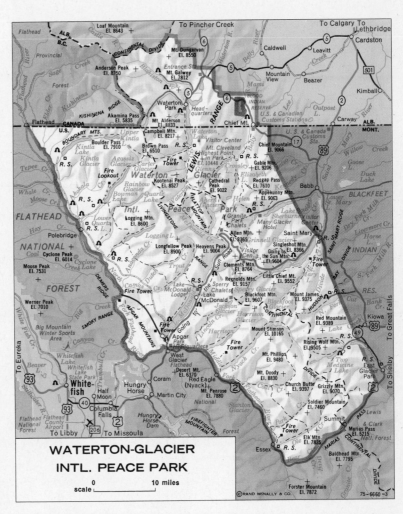

WATERTON-GLACIER
INTL. PEACE PARK

scale 0 — 10 miles

GRAND CANYON

Established as a national park, 1919

"Do nothing to mar its grandeur," said President Theodore Roosevelt after his first trip to the Grand Canyon in 1903. "Keep it for your children," he urged, "and your children's children, and all who come after you, as the one great sight which every American should see."

One would think the awesome Grand Canyon has forever been regarded in this manner, and by everyone, not solely because it staggers the senses, but as a moody, crumbling composite of rock that could hardly be adapted to "practical" purposes. Strangely, however, there have always been some ambitious souls believing they could harness the Colorado River and improve on nature's masterwork.

A few, who felt the Grand Canyon should be entrusted to them for exploitation of mineral resources, blocked establishment of the national park for 30 years. Others wanted to control a tourist toll road on Bright Angel Trail, and also to string a cable car down into the canyon, or even from one rim to the other. To this day, proposals are advanced to dam the Colorado River and thus "civilize" this wild country. The majority, however, still heed Roosevelt's plea. The visitor at the brink of the mighty abyss feels himself humbled, cleansed of self-interest, swept up by the spirit of what John Burroughs called "the world's most wonderful spectacle, ever changing, alive with a million moods," and hopeful, like Mr. Roosevelt, that it will always remain so.

In form, size, glowing color, or geological significance, nothing approaches the Grand Canyon of the Colorado River. Although it is 217 miles long, only about 100 miles are within the park, which covers 674,287 acres. From rim to rim, the park portion varies from 4 to 18 miles in width. Measured from the North Rim, which averages about 1,200 feet higher than the South Rim, it is 5,700 feet deep—substantially more than 1 mile straight down.

The North and South rims are only 9 miles apart (214 miles apart by road), but they are distinctly different—two of many worlds within the universe of the

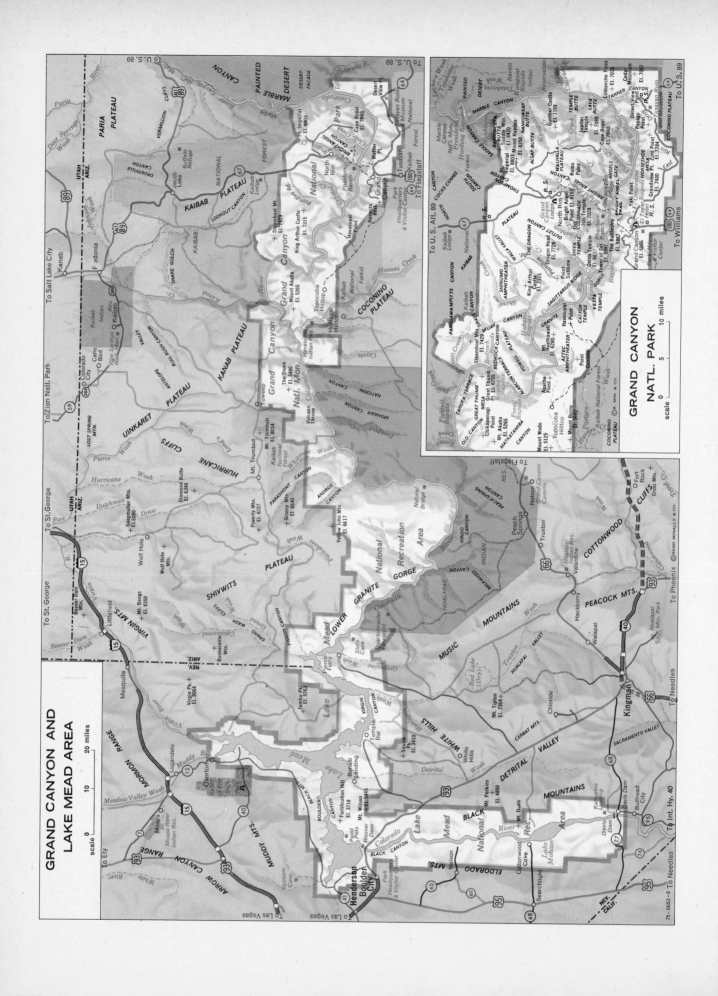

GRAND CANYON AND
LAKE MEAD AREA

scale
0   10   20 miles

GRAND CANYON
NATL. PARK

scale
0   5   10 miles

©R. MN. & CO.

Grand Canyon. The North Rim extends into the Canadian zone of climate, vegetation, and plant life and, at 9,000 feet, into the sub-Arctic Hudsonian zone. The famous blue spruce on the heavily forested North Rim are not seen at all on the other side of the canyon, which is more typical of the arid Southwest. Nor is the white-tailed, black-bodied Kaibab squirrel. On the other hand, the Abert's squirrel, grizzled gray of body and tail, with white underparts, is strictly a South Rim dweller. The two color phases never meet.

The first sight of the Grand Canyon excites the visitor's appetite to see more, and the first answers to his questions stimulate the curiosity to ask a thousand more questions. The sequence begins with rock and the formation of the canyon, and the end is the story of the earth and every science and romance related to it. As canyons go, the mighty chasm is young. The down-cutting process began only nine million years ago. The stream that preceded the Colorado, in the evolution of rivers, meandered over a broad plain until a general rising of the land caused it to flow more swiftly. Instead of being displaced, it cut downward. According to traditional theory, the slow rise was concurrent with the lifting of the Rocky Mountains, which gave the river greater run-off, and consequently more carrying and cutting power. As the canyon walls grew steadily higher, the Colorado deepened its course. A recent theory, endorsed by most experts on Colorado Plateau geology, declares that the Colorado River once drained eastward and was separated by the Kaibab Plateau from another drainage to the west. Then the land uplift near the present Arizona-New Mexico border blocked the flow of the Colorado, forming a large lake.

When the western drainage eroded headward, it tapped the waters of the lake, and the period of canyon cutting began.

Century after century the walls have weathered, crumbled, tumbled their shreds of sand, gravel, mud, and rock into the water, and have given the river tools for scouring and gouging. The canyon has widened and changed. It is never twice the same, one day to the next. Its appearance varies with the hour of day.

The rock layers exposed to view are pages in the textbook of earth's history, spanning two billion years. The uppermost stratum, Kaibab limestone, is of Permian age, formed approximately 180 million years ago. Below it lies Coconino sandstone, the solidified remains of sand dunes, in which fossilized footprints indicate a lizard type of life. Next are Hermit and Supai shales, with traces of amphibians and fossil ferns. The course of history can be traced through one layer to another to the sharp-angled mountains formed from Late Precambrian rocks. At the bottom of the inner gorge of the Grand Canyon are among the oldest rocks exposed anywhere on earth, the hard black rock of the Early Precambrian Age, which came before any form of life on earth.

All human affairs are dwarfed by these older, natural forces. The records of history date only to 1540, when the Spaniard Don Lopez de Cardenas was led by the Hopi Indians to the great gorge. It was John Wesley Powell, explorer, geologist, mapmaker, and hero of the West, who made a daring voyage of a thousand miles through the canyons of the Green and Colorado rivers in 1869—a modern odyssey, worthy of the ages, in the Grand Canyon.

THE PRACTICAL GUIDE: SOUTH RIM
This side is easier to reach, more heavily visited. Stay at least two days here, if only to watch the magic changes between dawn and dusk. Do the usual things, if this is your first visit, but then go on to the *unusual* opportunities available to explore Grand Canyon.

South Rim Drives from Grand Canyon Village give the introduction, covering 35 miles with excellent views and linking the main focal points. Two free transportation systems operate at Grand Canyon: a Village shuttle supplemental to private cars and a West Rim tour—the West Rim is closed to private cars.

Visitor Center. This building, 1 mile east of the village, is an important stop for orientation exhibits and dioramas. At **Yavapai Museum,** a ranger-naturalist gives daily talks.

Farther east, the drive leads to **Tu-sayan Ruin and Museum,** a small prehistoric pueblo which tells the story of Pueblo people who inhabited and left the Grand Canyon before the white man came; **Lipan Point,** with a view of the winding river and the San Francisco Peaks to the south; and the **Watchtower** at Desert View, perched on the brink of the canyon, 25 miles from the village, with views of the Painted Desert, Kaibab National Forest, and, through telescopes, the surrounding Indian country. The West Rim Drive leads 8 miles to **Hermit's Rest,** passing excellent lookouts and the head of Bright Angel Trail. Late each afternoon, year-round, at **Hopi House,** a small group of Hopi Indians perform ancient ceremonial dances. The sunsets from **Hopi Point** are famous.

A trip to the reservation of the Havasupai Indians is a separate excursion from the generally visited South Rim area. This is an attraction unique in the United States, a desert oasis with the turquoise-blue waters of Havasu Creek cascading in spectacular waterfalls. It takes about a half-day's drive (via US 66 and dirt road turnoff 7 miles east of Peach Springs) to Hualapai Hilltop, the point of entry. Access from there to the reservation, 2,000 feet below, is over a precipitous trail, and must be covered on horseback or on foot. Havasu Canyon is of special interest to geology students, botanists, bird-watchers, and anthropologists. The Indian community, Supai Village, entirely within the boundaries of the national park, is bordered by near-vertical red-rock walls. There are two tourist lodges with kitchen facilities in the village, and a National Park Service wilderness campground 3 miles down the canyon. The Havasupai serve no meals. Prepare to do your own cooking; some groceries may be purchased in the tribal store. Arrangements for horses and lodgings must be made in advance by telephoning or writing Havasupai Tourist Information, Havasupai Tourist Enterprise, Supai, Arizona 86435. Legislation has been proposed in Congress to transfer 91,000 acres of Grand Canyon National Park and Monument in "trust title" to the Havasupai Indians. This would endanger the environment of the park, since the Indians would have legal right to develop or exploit the land in any way they might decide, as long as they do not sell it.

Tour operators. Going by muleback to **Phantom Ranch** is a one-day trip that provides a popular way of viewing the canyon from the ground up. The trip begins down the celebrated twisting **Bright Angel Trail** between Grandeur and Maricopa points to the Tonto Plateau and Plateau Point.

Even more adventuresome is the two-day trip into the inner gorge, stopping overnight at the small guest ranch, alongside Bright Angel Creek, with cabins and swimming pool. The ride down over switchbacks cut into the sheer cliffs seems forbidding, but the sure-footed mules haven't lost a rider yet in over 50 years, perhaps because all riders must be over 12 years old and weigh under 200 pounds. After lunch at Indian Garden, a cottonwood oasis, the trail reaches the level of the roaring Colorado, crosses the narrow Kaibab Suspension Bridge, and continues a mile farther to the ranch—in time for a swim before dinner. The temperature is 20 degrees warmer than on the South Rim, 4,500 feet above. The next morning, you start the return trip by the **Kaibab Trail,** equally colorful but a little shorter, reaching the South Rim at Yaki Point, 3½ miles east of the village, in time for lunch. Advance confirmed reservations for muleback trips should be made, and are necessary May–October. Write Fred Harvey Company, Grand Canyon, Arizona 86023. If you don't have a reservation, make it your first point of business on arrival. In addition to muleback, bridle trails run through the pine forests along the South Rim, and horses (with a guide) may be rented for regularly scheduled summer trips.

Accommodations. Lodgings at the South Rim cover a wide range, including rustic Bright Angel Lodge, well known El Tovar Hotel, modern Yavapai Lodge, and Auto Lodge cabins. For reservations write Fred Harvey Company, Grand Canyon, Arizona 86023.

Camping. Camping below the rims is a rewarding experience, if planned with

plenty of time. Hikers can be accommodated at Phantom Ranch (when advance reservations are made). Going on foot is challenging to those in excellent condition. On the Bright Angel Trail, water is available in summer at two points between the South Rim and Indian Garden; from there to the river, the hottest part of the trip, none is available. On the steeper **South Kaibab Trail,** 7 miles to the river from the rim at Yaki Point, no water is available. Plan to carry an adequate water supply, a gallon a day per person. The toughest part comes at the end with the uphill climb, but the hiker with stamina can hook up to the **North Kaibab Trail** at the river and make his way to the North Rim, a distance of 14 miles. Campers must make advance reservations directly with park officials, either by mail or telephone, for the 225 campsites at the walk-in campgrounds in the Inner Canyon. Four campgrounds are along the way between Phantom Lodge and the top. Anyone can take a shorter trip into the canyon on the Bright Angel Trail or the Kaibab Trail, but allow ample time to return to the rim before dark. A trailer court, with hookups, is near the Visitor Center.

Seasons. Facilities on the South Rim are open all year. While the summer is crowded and advance reservations imperative, the park is pleasant and congestion-free during winter. Temperatures drop below freezing at night, but during the day the mid-40s and mid-50s are the rule. Amtrak trains arrive at Flagstaff in time to connect with bus service to the canyon.

Main Gateways to the South Rim are Williams and Flagstaff, less than two hours by car. Bus lines run frequently from these two cities. US 89, a major north-south route, provides access to the park at Cameron, Arizona. Airlines serve Grand Canyon directly by means of an airport 8 miles south of the park; each flight is met by a bus from Grand Canyon Village. The Santa Fe Railroad began service in 1901, virtually opening the park to large-scale tourist travel; before that time the only entry had been by stagecoach, bouncing over Indian trails, creaking from rut to rut. There is no longer any train service, but passengers on the Superchief–El Capitan come to Grand Canyon by bus from Flagstaff.

THE PRACTICAL GUIDE: NORTH RIM

Being less accessible, this side is not often congested. It affords different views and a different feeling. The vistas are spectacular, and the cool Kaibab Plateau is covered with beautiful forest, where families of deer roam late in the day,

and flowers of mountain and field meet, including iris, forget-me-not, lupine, and Indian paintbrush.

Gateway to the North Rim is Jacob Lake, Arizona, where a paved road leaves US 89A. Bus service runs regularly mid-June through August from Cedar City, Utah, through Kanab, and Fredonia, Arizona.

Cape Royal Drive from Grand Canyon Lodge extends 26 miles to **Cape Royal,** with choice stopping places en route. **Point Imperial,** 3 miles off the main road, is the highest point of the entire canyon rim, at 8,801 feet, with excellent views over the Painted Desert, Marble Canyon, and the Little Colorado River. Along the last part of the drive, the roadway is bordered with fragrant locust. In case you come without a car, a sightseeing bus trip is made every afternoon, with a nature talk at Cape Royal. A less developed, but no less scenic, road leads through the north Kaibab Plateau Forest to **Point Sublime,** 16 miles west of the entrance highway; there the inner gorge is closer than at any other spot along the rim.

Bright Angel Point is the tip of the promontory jutting a mile into the canyon, flanked by Roaring Springs Canyon and the Transept. A self-guiding nature trail from the shelter is an easy walk of three-tenths of a mile.

Naturalist program. The Transept Trail walk, led by a ranger-naturalist, is a popular 1-mile stroll. The daily schedule also includes geology talks at Cape Royal, evening campfire programs at the campground near the inn, and illustrated programs indoors at the lodge. Similar activities are conducted at the South Rim.

Whitewater adventure. There are many ways to see the Grand Canyon, but perhaps none as thrilling as from a rubber raft navigating the turbulent Colorado River. Shooting the rapids, camping on the river banks, photographing the spectacular sheer rims and low deserts are components of the exciting cruises that run 10 to 14 days. Trips usually carry 16 to 20 persons. Campsites are set up at white sand beaches near pools and waterfalls. These trips are not recommended for children under 12. Make plans and reservations well in advance; commercial and private float trips on the Colorado River are now limited in number. Write Grand Canyon Expeditions, P.O. Box 21021, Salt Lake City, Utah 84121, or Georgie White, 435 West Laconia Boulevard, Los Angeles, California 90061.

Tour operators. Muleback trips into the canyon include a one-day outing on a trail, cut from solid rock, to **Roaring Springs.** The two-day trip to Phantom Ranch is filled with superb scenery, stopping on the way down at aptly named **Ribbon Falls,** 4,000 feet below Bright Angel Point—and 30 degrees warmer. The last 5 miles are the hottest, but under shade following the course of Bright Angel Creek. For muleback trip reservations, write Mr. Jack Church, North Rim Rural Route, Fredonia, Arizona 86022. Morning and afternoon saddle-horse trips are scheduled along the rim during the summer.

Accommodations at the North Rim. Grand Canyon Lodge provides modest facilities, supplemented by North Rim Inn.

Camping. A campground (with showers and supply store) is located near the ranger station and inn.

Seasons. The North Rim is open mid-May to mid-October. Evenings are cool even during the summer. During winter heavy snows close the access roads. However, from September until mid-October, days are mild and clear, and golden-leaved aspen mantle the hillsides; a choice time for the adventurous traveler.

Temperatures in the canyon in summer may rise to as high as 124 degrees. Heat exhaustion is common. Hiking conditions are best in spring and autumn when weather is mild on the rims and within the canyon.

Nearby. Adjacent to both North and South Rims are units of the **Kaibab National Forest,** 1,700,000 acres of forest and rangeland, containing an abundant and famous herd of mule deer. Adjoining the national park on the west is **Grand Canyon National Monument,** which contains the remotest portions of the Grand Canyon, and is an ideal target for the rugged traveler. The most outstanding location is at Toroweap Point, 3,000 feet above the snakelike Colorado River, on a sheer, vertical wall. It is reached by driving southwest from Fredonia through the Kaibab Indian Reservation on a graded road to Tuweep, and then 5 additional miles on an unimproved road. A small campground is near the point, but there is no water supply, and the last food available is at Fredonia.

Bryce and Zion National Parks are related geologically to the Grand Canyon and are linked by highway with the

North Rim. Phases of the Colorado River story unfold upstream at **Glen Canyon National Recreation Area,** across the Utah-Arizona border, and downstream at **Lake Mead National Recreation Area,** across the Arizona-Nevada border. Driving south on US 89, the traveler can visit **Wupatki National Monument,** preserving prehistoric Indian pueblos, and **Sunset Crater National Monument,** a volcanic crater active as recently as A.D. 1064.

Flagstaff, at the foot of the San Francisco peaks, is a growing, changing city of the West. The **Museum of Northern Arizona** is like a companion piece to the Grand Canyon, one physical and visual, the other devoted to arts, anthropology, and the study of natural sciences. Flagstaff also is a gateway to the large **Navajo and Hopi Indian reservations** that border the Grand Canyon to the east.

Recommended reading. *Exploration of the Colorado River and Its Canyons,* by John W. Powell, and *The Grand Canyon,* by Joseph Wood Krutch.

For further information write Superintendent, Grand Canyon National Park, Box 129, Grand Canyon, Arizona 86023.

GRAND TETON

Established as a national park, 1929

A cluster of huge peaks, 40 miles long, rises from the level plain called Jackson Hole and dominates the landscape. No matter where you are in the vicinity, no matter what your approach, those snow-crested mountains claim your eye. You will know, without being told, that this is one of the boldest spectacles of natural scenery in America.

There are many ways of looking at the Tetons. Some mountain ranges are taller and more massive, but the Tetons afford an infinite variety of perspective because they rise, without foothills, abruptly from the earth. From the west side of the mountains, in Idaho, they may seem like towering spires parading against the sky. From their bases within the park they spread their images across large, forest-bordered lakes. On the mountain trails along their flanks, they become a network of rock gardens filled with glaciers, waterfalls, and wildflowers. And always they change color with the hour of day.

The Tetons are a great block of the earth's crust, thrust upward along a fault, or crack; then worn down by water, wind, and frost, and later by glaciers crunching through stream-cut canyons. Eleven of these "fault-block" mountains rank as major peaks, with the tallest, Grand Teton, rising 13,766 feet above sea level.

The frontispiece of the sheer, jagged peaks, the high basin known as Jackson Hole, is part of the treasure of the 310,418-acre national park. John Colter, who in 1806 left the Lewis and Clark expedition to trap beaver and explore the country, was probably the first white man to come this way, where only Indians had passed before to hunt elk. Then followed the mountain men, the traders, trappers, and the cattlemen. Not until the 1880s did homesteaders arrive, but they learned the country was too high, cold, and barren for successful farming.

The valley, about 50 miles long, varying in width from 6 to 12 miles, is rimmed by mountains—the high plateaus of Yellowstone National Park on the north, and the Mount Leidy Highlands and Gros Ventre Range on the east and south. It is bisected by the Snake River flowing through Jackson Lake, then through sagebrush meadow and forest and between steep bluffs.

The park is an exceptional wildlife sanctuary. Moose, the largest and least wary member of the deer family, are often seen. Antelope, buffalo, elk, and mule deer—the big game for which Jackson Hole has been famous since the era of the mountain men—are as large as life. Streams and lakes abound in fish and waterfowl.

The story of the park is hardly complete without reference to the role of the late John D. Rockefeller, Jr. He first came to visit this country in 1926 and was deeply impressed. In years that followed, he purchased 30,000 acres of the Jackson Hole Basin and presented them to the government for preservation as a sanctuary of nature. The John D. Rockefeller Memorial Parkway, extending the full length of Grand Teton National Park, has been named in his honor.

THE PRACTICAL GUIDE

You can see the mountains on a breezy drive-through, but you can do the same from the pages of a picture book with less effort. Give yourself a chance to really appreciate this park; even on a short tour, plan to spend at least one full day. The Tetons are filled with the widest range of activities, whatever your interest may be.

Signal Mountain Overlook, accessible by automobile, provides the best orientation. Turnouts along the way up offer picture-taking vistas. The summit commands a panoramic view over the Snake River valley. It lies off the **Teton Park Road,** which leads to campgrounds, fishing sites, and most mountain trails. **Jackson Hole Highway,** parallel to the Snake River, is one of America's most scenic roads, with wayside turnoffs and displays, and is part of the valley motor loop.

Hiking trails are the means to fully exploring and appreciating the Tetons. Short hikes of half-day or all-day duration are rewarding and worthwhile. A good get-acquainted hike will take you to **Hidden Falls.** It can. begin and end with a boat trip across beautiful **Jenny Lake,** at the foot of the Cathedral group, to Cascade Canyon. Overnight trips permit leisurely viewing of mountain flora, varied wildlife, and expansive mountain vistas. The well-conditioned person has no difficulty hiking from the 6,500 foot valley floor to the **Skyline Trail,** about 4,000 feet higher, where it becomes possible to make a loop trip completely encircling the Grand, Middle, and South Tetons and adjacent high peaks. The **Indian Paintbrush Trail** climbs from the south end of Leigh Lake to the upper end of Paintbrush Canyon, bordered with paintbrush and other wildflowers, and with fine views of the lakes beyond the mouth of the canyon. Over 200 miles of trail furnish a wide variety of hiking—through the valley, to high mountain lakes, and craggy passes above timberline. One part of the Teton Range, from **Leigh Canyon to Berry Creek,** is wilderness in the truest sense, being almost devoid of trails. The expert hiker who wants to test his skill in this area can obtain helpful advice from a park ranger, but he must register before an off-trail trip. Warm clothing, comfortable hiking shoes, and a good sleeping bag are all essential for overnight hikes; water repellent clothing and equipment are useful in the event of sudden summer squalls.

Horseback riding opportunities are among the finest in the world. Even children can enjoy an hour or two on a saddle-horse trip around the lakes, starting from the park concession corrals at Colter Bay, Jenny Lake, or Jackson Lake Lodge. Better riders can spend a full day on the high trails, or arrange pack trips through the concessioner or guest ranches in the valley.

Mountaineering begins where trail hiking leaves off. The Exum Mountain Guide Service and School of Mountaineering (113 Woodland Drive, Pinehurst, Idaho 83850, during winter; Moose, Wyoming, June 20 to Labor Day), headquartered at Jenny Lake, is probably the best place in the Rocky Mountains for beginners. Rates are modest, and even on the first day you practice crawling upward like a spider and swinging from a clifftop in a 20-foot rappel. Two days of instruction are required to go on the guided overnight climb of Mount Owen, Mount Moran, or the Grand. In a single year about 3,000 climbers make the ascent of the Grand, over at least 16 basic routes, ranging from relatively easy (with guides) to some of the finest rock climbing in the nation. Mountaineering, however, can never be taken lightly. All climbers are required to register in person at the Jenny Lake Ranger Station. Solo climbing is not permitted. The climbing season usually extends from June 15 to September 15, the brief summer season at high elevations between snows and storms.

Fishing in wild streams and lakes is typical of recreational angling in the northern Rockies. Cutthroat and brook trout may be taken with an artificial fly during most of the summer and autumn, but mackinaw trout in Jackson and Jenny lakes can best be caught by trolling with heavy tackle. A Wyoming license can be obtained at tackle shops for the season or a five-day period.

Wildlife shooting—with camera. One of the great sports in the Tetons, especially for children, is observing animals in their natural state. These creatures are part of the rich legacy of the West, and pictures of them are among the best possible souvenirs. It will help to have a telephoto lens. For safety's sake, keep your young photo fans (and grown-ups) a considerable distance from all animals, especially the moose.

Near the south entrance to the park a small number of elk can be seen during the summer in an enclosure at the **National Elk Refuge,** which is maintained primarily for the winter care of the Jackson Hole elk herd. Most of the flock of this handsome native deer, second largest to the moose, spend the summer grazing in the high range beyond view. Moose can be seen at any season in the early morning and at dusk along river bottoms and in fragrant meadows. There aren't many mule deer in the park, but hikers may see them, or their tracks, along the trails. The sleek pronghorn sometimes appear in small bands on Antelope Flats during summer. Bison are maintained in a pasture just east of Oxbow Bend; this is where white pelicans often stop on their migrations in spring and fall. One of the great prizes of the bird-watcher and photographer is the shy and rare trumpeter swan, sometimes seen in the elk refuge and other times on Christian Pond east of Jackson Lake Lodge.

An aerial tramway, completed in 1966, immediately adjacent to the park's south boundary, rises to an elevation of 10,446 feet on the slopes of Teton National Forest. In winter it provides the longest single vertical drop of any ski area on the continent. But throughout the year the panoramic views encompass hundreds of miles, including the national park, the Yellowstone country, the Idaho Mountains, and the Wind River Range of the Continental Divide to the east.

Float trips on the Snake River give a sample of adventure on a western stream. Rubber rafts, piloted by expert guides, make the 30-mile trip from Jackson Lake Lodge every day during the summer, passing undisturbed wildlife—including coyotes, elk, ducks, herons, and probably eagles feeding their young in a high nest—with a stop for lunch in a beautiful picnic area. You can put a canoe into the water at **String Lake** and be immersed in solitude, free of outboard motors.

Scenic boat rides are operated on **Jackson Lake,** the valley's largest and deepest body of water, to the far shore, where you look deep into wilderness country. And on Jenny Lake, rental boats are also available. If you bring your own boat, you must obtain a permit at park headquarters; motor-propelled craft are allowed only on Jackson, Jenny, and Phelps lakes. For strictly boating recreation, larger and better bodies of water are located within driving distance, outside the national park.

Menor's Ferry, near park headquarters, is a reconstruction of the pioneer vessel that began operating across the Snake River in 1892. Exhibits tell about the settlers and their early transportation. When water level permits, ranger-naturalists conduct demonstration rides.

Naturalist programs will contribute to the enjoyment and appreciation of the park. Illustrated talks or color films are presented in the campgrounds each evening during the summer and twice weekly at Jackson Lake Lodge. Guided nature walks are conducted every day, and all-day hikes, three days a week. The three visitor centers complement each other in telling the story of the Tetons: **Moose,** the fur trading era; **Colter Bay,** Indian Arts Museum, displaying the varied art forms of the American Indian, from the David T. Vernon collection; and **Jenny Lake,** mountaineering, geology, flora, and fauna. Pick up a printed copy of the naturalist program.

Accommodations. Jenny Lake Lodge, in a shaded setting, consists of splendid one- and two-room cottages, for the higher-priced trade. The Sunday night buffet is one of the dining treats of Wyoming (reservations advisable). Jackson Lake Lodge, in the center of activities, is a large, modern motel-type facility with swimming pool. Dining room and coffee shop are open to all park visitors. Its Stockade Room is a welcome rendezvous for relaxation at sunset. Colter Bay Village has two singular types of accommodations designed for family use: tent-cabins, a combination of log and canvas, with stove, grill, screen window, and bunks (camping gear for rent, or bring your own); and rustic log cabins, originals of pioneer settlement days, assembled in one area and furnished with appropriate but modern facilities. The above are operated by the principal concessioner, Grand Teton Lodge Company, Jackson, Wyoming 83001 (winter address, 209 Post Street, San Francisco, California 94108); advance reservations are advisable, particularly during July and August. Other lodges and guest houses, some with housekeeping cabins, are scattered throughout the park area. These include Signal Mountain Lodge, Leek's Lodge, and Highlands Lodge. Most provide riding horses. Motels and hotels are located in and near the town of Jackson.

Camping. Five public campgrounds are maintained by the Park Service: Colter Bay (largest and most developed,

with coin laundry, general store, cafeteria), Lizard Creek, Signal Mountain, Jenny Lake, Gros Ventre. In addition, the concessioner-operated Colter Bay Trailer Village has trailer sites with power, water, and sewer connections. Limit of stay at all campgrounds is 14 days, except at Jenny Lake, where the limit is 10 days. Twelve developed campgrounds in adjacent **Teton National Forest** are part of the total camping complex.

Transportation. Bus service operates daily from the park to Jackson, and service is also available to Rock Springs, Wyoming, for connections with Amtrak's San Francisco Zephyr. All buses are operated by the Grand Teton Lodge Company and leave on a regular schedule from the Jackson Lake Lodge. During summer, air service reaches Jackson daily from Salt Lake City, Denver, and Billings. Buses meet each flight. Automobiles can be rented at the airport (reservations advisable).

Seasons. Most activities are concentrated in the months of July and August, although the naturalist program begins in early June. Jackson Lake Lodge is open mid-June to mid-September, and is least crowded before July 4 and after Labor Day. Colter Bay has a longer season, May 30 to October 1. Flower months are June and July in Jackson Hole, July and August in the high country. Fishing is best in September, when days are sunny and clear, though snows may swirl around the summits. In autumn, elk are most easily observed and most exciting to watch. At this time of year, when golden aspen glitter on the hillsides, the mature bulls round up their harems of cows. Valleys ring with clashing antlers as rivals battle. The area about Signal Mountain and Burnt Ridge is the best part of the park to watch their activity and to hear the challenging bugle of the bull elks. This alone is worth the visit.

Winter is a season of majesty, undreamed of by the more than three mil-

lion visitors who come this way in summer. Roads are open from Jackson through the park and over Togwotee Pass, affording vistas of the mighty Tetons rising stark and white between the snow flats and a clear sky. The big aerial tramway above Teton Village is used by skiers as well as sightseers. Jackson Lake is frozen, but you can scoot over it in a snowplane. In early winter, depending on snow and weather, large bands of elk move across the open flats to their wintering area south of the park. During a severe winter as many as 11,000 elk have concentrated in the refuge, part of an old migration route, which is now critically blocked from farther southward movement by the settlement of man. To winter visitors, the spectacle of this mass of wild animals, many still bearing enormous racks, is the thrill of a lifetime. The public is invited to ride horse-drawn sleds (small fee) into the midst of the herd to see them being fed.

Nearby. The national park is part of an immense western outdoor recreation region. It includes Yellowstone National Park, Teton, Shoshone, and Targhee national forests. The closest, the Teton National Forest, encompasses three sides of Jackson Hole, with elevations up to 12,165 feet, plus the headwaters of the Yellowstone River and the South Fork of the Snake. Swimming is available at **Granite Hot Springs,** south of Jackson, and **Huckleberry Hot Springs,** north of town. **Jackson** itself, a historic western supply point, still has its wooden boardwalks leading to restaurants, saloons, and craft shops. This is a year-round vacation crossroads for dude ranchers, fishermen, campers, and for hunters and skiers.

Recommended reading. *One Day at Teton Marsh,* by Sally Carrighar; *Across the Wide Missouri,* by Bernard De Voto; and *Creation of the Teton Landscape,* by J. D. Love and John C. Reed, Jr.

For further information write Superintendent, Grand Teton National Park, Moose, Wyoming 83012.

Map on page 119.

GREAT SMOKY MOUNTAINS

Authorized as a national park, 1926

Astride the common border of North Carolina and Tennessee, unbroken for a distance of 70 miles except for one transmountain road, the Smokies stand as the masterwork of the Appalachian highlands. Fed by the fertile land and nourished by rain and rushing streams, plant life is luxuriant and varied, with more kinds of trees than in all of Europe.

The park covers 517,014 acres, embracing some of the oldest mountains on earth. Their foundations were laid on the floor of a shallow sea over 500 million years ago. The loftiness of the mountains was produced during a long period of earth upheavals called the Appalachian Revolution, about 200 million years ago. The Smokies escaped the icy tongue of glaciers and gave sanctuary to many plant species fleeing the frigid North. As a result, it is today the meeting ground of northern and southern types of forests.

For hundreds of years the Smokies were part of the mountain empire of the Cherokee Indians, which at its height extended from Virginia south to Georgia and Alabama. They lived in harmony with nature in small communities along the streams, but once the advancing colonists—moving in one direction inland from Charleston, South Carolina, and in another down from Virginia and Pennsylvania—pressed their settlements into the hills the Indians were doomed. Still the Smokies, remote and inaccessible, remained beyond the touch of man. William Bartram, the celebrated naturalist of Philadelphia, came close in the course of his adventurous travels at the time of the American Revolution, but even he missed this highest mountain mass.

At first settlers took up the generous valleys and coves. On the North Carolina side John Jacob Mingus settled in the Oconaluftee Valley in 1792. He may have been the first white man to live in what is now the national park. Others followed in the 1800s, living in isolation, moving into the subvalleys, along creek branches, and up the steep hillsides to scrabble for a hard living. They grew almost everything they ate and made almost

everything they wore. Their remoteness was not shattered until the late 19th and early 20th centuries, with the installation of railroad lines by logging companies and syndicates.

The national park was a long time in coming to the Great Smoky Mountains. The idea was first advanced by Dr. Chase Ambler, of Asheville, who organized the Appalachian National Park Association in 1899. It was renewed in 1923 by Mr. and Mrs. Willis P. Davis of Knoxville. But establishing a national park in the southern Appalachians, or anywhere in the East, demanded a different approach than in the West. Essentially, western parks were carved out of land already owned by the federal government as part of the vast public domain. But in the Smokies, 85 percent of the total acreage was owned by 18 timber and pulpwood companies, while the remaining 15 percent was divided among a multitude of 6,000 small farmers and owners of summer homesites.

In 1924, however, the Secretary of the Interior appointed a special committee to survey the entire mountain region for the best location for a national park. Finally the committee reported that: "The Great Smoky Mountains easily stand first because of the height of the mountains, depth of valleys, ruggedness of the area, and the unexampled variety of trees, shrubs, and plants." In point of fact, legislation was enacted by Congress in 1926 to establish three national parks: Shenandoah, Smoky Mountains, and Mammoth Cave.

Raising money to purchase the land was another story. Under the legislation, the states were required to make the land available to the federal government. Efforts were led by State Senator Mark Squires of North Carolina, and Colonel David Chapman of Tennessee. Horace Kephart of Bryson City, North Carolina, well known as the author of *Our Southern Highlanders,* was another key figure. Through appropriation and contribution the two states raised a total of $5 million, half the required amount. On February 28, 1928, following an

urgent appeal from the National Park Service, John D. Rockefeller, Jr., noted for his philanthropy and interest in conservation, agreed to contribute up to $5 million through the Laura Spelman Rockefeller Memorial, named for his mother. Without his commitment, the park would never have come into being. With it, the land was acquired and the national park established. It was dedicated by President Franklin D. Roosevelt on Labor Day, 1940, with appropriate ceremonies conducted at Newfound Gap attended by a tremendous throng of 25,000.

The Smokies lie about one hour's drive from Asheville, North Carolina, or from Knoxville, Tennessee.

They are within a day's driving time of almost all the large cities of the East and Middle West. Hikers are invited to follow 650 miles of winding trails along clear streams and waterfalls. The Appalachian Trail follows the mountain crest the full 72-mile length of the park, with a chain of overnight trailside shelters. Then there are short trails passing forest giants hundreds of years old, and valleys alive with spring wildflowers and blooming summer plants. Road viewpoints unfold the vista of wilderness—the peaks rising above 6,000 feet and extending to the horizon like green waves, and the valleys screened by bluish or smokelike mist, from which the mountains derive their name.

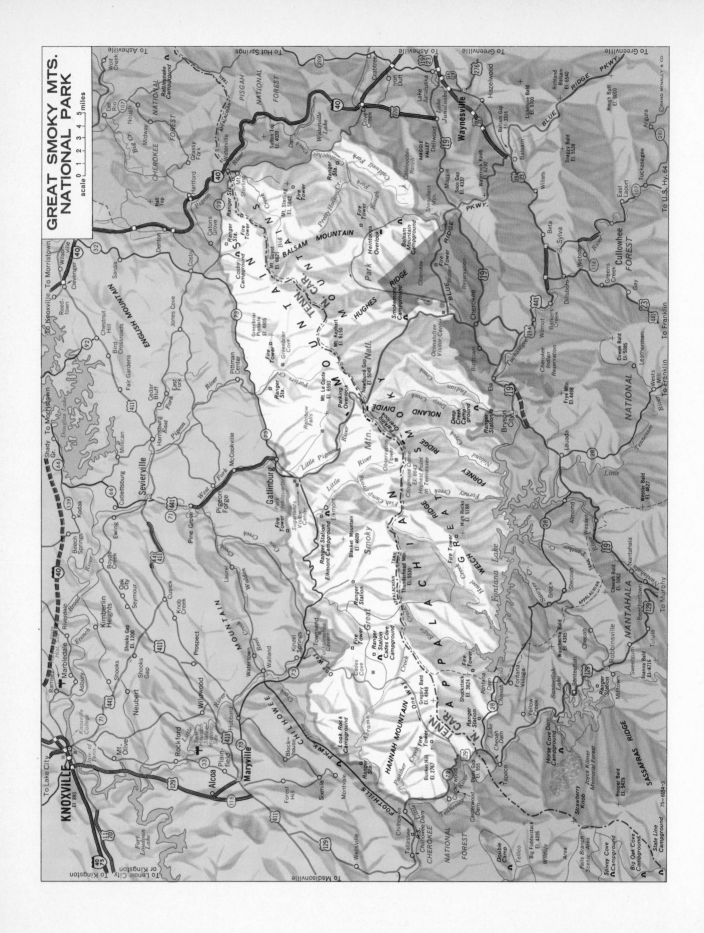

GREAT SMOKY MTS. NATIONAL PARK

scale 0 1 2 3 4 5 miles

THE PRACTICAL GUIDE

Plan for at least two days, unless you intend to take to the trails for a longer stay. Avoid the mistake of trying to "see" the Smokies only by driving over the transmountain road (US 441) and then departing. Great Smoky Mountain Tours, Inc., operates tours by bus from Knoxville and Asheville during the summer.

Visitor Center. When approaching from Tennessee, through Gatlinburg or Townsend, stop first at **Sugarlands Visitor Center** near park headquarters. On the North Carolina side, stop at the **Oconaluftee Visitor Center** to see the pioneer displays and 19th century farmstead. Nearby **Mingus Mill** presents a water-powered, turbine-driven gristmill as another page out of the past. Along the transmountain road, the major viewpoint is at **Newfound Gap,** where President Franklin D. Roosevelt dedicated the park. From here a 7.3-mile spur leads to Clingman's Dome, the highest point in the park (6,642 feet).

A number of trails begin from this road. From Alum Cave parking area you can hike to **Alum Cave Bluffs** (5 miles round trip), where rose-purple rhododendron bloom in mid-June. The expert hiker may climb the **Chimney Tops** (3 miles and three hours round trip), a high, rocky perch. The **Big Locust Trail** is an easy one. It passes through an area where settlers once cut the trees, piled the rocks, and cultivated the land; then it plunges through a virgin forest. From Newfound Gap, you can sample the **Appalachian Trail,** walking through a stand of Fraser fir and red spruce, a high island of Canadian vegetation, to Charlie's Bunion (8.6 miles round trip), one of the best points from which to enjoy the spreading wilderness below.

Many visitors enjoy hiking short distances on the **Appalachian Trail,** either from Davenport Gap at the eastern boundary; Fontana Dam, the southwest terminus; or from Clingman's Dome. The full distance takes six to eight days, with shelters and campsites spaced about a day's journey apart; each shelter provides bunks for at least 12 persons and is normally restricted to one night's use. A camping permit is required for camping along this trail. The eastern section is a graded four-foot standard horse trail; the western section, an ungraded, brushed-out footpath, rather rough in spots, but not difficult.

Cades Cove is one of the choicest spots of any national park. Drive the 11-mile loop road past open fields, frame churches, and homesteads where pioneer people lived. May through October the miller grinds corn at the Cable

Mill and you can purchase a bag at Becky Cable's store.

Park naturalists conduct many programs during the summer season. These include guided walks, ranging from two to five hours, motor caravans, and evening programs in the main campgrounds and at Sugarlands Visitor Center.

A leaflet titled "Visitor Programs," available throughout the park, will help you choose the activity that suits your interest.

Fishing season in the park extends from April 15 to September 15. Some 600 miles of stream flow through the park, many offering opportunities for rainbow and brook trout. Certain streams are managed for "fishing-for-fun" and portions of certain streams are reserved for children under 12.

Accommodations. Overnight lodgings for the noncamper are found at two locations inside the park. **Le Conte Lodge,** a secluded retreat (fine but not fancy) atop Mount Le Conte, is reached by foot or horse trail. Popular from spring through autumn, it provides a genuine national park experience. For reservations, write Le Conte Lodge, Gatlinburg, Tennessee 37738. **Wonderland Club Hotel** at Elkmont is small (25 rooms). It was here as a private club long before the park came into being and now operates as a public facility preserving the old-fashioned atmosphere, with good service and food in a quiet setting. It is open early June to Labor Day; reservations essential. Write Wonderland Club Hotel, Elkmont, Gatlinburg, Tennessee 37738. **Fontana Village,** near the southwestern edge of the park, is a unique family resort center with 300 cottages, and facilities for boating, swimming, golf, riding, and nature walks. Hotels and motels are available in many communities around the park between Asheville and Knoxville.

Camping. Campgrounds are scattered throughout the park, operating on first-come, first-served basis, with seven-day limit between June 1 and Labor Day. Smokemont Campground, on US 441, is usually jammed during the summer; consequently wise campers disperse to less congested sections, such as Cosby, Tennessee; Deep Creek and Cataloochee, North Carolina. Commercial campgrounds are located in communities around the park. Many campgrounds in Nantahala and Pisgah national forests, North Carolina, and in Cherokee National Forest, Tennessee.

Seasons. Spring weather can begin as early as January or as late as March. Hikers and campers should bring warm clothing for cool weather until May. Wild-

flowers usually are outstanding for the Spring Wildflower Pilgrimage, held annually at Gatlinburg the last weekend of April, with wildflower and botany lectures, photography seminar, birdwalks, and field trips in the park. The lowlands in summer are warm, the summits always cooler. Rainfall and thundershowers are likely, making a raincoat a must. For a rewarding experience, hike to Gregory's Bald in late June, when spectacular masses of wild azaleas bloom along the edges of this hillside meadow. Autumn weather is clear and invigorating, ideal for hiking. The beauty of the hardwood forest changing color is breathtaking. Winter is the time when hardy hikers and nature lovers achieve solitude. Most campgrounds are open all year, though some water supplies and comfort stations may be closed November to April. Permits for high mountain campsites and shelters are issued to experienced campers equipped with adequate footgear, clothing, and provisions.

Nearby. Mountain splendor and various recreational opportunities surround the national park. Just outside the park in North Carolina, the **Oconaluftee Village** and **Qualla Crafts Shop** display the handicrafts and history of the Cherokee people. They serve as a fitting prelude to an evening performance of the outdoor drama, **"Unto These Hills."** The **Blue Ridge Parkway** provides motoring adventure and picnic areas at high, cool elevations, with expansive vistas of the Smokies and other ranges. **Pisgah National Forest** includes 80 miles of the Appalachian Trail and the site of the historic "Cradle of Forestry in America" at the Pink Beds south of Asheville. **Nantahala National Forest,** the Cherokee "land of the noonday sun," has facilities for fishing, camping, hunting, and the beautiful Joyce Kilmer Memorial Forest, with towering giants 500 and 600 years old. **Fontana Lake** is the largest of a network of TVA and other reservoirs providing water sports. On the Tennessee side, the **Cherokee National Forest** is opening hundreds of camping sites, plus nature trails and scenic drives. Enthusiasts of Southern handicrafts will want to attend one of the annual **Craftsman's Fairs,** held at Asheville in July, and Gatlinburg in October.

Recommended reading. *Strangers in High Places* by Michael Frome, *Our Southern Highlanders* by Horace Kephart.

For further information write Superintendent, Great Smoky Mountains National Park, Gatlinburg, Tennessee 37738.

GUADALUPE MOUNTAINS

Authorized as a national park, 1966

The forested mountaintops; rugged, brushy slopes; and fringe of desert foothills lie at the south end of the Guadalupe Mountains, 110 miles from El Paso and barely below the border which Texas shares with New Mexico. The most prominent feature of the 79,972-acre national park established here is El Capitan, a sheer, thousand-foot, whitish-colored cliff. Directly north of it, Guadalupe Peak, 8,751 feet, is the highest point of the Lone Star State.

The Guadalupe Mountains stand like an island in the desert. Geologically speaking, they are considered a spectacular exposure of the world's most extensive and significant fossil reef. It dates from the Permian period, between 230 and 280 million years ago, when a vast saltwater basin occupied a large part of present Texas and New Mexico. In the shallower water, marine organisms formed a limestone barrier not unlike that which shelters the coastland of Queensland, Australia, today. Also of major geological interest is the tremendous earth fault on the abrupt west side of the park.

There is evidence that prehistoric Americans occupied these canyons as early as 12,000 years ago. Many pictographs are found in the caves and rock shelters. The first references in history were written by the Spanish conquistadores in the course of their journeys north from Mexico. They found Mescalero Apaches living in the area, finding their food source, no doubt, in the plants and game.

The first proposal for a "public" park in the Guadalupe Mountains was made in 1925, principally through the leadership of Judge J. C. Hunter of Culberson County, Texas. Judge Hunter purchased one section of land and had prospects of donation of an additional 6,000 to 8,000 acres from other owners for park purposes, but that initial project fell through. He continued to acquire land during the 1930s and '40s. The judge and his son, J. C. Hunter, Jr., used this territory west of the Pecos as a ranch for angora goats to produce mohair wool, but were careful to avoid overgrazing the land, in anticipation that one day it would become part of a national park. Even after the death of the judge in 1945, his son continued to expand the "Hunter Lands" in the Guadalupes.

New impetus was given in 1958 when Wallace E. Pratt offered to donate his ranch lands which included the mouth and north fork of McKittrick Canyon, an area rich in natural values. Mr. Pratt had been associated with Humble Oil Company as chief geologist and vice-president until his retirement in 1945. His donation of 5,632 acres was completed in 1961. Then J. C. Hunter, Jr., moved to offer 72,000 acres around McKittrick Canyon at a price of $1.5 million. "I hold title to the land," he declared, "but how can anyone consider himself owner of this magnificent country when these mountains have stood alone here for millions of years." When Congress, spurred by Senator Ralph Yarborough, of Texas, authorized establishment of the park in 1966, it picked up one of the greatest land bargains in history—a national park at $21 per acre. Following acquisition of mineral rights from other sources and the State of Texas, the park was formally established and dedicated on September 30, 1972.

The highlands of the park rise from about 3,000 feet in the Pecos Valley near Carlsbad, New Mexico. Within the space of a few miles three climatic zones are represented. The foot of the mountains is landscaped with agaves and cactuses. As elevation rises the vegetation changes to pines, alligator juniper, even Douglas fir in favorable settings, and groves of quaking aspen. On the highest peaks some spots show decidedly alpine characteristics.

Roasting pits found at all elevations indicate that early inhabitants followed the ripening of native plants from the valley floor in spring to the highest ridges in autumn.

Wildlife forming part of the scene today includes elk, mule deer, an occasional mountain lion, bear, wild turkey; a small band of native bighorn sheep may still remain in the region. More than 200 species of birds are found in the canyons and over the clifftops.

THE PRACTICAL GUIDE

Though planning is still underway, efforts have been made to open key features of the park. Roads cross only limited portions, but more than 60 miles of rugged, scenic hiking trails are open. So are several scenic sites, including the remains of a stage station on the Butterfield Stage Line. This is not an area for casual touring, but if you are willing to plan and prepare it will offer significant reward.

Information Station. Center of activities, the park station, is located 1 mile east of Pine Springs, Texas, and 55 miles southwest of Carlsbad, New Mexico. You'll find it on US 62/180. It is open 7:30 a.m. to 6 p.m. Friday through Sunday, 8 a.m. to 4:30 p.m. Monday through Thursday. A guided walk is conducted into Pine Canyon, 1½ miles away, each Friday, Saturday, and Sunday at 6 p.m.

McKittrick Canyon trips are arranged via shuttle bus service that is offered hourly to the mouth of this outstanding scientific and scenic area, from US 62/180, Wednesday through Sunday from 8 a.m. to 4 p.m. McKittrick Canyon was the first important section presented to the government for the park. You'll see rare plant communities on the lower floor of the canyon. The walls reveal segments of Capitan Reef and fore-reef and back-reef marine deposits, remnants of the inland sea formed during the Permian period. The trail covers 3½ miles. Hikers are expected to be out on the last bus.

Hiking trails here are not for the novice. Unless experienced in this type of country, content yourself with one-day hikes. Large parts of the trail system are in poor condition, with some routes ill-defined. The hike to **Devil's Hallway** leads up the floor of Pine Canyon; it takes about six hours on a rocky, scenic route.

The **Guadalupe Peak** hike is a strenuous 8-mile round trip over a primitive trail—the thrill of reaching the top is worth the effort.

Accommodations. Modern overnight facilities are located in Carlsbad, New Mexico; Whites City, New Mexico (35 miles northeast, near Carlsbad Caverns National Park); and Van Horn, Texas (65 miles south).

Camping. Pine Canyon Campground, a small, temporary facility, is located at the entrance to Pine Springs Canyon. Water may be obtained at the Information Station, 1½ miles away. Several private campgrounds are nearby. If traveling through you may want to stop at the roadside picnic area provided by the State of Texas in scenic Guadalupe Pass. If you are planning to camp in the backcountry, register at the Information Station, where you can purchase a good topographic map of the high country and obtain a permit for one of the designated camping areas. Be sure you have proper equipment, including sturdy boots and adequate water. Keep your eyes open for rattlesnakes, especially during their early morning and evening feeding hours. Just give the snakes a wide berth and let them be.

For further information write Superintendent, Guadalupe Mountains National Park, c/o Carlsbad Caverns National Park, 3225 National Parks Highway, Carlsbad, New Mexico 88220.

HALEAKALA

Authorized as a national park, 1960

In the Polynesian portion of the United States, an ocean's distance from the mainland, the "Valley Island" of Maui was formed by two volcanoes rising from the sea. In 20 million years a small part of the island has been tempered into fertile fields, now growing sugarcane and pineapple, but the mammoth crater of Haleakala bears eloquent witness to the volcanic explosions of the Pacific.

Haleakala means "House of the Sun." According to the legend, the demigod Maui captured the sun and held it prisoner here in order to give his people more daylight hours. Legend or not, the sun has helped to produce unusual native plants among the multicolored cones, cinders, pumice, and ash.

The plant most characteristic of Haleakala is the rare, yucca-like silversword, which grows as a mass of silvery, saberlike leaves; when full grown its flower stalk produces a hundred or more vivid purplish blooms. Once the seeds of this bloom mature, the plant dies.

Haleakala was a spiritual and cultural focal point for Hawaiians for perhaps a thousand years before Captain Cook arrived in the islands. In fact, the remains of an ancient hand-laid stone road may be seen within the crater. The Park Service has recently discovered the bones of what may be Hawaiian chiefs, secreted high on the crater slopes in a rugged lava bed. Some archaeologists suspect that Hawaiians have occupied the crater for religious purposes. Rangers still find food offerings wrapped in ti leaves left by Hawaiians in the sacred areas of the crater.

Missionaries, seafarers, and surveyors visited Haleakala in the 1800s. The most famous American to describe it was Mark Twain, in *Roughing It.* He was so enthusiastic about this site that in 1881 he wrote to Charles Warren Stoddard: "If the house would burn down, we would pack up the cubs and fly to the isles of the blest, and shut ourselves up in the healing solitudes of the crater of Haleakala and get a good rest. . . ."

It was Lorrin A. Thurston, grandson of missionaries and publisher of the *Pacific Commercial Advertiser,* who led the effort to establish a national park of Hawaii's volcanoes. In 1907, the Hawaii legislature invited no less than 50 members of Congress and their wives to see the proposed park area at first hand. Their visit included a fancy dinner cooked over hot lava vents at the edge of Halemaumau. In 1912, Dr. Thomas Jaggar, lately hired as director of the Hawaiian Volcano Observatory, joined the campaign. He and Thurston were tireless boosters of the park idea. In 1916, with little controversy generated, Congress voted to authorize the new Hawaii National Park, consisting of three separate sections: Kilauea, Mauna Loa, and Haleakala. In 1960, Haleakala was established as a park in its own right, giving official sanction to what had been a sacred, unspoiled wilderness for perhaps 1,400 years.

Early in 1969, major portions of Kipahulu Valley became part of the national park through donations of land by Laurance S. Rockefeller and the Nature Conservancy. The addition includes the beautiful Seven Sacred Pools, 54 acres fronting on the ocean. The Kipahulu Valley, on the east slope of Haleakala volcano, provides ancient forests, waterfalls, and lava pools.

The park covers 27,824 acres, and when you reach the rim you realize that most of it is contained within the crater. It is 7½ miles long, 2½ miles wide, and 21 miles around. The floor of the crater, the heart of the park with its richly colored cinder cones, lies 3,000 feet below the summit, covering an area of 19 square miles. The last volcanic action on Maui occurred in the 1700s (outside the crater), but earthquake activity is still recorded and felt at Haleakala.

The view from the observatory at the summit, 10,023 feet, is one of the major spectacles of the Hawaiian Islands. On a clear day you can look over the waters of the Pacific to the "Big Island" of Hawaii, 40 miles away, and in the opposite direction even farther to see the other neighboring islands of Lanai, Molokai, and Oahu lying to the northwest.

THE PRACTICAL GUIDE

Passenger planes make several flights daily (35 minutes) from Honolulu to Maui. Arrangements for tours can be made at Kahului Airport or at Maui hotels. All-day trips usually include lush Iao Valley. If you rent a car, the shortest distance from the airport to the park is 26 miles, traveling upward from sea level to the highest paved road in the mid-Pacific. For the full enjoyment of the park, plan two or three days, hiking or horseback riding, and stay overnight in the cabins within the crater, which are reached only by hiking or on horseback.

The real adventure is within the crater itself. There are no roads, but 30 miles of well-marked trails show how plant life increases as you descend and move eastward. Here you find rare birds like the Hawaiian goose, or nene. Though it has entirely forsaken the water, its feet retain some webbing. This native bird was reintroduced to the island near Paliku Cabin in 1962, in a cooperative project by the State of Hawaii, the U.S. Fish and Wildlife Service, and the National Park Service.

Visitor Center. A mile beyond the entrance, a ranger at park headquarters will help you plan your visit. Even if your time is limited, he will suggest a drive to the crater rim viewpoints, which rise steadily upward to the summit.
Kalahaku Overlook contains an area of silversword, enclosed to protect them from troublesome goats roaming loose and from thoughtless visitors. Growing throughout the Kalahaku Valley are rare plants, including the greensword, closely related to the silversword.

Red Hill Overlook, the highest point of the rim (and on the island), affords an excellent vantage for picture taking, especially at sunset.

Two hiking trails lead into the crater, Halemauu at 8,000 feet and Sliding Sands at 10,000 feet. Most persons enter via Sliding Sands and return via Halemauu, and are encouraged to do so. Arrangements can be made with the park concessioner to carry a party's food and other equipment on a pack animal to cabins in the crater. For safety reasons, a permit is required for all trips into the crater.

Paliku, a lush oasis deep inside the northeast corner of the crater, caused by clouds moving up the windward slopes and spilling over the rim. Here the nene feeds upon grasses, leafy plants, and berries in open or semiopen areas.

Tour operators. Saddle tours of one or more days into the crater are provided by the park concessioner with advance arrangements. The Park Service recommends the two-day trip, with an overnight stay in the cabin in order to observe native birdlife and have adequate time for photography. For rates and reservations, write Frank Frietas, Makawao, Maui, Hawaii 96732.

Accommodations. Three cabins located in different sections of the crater floor are maintained by the Park Service for visitors' use at a small charge. Each has 12 bunks, drinkable water, cookstove, firewood, and kerosine lamps. Reservations must be made in advance, by writing to the park superintendent, with 3-day limit during summer and holiday periods.

A number of resort hotels and cottages are located on the island.

Camping. One campground is located near the park entrance in the Hosmer Grove, surrounded by introduced trees and native shrubs.

Seasons. Rarely does temperature on Maui fall below 55 or rise above 90—rarely above 80 in the mountains. Come prepared for cool, windy weather at the high park elevation. Summers usually are clear, winters more cloudy and rainy, though rain may be expected at any time. At night, temperatures will drop into the low 40s, or high 30s, even during summer.

Nearby. All of Maui is designed for resort activity and sightseeing. Camping is permitted without charge in public parks, with four-day limit; permits are obtained by writing Superintendent, Maui County Department of Parks, 1580 Kaahumanu Avenue, Wailuku, Maui, Hawaii 96793. Seven parks are located on beaches along the shoreline, including **Waiehu Beach Park,** with excellent shelling and fishing. The drive between **Hana** and **Wailuku,** on the coast below Haleakala, offers unusual beauty in heavily foliaged gorges, fishing settlements, and small villages.

For further information write Superintendent, Haleakala National Park, Box 456, Kahului, Maui, Hawaii 96732.

HAWAII VOLCANOES

Established as a national park, 1916

Amidst a luxuriant subtropical forest with rare plant life, cinder cones spewed from both ancient and streaming live volcanoes remind any who have forgotten that the earth is in charge of its own destiny, and still building, even in the playgrounds of the Pacific.

Ever since man has watched them, mighty Mauna Loa and Kilauea have been intermittently active. The most spectacular eruption in Hawaii's recorded history occurred as recently as November 1959, when a line of lava "fountains" sprang from Kilauea Iki, the large pit just east of Kilauea Crater. One "fountain" grew until it was gushing molten lava mixed with sulfurous steam to a fantastic height of 1,900 feet, destroying a campsite and many acres of the bordering Tree Fern Forest. But the very next year, 500 new acres of land were added to the island as lava spilled from the Puna rift zone (outside the park) into the sea. Eruptions have occurred since then, including one as recently as February 1969, at Aloi Crater along the Chain of Craters Road.

Mauna Loa, whose dome, 13,680 feet above sea level, is visible to air travelers a hundred miles or more away, announces its eruptions with tremors in the earth. Its lava flows occupy more than 2,000 square miles of Hawaii, the "Big Island." Its 1949 eruption continued for almost five months. A year later it spewed one of the most voluminous flows in history, producing about one billion tons of lava in 23 days.

Both Kilauea and Mauna Loa are within the 229,177-acre national park. These young volcanoes, which may have been formed only within the last million years, grow with energy, keeping ahead of the ever-present agents of erosion. Despite their seeming ferocity, they are relatively gentle giants that seldom become dangerously explosive even while liberating tons of molten rock from vents and cracks.

Whenever a new eruption occurs, Hawaii residents rush out to view the magnificent fiery display. Parking lots on the rim are quickly filled and airplanes buzz overhead.

The Hawaiian Volcano Observatory, the only one of its kind in the nation, is located on the rim of the west wall of the Halemaumau pit. It was established by Dr. Thomas R. Jaggar in 1911.

Through the studies of volcanologists (geologists who specialize in volcanoes), much is known about the Hawaiian activity. The two great volcanoes are called "shields," being shaped much like inverted saucers. Despite their youth, their history goes back millions of years, when the floor of the Pacific Ocean trembled and cracked. Lava and hot gases were released, building steadily upward until the volcanic chain of the Hawaiian Islands was created. With each succeeding eruption a new layer spread itself upon the old. Finally came the island of Hawaii, 93 miles long and 76 miles wide. It is almost twice as large as all the other islands combined. From its base on the ocean floor to the highest point atop Mauna Kea this mountain measures 31,784 feet. Some say this makes it taller than Everest. No matter how you look at it, the mountain island, with its fascinating terrain, exposes the handiwork of the subterranean inner earth to the outer world.

THE PRACTICAL GUIDE

Passenger planes make several flights daily from Honolulu to the Big Island, with jet service reducing time en route to about 35 minutes. Direct flights operate to and from Hilo and the mainland; the number is expected to increase substantially. The national park is included in the itinerary of guided tours, which range from one to three days. Cars can be rented either at General Lyman Field, Hilo, or at Kailua-Kona.

Visitor Center. Park headquarters are off Hawaii 11, the Mamalahoa Highway, connecting Kona and Hilo. The park museum in the headquarters contains exhibits, maps, models, and paintings on the story of the park; color films of recent eruptions are shown three times daily. It is named in memory of Dr. Thomas A. Jaggar, who established the Hawaiian Volcano Observatory in 1911. A second Visitor Center is located at Wahaula Heiau near the Kalapana entrance, with exhibits devoted to the story of the early Hawaiian people.

Crater Rim Drive leads clockwise from park headquarters past the scenic **Byron Ledge Overlook** to the **Thurston Lava Tube,** formed when the outer crust of lava hardened and the inner portion flowed away. You can explore the tunnel-like formation for a distance of about 500 feet. Nearby thrives the glorious **Tree Fern Forest,** undisturbed by lava activity for many centuries. Rains average about 100 inches annually, sustaining a growth of many varieties of ferns, overtowered by a dense growth of tropical ohia trees. Whenever the ohia blooms, one finds the apapane, a small nectar-sucking bird as red as the lehua (the feathery ohia blossom), but with black wings and gray belly. Equally abundant in the forests is the amakihi, a small yellow-green insect gatherer, and the elepaio, a perky flycatcher. The road dips into the crater to a parking area at the brink of the **Halemaumau pit,** called the "house of everlasting fire"—

although the splashing lava lake phase actually terminated with the steam explosion of 1924.

Northwest of the Hawaiian Volcano Observatory, in the direction of Mauna Loa, lies **Kipuka Puaulu,** or "Bird Park," a typical "island" of old surface surrounded by young lava flows. A nature trail leads into a forested section, an arboretum of 40 varieties of trees, some peculiar to the island of Hawaii. A few are the only living representatives of their vanishing species. On fresh rock surfaces of the younger lava flows the sturdy ohia, the colorful aalii, and pukeawe shrubs pioneer a new forest. Perhaps the final point of interest on Crater Rim Drive is the **Byron Ledge Overlook** at Kilauea Iki crater, scene of the 1959 eruption. From this viewpoint you can look across the crater and view the cinder cone, part of the main caldera, and, on a clear day, Mauna Loa.

Kau Desert, the leeward slope of Kilauea Crater, also on the rim road, receives very little rain from the trade winds but is soaked occasionally by a heavy general storm. Weird naked lava formations are most easily seen here where they are not overgrown by forest.

Mauna Loa Trail provides one of the most unusual hikes in the national park system. The route to the summit, at 13,680 feet, is 18 miles one way. Two or three days should be allowed. From the mountain parkland the trail rises through the fringe of straggling mamanis and railliardias. Above 10,000 feet, it enters the vast expanse of barren lava fields, winding between pumice cones and along lava-splattered cracks. Ice lingers in the cracks all year. Hikers can stay overnight at park cabins at Red Hill, 10,000 feet, and on the summit. Another good backcountry trip is the **Halape Coastal Hike,** about 8 miles round trip to the coastal section of the park, with camping in a breezy coconut grove. The park has over 150 miles of foot trails.

Photography. Park headquarters area receives about 100 inches of rain yearly. This means many days are overcast and dark. Fortunately, a rough pattern is predictable—most early mornings are clear and bright, but by noon the northeast trade winds have blown in a dense cloud cover. At the park museum many photographers take pictures of the models, dioramas, and paintings. If you are fortunate enough to arrive during an eruption, you will find high-speed color film and a telephoto lens useful.

Accommodations. Volcano House, at 4,000 feet elevation on the rim of Kilauea, is a modern, comfortable lodge, a good stop for lunch or overnight.

Camping. The operator of the same concession has low-cost camper cabins at Namakani Paio Campground. The park maintains three campgrounds (the newest is at Kawoawoa near the coast).

Seasons. Seasons are not pronounced in semitropical Hawaii, but the weather can be cool at any time at the high elevations in the park. Rainwear will be useful, as there is heavy precipitation.

Nearby. Five miles from the Kalapana entrance to the park, **Harry K. Brown County Park** provides picnicking and overnight camping. **City of Refuge National Historical Park,** at Honaunau on the Kona coast, which became part of the national park system in 1961, contains an ancient burial temple of Hawaii's kings and interprets the story of the early Hawaiian settlers. An interesting horticultural area, **Akaka Falls State Park,** distinguished by its varied tropical plants, trees, and shrubs, is located north of Hilo near the sugar fields of Honomu.

A visit to Hawaii Volcanoes should be linked with a stop at Maui to see **Haleakala National Park;** both of these areas formerly constituted Hawaii National Park.

For further information write Superintendent, Hawaii Volcanoes National Park, Hawaii 96718.

HOT SPRINGS

Established as a national park, 1921

Entirely different from all other national parks, this area of 5,765 acres comprises 47 mineral hot springs, with beneficial qualities believed sampled by Hernando de Soto, and by Indians even before him. When the government established the springs as a federal reservation in 1832, it was the first step to hold places of special interest in trust for all—which later led to the national park idea.

In that period of the 19th century resorts with medicinal bathing ("spas") were extremely popular. The idea of the bath as a recreational pursuit goes back in history to the ancient days of the Greeks, Romans and Saxons. In fact, Bath, the most famous spa in England, had its beginning when the Romans discovered the healing qualities of the waters; the remains of the luxurious baths are now Britain's most significant Roman relic. From Europe the spa idea was transplanted to America as a mark of culture. Southern planters and Northern commercial leaders resorted at the springs in western Virginia. George Washington is known to have frequented Berkeley Springs in particular.

Virtually all these areas were reserved for the wealthy and aristocratic. Establishment of the Hot Springs Reservation in behalf of the people was a fitting action in a growing republic. Nevertheless, the area remained largely in private holdings, with titles in litigation for years. In 1870, Congress set up legal procedure for settling titles and claims to titles. The national park was established in 1921, through the influence of Stephen T. Mather, as a successor to the reservation that had existed previously.

The park's 47 hot springs are along a fault, or ancient break in the earth's crust. What makes the waters hot? The prevalent theory is that rainwater sinks into the earth, then rises along tilted layers of rock to emerge through the fault at the southwest base of Hot Springs Mountain. However, another theory suggests that the water escapes and rises to the surface from cooling, molten rocks in the earth's interior. From whatever source, more than a million gallons of water flow from the springs, with an average temperature of 143 degrees Fahrenheit. Waters from all the springs are practically identical in chemical content. The water from two springs can be seen emerging naturally. From the 45 other springs the water is collected in common reservoirs for exclusive use in the bathhouses of the national park.

Because the park is small and nearly surrounded by a busy resort city, the 18-mile network of hiking trails and the undisturbed woodland are a pleasant surprise to those who find them. A dense forest covers the steep, rocky hills of the park, with wildflowers blooming most of the year. More than 110 species of birds have been identified. The altitude of the park varies from 600 feet on the valley floor to 1,200 feet on the summits.

Only physicians approved by the National Park Service are allowed to prescribe the waters of the hot springs. While the baths may be taken without the advice of a physician by securing a permit at any of the bathhouses, examination by a physician is recommended. Seventeen concessioner bathhouses operate under a specific series of regulations which have been approved by the Secretary of the Interior.

THE PRACTICAL GUIDE

Park Museum, Central and Reserve Avenues, explains the varying theories on the origin of the hot springs in the geologic past. **Display Springs** are not sealed and still emerge naturally; they are located adjacent to the **Promenade,** a landscaped brick-paved walk.

The rugged hill country around Hot Springs abounds in hunting, fishing, canoeing, and hiking opportunities. Three man-made lakes are in the area.

Accommodations. Hotels, motels, and tourist homes are located throughout the city.

Camping. The 57-site Gulpha Gorge Campground is set in a beautiful valley 2 miles from the center of Hot Springs.

Seasons. Unlike many parks, the season at Hot Springs covers the entire year. Winter temperatures are mild, allowing for outdoor activities, except at infrequent intervals. Spring and fall offer special features for nature enthusiasts and photographers. Fall colors abound in October, especially along the West Mountain Scenic Road.

For further information write Superintendent, Hot Springs National Park, Box 1219, Hot Springs, Arkansas 71902.

ISLE ROYALE

Authorized as a national park, 1931

No roads, no cars. The only loud noise is the sound of an outboard motor offshore, unless you listen hard to orchids poking from the underbrush, or to the nocturnal serenade of the wolves exulting in the survival of a last stronghold. The largest island in Lake Superior is a natural sanctuary, attracting creatures that can fly, swim, or drift across the water barrier. It is also a superlative outdoor laboratory for the study of ecology, a modern science concerned with the interwoven web of life-forms and their environment. This is indeed a national park worthy of its name.

Beaver, muskrat, mink, and weasel are common. So are the snowshoe hare, squirrel, and red fox. The bald eagle, osprey, pileated woodpecker, 25 kinds of warblers and, most frequently seen, the herring gull—these have made their way across the 45 miles of water from the nearest Michigan shore, or the 15 miles from Canada. But not so for the deer, bear, porcupine, and skunk, unable to bridge the water. Moose, often seen along streams or on the shores of inland lakes, were not on the island before 1900, but when the lake froze in about 1912, a number of them may have ventured over the ice. In the winter of 1948-49, the wolves made their way across, arriving at a time when they were needed. The moose herds had grown overabundant, and the ecology of the island demanded a thinning of the species, which the wolves provided through predation, culling the diseased weaklings and fulfilling their role in the balance of natural forces.

Studies of the wolf-moose relationship at Isle Royale have achieved much recognition in the world of biology.

Ancient Indian mining pits are found at various locations in the park, and radio carbon tests show that these pits date back 3,800 years or more. Copper mined by hammerstone in the prehistoric age was used on the trading trails throughout the Great Lakes.

Isle Royale National Park, with its 539,280 acres of forested wilderness, fjordlike harbors, beaver ponds, innumerable lakes, and surrounding islets, is for people, too. Because it is accessible only by boat, it provides unforgettable vistas along the rugged wave-swept shores and a feeling of serenity on backcountry trails carpeted with spruce or fir needles. A chain of outstanding campgrounds extends almost the full 45-mile length of the island and across its 9-mile width. Attractive and comfortable accommodations are provided at lodges at both ends of the island, with many opportunities for photography, fishing, and the study of nature in all its moods.

Old lava flows formed the early rocks of Isle Royale, but during the glacial period in the last million years the island was buried beneath a mile-thick sheet of ice. Even during the early melting and retreat of glaciers, it remained submerged; but as the level of Lake Superior lowered with the opening of new outlets, the underwater ridge finally emerged as an island. Although soil on the stony foundation is only a few inches to a few feet in depth, Isle Royale today is a wonderful meeting ground of hardwood trees and conifers sheltering several hundred species of wildflowers.

THE PRACTICAL GUIDE

There are ways of getting here on a short tour, which anyone taking the great circle loop around Lake Superior should consider. However, if you stay at least one unhurried week you will spend every minute of it to advantage. A boater planning to navigate his own craft across Lake Superior must prepare to cope with a tough inland sea, which can be dangerous. Boats under 20 feet are best left home or transported to the island on the regularly scheduled passenger boat trips. The waters are definitely not for swimming.

Reaching the island. The "main highway to the park" is *Ranger III,* the National Park Service motor ship, 165 feet long, which makes three round trips weekly. It sails from Houghton on Michigan's Upper Peninsula, 70 miles away, on Tuesday, Thursday, and Saturday, returning one day later. There is also commercial float-plane service from Houghton. Charter planes are available from Houghton and Grand Portage as well. The privately owned *Isle Royale Queen II* makes a round trip daily from Copper Harbor to Rock Harbor Lodge. From the west, the *Wenonah,* operated by Sivertson Brothers, makes a round trip daily from Grand Portage to Windigo Inn, a distance of 20 miles, leaving 9:30 a.m. June 20 to Labor Day. Boat operators will transport your small runabout or canoe. Gasoline may be purchased at Rock Harbor and Windigo marinas.

Windigo Mine. This ruin of an old copper pit was mined by white men until about 1899. A fine trail leads from Washington Creek, near Windigo Inn, along the river to the mine.

Hiking. The national park is laced by more than 120 miles of foot trails. The **Greenstone Ridge Trail** extends 40 miles from Rock Harbor Lodge to Washington Harbor, following the backbone of the island. The trip should be planned to cover several days.

Even if you don't go all the way, you can get a good sample by hiking to Mount Franklin, then continuing to **Ojibway Lookout,** with a superb view from the tower of many lakes and, on a clear day, the Canadian mainland standing out 15 miles north. There are other fine trails as well. One leads to the mellowed and abandoned **Rock Harbor Lighthouse,** built in 1885 to guide boats into the harbor during the early copper mining days. Another goes to **Monument Rock,** a towering 70-foot pinnacle carved by waves and ice, then continues past ancient beaches and a copper mining site, used by prehistoric Indians, to **Lookout Louise,** for one of the most beautiful views in the park. Ask about the "Wilderness Trails" patch you can win to wear on your jacket. Almost all campsites are equipped with Isle Royale shelters, a screened version of the famous three-sided Adirondack shelter.

Tour operators. A good way to make the round trip over the whole island is to go one way by trail and the other by boat. The *Voyageur,* privately owned, circumnavigates the park two or three times weekly. You can board it at Rock Harbor Lodge and travel to Windigo, or vice versa; or you can arrange to have it pick you up at your lakeside camp. Write Sivertson Brothers Fisheries, 366 Lake Avenue South, Duluth, Minnesota 55802.

There usually are enough shelters for all campers, but be prepared to use your own tent. A park ranger will advise which shelters are available; the limit is 15 days at most sites, a shorter period at others.

Fishing and Boating. Motor launch trips can be arranged at Windigo Inn or Rock Harbor Lodge. Boats can be rented at both locations. A modern marina for small boats and private cruisers is located at Rock Harbor. About 50 kinds of fish are found on inland streams, bays, and lakes and in Lake Superior. No fishing license is required for inland waters of the park. Lake trout are taken in Lake Superior by trolling over reefs and along the shore. Inland lakes teem with northern pike and perch.

Naturalist program. Naturalist-guided walks are conducted from Rock Harbor Lodge and Windigo. Illustrated talks on geology, flora, fauna, or climate are conducted each evening at 8:30 at both of these places and at Daisy Farm Campground. A slide talk is presented on each voyage aboard the *Ranger III.*

Accommodations. Rock Harbor Lodge has 12 attractive twin-unit housekeeping cabins, suitable for families, plus lodge rooms. Dining room and snack bar are open to the public. Windigo Inn, at Washington Harbor, has lodge rooms. Atmosphere is friendly and informal. Reservations should be made at least three weeks in advance. Write National Park Concessions, Inc., Isle Royale National Park, Houghton, Michigan 49931 (before June 1, c/o Mammoth Cave, Kentucky 42259).

Camping. Camper supplies are sold at the lodges. Twenty-two campsites are along the shores and on inland lakes.

Seasons. Weather is cool and the travel season short, from mid-June until shortly after Labor Day. Fog is common during June and early July. Mosquitoes, blackflies, and deer flies can be a problem early and midsummer, although shelters are screened. Temperature during the day seldom rises above 80 degrees, and nights always are cool. Warm clothes are as important as insect repellent. Maples, aspen, and birch turn color early in September.

Nearby. Michigan's Upper Peninsula is the center of an old copper mining industry. The **Museum** at the **Michigan Technological University** at Houghton contains a large collection of minerals. **Fort Wilkins State Park,** northeast of Copper Harbor, surrounded on three sides by palisades, contains the restored buildings and historical museum relating to a remote army post established in 1844 to prevent disturbances among the miners and Indians. Anyone coming from Grand Portage should visit the **Grand Portage National Monument,** on the site of the "great depot," where voyageurs transferred supplies from Lake Superior to the border-lake canoe route during the fur trading days.

Recommended reading. *The Wolves of Isle Royale,* by David L. Mech.

For further information write Superintendent, Isle Royale National Park, Houghton, Michigan 49931.

LASSEN VOLCANIC

Established as a national park, 1916

At the southern end of the lofty Cascades, the most recently active volcano in the United States, except for those in Alaska and Hawaii, forms the core of a national park where snow sometimes falls lightly in summer on blue lakes and evergreen forests. In January, cross-country skiers take to the high, timber-free slopes and visit steaming fumaroles, hissing hot springs, and boiling mud pots. Thus visitors can enjoy the park in any season.

Lassen Volcanic is the smallest (106,372 acres) of the five national parks in California, and is also the least known, but is a beauty spot nonetheless, being in the heavily wooded northeast part of the state where the Sierra Nevadas meet the Cascades.

The towering mass of Lassen Peak, 10,457 feet, is part of the fraternity of volcanic giants, in company with Mount Baker, Mount Rainier, Mount Hood, and the ancient Mount Mazama of Crater Lake, and Mount Shasta. The last series of eruptions began in the spring of 1914, after at least 400 years of quiet slumber, and continued over a period of seven years. In 1915, red tongues of lava spilled through a notch in the crater rim, flowed down the western slope 1,000 feet, and hardened in place. But on the northeast flank, hot lava melted the deep snowpack, causing a mammoth river of mud to rush downhill carrying 30-ton boulders in its path. Three days later, a column of vapor and dust rose more than 5 miles in the sky, while a low-angle blast struck the northeast flank again, widening the path of destruction to more than a mile, mowing down trees and all life in its path for a length of 5 miles. It was these eruptions that drew nationwide attention and hastened the establishment of the national park in 1916.

The first recorded observation of the area had been made by an expedition led by Don Luis Arguello in 1821. The name "San Jose" was given to the mountain. Six years later Jedediah Smith, the intrepid explorer, named it "Mount Joseph," but he actually had the whole range of mountains in mind. Then, in the 1840s, Peter Lassen, a Danish pioneer, filed for a land grant from the Mexican government and established a ranch. Both the peak and the county now bear his name.

The geology of the volcano had been studied for more than 30 years (notably by J. S. Diller of the U.S. Geological Survey) before establishment of the park. In 1907, President Theodore Roosevelt signed a proclamation setting aside Cinder Cone and Lassen Peak as national monuments. Then, following the eruptions of 1914-1916, Lassen Volcanic was established as the 13th national park.

Lassen is the remnant of a larger, higher volcano called Mount Tehama, the top of which collapsed, creating a great bowl, or caldera, similar to the one in nearby Oregon containing Crater Lake. Lassen Peak began as lava squeezed upward on the slope of old Tehama. Too thick to flow like liquid, it plugged the vent from which it came and formed a rough, rounded mass called a "plug dome." After formation of the plug dome, Lassen remained relatively calm, although smaller eruptions took place before the big blasts that began in 1914. Lassen is now dormant, but scientists believe that in the future new eruptions may be possible.

THE PRACTICAL GUIDE

Many important scenic and volcanic features can be seen from the 30-mile-long Lassen Park Road, which half encircles Lassen Peak, so it can easily be included as a half-day side trip while driving north or south on I-5 (California 99) or US 395. Most of the eastern half of the park is superb hiking and camping country. More than 150 miles of marked trails lead to old volcanoes, thermal features, lakes, and other natural features.

Manzanita Lake, near the northwest boundary, is rimmed with firs and pines. At least six types of pines are found in the park: Jeffrey, ponderosa, sugar, western white, and lodgepole at lower elevations, plus whitebark pine, which climbs and struggles to survive at 10,000 feet. Willows and thin-leafed alder dip their roots into the clear waters of the lake. **Manzanita Lake Visitor Center** and nearby concession facilities were closed during 1974 due to a geologist's discovery of the instability of rocks and cliffs of Chaos Crags to a degree that might endanger the safety of visitors. A new location has not yet been determined.

Chaos Crags and Jumbles, along the Park Road. The Crags, like Lassen Peak, are towering, plug-like masses pushed up through vents a few thousand years ago. Violent steam explosions from the base of the Crags caused avalanches, forming the hummocky Jumbles. The small coniferous trees growing around them are known as the Dwarf Forest, part of nature's effort to heal the scars of its own violence.

You can see a young pine forest taking hold of the soil while you drive 2½ miles through the **Devastated Area,** which was denuded of all vegetation in the volcanic blast of 1915.

Summit Lake. This is a good starting point for hikes and horseback riding to the lakes in the wilderness eastern portion of the park. Saddle and pack trips can be arranged.

Lassen Peak Trail. It starts from near the summit of the Park Road at 8,512 feet elevation. The climb is 2½ miles and takes four to five hours round trip, but the view from the summit is worth the effort. Overlooking craters, blue lakes, and forests, this is the high point of a visit to Lassen Volcanic.

The trail from **Kings Creek Meadows** to the falls, 1.3 miles, shows Lassen's wildflowers at their best, including crimson snow plant, leopard lily, paintbrush, lupine, penstemon, and bleeding heart.

Bumpass Hell is the destination of a 1.3-mile walk worth taking for the name alone. It leads from the Park Road through an alpine wildflower area to the largest display of hot springs in the park, with bubbling mud pots testifying to underground turbulence. It was named for an early hunter, whose tragic mistake

61

in placing one leg into a boiling pool should be fair warning to stay on trails and skip the shortcuts in the thermal areas or on any other trails in the park.

Sulphur Works is 2 miles from the southwest park boundary. A self-guiding trail leads through an area where seething gases and heat are emitted from within the caldera of ancient Mount Tehama.

Cinder Cone is one of the outstanding volcanic features of the park, which justified its separate establishment as a national monument in 1907. It is believed to be the source of "fires" and "flaring lights" in 1850-51, which were seen as far off as 160 miles. Black in color, bare of vegetation, it lies surrounded by multicolored heaps of volcanic cinder and ash, called the Painted Dunes, and looks as though it were formed yesterday. Cinder Cone is reached either by hiking or riding horseback from Summit Lake, or by hiking from **Butte Lake** in the northeast corner of the park. Fantastic Lava Beds is a mass of rough blocky lava flows that

originated from the base of Cinder Cone.

Skiing. Activities center near the park's southwestern entrance, where ski tows are operated for both beginners and advanced skiers, usually from December through the middle of April. The concessioner operates a bunny tow for children, intermediate rope tow, and 1,100-foot disc lift. Heavy snow closes the main highway from early November to June. (Note: the ski trip to Bumpass Hell and high country is for experienced skiers only.) Ice skating is often good on Reflection Lake in early winter. The road is kept open from the northwest entrance to the Visitor Center.

Fishing and Boating. Rowboats and canoes can be used on most lakes (except Reflection, Emerald, Helen, Boiling Springs). In the spirit of backcountry recreation, motorboats are prohibited on all lakes in the park. Many lakes and streams have an abundance of rainbow, brook, and brown trout; a California fishing license is required.

Naturalist programs. Features of Lassen Volcanic are best enjoyed and un-

derstood by participating in naturalist-conducted trips. Campfire programs are conducted during the summer at Crags, Summit Lake, and Butte Lake campgrounds, and a variety of guided walks are led in those areas.

Accommodations. Manzanita Lake Lodge, with housekeeping cabins, cabins, and hotel bungalows, has been closed pending relocation. Drakesbad Guest Ranch, a resort in Warner Valley, is a good base for riding and pack trips. For rates and reservations write Lassen National Park Company, Manzanita Lake, California 96060. A number of privately owned resorts are nearby on California 36, 44, and 89.

Camping. Three campgrounds are located on the Park Road (Summit Lake, Kings Creek, and Southwest). Campgrounds at Summit Lake and Butte Lake on the Lassen Park Road have spaces for trailers and some modern conveniences, but no hookups for electricity, water, or sewage. The Sulphur Works campground has modern conveniences too, but you must walk about 100 yards from the parking area to the site. Summit Lake is best for backcountry hiking and horseback riding. Kings Creek is open only five or six weeks during summer. Other campgrounds are at Horseshoe Lake, Juniper Lake, and Warner Valley, on dead-end spur roads. Camping is permitted mid-May to October, depending on weather. The camping limit is 14 days.

Seasons. Summer is the main season. Overnight accommodations in the park are open mid-June to mid-September. During that period there are daily bus trips by the Lassen National Park Company to the Greyhound depot in Redding. Wildflowers burst into bloom in early summer, but the show continues until September. Ski activities are centered in the winter-use building. Nearest lodgings are at Mineral Lodge, 9 miles from the south entrance.

Nearby. Many campgrounds and recreation areas lie within the 1,147,000 acres of **Lassen National Forest.** A major campground is located southeast of the park on the west shore of **Lake Almanor** (elevation 4,550 feet), one of the largest artificial bodies of water in California, noted for its abundant trout. Other camping and picnic areas are conveniently located north of the park along **Hat Creek.** At **McArthur-Burney Falls Memorial State Park,** 11 miles north of Burney, Burney Falls is a cataract of singular beauty.

For further information write Superintendent, Lassen Volcanic National Park, Mineral, California 96063.

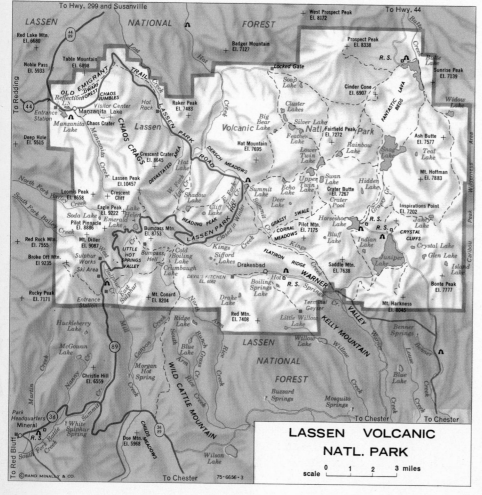

LASSEN VOLCANIC NATL. PARK

scale 0 1 2 3 miles

MAMMOTH CAVE

Authorized as a national park, 1926

It was discovered in 1798, and it became an attraction of wide renown and lasting appeal. Edwin Booth, the Shakespearean actor, once recited Hamlet's soliloquy in an underground chasm now called Booth's Amphitheatre. Ole Bull, the celebrated Norwegian violinist, performed here in 1851—the same year Jenny Lind, the Swedish nightingale, shattered the subterranean stillness with her golden voice. Those were thrilling days, when visitors eagerly toted whale-oil lamps, and ladies were advised that "bloomers or Turkish dress" constituted proper attire, and many came from afar to explore "the greatest cave that ever was."

Mammoth Cave still provides a full quota of thrills. It consists of many miles of charted passageways filled with spectacular rock formations and domes, though how large it really is nobody knows. Several levels have been explored, but many underground streams are still at work, shaping more passages.

The national park, about 100 miles from Louisville and the same distance from Nashville, Tennessee, covers 51,311 acres. It lies near Bowling Green in south central Kentucky, where the limestone terrain is pitted by depressions called sinkholes. Some geologists call the area the Southern Sinkhole Plain, but local people are apt to refer to it as the "Land of 10,000 Sinks." The formation of the sinkholes and Mammoth Cave are intimately related. Over millions of years rainwater, containing small amounts of carbonic acid, seeped into the ground dissolving limestone layers, causing the surface to collapse, and developing an underground river system. As the streams cut deeper and deeper into the lower depths, upper levels were drained and became dry. In places rocks fell from the ceilings enlarging the caverns. After the upper parts became filled with air, seepage played a new role as the means of dissolving and depositing limestone, a miniscule amount at a time, to form travertine, or cave onyx, in thousands of intricate and artistic patterns, including stalagmites, stalactites, draperies, and cascading flowstone. Mammoth Cave was the first known cave to contain gypsum, restricted to drier portions, where slow leaching of calcium sulfate through porous limestone forces the gypsum crystals outward into the cave. Then they grow and often curve, much like ice crystals from a wet soil during winter, sometimes crusting an entire wall or ceiling.

These subtle processes of nature have been under way for a period longer than man can imagine. They continue to form new caves, to decorate the older ones, and to enhance the visual beauty of the mammoth underground that has delighted visitors since its discovery. For many years the cave was in private hands; part of it once was used as a tuberculosis sanitarium.

Scenic hills and valleys on the surface are part of the attraction of the park. A wide variety of birds and wildflowers enliven the forest of hardwood trees. Whitetail deer, woodchucks, cottontails, and squirrels are likely to be encountered. The Green River, joined by underground streams, winds 25 miles across the park. It is the key to the active circulation of underground and surface waters, assuring that new passages will continue to be formed at the lower levels of Mammoth Cave for a new world of hidden beauty.

THE PRACTICAL GUIDE

You can see the cave on one of the guided trips conducted every day, ranging from one to six hours, and then be on your way. But don't overlook the good overnight accommodations and campgrounds, and the opportunities for boating and fishing on the Green and Nolin rivers.

Watch your step in approaching the national park. Solicitors employed by privately owned caves wear official-looking uniforms and operate from little "ranger stations" on the road. The only place where you can purchase tickets for Mammoth Cave is at the Visitor Center in Mammoth Cave National Park, except during the summer, when tickets for the Historic Tour must be purchased at a kiosk located along the trail to the Historic Entrance.

Visitor Center and cave trips. Trips into the cave are conducted every day of the year. Prices and schedules are available at the Visitor Center, where displays interpret the natural history. Only persons accompanied by a National Park Service guide may enter the cave. Trails are solid and reasonably smooth. The temperature is 54 degrees all year; carry a sweater or jacket. Low-heeled shoes are a must for comfort. The pace underground is leisurely, with frequent rest stops, but if you have any doubts about your endurance, settle for one of the shorter trips. All trips can be considered somewhat strenuous.

Frozen Niagara Trip (½ mile, one hour) displays a variety of formations. Among others is Frozen Niagara, the largest travertine formation in the cave, a fine example of flowstone, formed through centuries of deposition from water flowing over rock formations instead of dripping from them. Then you look down at Crystal Lake, a small green pool formed by a stalagmite dam.

Historic Trip (2 miles, two hours) is a conducted tour September to May and is a self-guiding tour during the summer, with park guides and interpretive signs along the route to help you. Enter through the natural opening near the Visitor Center, then see the **Rotunda,** scene of saltpeter mining during the War of 1812, and Indian artifacts. The trip continues to **Mammoth Dome,** aptly named. The famous blindfish in underground streams are displayed along the route.

The Scenic Trip (4 miles, four hours) takes you to some beautiful gypsum formations. The group stops for a good lunch 267 feet underground in the **Snowball Room,** which is worth the price of the admission, with its clusters of gypsum that resemble snowballs on the ceiling. Then it cuts through **Frozen Niagara,** the spectacle in travertine.

Lantern Trip (3 miles, three hours) is unique. It gives the thrill of times past, before the cave was electrically wired. Trips scheduled four times daily during the summer are limited to 40 persons.

Wild Cave Trip (5 miles, six hours) is scheduled during summer and on weekends throughout the rest of the year. This rugged spelunking adventure, which extends through crawlways and unimproved passages, requires the aid of hard hats and headlamps. Not suited for persons under 16.

Tour for physically handicapped (½ mile, one and one-half hours) is available to persons confined to wheelchairs. Inquire at the Visitor Center for details.

Green River Cruise. The *Miss Green River,* a 120-passenger twin diesel-powered cruiser, makes several cruises daily. The twilight cruise reveals not only the forests along the riverbanks, but deer, beavers, turtles, and a snake or two, all completely at home. Cruises last one hour.

Cave Island Nature Trail. It begins and ends near the Historic Cave entrance, winding through the woods for about a mile. In addition, there are more than 7 miles of hiking trails keyed to geology, botany, and zoology. As part of the interpretive program, several guided walks are conducted daily during the summer. Evening programs illustrated with slides are given nightly at the amphitheater.

Fishing is permitted all year with throw lines, pole and line, rod and reel. No license required. Swimming is discouraged because of unsafe conditions along the river.

Kentucky Craft Shop features outstanding weaving, pottery, metalcrafts, baskets, brooms, and wood carvings. Here you can acquire a dulcimer, the prized musical instrument made in the Kentucky mountains.

Accommodations. Some of the best in the National Park System are the Mammoth Cave Hotel and the Sunset Point Motor Lodge at the edge of the forest. There also are older hotel rooms and plain cottages. For rates and reservations write National Park Concessions, Inc., Mammoth Cave, Kentucky 42259. Motels are located in nearby Cave City, Park City, and Horse Cave.

Camping. The campground of 145 sites, southeast of the Visitor Center, is adjacent to laundry, supply store, and showers, which are open during the summer. Limit of 14 days, June 1 to Labor Day.

Seasons. This is a national park worth visiting any time of year. In spring, the hardwood forest is filled with wildflowers. In summer, the coolness of the cave provides visitors with natural air conditioning; nights in the park are cool and comfortable. Autumn is the time of brilliant color changes, when days are mild and clear and nights crisp and chilly.

Nearby. Ten miles north of the national park, **Nolin Lake Reservoir** formed behind Nolin Dam, completed in 1963, has over 6,000 acres of boating and fishing waters.

North and east of Mammoth Cave lie **Abraham Lincoln Birthplace National Historic Site** and the **Bluegrass** country around Lexington.

For further information write Superintendent, Mammoth Cave National Park, Mammoth Cave, Kentucky 42259.

MESA VERDE

Established as a national park, 1906

The tableland runs 15 miles long and 2,000 feet above the valley to the north. Its rimrocks command the horizon for more than a hundred miles, up through the purple Rockies and down across the stark desert of the Four Corners. On its south side, this table mountain is honeycombed with deep canyons. In long crannies and huge arching caves within these canyons and on the mesa tops stand hundreds of villages. They bespeak a lost world that struggled to survive in a harsh environment, flourished for a time, and was abandoned two centuries before Columbus.

The fascination of Mesa Verde, above all, is inherent in its mysteries. Enthusiasts sometimes ascribe to these cliff dwellings superlatives such as "the largest," "the earliest," or "the most important." All of these may be true, and none may be true, for the only constant in history, as in nature, is change. From these ruins archaeologists, who are the modern heroes of this national park, have given their best interpretation of a creative chapter in the story of prehistoric America, but their evaluations change as they acquire new knowledge.

The park covers 52,036 acres in the southwestern tip of Colorado. The region initially was occupied about the beginning of the first century A.D. by nomadic hunters turning to the land. At first they seem to have ignored the Mesa Verde, choosing instead the stream valleys for their villages. During the sixth century, however, they took up residence among the heavy forests of juniper and pinyon on the mesa tops. Here they found a permanent supply of water, arable soil, and shelter from the elements. These Indians remained for 800 years, during which time they advanced their culture and refined their arts, architecture, agriculture, and industry. From pithouses and crude pueblos they progressed to great structures in the sheer rock, to which we have assigned such names as Cliff Palace and Balcony House—towers, terraces, whole towns built in the caves. Toward the end of the 13th century they left their houses empty in the cliffs, their Temple to the Sun un-

finished, and wandered away, searching for water, and to mingle with other tribes in the Southwest. Their blood lines could well be carried down to many of the modern Pueblo Indians along the Rio Grande in New Mexico and west to the Hopi country in northern Arizona. As to why they deserted their villages, despite our desire for simple answers, there is no simple answer. A severe drought occurred, but the people had overcome worse water shortages earlier. They may have departed because of nomadic raiders, pressure from internal dissention, or a combination of many factors. The abandonment was gradual, over a long period of time; the precise reasons are part of the puzzle of archaeology and history.

The early period of exploration to unravel the mysteries began in 1859, with a series of geological surveys. In 1874, William H. Jackson, the famous frontier photographer of the Hayden Survey, visited, photographed, and named Two Story House in Mancos Canyon, at the southern tip of Moccasin Mesa, doing much to make the ruins known to the public. During the last quarter of the 19th century it was common practice for local ranchers to graze cattle in this area. B. K. Wetherill and his five sons became intimately familiar, through their cattle-herding activities, with Mesa Verde and its treasures. In 1888, Richard Wetherill and Charles Mason discovered Chapin Mesa. In 1892, Baron Gustavus Nordenskiold, of Sweden, guided by the Wetherills, recorded 22 cliff dwellings and performed major excavations; some of the materials he took to Europe now form part of the collection of the Finland National Museum.

As the ruins became known, they were increasingly ravaged by cowboys and others in search of salable artifacts. In protest against the vandalism, scientific and educational institutions urged that protective measures be taken. In 1891 the Colorado legislature memorialized Congress for the establishment of a national park on a part of the Ute Indian Reservation. Legislation to achieve

that goal was introduced but continually failed (partly in dispute over whether mining should be permitted) until 1906. In the same year that saw passage of the Antiquities Act, Mesa Verde National Park was established for the purpose of preserving the prehistoric cliff dwellings. Unfortunately, the park included almost none of the ruins it was supposed to preserve. The most valuable, including Cliff Palace, were on Ute deeded lands.

In 1906, the Secretary of the Interior called for an archaeological survey, to be conducted by the Smithsonian Institution, to determine exactly what ruins situated on Ute lands should be embraced in the park and what the boundaries and acreage should be. But the Utes refused to trade until 1913, when they finally agreed to accept a much larger acreage of their own selection. The boundaries were again changed in 1931, 1932, and as recently as 1963 to insure protection of the mesas and their ruins.

Among the prominent figures in the early history of the park were Mrs. Gilbert McClurg, who organized and promoted the Colorado Cliff Dwelling Association; Dr. J. W. Fewkes, of the Smithsonian Institution, who conducted extensive excavations and repairs over a period of years; and Dr. Jesse Nusbaum, who served as a young photographer on the 1906–07 Smithsonian survey. Dr. Nusbaum was just beginning a distinguished career in the field of archaeology which included service as superintendent of Mesa Verde National Park.

A great deal has been learned about the changes in the ways of people while they dwelt here. Their life span at Mesa Verde is divided into four ages. The first is called the Basketmaker Period, when shallow caves furnished shelter, and corn and squash were raised in small fields on the mesa top. Basketry, the earliest American craft, characterized this era, and woven baskets, bags, sandals, and containers of all sorts were created. Sometime after A.D. 450 their culture advanced into the Modified Basketmaker Period when their architecture included development of the pithouse, a semi-subterranean room with low walls and a flat roof of mud-covered poles and sticks. Transition to Modified Basketmaker coincides with the initial occupation of the Mesa Verde.

There were all sorts of variations in the shape of the pithouse—circular, D-shaped, square with rounded corners; antechambers with doorways; ventilator tunnels with vertical shafts; and ladders giving access through a smokehole in the rooftop. The Modified Basketmakers replaced some of their baskets with pottery, which enabled them to add beans to their diet by cooking in fireproof vessels.

The Developmental Period, a time of experimenta-tion, saw the emergence of a new type of house, a rectangular structure with vertical side walls and flat roofs. Houses were joined to form compact groups around open courts, where daily activity went on. Instead of pithouses, people built underground pitrooms in the courts, stylized ceremonial rooms called kivas. These provided the men with a combination clubhouse and religious chamber, a type still used by Pueblo Indians. This was a period of expansion, flourishing arts and crafts, and the introduction of cotton, along with the use of the true loom. They built an ingenious chain of ditches to conserve water atop Chapin Mesa and to save the time it took to haul water from springs below.

Then came the climax of Mesa Verde culture, the golden age called the Classic Pueblo Period, from A.D. 1100 to 1300. At first the people lived in well-built stone pueblos on the mesa tops. Nearly all house walls were double, the outer walls being massive (possibly as a protection against raiders). It was the sophisticated age of fine craftsmanship, beautiful black-on-white pottery made without the aid of a wheel, turquoise jewelry, and woven cloth.

Strangely, at the same time, the gradual emigration to the south began. In the last phase, the twilight of Mesa Verde, architectural monuments were constructed in the most spectacular locations, on the cliff ledges and in the caves. Walls of houses and kivas occasionally were covered with handsome designs, sometimes colored red, white, yellow, and black. Pottery pitchers, bowls, and other pieces were elaborately decorated.

Of hundreds of silent cities in the cliffs, actually few have been scientifically studied. A major archaeological project started in 1958 on Wetherill Mesa, a mile wide and 10 miles long, has finally been completed. It was opened to visitors in 1972—the first new area since the park was established in 1906.

THE PRACTICAL GUIDE

During summer, since large crowds jam the park, visits to the ruins are rationed by means of a ticket system. It may take a visitor two or three days to see all of the major ruins.

Park entrance. The center of activities lies 21 miles ahead. This is the place to decide whether to make overnight reservations in the park (if there are vacancies), to head for the campground, or to spend a few hours and travel on.

Park Point Fire Lookout, one of five numbered stops at points of interest along the entrance road. At 8,572 feet above sea level, this is the highest elevation in the park. It opens views into Arizona, Utah, New Mexico, and Colorado, the states sharing the Four Cor-ners. The mighty landmark of the desert, Shiprock, on the Navajo Indian Reservation, rises 1,400 feet. Viewed at sunset, it shimmers in the alpenglow, looking more like a ship than a rock.

Park Museum. A series of outstanding dioramas, accompanied by baskets, feather cloaks, jewels, and mummies found during excavations, reveal the successive cultures of the cliff dwellers. At the museum visitors learn the ground rules for visiting the dwellings, which have been dangerously weakened by time; cliff dwellings are visited only with rangers on guided trips, or when marked "open for visitation" with a ranger posted on duty; mesa top ruins, which are less susceptible to damage, may be visited unaccompanied.

Ruins trip, led by a ranger, on Chapin Mesa. Check the museum for the daily schedule. This is your chance to enter the inner sanctum of the American Stone Age. **Spruce Tree House,** best preserved and one of the largest cliff dwellings in the park, contains 114 living rooms, of which 8 are kivas. **Cliff Palace,** the largest and most famous community dwelling, was discovered by Richard Wetherill and Charles Mason in 1888. Built under the protection of a high vaulted cave roof, it contains more than 200 rooms, of which 23 are kivas. Houses rising in some sections to four stories were home to as many as 200 persons. **Balcony House,** in a high cave on the west wall of Soda Canyon, demonstrates architectural detail and construction skills in a choice defensive setting.

Ruins Road drive. Two self-guiding loops cover 12 miles and provide views of many cliff dwellings with roofs still intact after a thousand years. Ten excavated mesa top ruins may be visited. They demonstrate the entire range of architectural development in the sequence in which they were constructed, starting with a Modified Basketmaker pithouse of the late 600s. The road passes **Square Tower House** (not open), with a tower rising to a height of four stories, built against the near-perpendicular wall of Navajo canyon, with the cliff forming its back wall. **Sun Point Pueblo** is interesting because its inhabitants, in the late Classic Pueblo Period, deliberately tore down the roofs and walls and used them to build a cliff dwelling in a nearby canyon. The last stop is **Sun Temple,** a great ceremonial structure also of the late Classic Pueblo Period, built in a D-shape on a promontory over Cliff and Fewkes canyons. No part of the building was roofed, and only some stone-working tools were found within.

Wetherill Mesa is second only to Chapin Mesa for the impressive concentration of cliff dwellings. Wetherill is spectacular but fragile; it cannot stand heavy or uncontrolled visitor use. At the Visitor Center at Navajo Hill you can board a free bus for the 12-mile ride to Wetherill. Then you switch to an open-sided minitrain for a leisurely trip along a narrow path through the pinyon-juniper forest to see the impressive ruins dating from the 12th and 13th centuries. Stops are made for guided tours of the Long House, the largest ruin on the mesa, Mug House, and Step House.

Tour operators. Conducted bus trips of two or three hours around the ruins are run by Spruce Tree Lodge.

Hiking is restricted in Mesa Verde because of the fragile nature of the ruins. Pictograph Point Trail leads from the museum around the base of the cliff on the east side of Spruce Tree and Navajo canyons, but you must obtain a written permit from the chief ranger's office. Longer trails are located in Morfield Canyon area, but even for these you must register with the campground ranger. Hiking is best done in areas outside Mesa Verde, and visitors should acquaint themselves with the Federal Antiquities Act, adopted in 1906 in order to curb "pothunting" and vandalism in this and similar areas. Under this act, it is a federal offense to remove, injure, damage, or destroy "any historic or prehistoric ruin or monument, or any object

of antiquity" situated on federal lands. Children should be advised firmly that every piece of pottery, bone, and stone plays a part in telling the story and that regulations are strictly enforced.

Horseback trips. Saddle horses can be rented at the concession in Morfield Canyon for wrangler-guided rides of one, two, and four hours on mesa top trails that lead to unexcavated ruins and broad canyons.

Evening campfire programs are held at the brink of the canyon each evening at 8:30 p.m., early June to Labor Day; 8 p.m. thereafter (weather permitting). Programs are also presented nightly at the Morfield campground amphitheater. There is an archaeology lecture, and a Navajo dance team frequently performs tribal dances and chants.

Photography. The cliff dwellings are best photographed in the afternoon, for most caves face west-southwest. Large mesa top ruins are good any time of day. Excellent scenic views are obtained from Mancos and Montezuma Valley overlooks and Park Point.

Accommodations. Modern motel-type accommodations are located at **Far View Terrace** on Navajo Hill, a ten-minute drive from park headquarters. **Spruce Tree Terrace** sells snacks and picnic supplies and rents a number of cabins. **Point Lookout Lodge,** at the park entrance, provides economy family cabins and some trailer sites in a forested area, and a small cafe. Write Reservations Manager, Mesa Verde Company, Mesa Verde National Park, Colorado 81330. Outside the park, accommodations are plentiful at Cortez, 10 miles west, and Durango, 38 miles east.

Camping. Morfield Canyon Campground, 5 miles from the park entrance, at 7,800-feet elevation, has 415 modern campsites, most of which accommodate trailers. The campground runs on first-come, first-served basis, with a 14-day limit during the summer. Morfield Village, operated by the park concessioner, includes supply store, coin-operated laundry, showers, and carry-out snack shop. Service stations are located at Navajo Hill and Morfield Village.

Seasons. Accommodations are provided early May to mid-October (limited basis after Labor Day), but an interpretive program is presented year-round, with trips scheduled to at least one cliff dwelling, weather permitting. The park is open all year; after October 15 you may visit the museum and drive one loop of the ruins road, viewing cliff dwellings from canyon rims and visiting the mesa top ruins. Summer days are warm, evenings chilly. Freezing weather

arrives early at this high elevation.

Frontier Airlines operates daily flights to both Durango and Cortez, where rent-a-car service is available. Bus service from Durango to the park center is scheduled twice daily by Continental Trailways, May to mid-October.

Nearby. Three important points should be made: first, **San Juan National Forest** to the north offers excellent fishing, hunting, backcountry trails, and numerous small campgrounds, all within two hours drive of Mesa Verde. Check for locations at ranger offices in Cortez, Mancos, and Durango. The metropolis of the San Juan Basin, Durango, is the starting point of the **Silverton,** historic narrow-gauge passenger railroad running daily during the summer to the old mining town of Silverton, a wonderful journey through the deep canyons of the Animas River. The train operates from the last Saturday in May to the first Sunday in October. During summer (late June through August) it is crowded, reservations are necessary. Contact Denver and Rio Grande Western Railroad, Durango, Colorado.

Second, though Mesa Verde was isolated and hard to reach for many years, new paved highways have shortened the driving time to one day from Denver and Salt Lake City. Grand Canyon is a five and one-half hour drive, and Santa Fe approximately five hours. Road improvement across Monument Valley, Arizona, links Mesa Verde with spectacular frontier scenery of the Four Corners country.

Third, Mesa Verde will be appreciated more when you visit and compare it with national monuments of the region. A dry climate and the use of stone and adobe by ancient architects have combined to produce extremely well-preserved ruins. Because of the excellent stage of preservation and the impressive structures, more archaeological sites have been incorporated in the National Park System in the Southwest than in any other part of the country. National monuments in the vicinity of the Four Corners are **Aztec Ruins,** New Mexico, a great prehistoric American town of the 12th century; **Chaco Canyon,** New Mexico, representing a high point of the ancient Pueblo civilization; **Hovenweep,** a network of towers and pueblos spread across Colorado and Utah; **Navajo,** Arizona, three of the largest, most elaborate cliff dwellings, and **Canyon de Chelly,** Arizona, fantastic ruins in red cliff and cave country, where modern Navajo Indians have homes and farms.

For further information write Superintendent, Mesa Verde National Park, Colorado 81330.

MOUNT McKINLEY

Established as a national park, 1917

The early Indians knew Mount McKinley as *Denali*, "the high one." To others it is simply *the* mountain. However you look at it, Mount McKinley constitutes a massive monument to the forces of nature.

But the mountain does not stand alone.

It is part of a national park covering almost two million acres (second only to Yellowstone in size), an immense sanctuary of glaciers, forests, tundra, and blue lakes, where the visitor is overcome by stark beauty edging the Arctic Circle, and where he senses the struggle for survival by magnificent wildlife, caribou, Dall sheep, grizzly bears, moose, and wolves among them, in a region of *their* civilization scarcely touched by ours.

The overpowering feeling is one of largeness and naturalness, which is Alaska's special gift to the nation. "Can one describe such a scene and such an environment to wander about in?" once wrote the master of wilderness, Olaus J. Murie. He could find no words, except to add that for him Mount McKinley National Park was the greatest scenic experience on the North American continent.

The park terrain rises from about 1,400 feet to 20,320 feet, the highest point on the continent, at the summit of Mount McKinley. There are other major peaks like Mount Foraker, or "Denali's Wife," called *Sultana* by early Indians, 17,400 feet, also taller than anything in the "lower forty-eight"; Mount Silverthrone, 13,220 feet; and Mount Russell, 11,670 feet. Many glaciers, up to 30 and 40 miles long, are still active on these and other mountains inside the park. One of them, Muldrow Glacier, the largest northward-flowing glacier in Alaska, stretches from between Mount McKinley's twin peaks to within a mile of the park road. The whole landscape is influenced by glaciation of the past and present, with broad, U-shaped valleys, small kettle lakes, old and new moraines.

White and black spruce are the chief evergreens growing in the park, with cottonwood and willow along the stream beds, dwarf birch on the lower mountain slopes, quaking aspen and Alaska birch interspersed with the spruce. Most of the park, however, lies above timberline, which varies between 2,500 to 3,000 feet. The vegetation becomes alpine tundra—lichens, mosses, tough grasses, sedges, a variety of dwarfed, matlike plants capable of surviving in severe climate, and also of producing a surprising display of delicate blossoms.

Lichen proves useful, maybe not immediately to man in this setting, but as a food source to the wildlife community that man protects. Caribou, the most numerous large animal in the park, feeds on such humble plants during its annual stay here, and the concentration of caribou in great herds form a spectacle that no human observer can ever forget. It is not uncommon to see a band of 300 to 400 animals advance in a broad front over the tundra to their wintering grounds farther north.

A more leisurely migration of this native American reindeer takes place in September, when the animals have their heavy winter coats. The bulls have grown their resplendent antlers and striking white capes—the handsome fellows are gathering their harems in the time of the rut.

In all the National Park System, the barren-ground caribou can be seen only here. Occasionally, with good fortune, it is possible to catch sight of wolves at the edge of a caribou concentration, preparing to play their roles in the endless wilderness drama of predator and prey. The Dall sheep, a species of bighorn, looks like a white speck on the higher slopes, as it safeguards itself by climbing to crags beyond the wolf's reach; it too cannot be found in another national park. It is fascinating to watch the Dall's short, springy, and muscular jumps when running over the flats. The Dall is obviously unsuited to level terrain, in contrast to its graceful efficiency in its own element on the upper cliffs.

Since the "1910 Sourdough Expedition," Mount McKinley has been successfully climbed by more than 100 parties. Over three-fourths have been in the last ten years, a period of increased mountaineering activity.

But many routes have been scaled only once or twice. The mountain rises nearly 17,000 feet above the surrounding country and all above 7,000 feet are enveloped by snow and ice—tough for climbers, spectacular for scenic enjoyment.

The mountain has two peaks: the South Peak, the upper summit, 20,320 feet; and North Peak, 19,470 feet, two miles away. It is so brilliant a landmark that it can be seen on clear days from Anchorage and Fairbanks, though it often is obscured by low-hanging clouds.

In early Territorial days this was rough, untracked country, testing the skills of sourdough prospectors, hunters, geologists, and naturalists. Even after establishment of the national park in 1917 as a great wilderness reserve, it remained inaccessible. Only since 1957, with completion of the 161-mile Denali Highway from Paxson as a spur off the Richardson Highway, has it been possible to reach the park by efficient means other than the Alaska Railroad or airplane.

The completion of Alaska 3, between Anchorage and Fairbanks, in 1972, virtually ended the park's remoteness. Now other means must be taken to preserve it.

THE PRACTICAL GUIDE

You'll have 16 to 20 hours of daylight during summer; use them all. Some of the best weather is in early morning, about 3 a.m. Many visitors spend one night as part of an Alaska tour and then depart the next day. However, this great park is worthy of at least two or three days in order to really catch the flavor of the arctic wilderness, wander over the tundra, the vast river bars, and through the black spruce forests. Binoculars are essential to observe animals. Insect repellent is advised for anyone planning a hike.

The park road extends 90 miles from its connection with the Denali Highway, but private vehicles beyond Savage River bridge (milepost 14.5) are restricted to those people with camping reservations. Once at designated campsites they, and others, may use the free shuttle bus system. The gravel, curving park road does not lend itself to a heavy volume of traffic, and protection of the environment is an even more important factor. Shuttle buses operate frequently; they drop off and pick up visitors at virtually any point along the highway.

Trains, planes, buses. The Alaska Railroad provides daily service in summer from Fairbanks (four hours) and Anchorage (eight hours). Light plane flights to the small McKinley Park Station airstrip can be arranged in Anchorage or Fairbanks.

Visitor Center. Eielson Visitor Center, 65 miles west of the entrance, elevation 3,730 feet. Glass-enclosed exhibit rooms face Muldrow Glacier and the towering twin peaks. The displays interpret glacial geology and the mountain-climbing history of the park. The first climbers were sourdoughs impelled by the simple urge to make the top the hard way and see what it was like.

McKinley Park Station, gateway to the park, with service station, store, campground, hotel, and park headquarters. The mountain becomes visible, on clear days, about 8 miles farther on.

Teklanika River, 27 miles from the entrance, typifies glacial rivers flowing north from the Alaska Range, over numerous channels and wide gravel bars, creating a braided course. The milky cast derives from glacier-ground rock flour.

Igloo Canyon, an excellent locale for animals, particularly Dall sheep. Learn to spot animals by looking for contrasts of color and form in the landscape.

Sable Pass, elevation 3,900 feet, the best place to observe grizzly bears browsing on lush grass or ripping tundra for its succulent roots. Though most common here, bears may be seen anywhere in the park, roaming the spruce forests, aspen thickets, over the bare mountain slopes. A feeding grizzly is not impressive looking, seemingly slow moving, but it can run faster than a horse and demonstrates pride in being called *Ursus horribilis*. He's powerful—stay away. The best place to see moose is in the **Savage River area,** though they may be seen anywhere along the road. They spend a great deal of time in lakes and ponds searching for summer food. The moose should not be approached closely, either.

Highway Pass, where the most breathtaking view of the mountain bursts upon the motorist coming over the rise. The full sweep hits your eye, to the snow plume of the **South Peak.** For the rest of the way you are almost constantly in view of the peaks, always changing, but always dominating the landscape. The best time of day to see Denali is between 3 and 6 a.m. The mountain often clouds up rapidly later in the morning and may be hidden by noon. Caribou are common from this pass westward.

Stony Hill Overlook. Wildflowers spread across the fields in June and early July—which here means springtime. These include the state flower, forget-me-not, as well as arctic poppy, densely carpeted white dryas, white and pink pyrolas, and heather.

Wonder Lake, close to the northern boundary of the park, where you can photograph and dream over reflections of the mountain. It was near here that Olaus Murie, while exploring with another distinguished biologist, his brother, Adolph, discovered his "greatest scene." He wrote: "We looked before us, across the wide valley to the white Denali and the snowy Alaska Range rising high on the horizon. To be on that ridgetop, to look at what was before us!"

Hiking, backpacking. Register at park headquarters and obtain a backcountry use permit for off-highway camping. Always check with the superintendent's office or with a ranger for current information on wilderness travel. Certain areas may be restricted due to critical wildlife habitat. Cross-country travel is complicated by heavy patches of brush, tundra, marshes, and dangerous stream crossings.

Tour operators. The McKinley Park Hotel runs a bus tour daily during summer as far as the Eielson Visitor Center. It starts at 4 a.m., with a box lunch included. The driver stops briefly for good views of wildlife, and accommodates photographers as much as his schedule permits before returning to catch the 1 p.m. train to Anchorage.

Photography. Long hours of daylight provide plenty of time for picture taking. Days are often cloudy, obscuring the mountain, but cloudy days can be excellent for wildflower photography. Try to interpret the three life communities of the park: northern forest (or taiga), tundra, and perennial snowfield.

Accommodations. Near the entrance station. **McKinley Park Hotel** provides overnight lodgings. The sourdough breakfast of hot cakes, eggs, and bacon will soften the blow of rising at 2 or 3 a.m. Dinner of king crab or salmon steak will prepare you for another morning at the same hour. Naturalist-guided walks and lectures are given daily at the hotel area. For rates and reservations write McKinley Park Hotel, McKinley Park, Alaska 99755. (Between October 1 and May 14 write Outdoor World Limited, 2725 Sandhill Road, Menlo Park, California 94025.)

Camping. Camp Denali, just north of Wonder Lake, outside the park, offers one of the finest experiences in Alaska for lovers of nature. This delightful wilderness retreat has tent cabins equipped for housekeeping and rustic chalet cabins with family-style meals in the dining room. Daily guided trips combine hiking and driving to points of interest in the park and historic Kantishna, once a booming mining town. Special sessions are scheduled in wildlife photography and nature lore. Three and four day "Sourdough Vacations" are popular. Write Camp Denali, McKinley Park,

Alaska 99755 (September 11 to May 31, Camp Denali, Box 526, College, Alaska 99735).

Seven campgrounds are well spaced along the park road; best facilities are at Savage River and Wonder Lake; none have house-trailer facilities. Warm clothing, waterproof shelter, and mosquito repellent are important. Bring camp-stoves since firewood is not plentiful. Permits to camp beyond Savage River bridge are available by writing the park superintendent or at park headquarters. Three campgrounds between the park entrance and Savage River are available on a first-come, first-served basis.

Seasons. Spring arrives late, in June and early July, with wildflowers, nesting birds, 24 hours of daylight—and mosquitoes. After August 15, you have a share of two seasons. The atmosphere is crisp and clear; animals appear in their glossy winter coats, and mos-

quitoes are gone. Leaves of the very few hardwood trees turn gold and orange, while the alpine tundra turns into a vast Persian carpet of gold, red-orange, purple, brown, and green. Nights at this time of the year are dark, often chilly.

The park road and public facilities are usually open from late May to early September. Summers are moderately warm, wet, cloudy. Come prepared with clothing for temperatures from freezing to 80 degrees.

Best Buys. Silk screen prints by two talented local artists—wildlife by William Berry, birds and wildflowers by Ree Nancarrow.

Recommended reading. *Two in the Far North,* by Margaret Murie; and *A Naturalist in Alaska,* by Adolph Murie.

For further information write Superintendent, Mount McKinley National Park, McKinley Park, Alaska 99755.

MOUNT RAINIER

Established as a national park, 1899

About 40 square miles of icy, glacial rivers cap Mount Rainier, the loftiest volcanic peak of the Cascade Range. They flow downward from the 14,410-foot summit of Columbia Crest to timberline at about 6,500 feet, and contribute to lakes and waterfalls in the midst of flowering meadows. In the valleys around the base of the mountain, heavy precipitation spurs the growth of dark, cathedral-like forests of the mighty and wonderfully proportioned Douglas fir, Western hemlock, Western red cedar, Sitka spruce, Pacific silver fir, and other giants of the Northwest.

Rainier is a gleaming landmark visible for hundreds of miles in all directions when the weather is clear. It is the fifth highest peak in the United States south of Alaska, rising higher above its base than any other in the "lower 48." At close range, however, the mountain is a rendezvous for hikers, mountain climbers, wildflower lovers and birdwatchers, auto-tourists, campers, and for those interested in observing the rivers of ice called glaciers.

The broad dome of Mount Rainier is a kingdom of glaciers. The Emmons Glacier, about 4.3 miles long and 1 mile wide on the northeast flank, is the largest glacier by overall size in the United States south of Alaska, while the Carbon Glacier, on the north face of the mountain, is the longest—6 miles. The glacier system of Rainier, though a mere remnant of its former size, is recognized as the country's most extensive "single peak" glacial system outside of Alaska. It contains a total of 41 glaciers, including 26 named glaciers and 10 others that are of major proportions.

In this national park, covering 235,404 acres, the visitor can learn some of the simple truths (that are known) about glaciers and their behavior. On the Nisqually Glacier, the body of ice has been determined to move from 50 to over 400 feet per year at the 6,000-foot level. Movement varies within each glacier; the masses of ice move downward by virtue of their own weight, faster at the center than along the edges, and are influenced by the steepness of slope. Most glaciers of the world have been receding and growing shorter, as the case had been at Mount Rainier from the late 19th century until recent years. Slowly vegetation crept into the barren areas. In recent years, however, the major glaciers on Rainier reversed the trend and expanded, advancing downhill.

A glacier actually is a body of ice formed in a region where snowfalls exceed melting. The ice then moves slowly down the mountain valley like a viscous fluid. The beauty of Mount Rainier as a glacial laboratory is that you can see the rivers of ice in action and the effects of their movements. The glacier churns and moves the earth's mantle and pieces of bedrock; it rasps the firm rock in its path, leaving it smooth; it carries away the plowed-off and filed-off debris, plus rock fragments fallen from the mountain slopes. Around the base you can identify glacial moraines, representing the accumulation of earth and rock dust where they are finally deposited. You can observe how glacial debris, plucked and scoured from the mountain cone, is transported downstream.

The formation of Mount Rainier and its glaciers are

recent events in the history of the earth. The last extensive glacial movement of the Ice Age, far beyond the present park boundaries, ended possibly only 10,000 years ago. The eruptions that built the mountain occurred within the last million years, part of the series of Cascadian upheavals that produced a chain of volcanic cones from Mount Baker at the Canadian border to Lassen Peak in northern California. The last violent outburst occurred about 2,000 years ago, spewing pumice over the glacial-clad slopes, and there is still a little steam activity to show the volcano is dormant rather than dead.

Climate is a major influence upon Mount Rainier. It becomes more severe with rise in elevation, so that Longmire, elevation 2,760 feet, receives about one-third as much snow as Paradise, elevation 5,500 feet, which has averaged about 575 inches a year. The snow feeding Mount Rainier's glaciers originates as clouds over the Pacific Ocean. Rising to pass over the mountains, westerly winds are cooled, and the condensing moisture falls as rain and snow.

At lower elevations, the heavy moisture produces a luxuriant growth of trees and wildflowers, equally as lovely as the more celebrated flowers of the mountain meadows. The species of the deep woods, such as the three-leaf anemone, long tube twinflower, Pacific trillium, calypso, and spring beauty, actually outnumber those typical of the higher elevations. But almost anywhere you go there will be blossoms, right up to the edge of the snowbank and sometimes up through the snow. In this setting wildlife thrives in more than 50 species of mammals and 130 species of birds. Among the unusual, mountain goats are seen in bands along the rocky crags between 6,000 and 9,000 feet during summer and down to 3,000 feet during winter. The hoary marmot, a large furry rodent, often suns himself on rocky slopes from 5,000 feet to timberline. Mammals in the park include elk, deer, raccoon, and cougar.

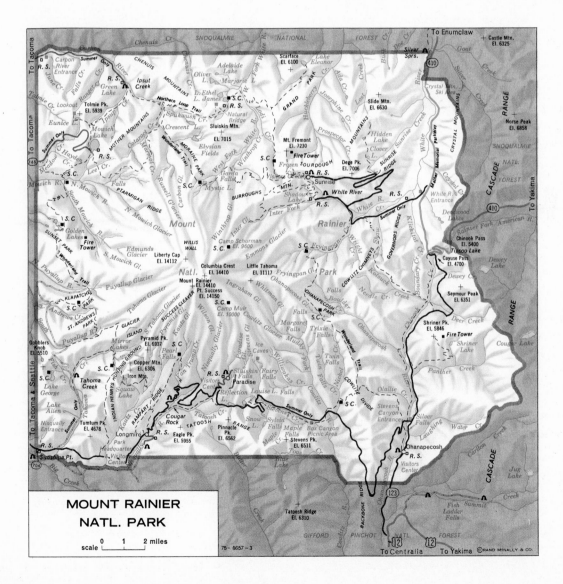

MOUNT RAINIER
NATL. PARK

scale 0 1 2 miles

THE PRACTICAL GUIDE

Mount Rainier National Park is a good one-day automobile trip from Seattle or Tacoma, both about two hours driving distance. Hikers, mountain climbers, and campers enjoy longer stays.

Visitor Centers. The four visitor centers of the park are at Longmire, Paradise, Sunrise, and Ohanapecosh. The new Visitor Center at Paradise includes ski equipment, refreshment facilities, interpretive displays, and naturalist programs.

Wonderland Trail completely encircles the mountain, a distance of 90 miles, with campsites spaced about 8 to 12 miles apart. Parts of the trail can be enjoyed a day or two at a time, or even on a half-day hike, being linked with spur trails to the park road system. The 30-mile section between **Paradise** and **Sunrise** passes lakes, waterfalls, and the glacial-formed Box Canyon of the Cowlitz River. From Sunrise to **Carbon River,** 16½ miles, hikers enter the deep backcountry to see Winthrop Glacier, Mystic Lake at 5,800 feet, and through Moraine Park at the foot of Carbon Glacier. From Carbon River around to **Longmire,** the trail crosses one stream after another while passing the Mowich Glaciers, Golden Lakes, and between the fingers of Tahoma Glacier.

Northern Loop Trail, a branch off the Wonderland Trail, winds from Sunrise at 6,400 feet elevation, through the meadows of Berkeley Park, carpeted with paintbrush, lupine, mountain buttercup, and other flowers, across the southern tip of the beautiful Chenuis Mountain to **Ipsut Creek Campground** on Carbon River, a distance of 17½ miles. More than 300 miles of trails of varying distances offer hikers and trail campers breathtaking views and experiences to remember. Don't forget to obtain a backcountry use permit for all overnight camping.

Stevens Canyon Road, completed in 1957 as part of the 117-mile road network in the park, is an outstanding scenic drive of the Northwest. The park has five approaches: via the **Nisqually,** or southwest entrance; **Carbon River,** or northwest entrance; **Ohanapecosh,** or southeast entrance; **Chinook Pass** entrance, on the crest of the Cascade Range at the east boundary; and **White River** entrance, off the beautiful Mather Memorial Highway from the northeast. An attractive route for motorists leads from the Nisqually entrance to **Longmire,** the park headquarters, then 13 miles past Cougar Rock campground and Christine Falls to **Paradise Valley,** with subalpine fir, mountain hemlock,

and fields of wildflowers. Continuing east from Paradise, Stevens Canyon Road passes beautiful Reflection and Louise lakes, with vistas of the rugged Tatoosh Range and Mount Adams. It intersects the East Side Road north of Ohanapecosh; you can turn north to Tipsoo Lake near Chinook Pass or continue north to the White River entrance, leading into Sunrise, the highest point reached by improved road in the State of Washington, facing Emmons Glacier.

Mountain climbing is one of the thrills of this national park, which served as training grounds of the 1963 American Mount Everest expedition. The concession guide service conducts a varied program for both novices and experienced mountaineers. The best is the climb to the summit, a long, strenuous ascent over moderately difficult terrain. With good conditioning and proper training, previous climbing experience is not necessary to reach the top. Part of the pleasure of the trip is just participating in the snow- and ice-climbing school (about half a day). The climb takes two days. It begins with the climb to **Camp Muir,** a rock shelter at 10,000 feet. Early next morning, about 1 a.m., the climbers continue to the summit, this time roped together. They try to get to the summit and back before the sun brings icefall dangers. Climbing gear is available for sale or rent at Paradise. About 2,500 climbers reach the summit each year over several routes. But it takes an expert guide or leader to spot treacherous crevasses and crumbling lava. Routes are officially open May 30 to Labor Day; all parties must register and give evidence they are properly qualified and equipped. An interesting easier climb, if snows are not too deep, is the 2½-mile guided trip to the **Paradise Glacier Ice Caves,** vast caverns with unusual ice-crystal coloring, which is conducted twice daily in summer; clothing and boots furnished.

Skiing. During winter months the high country becomes a fairyland blanketed by winter snows. Rope tows operate weekends and holidays at Paradise. The five rope tows range from 300 to 600 feet, with combined capacity of about 400 skiers per hour. One ski trail runs about a mile long down to the Narada Falls area, and there is a respectable amount of cross-country skiing, but the country can be hazardous. Major ski developments with mechanical lifts are located nearby in the **Snoqualmie National Forest.**

Fishing. All waters are open, except those posted, without a license. Lakes are open July 4 to October 31; stream

fishing conforms to the state fishing season. Glacial streams and upland lakes are generally too cold to support much aquatic life, but some remote lakes and clear streams provide fair to good trout fishing. Boats without motors are allowed in most lakes, but you must have a written permit from the superintendent. Swimming conditions are poor.

Naturalist program. Guided nature walks and evening illustrated talks are conducted at Paradise, Longmire, Sunrise, Ohanapecosh, and Ipsut Creek.

Accommodations. Overnight lodgings inside the park are provided in the National Park Inn, at Longmire, from May until October, and Paradise Inn, at Paradise, during the summer. These plain hotels are owned by the government but concession-operated. For rates and reservations write Rainier Hospitality Service, Box 1136, Tacoma, Washington 98401. Motels, restaurants, and grocery stores are located on the approach roads to the park. On the east side, new and improved resorts are found along the Mather Memorial Highway, at White Pass, and Packwood. The largest as well as the newest resort development in Washington State, Crystal Mountain, provides excellent overnight accommodations on the east side just outside the park. Summer accommodations include Silver Skis Chalet, a contemporary building with family apartments and heated swimming pool. The dining room, called the Crystal Inn, serves outstanding

seafood specialties of the Northwest.

Camping. The main campgrounds inside the park are at Longmire, Cougar Rock, Ohanapecosh, White River, and Sunrise. Paradise and Sunrise campgrounds are open as overflow campgrounds on weekends only. For those who want solitude and more primitive conditions, small campgrounds are at Tahoma Creek, Sunshine Point, Ipsut Creek, and Mowich Lake. Limit is 14 days, no trailer utilities. Camping is permitted in remote areas of the park, but obtain a backcountry use permit. Other campgrounds are adjacent to the park in Snoqualmie National Forest.

Seasons. Views of the mountain and glacier are obscured much of the year by clouds and fog, but warm, clear weather may be expected during the height of the summer season from about July 1 to early September. Two wildflower climaxes occur, one in early July and the other during August. Paradise Inn is open late June until Labor Day; at lower elevation, the Longmire concession provides rooms and meals from early May until October. Daily bus service to the park operates from Seattle and Tacoma from late June to early September. Indian summer weather sometimes continues well into October, when the season is enlivened by bright red berries of mountain-ash, brilliant reds of vine maples, and other colors in the forests. Most roads, including Stevens Canyon, are closed for the winter

after the first heavy snowfall, usually about November 1. The roads from Nisqually entrance to Paradise and from the northeast boundary through Ohanapecosh are open all year, although snow conditions may cause them to be closed for short periods; be sure to carry tire chains. During late winter and early spring, snowstorms are interspersed with many clear, warm days.

Nearby. Named in memory of the first director of the National Park Service, **Mather Memorial Highway,** a 50-mile scenic drive on Washington 410, starts at the boundary of the Snoqualmie National Forest southeast of Enumclaw, continues through the park to Chinook Pass, then down the American River. **Federation Forest State Park,** 15 miles north of the White River entrance on Washington 410, contains a museum and interpretive center on the natural history of White River Valley. **Crystal Mountain,** a great new ski center and year-round resort, provides one of the finest views of Mount Rainier and the whole Cascades from the top of the chairlift—a vista embracing Mount Baker to the north, Mount Adams to the south in Washington, Mount Saint Helens, and Mount Hood in Oregon. Paths lead from Crystal Mountain to the **Washington Cascade Crest Trail,** which follows the backbone of the range.

For further information write Superintendent, Mount Rainier National Park, Longmire, Washington 98397.

NORTH CASCADES

Established as a national park, 1968

Washington's third great national park was established in 1968. The region is often called the "American Alps," and is one of the last of our primeval landscapes. The most prominent structural features of the Cascades—the volcanoes—are considered the largest freestanding objects in the contiguous United States.

This country had long been known to the Indians. The first white men who ventured into the North Cascades undoubtedly were trappers and hunters. In addition to a great variety of furbearers and game animals, they found a breathtaking land of alpine scenery, snow-capped peaks, cascading streams, and western foothills covered with dense softwood forests. In 1814, Alexander Ross, backed by fur-trading interests, went over Cascade Pass in search of a short route to the Pacific.

Then gold and other metallic ores—including silver, copper, lead, mercury, iron, and chromium—were discovered sometime prior to 1850. Prospectors and fortune-seekers were immediately attracted to the region. George Brinton McClellan searched in vain during 1853 for a wagon route over the Cascades. The gold-mining activities rose and fell until they finally ended in the early 1900s but, with very few exceptions (such as George Holmes in the Ruby Creek area), the only profits were made by those selling food and equipment to the miners. The net effect was to stimulate river transportation, trail improvement, and settlement by hardy souls. Mrs. Lucinda Davis, who had mining claims up the Cascade River, moved to Cedar Bar in 1897, near the present town of Diablo, opened an inn, and became the first woman to climb Sourdough Mountain and Davis Peak. Tommy Rowland, who had a cabin on the upper Skagit, gave place names to such features as Mount Prophet and Elija Ridge. The Weaver family, early residents in the Stehekin area, gave their name to Weaver Point, and the Purple family gave theirs to Purple Creek. The harvest of timber from the dense Cascade forests also began around the mid-1800s, but it was decades later that large-scale commercial logging became important.

An abundance of high-quality water, stemming partly from melting snowfields and glaciers, was another resource that was recognized. In 1919, Seattle City Light started its hydroelectric developments, which led eventually to construction of the towns of Diablo and Newhalem.

In 1899 Mount Rainier National Park was established out of the old Mount Rainier Forest Reserve. During the years following many proposals were advanced for additional areas of national forests in the North Cascades to be transferred to the National Park Service in order to insure protection of virgin areas. Perhaps the first was made in 1906 by the Mazamas, a well-known club of outdoors enthusiasts, for a national park in the Lake Chelan region. A similar proposal was made two years later for a national park to be centered on Mount Baker.

Legislation was introduced in Congress as early as 1916 and a number of studies of recreational potential were made, including one by the National Park Service in 1937. The critical need for action did not become obvious, however, until the 1950s. In his classic work, *The Wild Cascades,* Harvey Manning recalls that as recently as 1948 he and other outdoorsmen felt "the wilderness was inexhaustible, and if one valley was logged, or two or three or a dozen, we could always escape to what seemed uncountable virgin valleys remaining." Then the growing obbligato of bulldozers, chain saws, and logging trucks changed everything.

The North Cascades Conservation Council, headed by Patrick D. Goldsworthy, and the Sierra Club, led by David Brower, mounted a major national campaign that could not be denied. In January 1963, the Secretaries of Interior and Agriculture (responsible for parks and forests, respectively) agreed to form a study team to review administration of the North Cascades. Despite the political power of the timber industry and resistance of the Forest Service, the study team report of October 1965 recommended establishment of a new North Cascades National Park, though not as large as conserva-

tionists had wished and with some key features, such as Mount Baker, omitted. In February 1966, appropriate legislation was introduced in both houses of Congress, hearings were held in Washington, D.C., and Washington State in 1967 and 1968, and in the latter year the bill was passed establishing a national park and two national recreation areas, Ross Lake and Lake Chelan,

totaling 674,000 acres. On October 2, 1968, President Lyndon B. Johnson signed the bill into law.

Visitors will find the North Cascades a range of giant faults and massive overthrusts and thoroughly complex geology. Formed of weather-resistant rocks, the high stretch of the Cascades intercepts some of the continent's wettest prevailing winds. The resulting precipitation has produced a network of hanging glaciers and icefalls, ice aprons and ice caps, hanging valleys and waterfalls. Works of ice make the North Cascades a rough, tall country, and a steep one from valley to summit. Some of the finest mountaineering opportunities in the United States are found here.

Between the moisture-laden west side and the dry east slopes, plant communities show a tremendous variation, ranging from subalpine conifers, green meadows, and alpine tundra, back down to pine forests and sunny-dry shrub lands. They combine to form a vast array of unimpaired wilderness life communities; the national park was established to keep them free.

Mountain goats, deer, and black bears are frequently seen in the wilderness. Other wildlife include the wolverine, marten, fisher, grizzly bear, cougar, and moose. White-tailed ptarmigans and a host of smaller birds and mammals make this harsh land their home. In winter, large numbers of bald eagles congregate along the Skagit River to feed on salmon.

The national park covers 504,785 acres in two units, each with a major wilderness as its core; Ross Lake National Recreation Area separates the two. The northern unit, bordering Canada, includes Mount Shuksan and the Picket Range, composed of glaciers, granite peaks, high lakes, and remote valleys. The southern unit includes the "Eldorado high country" and the Stehekin River valley, one of the finest glacier-carved canyons in the Cascades.

The Ross Lake Recreation Area covers 105,000 acres between the Pasayten Wilderness of the Forest Service and the two units of the national park. Lake Chelan National Recreation Area covers 62,000 acres at the head of the lake and in the lower Stehekin Valley.

THE PRACTICAL GUIDE

The major access to the park is on Washington 20, the North Cascades Highway, a link between Okanogan and US 97 in north central Washington and Mount Vernon on I-5 on the Pacific Coast.

Besides the cross-park route, access to the periphery is possible via Washington 542 from Bellingham on the west, Highway 3 in Canada from the north, and by boat or float plane service daily from Chelan (north of Wenatchee on US 97) at the southern end of 55-mile-long Lake Chelan. There are almost 350 miles of trails in the park and adjacent recreation areas.

Ross Lake. Access to Ross Lake is gained via a 3½-mile trail starting at the Diablo Lake Resort, or from the Ross Dam powerhouse at the head of **Diablo Lake** along a 1-mile gravel road. At the Ross Lake Resort, you can make arrangements to take a boat trip toward the Canadian border. The lake is 24 miles long and 2 miles across at its greatest width. On the west rise the peaks of the Picket Range; farther north, Little Jackass Mountain and the Canadian peaks beyond the head of the lake. The Skagit River empties from Ross Lake into Diablo Lake. You can go on foot from Colonial Creek campground on Diablo Lake to a variety of areas. A strenuous 7-mile hike leads to **Sourdough Mountain,** looking up at towering peaks and glaciers. Contrary to popular belief, most of this country can be hiked, but the rugged ridges that cut up the country are not to be tried except by those with a rock-climbing background.

About 345 miles of hiking and horse trails exist throughout the four units of the North Cascades complex. North from Diablo Lake you can go up Big Beaver Creek to Whatcom Pass and the high lakes—this trip does not require rock-climbing experience. Neither does the shorter hike to Ruby Mountain.

Diablo Lake, which covers 910 acres to the northeast of Newhalem in the Skagit Valley, lies between the north and south units of the park. An impressive trip to the south—not strenuous, but two or three days for most walkers—leads up **Thunder Creek** and over **Park Creek,** then down to **Lake Chelan.** This trip passes close to spectacular glaciers and the lofty peaks of the Eldorado wilderness, such as Eldorado, Forbidden, Buckner, and Goode. An alternative to this route is to drive from the west to Marblemount on the Skagit River, then 22 miles along the Cascade River, stopping 2 miles short of Cascade Pass in the scenic climax of the range. The short hike to the pass takes one through an alpine world of flowering meadows, sheer cliffs, and glaciered peaks, and the headwaters of two wild rivers flowing east and west. Cascade Pass is one of the most popular areas.

Lake Chelan furnishes the classic approach to the range. The passenger ferry, *Lady of the Lake,* operates daily, with the five-hour trip a treat in itself, like a voyage on a Swiss lake. Chelan, set in a glacial trough, is 1,642 feet deep and varies from ¼ mile to 2 miles wide, flanked by forested slopes and wilderness peaks. At the head of the lake are Stehekin, both the town and the outlet of the river. The Stehekin country offers opportunity for an enjoyable experience in camping, riding, and fishing. Lodges and restaurants now provide accommodations. Climb aboard the shuttle bus at Stehekin Landing and ride up the road into the park. You can get off at any of a number of trailheads. Between arrival and pickup, a party may walk along forest trails, climb peaks, or fish the rivers and lakes. One of the easy trips leads from **Cottonwood Camp** into the meadows of **Horseshoe Basin.** For a summit day there is again Cascade Pass, but strikingly different from the ones travelers know from approaches through the logging-scarred valleys of the west.

Fishing and hunting. Besides the two big lakes, many small lakes and countless streams tempt the fisherman with rainbow, eastern brook, cutthroat, and Dolly Varden. Hunting is permitted within the two recreation areas, in accordance with state laws, but not in the park.

Seasons. At lower elevations and on the big lakes, the season extends from early April to mid-October, at higher elevations from mid-June to mid-September. The western side of the range receives more rain and has more lakes and streams; consequently days are cooler. On the east side the combination of more sunshine, warm rock surfaces, and sparse vegetation offer the warm days and cool nights of a typical dry climate.

Recommended reading. *The Wild Cascades,* by Harvey Manning.

For further information write Superintendent, North Cascades National Park, Sedro Woolley, Washington 98284.

OLYMPIC

Established as a national park, 1938

The mountains of the Olympic Peninsula stand first in line to meet the sea that crosses half a world.

The mass of open peaks embraces the moisture-filled Pacific winds, wringing from them rain, snow, and mist, and so begins (or continues) the endless cycle of water from a distant ocean exercising its influence on the land.

From glaciers and snowfields it flows downward through rushing streams, over forest slopes, and outward past a sandy beach, returning to its source and a renewed journey. But along the course of the water cycle momentous happenings combine to tell the story of 897,885-acre Olympic National Park in Washington.

The finest achievements of heavy precipitation are represented in the valleys along the Pacific, the Bogachiel, Hoh, Queets, and Quinault, the serene botanical gardens called rain forests, comprising the entire sweep of plant progression from fungi, mosses, and lichens to immense trees 300 feet high and a thousand years old. Similar forests parallel the ocean from Alaska to California, but none is more luxuriant than those here.

The Olympic Peninsula, the "upper left-hand" corner of the West, lies in semi-isolation, bordered by the waters of the Pacific, the Strait of Juan de Fuca, the clustered cosmos of Puget Sound, and the Hood Canal. It presents a marvelous geological story, with about 60 living glaciers in the high country. Six major glaciers, some blue, some white, are on 7,965-foot Mount Olympus alone. It gets the greatest precipitation of any spot in conterminous United States, perhaps 200 inches, most of it in the form of snow.

The glaciers of today are reminders of massive sheets of ice which plowed, scraped, and scoured the earth in at least four surges spread over millions of years. The last mighty glacial movement retreated northward only 11,000 years ago.

Below the glaciers are alpine meadowlands. The northern side of the park, including Hurricane Ridge and Mount Angeles, a mile above the sea, is especially rich in mountain wildflowers, the meadows being carpeted with glacier and avalanche lilies, lupine, white buckwheat, columbine, asters, Indian paintbrush, and others. Eight species of herbaceous flowering plants are found in these high mountains and nowhere else.

Growing conditions in the moderate climate have been so favorable since the last glacial age that the Olympic Peninsula, below the meadows, has bloomed into a forest of evergreen giants. Within the national park are record-making trees, or near-record-making trees, of the "big four" Olympic species. Western red cedar, growing largely in moist valley bottoms, reaches heights of 175 feet. It has a cinnamon-red, fibrous bark, and flat, lacy sprays of almost fernlike leaves. Western hemlock, a little smaller, grows at elevations up to 3,000 feet. It is a tree of dignity, of dark russet-brown bark, showing abundant and very short cones at the end of its branches. Then, in the rain forests, there is the energetic, lordly Sitka spruce. It towers over most other trees and can be easily recognized by its sharp, silvery-green needles. The mightiest of the big four is the Douglas fir, exceeded only by the redwood and giant sequoia in size of all trees on the continent. This stately, wonderfully proportioned tree grows to heights of 250 feet and sometimes 300 feet. In age, the larger trees may be from 400 to 1,000 years old. The Douglas fir was discovered by Dr. Archibald Menzies, in 1791, on the west coast of Vancouver Island, but was named for David Douglas, the roving Scottish botanist, who brought a specimen back to England. For many years the timber tycoons of the Olympic Peninsula have strived to obtain legal right to log these ancient monarchs, but the nation has continued to recognize that there are other destinies for trees than "board feet" of timber.

The Olympic area first received national recognition because of its wildlife, particularly the Roosevelt, or Olympic, elk. These large members of the deer family grow as heavy as 900 to 1,000 pounds. Between 4,000 and 5,000 live in the park, mostly on the west side, constituting the largest remaining herd of their kind anywhere. Though many of them migrate in summer to the high country, they leave footprints in the hardened mud, teeth marks on browsed trees and shrubs, and telltale elk pellets scattered in clusters over the ground to show where they have been.

Of more than 50 different species of wild mammals, black-tailed deer are frequently seen in the lowlands as well as in mountain meadows. Black bear, cougar, and Rocky Mountain goat are other fairly plentiful large mammals. A smaller animal worth looking for is the Olympic marmot, or "whistler," a distinct species which lives only here.

Wildlife of another sort frequent the 50-mile-long coastal portion of the park called the Pacific Coast Area. Five species of seals, plus sea lions and whales, the flippered animals, frolic in the offshore waters or on the rocks. Thousands of marine birds nest on small islands and the strip lies within one of the major flyways of migrating birds. Persistent waves and the encroaching sea continue the endless process of sculpture—carving seascapes on tree-studded islands, rocky arches, and crescent beaches.

THE PRACTICAL GUIDE

Spend at least two days to see the highlights of the park as part of a tour of the Olympic Peninsula. You can combine it with ferry cruises across Puget Sound and to Victoria, British Columbia.

Visitor Center and Museum, the main Visitor Center, is located at the southern edge of **Port Angeles,** gateway to the most accessible portions that lie along the north side. Here you start the **Heart O' the Hills Road,** 18 miles of paved road from sea level to 5,229 feet. Trailers should not try to make it beyond the campground, 5.4 miles from US 101. Halfway up, at **Lookout Rock,** vistas unfold across the Strait of Juan de Fuca; on a clear day you can see the snowy mass of Mount Baker in the northern Cascades.

Hurricane Ridge, upper terminal of the main road. Superb views of the Olympic Mountains are framed through the windows of Hurricane Ridge Lodge. The **Big Meadow Nature Trail** is a leisurely walk that anyone can take and enjoy. Or, drive 8 miles more on a narrow unpaved road (open during summer only) to **Obstruction Point,** elevation 6,450 feet, which places you at the threshold of the heart of the high country, with the best view of mighty Mount Olympus available by road. This is the starting point of fine hiking trails, including one to **Deer Park Campground,** passing wildflower meadows—with a good chance to observe Columbian black-tailed deer and Olympic marmot. Fifteen roads enter the park like the spokes of a wheel, but none is permitted to penetrate the core of wilderness. "Where the roads end," according to park enthusiasts, "trails begin." Over 600 miles of trail thread the park, permitting short, easy trips of a day or less and more difficult hikes of a week and more. Trailside shelters often enable hikers to travel light, without the weight of a tent, but it is prudent to carry rain clothing or lightweight shelter material. Trail shelters are not always vacant when needed.

Lake Crescent, largest lake in the park, nestled between the forested slopes of Pyramid and Mount Storm King. US 101, west of Port Angeles, follows the shore of the lake for 10 miles. From the western end of the lake, a road follows the Soleduck River to **Soleduck Campground,** the beginning of trails to **Seven Lakes Basin,** in the subalpine zone, and other high country of exceptional beauty.

Rain Forest Nature Trail is at the end of Hoh River Road on the west side of the park. The river is often swollen with "milky" silt from the glaciers on Mount Olympus, but it is only one feature of the forest, where precipitation averages 140 inches yearly. This forest is a complex community of many living things. The forest litter contains a thriving population of mice, shrews, salamanders, and insects. Sitka spruce is the most characteristic large tree of the rain forests, and here it reaches its greatest size; one of the largest anywhere (though the record holder is outside the park), 41 feet, 8 inches in circumference, is located about 3½ miles up the trail from the Hoh Rain Forest Visitor Center. At least 70 kinds of mosses are present, some covering rocks, others growing like airplants from the limbs of trees, draped in fragile beauty like mysterious poetry of the forest. Roosevelt elk are sometimes seen in the vicinity of the Visitor Center and along the trails.

Kalaloch, in the Pacific Coast Area. Nine short trails lead from the highway to the beach, where ocean waves have worn back the land. In this laboratory of life between-the-tides, colorful hydroids, sea urchins, and anemones thrive in pools where the shore is rocky and protected from strong waves. Densely clustered mussels and barnacles cling to rocks near shore, while crabs scurry for shelter beneath them. Other creatures prefer the sandy beaches. On a weekend in clam season, when the tide is low, Kalaloch Beach becomes pockmarked with holes and bumpy with piles from the "guns" (spades with long, narrow blades) of clam diggers in quest of Pacific razor clams (Siliqua patula), a delectable, meaty shellfish which grows from California's Pismo Beach to the Aleutians. The clam is a fascinating creature that feeds on diatoms and microscopic animals. Its chief protection from man is rapid movement—it can dig its way several feet into the sand at a rate of up to nine inches per minute. On a hike along the shore several bald eagles might be seen flying from their nests in the top of tall snags; other birds are always present, including gulls, crows, oyster catchers, and cormorants.

Three Indian villages are encompassed by the Pacific Coast Area, while a fourth abuts it on the south, reflecting little of the ancient Olympic culture. In times past their dugout canoes were among the finest made by any aboriginal people; these they used in harvesting the resources of the sea, fishing for salmon, and hunting for whales. Customs and clothing have changed; little of the old tradition survives, but the main source of livelihood still is fishing.

Naturalist program. The three Visitor Centers (Visitor Center and Museum, Storm King at Lake Crescent, and Hoh Rain Forest) offer an important introduction to the park—enhancing one's understanding as well as enjoyment. During summer months short walks are conducted daily by naturalists at Hurricane Ridge, the Hoh Rain Forest, and along the coastal beach. Excellent evening programs, illustrated with slides or movies, are given at the seven major campgrounds after the sun goes down, on subjects ranging from "Whales and Their Ways" to "Glaciers of the Olympics." No better family entertainment in Washington State, and the values are lasting.

Fishing. The extensive streams and lakes contain rainbow, brook, cutthroat, and the anadromous steelhead trout. No license required, but check regulations.

Accommodations. A variety of motel-type lodges and housekeeping cabins are available at several localities inside the park. The largest is Lake Crescent Lodge, at the foot of Mount Storm King, with access to fishing, boating, and hiking. Other facilities are found at Kalaloch Beach and La Push in the coast area. In addition, there are hotels, motels, and resorts in Port Angeles and elsewhere on the peninsula outside the park.

Camping. Campgrounds are maintained near the end of, or adjacent to, nearly all the entrance roads in the park. Most have complete camping facilities during the summer, but without hookups. Camping near the beaches of the Pacific Coast Area is pleasant during dry weather, and there is ample firewood. Many other campgrounds can be found on the peninsula outside the park in state parks, the Olympic National Forest, and on private lands owned by large timber companies.

Seasons. This park has special features to admire in every season of the year, even though snow closes high country roads and trails from late fall to early spring. Port Angeles and the northern side of the peninsula are served by bus throughout the year from Seattle; Puget Sound Airlines makes three round-trip flights daily during the summer; rental cars are available; and ferry service is maintained across Puget Sound. Winter is best for spotting elk, and for quiet walks along the ocean beach (where lodgings are open all year). Hurricane Ridge is open weekends for skiing (with the aid of three rope tows). By late May all accommodations and the 15 developed campgrounds are open, and by June wildflowers start marching up the mountains.

Summer is mostly cool and sunny, though rainproof garments are a must for hikers and campers. September and October are often delightful, with Indian summer; in late fall spawning salmon may be seen in many rivers, performing the grand and final act of their lives.

Scheduled and charter tours are offered during the summer by Gray Line and North Olympic Tours, both of Port Angeles.

Nearby. US 101, the broad Olympic Highway, nearly encircles the peninsula. It begins at the southern tip of Puget Sound, in **Olympia,** where the state capitol is handsomely landscaped, and restaurants are famous for oyster dinners. Along the way are many campgrounds and scenic areas in **Olympic National Forest.** On the east side, **Mount Walker Summit** looks deep into the ridges and valleys of the high Olympics, and off to the Strait of Juan de Fuca and the distant Cascades. In the southwest corner of the national forest, along the shore of **Lake Quinault,** are three campgrounds, summer homes, and the Lake Quinault Lodge, with fishing, boating, and swimming enhanced by the surrounding dark forests. Within walking distance is the rain forest of the Quinault Natural Area, including the famous "Big Acre," the greatest known stand of Douglas fir in the United States; a replica is shown in diorama in the Hall of North American Forests at the American Museum of Natural History in New York. **Port Angeles,** fishing center and northern crossroads of the peninsula, is linked by ferry with **Victoria,** a proper British city with gardens that are almost as lovely as nature's botanic splendors in the Olympic wilderness.

Recommended reading. *Exploring the Olympic Peninsula,* by Ruth Kirk.

For further information write Superintendent, Olympic National Park, 600 East Park Avenue, Port Angeles, Washington 98362.

PETRIFIED FOREST

Established as a national park, 1962

Once a forest grew on what is now the high plateaus of northeastern Arizona. There were dense beds of ferns, mosses, and trees thriving in marshlands and along streams. Conifers flourished in scattered groves on hills and ridges above the water.

That was about 200 million years ago, in the Triassic period, when this region was a low-lying swamp basin. The scene has changed since then. The land receives less than ten inches of moisture yearly. Most plants are small and inconspicuous (though many have delicate, beautiful flowers), with only junipers and cottonwoods seen here and there. But the logs of petrified wood are often brilliant and vivid, reflecting nature's own artistry.

Indian ruins and petroglyphs show that ancient man dwelled in these environs. The Anasazi, prehistoric farmers who inhabited the area from about the time of Christ until A.D. 1450, shaped the petrified wood into tools and weapons, and used the brilliantly colored pieces as trade items with neighboring peoples.

Curiously, Spanish explorers into northeastern Arizona left no written record of interest in the petrified wood, probably because of their preoccupation with the search for mineral wealth. Though American traders and fur trappers repeatedly crossed the area in the early 19th century, they showed no interest in the fossil wood deposits either. The first written reports of note apparently were made by American military and railroad surveys following the Mexican War. Still, the area remained almost unknown until the coming of the railroad and settlers late in the last century. Then began a rush for riches by souvenir hunters, gem collectors, and commercial jewelers that might have destroyed in two or three decades the treasures that nature had taken millions of years to create. Large quantities of wood were either dynamited for gems or freighted to stations at Adamana and Billings (Bibo) for shipment to the East. The erection of a stamp mill to crush the logs into abrasives stirred public opinion into demanding federal regulations to protect these fossil deposits.

Though Arizona was not yet a state, its territorial legislature petitioned Washington in 1895 to have Chalcedony Park, as the Petrified Forest was then called, set aside as a national preserve. Action came slowly; not till 1906, with passage of the Antiquities Act, was the area proclaimed a national monument. Three individuals deserve particular mention for their efforts. Will C. Barnes, of Holbrook, introduced the original petition in the territorial legislature, then followed up with a personal visit to Washington. Dr. Lester C. Ward of the U.S. Geological Survey conducted a reconnaissance of the fossil forests and pronounced them worthy of preservation. President Theodore Roosevelt responded to the plea by declaring the area a monument. In 1962, private land holdings within the boundaries were acquired and Petrified Forest was made a national park.

It covers more than 94,189 acres and is part of the Painted Desert, a wide arid land of plateaus, buttes, and low mesas—low in water and plant growth, but lavish in displaying many hues in bands of sandstones, shales, and clays. The national park consists of six separate "forests," with great logs of agate and jasper lying on the ground, many of them broken into fragments. It is believed the trees were transported by flooding streams from the surrounding highlands and buried under mud and sand, then covered over by layers of silica-rich volcanic ash. The silica and other minerals gradually filled in the wood cells until the logs had virtually turned to solid stone. Traces of iron, manganese, and carbon stained the silica to form the present rainbow colors. After the forest was buried and several periods of mountain-making had lifted the land thousands of feet, wind and rain removed the covering sediments to expose a portion of the logs. Many other logs are believed to be below the surface, to a depth of 300 feet.

That life once thrived in this arid, isolated land seems difficult to accept. Yet occasionally the bones of giant amphibians and reptiles are washed from their long-hidden burial places in the soft rock.

THE PRACTICAL GUIDE

Main points of interest lie along a 28-mile road running north–south through the park between I-40 (US 66) and US 180. Short drives to several places back from the main road may increase the distance of the complete trip to about 34 miles. You can see the main features and wayside exhibits within one and a half to three hours. If you are driving west, there is no need to double back, for the town of Holbrook lies 24 miles from the north entrance and 18 miles from the south entrance. Eastbound parties should simple reverse the order, leaving I-40 (US 66) at Holbrook and proceeding to the south end of the park via US 180. After driving north through the park, rejoin US 66 from the north boundary. Gallup, New Mexico, lies 70 miles east.

Visitor Center. At the Visitor Center, exhibits include outstanding specimens of polished petrified wood, fossils, minerals, and diagrams explaining how wood becomes petrified. A spur road to the **Long Logs** reveals the "logjam" character of deposits, with logs piled helterskelter upon one another. A partially restored pueblo, the **Agate House,** built centuries ago of petrified wood chunks, overlooks the Rainbow Forest at the end of a foot trail.

Rainbow Forest is near the south entrance. Many trunks exceed 100 feet in length; the ground is strewn with chips of onyx, agate, carnelian, and jasper.

Jasper Forest was named for the opaque colors of some of the petrified wood here. A parking viewpoint located on a ridgetop faces great masses of log sections strewn on the valley floor. Nearby **Agate Bridge** is a mammoth single log, with over 100 feet exposed and both ends encased in sandstone. A deep ravine has gradually been carved into the sandstone, leaving the log looking like a natural bridge. North along the park road lies the beautiful **Blue Mesa.** Colorful banded buttes, mesas,

and cones clearly reveal the ancient layers of marsh. Erosion nibbling at the soft earth has left some petrified logs stranded in unusual postures on slender pedestals.

Newspaper Rock, a massive sandstone block, is filled with picture writings of prehistoric Indians. The signs and symbols have never been interpreted, but probably represent clan symbols, religious symbols, and simple doodling. Nearby lies the **Puerco Indian Ruin,** the remains of a pueblo occupied in the 14th century. It consisted of about 150 rooms around a large courtyard.

Painted Desert. First, stop at the **Administration Building,** near the north entrance, to see the displays. Then take the 6-mile loop drive along the desert rim, where several overlooks offer spectacular views and photographic opportunities. The most amazing property of the Painted Desert is the everchanging quality of its colors. Minute quantities of iron oxide have stained the layers of land many shades, ranging from harshly gaudy red to softly soothing blue. Colors are most vivid after a rain in early morning or late evening. **Pilot Rock,** 6,235 feet, the highest point in the park, lies to the northwest. **Black Forest,** a concentrated deposit of dark petrified wood, is not accessible except by hiking —try it only if you are conditioned to the desert, and first notify a ranger of your plans.

Souvenirs for sale. Samples of polished petrified wood, found on private land *outside* the park, may be purchased at the Painted Desert Oasis and Rainbow Forest Lodge. These establishments, about 26 miles apart, are located near the park entrances. Both are open every day of the year to sell souvenirs, lunches, refreshments, and gasoline. Children should be restrained from attempting to pick up loose petrified wood in the park; if each youngster took one piece, there would be little left in 20 years for *their* children to see and enjoy.

Though commercial exploitation has been halted, theft by park visitors poses a threat just as dangerous. For this very reason, federal law prohibits removal of any petrified wood from the park, no matter how small the piece. Obey the numerous warning signs; don't run the risk of being arrested, with possible fine or even jail sentence as a result.

Photography. Colors are most vivid to record after a rain. Early or late in the day are the best times for pictures, because shadows provide contrast, and the warmer light intensifies the red colors of the soil.

Seasons. This is high country, ranging from 5,300 to 6,200 feet in elevation. During the winter, be alert for icy spots on the highway. During spring, the showy blossoms of yucca, cactus, and mariposa lily will be on display, followed by blooms of paintbrush, aster, and other plants during summer.

Nearby. There are no overnight facilities inside the park, and camping is not allowed. Campgrounds are in the **Sitgreaves National Forest,** over 50 miles south; **Coconino National Forest,** nearly 100 miles to the west; and in the Indian lands to the north. Motels and restaurants are located at Holbrook and other nearby communities. The closest to the park, coming from the east, is at Navajo, 15 miles away. Ask a park ranger about road conditions and facilities on Arizona 63 to **Ganado** and **Chinle** in the heart of the Navajo Reservation. **Canyon de Chelly National Monument,** near Chinle, is one of the fantastically beautiful areas of the Southwest. Inquire also about conditions on Arizona 77 across the Five Buttes into **Keams Canyon Campground** on the Hopi Reservation. About 100 miles due south of the park, **Hawley Lake** on the Fort Apache Reservation provides motel facilities, fishing, and recreation.

For further information write Superintendent, Petrified Forest National Park, Arizona 86025.

PLATT

Established as a national park, 1906

The smallest national park lies nestled in the foothills of the Arbuckle Mountains in southern Oklahoma, adjacent to the town of Sulphur, south of Oklahoma City. It is recognized mainly for the distinctive mineral waters of the area. Though containing only 912 acres, the park includes woods, streams, and waterfalls, as well as the freshwater and cold mineral springs.

In the 1830s, after incorporating the general area into Indian territory, the government settled the Choctaw and Chickasaw Indians in the vicinity. A company of town developers tried to use the presence of the 32 springs to build a health resort. One of the principals, R. A. Sneed, contacted friends in Washington, which led to the agreement of 1902 whereby the springs and creeks were purchased from the Indians and Sulphur Springs Reservation was established. In 1906, Congress directed that the name be changed to Platt National Park, in honor of the late Senator Orville Hitchcock Platt of Connecticut, who had been active in Indian affairs.

The validity of Platt as a national park has long been questioned. Legislation currently before Congress would repeal the Act of 1906 and establish a new Chickasaw National Recreation Area, combining Platt with the present Arbuckle Recreation Area into a single unit. Yet, although it possesses scant scenic spectacles and limited scientific significance, Platt's rolling hills and valleys offer examples of two distinct plant communities. The valleys, lower slopes, and some hills are wooded with an eastern hardwood forest, smaller and sparser than usual, because the park is near the western limit of that forest. Upper slopes and hilltops are examples of the prairie more typical of the West.

THE PRACTICAL GUIDE

Visitor Center. Travertine Nature Center, in the eastern end of the park, contains interpretive displays featuring live snakes, frogs, lizards, insects, plants, and fish native to the area. The center is the main visitor information point and start of several nature trails through the Environmental Study Area, an outdoor classroom. During summer, guided walks, movies, a children's program, and evening talks are given each day. The center is open every day of the year except Christmas.

Perimeter Road, a 6-mile circuit drive, offers motorists a scenic view of the park. Thirteen miles of trail provide access to all points of interest in the park.

Bromide Hill, a steep wooded bluff easily reached by road or trail, offers a fine panoramic view. Along the horizon to the southwest lie the highlands of the Arbuckle Mountains and the lowland of the Washita River valley; to the east, most of the park can be seen stretching along the courses of the Rock and Travertine creeks.

Mineral spring waters may be used by all visitors, but should not be taken in quantity except on a physician's advice. The mud from some sulfur-water pools is said to help in treating certain skin diseases. In the eastern end of the park, Buffalo and Antelope springs were named because herds of these animals used to come from the surrounding prairies to drink.

Arbuckle Recreation Area is centered on a large man-made lake 6 miles southwest of the park, with a wide variety of fishing, boating, and water-skiing opportunities supervised by the National Park Service.

Accommodations. Motels and hotels are in the town of Sulphur, famous for its gushing artesian wells. **Vendome** is one of the largest flowing mineral wells in the world. **Veterans Lake,** owned by the town, covers about 117 acres and is well stocked with fish.

Camping. Three large campgrounds are located in the park, but campers are limited to 14-day stays during the summer season.

For further information write Superintendent, Platt National Park, Box 201, Sulphur, Oklahoma 73086.

REDWOOD

Established as a national park, 1968

Establishment of this national park by Congress in 1968 gave national recognition and protection at last to one of the natural wonders of the United States and the world. It assured for all time to come the preservation of an area representative of the finest remaining virgin growth of redwoods, with the incomparable scenery of the tallest trees on earth.

The coastal redwoods constitute a special province. In early geological times these trees were widely spread across North America. Today they are found only in a narrow band along the moisture-rich northern coast of California. As a living tribe, the redwoods are remnants of the age of dinosaurs; as individual creatures, some have been growing a thousand years or more. Preserving redwoods has long been the goal of many patriotic conservationists. The first successful effort came in 1902 with establishment of Big Basin Redwoods State Park, containing some of the largest remaining trees in the southern redwood belt near Santa Cruz. The establishment of Muir Woods, just north of San Francisco, followed in 1908 as a gift of land from Congressman William Kent to the federal government in honor of John Muir.

In 1918, the Save-the-Redwoods League was formed. In half a century, with matching funds provided by the State of California, it placed large acreages of primeval redwood forest in the California State Park System. Three of these parks—Jedediah Smith and Del Norte Coast Redwoods and Prairie Creek Redwoods— form the core of the new national park.

In its earliest years, one of the major objectives of the Save-the-Redwoods League was establishment of a Redwood National Park. During the 1920s and 1930s various studies were made, but legislative action did not materialize. The Douglas Bill of 1946 proposed establishment of a memorial national forest of 2.5 million acres with about 180,000 acres to be preserved according to park principles and conservation objectives, but the bill was never passed.

In 1963 and 1964, the National Park Service made a survey of the redwood region. Of the original growth forest of almost two million acres, only 15 percent remained. Of this volume, only two and one-half percent, or approximately 50,000 acres, was protected in state parks. At the annual rate of redwood logging, it was estimated that virtually all old growth redwoods not protected in parks would be gone within 20 or 30 years. Moreover, in one area along Redwood Creek researchers found a concentration of the tallest known living trees, one giant among them reaching 367.4 feet above the ground, and all on private land.

The coastal redwood is much like its cousin, the giant sequoia (see Sequoia National Park, page 98, and Yosemite National Park, page 121, for references to the latter and differences between the two). The redwood is the earth's tallest living tree, commonly growing more than 200 feet high, occasionally more than 300 feet. Trunks are 15 to 20 feet in diameter, with exceptional specimens up to 25 feet. The bark is cinnamon brown and deeply furrowed—the evergreen foliage on the short branches is light and feathery and soft green. The cathedral groves of these ancient giants have stirred and inspired men since they were first discovered when California was young.

THE PRACTICAL GUIDE

The 62,304-acre park is 46 miles long north and south and about 7 miles wide at its greatest width. It includes 30 continuous miles of coastal acreage in addition to the forests. Of the total acreage, 27,468 acres have been publicly held for up to 40 years in the three California state parks, which are expected to be transferred to the federal government. Until then, they will remain as completely separate units under California administration. The remaining 30,500 acres are former private lands, mostly redwood groves, coastal bluffs, and beach. It will take time for the National Park Service to acquire, occupy, and prepare these lands for public use. Until then, visitors are asked to understand and respect "no trespassing" signs that may be posted within park boundaries—a great many formerly private holdings will not be open for some time.

Be especially cautious of logging trucks. Intensive logging is underway in some key areas which conservationists have urged be added to the park. Information stations are located at Orick and Crescent City.

Visitor Center. Plan to stop at the Newton B. Drury Center, headquarters of the National Park at Crescent City (24 miles south of the Oregon border). Evening programs are scheduled during the summer months. Displays interpret the history and culture of the area. The two-story building was opened in the fall of 1973 and named for a former director of the National Park Service (from 1940 to 1951) who also served for many years as executive secretary of the Save-the-Redwoods League, which continues to raise funds for purchase of virgin groves. Mr. Drury was elected president of the league in 1971.

Orick, a small town close to the Pacific Ocean and 330 miles north of San Francisco, is the southern gateway to the park. About one-half mile north, turn onto **Bald Hills Road.** It passes through a towering stand of redwoods. You can park your car 2 miles up and walk to the site where the park was dedicated. Bet-

ter yet, take the hike along Redwood Creek. Continuing north, **Prairie Creek State Park** presents a superb botanical garden combining great coastal redwoods, Douglas fir, western hemlock, and Sitka spruce knit together with broad-leafed trees and many flowering plants. The park is almost a rain forest, with up to 100 inches of rain (falling mostly in the winter months).

The 1,100-acre Madison Grant Forest lies within the park boundaries. Here about 200 Roosevelt elk roam free and unfettered. They make excellent picture subjects, but you should avoid getting too close—for your own good.

The park ranges in elevation from 1,500 feet to sea level. The western slopes drop off abruptly at the **Gold Bluffs,** fronting the Pacific, an area of sand flecked with gold, rugged promontories, and huge waves breaking over the rocks. When visiting the ocean section of the national park, always respect the tide, to say nothing of heavy undertow and rocky shoals that make the beach one for watching rather than swimming and surfing. During summer a naturalist program is presented at Prairie Creek; a self-guided trail is also available.

The Emerald Mile, southeast of the state park, contains a concentration of the world's tallest trees, one giant reaching 367.4 feet. This stand is located on private land to be included in the national park, along with the heavily wooded watershed of Lost Man Creek. For the past three years the lumber company owning the tract has encouraged tours through the area, known as Tall Trees Grove. The scenic corridor will allow outdoorsmen to enjoy hiking or floating along more than 8 miles of Redwood Creek.

Driving north on US 101, the Redwood Highway passes through many miles of redwoods. Klamath, midway between Orick and Crescent City, is famous for its steelhead and salmon runs on the Klamath River. **Klamath Beach Road,** 11 miles long, covers some spectacular scenery. Fishermen can also try their

luck in the numerous streams of **Del Norte Coast Redwoods State Park,** 8 miles south of Crescent City. Del Norte contains four groves of redwoods, with steep slopes bearing the trees almost to the ocean shore. It is one of the rare places where the natural ecological transition from virgin redwood growth down to a wild ocean shoreline remains essentially undisturbed. The park is noted also for the profusion of azaleas blooming in May and June, that can be easily reached by foot trails.

A number of small beaches are unsafe for swimming, although the rocky coast, marked by heavy surf, does not discourage surf casters.

The northern boundary of the national park lies on the beautiful Smith River above Crescent City. Here **Jedediah Smith State Park** combines a dense outstanding forest of redwoods along Mill Creek. Because of its location at the eastern edge of the coast redwood belt, this park contains an interesting array of coastal and inland trees, including ponderosa pine, with a lush underbrush of rhododendron, azalea, fern oxalis, salal, and huckleberry. The entire park is laced with trails. **Stout Memorial Grove** contains the largest trees in the park, including the 340-foot Stout Tree, a giant among giants.

The Smith River in Jedediah Smith has a very long sandy beach for bathing, with picnic area nearby. The best chance for getting campsites in the park during summer is to arrive early. Horses can be rented privately nearby, and there are miles of riding trails. **Fishing** is excellent, for rainbow trout and cutthroats in spring and summer, then for large steelhead and salmon running from October to the end of February.

Camping. Campgrounds in Prairie Creek State Park usually are filled in summer, but a choice time to visit is from Labor Day through early November, when space is available and the deciduous trees are changing color.

For further information write Superintendent, Redwood National Park, Drawer N, Crescent City, California 95531.

ROCKY MOUNTAIN

Established as a national park, 1915

Rocky Mountain National Park embraces 400 square miles, the untamed portion of the Front Range, one of the highest regions of the country—rough, spectacular, and noble, deriving its name as the first wave of the Rockies to rise from the central Great Plains. The valleys are about 8,000 feet above sea level, but within the park are 59 peaks 12,000 feet in elevation or higher. Perpetual snows mantle the highest summits and valley walls. Small glaciers can still be seen at the heads of some of the high mountain canyons. Highest of all towers Longs Peak, 14,256 feet. A variety of trails make this a "climbing and hiking park." And when you drive to the summit on Trail Ridge Road, in the section between Iceberg Lake and Fall River Pass, you are at a lofty 12,183 feet, as high as a motorist can go anywhere in the national parks.

The park covers 261,986 acres. One hundred million years ago a great sea covered much of this area, with subtropical forests lining the shores. Gigantic forces within the earth caused an uplifting of the land under the sea. A highland was formed of rock layers and molten lava, which then was worn down slowly by water, wind, and freezing action. During the long period of upheaval and erosion, another series of uplifts, 40 to 60 million years ago, raised the mountain range still higher, giving the streams vigor to carve deep, sharp valleys. Then, about a million years ago, the Ice Age began and glaciers carved their characteristic U-shaped valley bottoms. They left enormous moraines—deposits of loose rock material—and other evidence of their work.

At least a thousand years ago Indians passed through, leaving arrow points, hand hammers, and even crude pottery fragments. In the past two centuries the park was the haunt of the Utes, then of the Arapahoes, who left their mark in trails still in use.

After the United States acquired the region through the Louisiana Purchase, explorers and adventurers passed near the park. Colonel Stephen Long in 1820 apparently was first. He was followed by William Ashley

in 1825. The intrepid John C. Frémont made two expeditions, in 1843 and 1844, and Francis Parkman was there in 1846. In 1859, during the Colorado Gold Rush, Joel Estes visited the area and the following year settled his family in the grassy meadow now known as the community of Estes Park. An Irish nobleman, the Earl of Dunraven, fell in love with this magnificent country in 1872 and resolved to build a great estate and game preserve. Through his feudal regime, many beauty spots were preserved. He publicized the region and entertained Albert Bierstadt, the celebrated artist of classic Rocky Mountain landscapes. In the 1880s a mining boom occurred on what is now the west side of the park; prospectors filed claims and operated out of little settlements like Lulu City, Dutchman, and Teller, but they found little pay dirt and the boom presently collapsed.

The national park idea caught on early in the 20th century. There were many supporters, but Enos Mills, naturalist, philosopher, and author stands out as the "John Muir of the Rockies." He wrote many articles and stirred wide support. The Colorado legislature memorialized Congress in 1913 and appropriate legislation was introduced in Congress. Considering the opposition of the Forest Service and some owners of land inside the park, the legislation moved surprisingly well. Another obstacle lay in the argument of influential senators and congressmen that the cost of maintaining parks was excessive and that they should be supported by the states rather than the federal government. This explains the proviso (later repealed), when the bill was passed, that appropriations for the park not exceed $10,000 a year. Enos Mills was rewarded for his years of hard work when he participated in the dedication ceremonies on September 4, 1915.

Forests and wildflowers on the mountain flanks reflect the story of the struggle of earth forces and the adjustment to varied environments. At the summits, tiny dwarf plants of the alpine tundra, like those of Siberia and northern Alaska, cluster densely together and carry the banners of life high above timberline, or treeline. Far below, pines, blue spruce, and aspen thrive in the sheltered valleys.

Between the two extremes, some 750 kinds of plants are spread over the wide range of elevations, soils, and exposures to the sun and moisture.

The lofty rocks are the natural home of bighorn, or mountain sheep—powerful, agile animals that symbolize Rocky Mountain National Park. You may also see elk, beaver, golden eagles, and hawks, depending on where you are and how perceptively you look. As far as these animals are concerned, the mountains are still their dwelling place and man is the outsider.

THE PRACTICAL GUIDE

Stay three or four days to sample the highlights, longer for a mountain vacation, at one of the campgrounds or resorts in the area. However, if you are in Denver, (65 miles away) with time to spare, take a bus tour (or rent a car) and head for the gateway of Estes Park and the Trail Ridge Road.

Gear your pace to change in elevation. At high altitudes the atmosphere is thinner than at sea level, increasing the work of heart and lungs. Motoring and normal sightseeing cause little problem, but strenuous hiking and climbing can, unless you are in prime condition. If you have a heart condition, do not overexert. Even climbers should start slowly, acclimating to 7,500 and 8,500 feet before heading for 12,000.

Trail Ridge Road climbs 5,000 feet on its winding course from Estes Park, at the east entrance, to the crest of the Front Range, then descends 4,000 feet to Grand Lake at the west entrance; yet this modern, high 44-mile road, following an ancient Indian trail over the Continental Divide, is comfortable and safe all the way. Dress warmly; while the air is light and dry, you are entering a cold-climate zone. Allow a minimum of three hours for the drive.

Visitor Center. Approaching from Estes Park, the new **park headquarters,** a beautiful low building of reddish-pink stone, should be your first stop to see the introductory movie and relief model. If coming from the west, start at the **Public Information Building** near the Grand Lake entrance.

From park headquarters you may decide to go up the old **Fall River Road,** narrow, winding, and completely safe if you stick to the 15-mile speed limit; it is intended for sightseeing and picture-taking at a leisurely pace. It joins the main road at Fall River Pass (so you can make a loop tour from Estes Park). If you go the main route, from Many Park Curve you see the whole central and eastern portions, dominated by Longs Peak. From **Rainbow Curve,** the Mummy Range is visible to the north. Soon you rise above timberline where fir, pine, and spruce

covering yield to rock and tundra, and reach the 4-mile section above 12,000 feet—one of the world's unforgettable motoring experiences. From **Rock Cut,** you get superlative views of glacial-carved peaks along the Continental Divide. From the lower end of the parking area, take the one-hour round trip by trail to the **Toll Memorial,** in the center of tundra meadowlands.

Don't rush your descent. Lunch at the **Fall River Pass** (11,796 feet). The **Alpine Visitor Center,** completed 1965, has exhibits devoted to the ecology of alpine tundra.

Continuing on the western side, at **Milner Pass,** 10,759 feet, you cross the Continental Divide, the backbone of North America. From Kawuneeche Valley, the road follows the Colorado River to **Grand Lake,** largest natural lake in Colorado.

Hiking and Climbing. Over 300 miles of trail thread the park to the famous and lesser-known scenic points. Some are designed for a half-hour's leisurely walk, others for strenuous exploring.

The energetic hiker who wants to become a climber does well to take a few lessons from the Rocky Mountain Guide Service and Mountaineering School, an approved park concession. For any hike to the summit of Longs Peak (8 miles from Longs Peak Campground), check first at the chief ranger's office or the nearest ranger station. For a climb up the "Diamond," toughest approach of all, the park superintendent must give approval. Severe storms come quickly in the mountains, striking climbers unused to the Rockies with surprise. Rangers require that you never climb alone, always attempt routes within your ability, and turn back when adverse weather or exhaustion threatens. Following this advice assures that you will climb again.

Trail riding. Most trails in the park can be traveled on horseback, including the **Flattop Trail,** a good day's ride across the Continental Divide between Estes Park and Grand Lake. The surroundings of the park being old cattle country, many ranches and hotels have horses and guides available for pack trips in the high country. Horses may also be rented

from livery concession at Glacier Basin and Moraine Park.

Naturalist program. To really know the fascinating natural history of these mountains, join one or more of the many hikes led by ranger-naturalists. These trips range from two hours to all day and open a new world of understanding. The naturalist will show where and how to look for beavers building dams, will help identify some of the 241 birds of the park, and will try to bring you within sight of mule deer grazing at the edge of forest or on the tundra. Campfire programs, usually illustrated with slides or film, are held at the main campgrounds and park headquarters. The Moraine Park Visitor Center serves as an interpretive museum.

Fishing. Fishing season above 9,500 feet runs from June 1 to October 31. Waters below 9,500 feet are open year-round, except as posted. A Colorado fishing license is required (but not for children under 15).

Tour operator. Circle bus trips are conducted from Denver during the summer travel season by the Colorado Transportation Company. The most popular is the 240-mile two-day loop to Estes Park, over Trail Ridge Road to Grand Lake (overnight stop), then returning to Denver over Berthoud Pass, twice crossing the Continental Divide. This company also makes connections at Denver with transcontinental airlines, railroads, and buses for service to the park area. Sightseeing trips through the park are scheduled daily during summer.

Photography. Because the most spectacular scenery of the snow-crowned mountains faces the east, morning light is best at most locations. The west side is good for pictures of streams, lakes, and ranches.

Accommodations. The two principal tourist centers are the villages of Estes Park and Grand Lake, which provide a full range of hotels, motels, cottages. If you want to sample the informal ways of the Rockies, you may want to try a dude ranch vacation. For a list of ranches in the vicinity of the park, write Colorado Dude and Guest Ranch Association, 2126

Estes Street, Denver, Colorado 80215.

Camping. Campgrounds inside the park operate on a first-come, first-served basis, with 14-day limit. No electric or sewer connections are available. The largest and most developed are at Glacier Basin and Aspenglen (on Fall River Road), and at Moraine Park. Timber Creek Campground, on the western slope, has similar facilities (fireplaces, flush-type comfort stations, running water, picnic tables). Wild Basin is situated at the beginning of the extensive Wild Basin trail network. Longs Peak is popular with those who plan to ascend the mountain. Trailers are permitted at all campgrounds except Endovalley, but are not recommended for Wild Basin because of narrow, winding roads. Camping is permitted at many other specified points in the backcountry; obtain a fire permit at a ranger station.

Other campgrounds are located in Shadow Mountain National Recreation Area on the west side. On the east side, two campgrounds are located close to Estes Park in the Roosevelt National Forest. Olive Ridge Campground is southeast of the park on Colorado 7, near Allenspark. Several private campgrounds are located near Estes Park.

Seasons. Spring reaches the lower altitudes in late April and advances upward in ensuing weeks. The scheduled official opening of Trail Ridge Road is Memorial Day. Sometimes it opens earlier, sometimes on that day, but then may be closed for a week by snow. Summer is the peak season, the time to enjoy the high country with its brilliant skies, warm sun, and sparkling streams. The state flower, Colorado columbine, is found in bloom June through August, depending on location, amidst a myriad of other wildflowers. September is a superb month in the Rockies, a time of clear, crisp days when aspen glitter golden on the hills. With good fortune you may hear a bull elk bugling and catch a glimpse of one on a hilltop with his handsome rack sharply outlined against a blue sky. Reduced rates are offered during autumn at many ranches. Winter activities (mid-December to mid-April) are centered at Hidden Valley, 10 miles west of Estes Park. The area is open weekends, Friday through Sunday. Activities include skiing, ice skating, platter sliding, and snowshoeing. Illustrated programs are presented at Hidden Valley Lodge.

Nearby. Bordering the park on the east, northeast, and south is **Roosevelt National Forest,** comprising almost 800,-000 acres, with choice lake and stream fishing, and active glaciers accessible by trail. Unique off-the-highway tours are

operated from Estes Park in four-wheel-drive vehicles to the forest observation tower at Panorama Peak, overlooking the Great Plains and mountain ranges extending from Wyoming to New Mexico. Big Thompson Canyon lies on US 34, the main road from Estes Park to Loveland; for 16 miles the road is flanked by a foaming, roaring stream and rugged rock walls. Across the Divide, bordering the southwest corner of the park, **Shadow Mountain National Recreation Area** complements majestic natural beauty with a scenic lake and mountain playground. Man-made reservoirs named Lake Granby and Shadow Mountain Lake are linked by channel to Grand Lake to form the "Great

Lakes" of Colorado. This area offers camping, riding, swimming, fishing, boating, and sightseeing boat cruises. Guided tours are conducted at the **Granby Pumping Plant** on Lake Granby, unfolding the story of the Colorado–Big Thompson Project, which diverts water via 13 miles of tunnel from the western slope under the great peaks of the national park for irrigation and hydroelectric power in eastern Colorado; power lines and terminals of the tunnel were kept outside the park, with natural features remaining in their pristine state.

For further information write Superintendent, Rocky Mountain National Park, Estes Park, Colorado 80517.

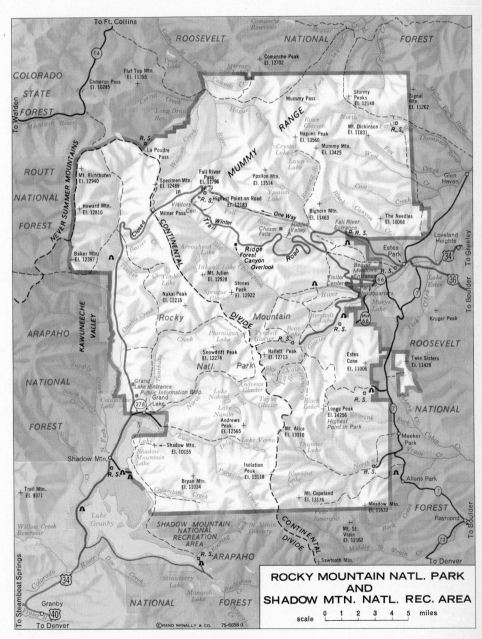

ROCKY MOUNTAIN NATL. PARK
AND
SHADOW MTN. NATL. REC. AREA

SEQUOIA and KINGS CANYON

Established as national parks, 1890

It was the Spaniards who long ago named the gallery of mountains that form the high backbone of California. They called it, in their poetic way, *Sierra Nevada,* which literally means "snow-covered mountain range." This has proven a fitting title for the range that extends from about Lake Tahoe southward for more than 250 miles, and especially for those parts of it which lie in Sequoia and Kings Canyon national parks, where these lofty mountains reach their climax in Mount Whitney, the highest point in the United States outside Alaska.

The two national parks, which are joined end to end and stretch 65 miles north to south, are virtually a single unit (and are so administered) of 846,946 acres, yet the features which define them as national parks are quite different.

Sequoia, the southernmost, is the oldest of California's five national parks, having been established in 1890 (fully five days before Yosemite). Its primary purpose then—as now—was to preserve 32 groves of giant sequoia trees, the largest of living things, the remnants of once widespread forests that covered a great portion of the Northern Hemisphere. The park came into existence through the efforts of conservationists just in time to arrest a wasteful logging era that seemed destined to destroy the abundant forests.

Kings Canyon was designated a national park in 1940, principally because of its high granite mountains and rugged canyons, around the core of the Grant Grove, which had been a tiny national park. It has goodly stands of the great trees and, in addition, the highest canyon wall in America—a sheer 8,350-foot rise from the South Fork of Kings River to the top of Spanish Mountain. All the backcountry is composed of peaks, gorges, rockbound glacial lakes, virgin forests, and flowering alpine meadows.

The giant sequoia (*Sequoia gigantea*) and its relative, the coastal redwood (*Sequoia sempervirens*), are the last surviving species of a large genus of ancient geological times. (Only two other species of trees closely resemble them—the bald cypress of our southern states and the cryptomeria of Japan.) The differences between these two trees? The giant sequoia grows only in scattered groves on the western slopes of the Sierra Nevada in central California, at elevations of 4,000 to 8,000 feet. The redwood grows near the Pacific Ocean along the northern California coast in a more or less continuous belt 450 miles long. It is the world's tallest tree and has a slender trunk, while the giant sequoia is the world's largest tree in *volume,* with an immense trunk and very slight taper. The cones and seeds of the giant sequoia are about three times the size of those produced by the redwood; it has a thicker, asbestoslike bark and heavier, more angular limbs.

Beneath the giant sequoia, or Big Tree, the forest floor is often covered with lupine, dogwood, hazelnut, chinquapin, and willow, creating the contrast of color in dark groves. In addition, magnificent stands of sugar pine, sometimes attaining a base diameter of 11 feet with finely tapered trunk rising more than 200 feet, ponderosa and Jeffrey pines, white and shasta fir, and incense cedar also thrive in Sequoia and Kings Canyon. But the sequoia, massive and vigorous, tower above all as patriarchs of the forest community. They can be seen now as John Muir found them here: "Giants grouped in pure temple groves, or ranged in colonnades along the sides of meadows."

The high country constitutes a vast region of unbroken wilderness, providing one of the outstanding experiences of the National Park System. A motorist catches glimpses of the wild country here and there by car and from overlooks, but by foot or horse trail you can put yourself into the midst of canyons, rivers, lakes, and meadows, as well as high on the Sierra Crest, ranging in elevation from 11,000 feet to the 14,495-foot summit of Mount Whitney. The hiker's principal boulevard is the John Muir Trail, which runs 218 miles from Yosemite Valley down through two national parks and three national forests, all of which preserve the feeling of the original California, the country where Indians roamed and fished, and where the Spaniards gazed on the plunging waters of the Kings River and named it *Rio de los Santos Reyes*—River of the Holy Kings. Surely it is impossible to look at this overpowering scenery without being moved to awe, if not to reverence.

THE PRACTICAL GUIDE

One can hike or ride for days on end without retracing his course. However, Sequoia and Kings Canyon is also an excellent place for a family to get started in wilderness backpacking on weekends. Auto visitors should plan on spending at least one day.

Visitor Center. Allow time to visit the Lodgepole Visitor Center and absorb the displays on the story of the trees and the geology of the parks.

Giant Forest embraces all phases of the giant sequoias within a small area, from tiny saplings to giants which have lived their lives and now, toppled by some wintry blast, lie with roots upturn. The growth is dense: eight sequoias can be counted within a radius of 50 feet, and four others, perhaps four feet in diameter, within a radius of 25 feet. But if you look closely and thoughtfully, every tree is a great one, with individuality and unique characteristics, presenting some new phase of size, persistence, or growth. The tenacity to life and incomparable resistance to destruction make the sequoia a giant of the tree world, yet it grows from seed about the size of a pinhead.

Within easy driving or walking distance of Giant Forest are a number of notable sights. **Moro Rock,** 2 miles by road or trail, is one of the great monoliths of the Sierra Nevada. From its top, or even its slopes, you can see both the ridges of the Sierra's backbone at the horizon and the silvery Kaweah River, 4,000 feet below and almost straight down. Not far away is **Crescent Meadow,** where an easy trail leads to **Tharp's Log,** headquarters of the pioneer white man of Giant Forest, Hale Tharp, who had been guided up the mountains by Indians. He built a cabin in a fallen sequoia log, which Muir called a "noble den." There is also **Beetle Rock,** from which the sunset views are gorgeous. If you don't mind hiking one-half mile downhill from the parking area and back up again, you can visit **Crystal Cave,** a small but beautiful marble cavern, open during the summer.

Rangers provide various guided tours.

Generals Highway, a scenic drive worthy of the superb country, connects the two parks, running 47 miles from California 198 at Ash Mountain in Sequoia to California 180 at Grant Grove in Kings Canyon.

General Sherman Tree, the largest of living trees, is found near the Generals Highway. It stands approximately 272 feet tall and 101.6 feet in circumference; there are higher trees but none of such bulk. Estimates place the age of this giant among giants at 3,500 years, during which period it has withstood wind, storm, fire, and lightning. But if this great tree is to continue to thrive, it becomes the responsibility of everyone to avoid causing damage of any kind. To protect the tree, the Park Service has built a low wooden fence around it, a gentle reminder that damage possibly can occur from heavy human impact. Actually, the beauty of the tree is best appreciated when viewed from a point where the visitor's eye can encompass its great size. Trees such as this continue to reproduce themselves, and thousands of young sequoias grow in favorable localities throughout the park, their lovely cone-shaped forms seeming like a mass of Christmas trees.

General Grant Tree, from which Grant Grove takes its name, is second in size to the General Sherman, measuring 267 feet tall with a circumference of 107.6 feet. Almost as large is the **Robert E. Lee Tree** in the same grove. A few minutes' drive leads to **Big Stump Basin,** filled with ghostly reminders of early logging. John Muir had pleaded for years to preserve the giant sequoias, but only after extensive devastation did he and others succeed. The **Hart Tree,** fourth largest known sequoia, stands in the **Redwood Mountain Grove,** west of the Generals Highway.

Cedar Grove, center of activity in Kings Canyon, is reached from General Grant Grove, on California 180, on a 28-mile drive through Sequoia National Forest and along the South Fork of the Kings River. The road descends through open country and past hillsides bright with berry bushes, then into the river canyon. From an overlook you can watch the brawling waters of the South and Middle forks form their junction. Beyond, one canyon vista succeeds another until the highway crosses the river at Boyden's Cave; then the route closely follows the foaming river. Six miles past Cedar Grove Ranger Station, the road ends at Copper Creek, or Roads End, beneath solid granite walls, one of the take-off points for the great expanse of high mountain country, which makes up over four-fifths of the two parks.

Single-day hiking trips of outstanding character can be made from Giant Forest, Crescent Meadow, Lodgepole Campground, Dorst Campground, and from Roads End. For instance, **Twin Lakes,** reached from Lodgepole, are famous for their unsurpassed setting at an elevation of 9,500 feet; if you have the time, Silliman Pass is worth the extra climb for its magnificent view.

Bearpaw Meadow, elevation 7,800 feet, is the destination of a choice overnight trip from Giant Forest, a distance of 11 miles over the **High Sierra Trail,** a close rival of the John Muir Trail for outstanding scenery. You can travel light and rent a tent cabin with meals provided (advance reservations), or pitch your own tent. The High Sierra Trail joins the John Muir Trail at Wallace Creek, 37 miles east of Bearpaw, offering many possibilities for side trips into the Great Western Divide country—Big Arroyo, Kern Canyon, and Mount Whitney.

The backcountry is accessible over about a thousand miles of trail, via 28 trail entrances. A High Sierra trip once was thought to be only for those of extraordinary strength and endurance, but you can have the vacation of a lifetime if you travel leisurely, with time to relax, fish, and enjoy nature along the way. By so doing you avoid overexertion in the rugged terrain and high altitude. At vary-

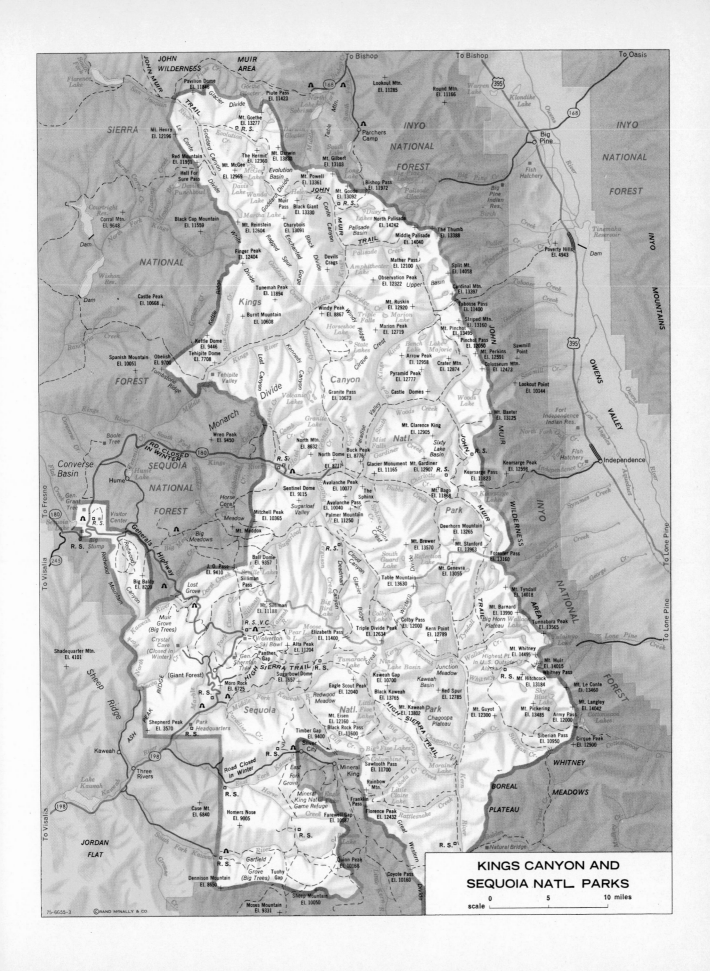

**KINGS CANYON AND
SEQUOIA NATL PARKS**

scale 0 — 5 — 10 miles

75-6655-3   © Rand McNally & Co.

ing elevations there are more than 1,200 kinds of trees, plants, shrubs, and flowers. The golden eagle nests on mountain crags, and nearly 170 other kinds of birds find a home in these parks. Deer are common—there are more deer in Sequoia than in any of the other western parks—as well as bear, mountain lion, bobcats, coyotes, marmots, and smaller animals. **Backpacking** is the most economical way to get around. Though strenuous, you can get into many places where horses and pack animals are barred because of grazing problems, and since the latest equipment is much lighter than it used to be backpacking is easier now. But stay on the trails and avoid trips alone.

From mid-June through mid-September, backcountry use is limited in Kings Canyon. The number permitted through the 16 major trailheads is adjusted each year, depending on the condition of the trails; it has been running about 500 per day. Permits are issued on a first-come, first-served basis, without charge. Check your schedule with a ranger so that someone knows where you are and when to expect you back. Camping and hiking supplies are available for rent at Giant Forest. You can also **rent a burro or mule** to do the heavy work. This makes it possible for families with small children, or those who can't carry the loads in backpacking, to enjoy the wilderness at small cost. You can make arrangements with packers, including setting up a base camp, or furnishing a guide and cook for an entire tour. **Horseback trips** over the hundreds of miles of pack trails are popular. Saddle horses are for rent in Giant Forest, General Grant Grove, Cedar Grove, and in Owens Valley. If you start from Cedar Grove, you will probably encounter more people on the loop trail over Glen Pass to Rae Lakes, returning through Paradise Valley, than anywhere else in the backcountry; because of the heavy horseback riding traffic the most critical grazing problems are along this route.

Many people enter the high country from Owens Valley, east of the Sierra. From Lone Pine a road leads to **Whitney**

Portal, elevation 8,367 feet, closest point by road to Mount Whitney, and the location of a pack station. The summit of the mountain can be reached by saddle and pack trip. The hiking trail up is considered fairly easy, but it is a long trip. Many other mountains in the two parks are popular with climbers, too, but consult with a park ranger before starting. Unfortunately, a summer rarely passes without several persons becoming seriously ill or injured.

Fishing. There are 800 miles of stream and 500 lakes, many with rainbow and eastern brook trout. The headwaters of the Kern are the native habitat of the highly prized California golden. You can buy a state fishing license at the stores.

Swimming is not only inadvisable, but can be dangerous.

Accommodations. Facilities inside the park cover a wide range. Giant Forest Lodge has cottages and tent cabins. Nearby Camp Kaweah has a motel, cottages, and housekeeping cabins with and without bath. Grant Grove Lodge has cottages and tent cabins, and Meadow Camp has plain housekeeping cabins. Reservations at all sites are recommended. Write Sequoia and Kings Canyon National Parks Company, Sequoia National Park, California 93262.

Camping. Campgrounds at five locations in the park (Giant Forest, Lodgepole, Dorst Creek, Grant Grove, and Cedar Grove) are well developed; all but Dorst Creek have stores. Lodgepole and Cedar Grove are best suited to trailers, though neither has electrical or sewer connections. Occupancy is limited to 14 days on a first-come, first-served basis. Year-round campsites are available at Potwisha Campground, at an elevation of 2,100 feet.

Seasons. Most accommodations in the park are open mid-May to mid-September and some until late October. Limited facilities are open at Giant Forest the remainder of the year. Entrances to the high mountain passes are seldom open before July 1, but the General Grant Grove section and Giant Forest area are open all year, and roads generally are

kept clear in winter. The Generals Highway is kept open during the winter between Lodgepole and Grant Grove. In winter the giant sequoias are draped with snowlike candelabra and express a liveliness that contrasts with their somber summers. There is nothing more eloquent than the wintry natural scene. In addition, skiing activities center at the Wolverton area, where varied slopes are designed for novices, intermediates, and experts. There is ice skating at Lodgepole in the early winter months. Ski equipment, snowshoes, and ice skates are available for rent. Though most visitors come in summer, April and May are months when the foothills are covered with flowering redbud, buckeye, and laurel. In autumn, dogwood, aspen, and oak enliven the landscape with their brilliant red, yellow, and orange foliage.

Nearby. More than 50 camping and picnic sites are located in **Sequoia National Forest,** which lies adjacent to the two national parks on the west. **Hume Lake,** on California 180 north of General Grant Village, offers recreational facilities, including swimming. **Stony Creek Campground,** lodge, and service station are located convenient to Kings Canyon National Park, south of Grant Grove on the Generals Highway. High mountain lakes and streams noted for golden trout enhance the forest's beauty. On the east side of the park, **Inyo National Forest** has nearly 900 natural lakes among its granite peaks towering from 12,000 to 14,000 feet. From **Big Pine** a road leads west to Palisades Glaciers, a mass of living ice flush against Bishop Pass in Kings Canyon. In contrast to this high, cool country, only 80 miles to the east of Mount Whitney is the lowest point in the Western Hemisphere, Bad Water, in **Death Valley National Monument** astride the California–Nevada boundary.

Recommended reading. *Starr's Guide to the John Muir Trail* and *Backpacking in the Sierra Nevada.*

For further information write Superintendent, Sequoia and Kings Canyon National Parks, Three Rivers, California 93271.

SHENANDOAH

Authorized as a national park, 1926

"Equal to the promised land in fertility, and far superior to it for beauty." So wrote Washington Irving of the Shenandoah Valley as it is seen from the mountain crest of the national park rising above it. Though deep in the Blue Ridge Mountains of Virginia, the park lies but 75 miles from the national capital, and less than one day's drive from New York, Cleveland, or even Charleston, South Carolina. To the populated East, it provides a natural refuge in the hills—95 percent of its 190,420 acres comprises rich and varied forests, 5 percent, lovely open meadows.

Sixty mountain peaks, ranging from 2,000 to 4,000 feet, reach up to blend their gentle summits with billows of bluish haze that give the mountains their name.

The highlands of Shenandoah (meaning "Daughter of the Stars" in an Indian tongue) are part of the same Appalachian range that stretches to the Acadian hills. Its Skyline Drive is a lofty vantage point for viewing the panoramas of the Shenandoah Valley, or Valley of Virginia, to the west and the rolling hills of the Piedmont Plateau to the east. For a distance of 105 miles, this stellar scenic route stretches like a ribbon down a bright tapestry, crossing and recrossing the ridgetop. In precolonial times, game and Indian trails ran along this same crest, and by the time of the Revolution the beauty of the Shenandoah area in the Blue Ridge was already known to Americans. The nine years of labor that went into construction of the drive forged the first link of a longer mountaintop boulevard that continues southward for almost 500 miles over the Blue Ridge Parkway to the Smokies, creating a spectacular drive.

These mountains record more than a billion years of history. Their granite "basement" rocks are among the oldest in eastern America, yet this antiquity explains the rounded, forest-covered feature of the Blue Ridge. Continuous erosion caused by wind, water, and frost stripped thousands of feet of material from the mountains as they were being uplifted, with rivers then transporting vast quantities of material to the sea.

Though the land is ancient, establishment of the national park is fairly recent. Shenandoah was first approved by Congress in 1926 (at the same time as Great Smoky), when Acadia was the only national park east of the Mississippi. But complete acceptance depended upon the people of Virginia acquiring the land and deeding it to the federal government. Unlike the western parks, these were not public lands, but privately owned, mostly by struggling mountain folks. It took almost ten years, but individuals like George Freeman Pollock, colorful owner of the mountaintop Skyland resort, lent enthusiasm and energy to help raise $1,200,000 (while another $1,000,000 was appropriated by the Virginia legislature) and make this beautiful highland a gift to the nation. Even a president's personal landholding—Herbert Hoover's fishing camp on the Rapidan—became part of the new park.

President Hoover enjoyed the region as a place where he could fish the quiet pools and riffles in the streams. Today the park is a hiker's, as well as a motorist's, paradise, with 200 miles of trails, including part of the Appalachian Trail; a delight for birdwatchers, who can find 200 species at one time or other during the year; and for wildflower enthusiasts, who may identify as many as 80 flowering plants in a day's walk.

103

THE PRACTICAL GUIDE

A worthwhile visit can be as long or short as you make it. If driving, key your time allowance to the speed limit of 35 miles per hour, and plan to leave your car at one or more of the overlooks to sample the trails.

Four main entrances lead to the park and Skyline Drive, including the north entrance at Front Royal; Thornton Gap, between Luray and Sperryville; Swift Run Gap, between Stanardsville and Elkton; and the south entrance, the link with the Blue Ridge Parkway, at Rockfish Gap, between Charlottesville and Waynesboro. Seventy-five parking overlooks give plenty of opportunity to observe the mountain slopes and surroundings in all their moods. From **Hogback Overlook,** on a clear day, you can count 11 bends in the Shenandoah River.

Visitor Center. If you enter from the north, stop at **Dickey Ridge Visitor Center,** where a sequence of color slides will describe the variety of park attractions and facilities. Also visit the large, new **Harry F. Byrd, Sr. Visitor Center** at Big Meadows. It interprets graphically the cultural story of mountaineers who formerly lived in the park area.

Short trail trips of wide variety enable everyone to gain intimate contact with park features. From Skyland, one of two major developed areas, you can hike the 1½-mile round trip **Stony Man Nature Trail.** This leisurely path leads through a good cross section of the nearly 100 species of trees in the park. It ascends the slopes of Stony Man Mountain to its craggy 4,010-foot summit, perched 3,000 feet above Shenandoah Valley. The 5-mile hike (allow half a day) to **Whiteoak Canyon** begins just south of Skyland, taking visitors through an ancient hemlock forest into a wild and water-splashed garden of rock, vines, and shrubs. Five miles farther south, the **Hawksbill Mountain Trail** (2 miles round trip) leads to the highest point in the park, 4,049 feet above sea level, clothed in remnants of a spruce-fir forest, more typical of northern New England or Canada. From Big Meadows, the largest of the developed areas, the **Swamp Nature Trail** is filled with pleasant surprises for amateur and even professional botanists; the 2-mile round trip includes a boggy habitat of swamp-loving wildflowers. The trail to "Old Raggedy," or **Old Rag Mountain,** leads to the most spectacular and fascinating peak in the park. It lies east of the main Blue Ridge chain, an imposing mass of granite, with a rocky, boulder-strewn ridge-crest nearly 5 miles in length. Hikers love it because of the unique Ridge Trail, which winds around massive boulders for

more than a mile, and even through a cave, before reaching the summit with expansive views in all directions. The 7.7-mile circuit hike is tough and takes a full day. The starting point for the hike, at the little town of Nethers (near Sperryville), is a drive of 30 miles from Skyland, 40 miles from Big Meadows. To reach the **Hoover Camp** on the Rapidan River, where the president's old lodge and a caretaker's cabin have been restored, start at Big Meadows wayside, just past milepost 51. The circuit hike, a little over 6 miles, is easy and scenic. Deer frequently can be seen grazing in the meadows.

The Appalachian Trail follows the mountain crest for 94 miles through the park, with numerous spur trails. It is possible to take the trail in large or small measures. Park your car at a picnic area, overlook, or parking area on the Skyline Drive and you can hike for an hour or a half-day. For overnighting without having to carry a tent, 21 open shelters, most with simple built-in bunks for six, are located along the trail in the park, available on a first-come, first-served basis. In addition, there are five locked cabins furnished with mattresses and blankets, stove, cooking utensils, and dishes. All you must bring are food supplies and an appetite. For reservations and rates, write the Potomac Appalachian Trail Club, 1718 N Street, N.W., Washington, D.C. 20036.

Horseback riding. Horses can be rented at Skyland or Big Meadows for an hour, half-day, or all day (a guide accompanies each trip). Heading to Whiteoak Canyon gives the feel of a real wilderness trail ride, but the horses are gentle enough for children. Overnight pack trips can be arranged.

Fishing for native brook trout is good in a number of beautiful mountain streams, April to mid-October. A Virginia license is required (three-day nonresident trout license, valid in the park only, is available at all major concession facilities). Rapidan and Staunton rivers and their tributaries are "fishing-for-fun" streams.

Naturalist program. Guided hikes are conducted daily, mid-June to Labor Day, to major points of interest like Hawksbill Mountain, Whiteoak Falls, Bearfence Mountain, and Limberlost. Trips may be cancelled because of weather or if fewer than five people appear to join the naturalist. Parents must accompany children under 12. Campfire programs, with group singing and illustrated talks, are given at Skyland, Loft Mountain, Big Meadows, Matthews Arm, and Lewis Mountain campgrounds. Self-guiding nature trails are popular; Dark Hollow is best enjoyed by those in good physical condition.

Tour operators. Virginia Trailways of Charlottesville operates bus tours through the park from late June through mid-October. In addition, Trailways Travel Bureau of Washington offers varying tour packages of Virginia, which feature Shenandoah National Park. Highlights of these trips include the **Caverns of Luray,** the largest in the state and among the most beautiful in the country; **Charlottesville,** distinguished by Thomas Jefferson's home and the campus he designed for the University of Virginia, and **Staunton,** where the birthplace of Woodrow Wilson has

been restored as a museum and shrine.

Accommodations. Splendid overnight lodges and dining rooms (specializing in Virginia foods) are located at Big Meadows and Skyland, with views of Shenandoah Valley and mountain ranges beyond. Some units are modern motel-type, but you may prefer the rustic cottages. Lewis Mountain has the southernmost accommodations, with cabins for 24 persons and a small restaurant. Advance reservations are desirable, early April through October. Write Virginia Sky-Line Company, Inc., P.O. Box 191, Luray, Virginia 22834. Restaurant facilities also are available along the Skyline Drive at Elkwallow, Panorama, and Swift Run Gap. Picnickers, hikers, and fishermen can pick up box lunches at Skyland and Big Meadow.

Camping. Campgrounds in the park are located at Big Meadows, Lewis Mountain. Loft Mountain, and Matthews Arm near Elkwallow in the north district. These operate on a first-come, first-served basis, with 14-day limit. Big Meadows and Loft Mountain have camper supply stores, pay showers, coin laundries, ice, and wood sales. Campers who fail to keep food (including ice chests) locked in car trunks may expect company—black bears searching for food. No utility connections for trailers, but sewage disposal stations are located at Big Meadows, Matthews Arm, and Loft Mountain.

Seasons. Skyland opens in April, Big Meadows in May, and both remain open till late October or early November. A section of Big Meadows campground is open all year, the others from May to October. The park itself is open all year, except when severe ice or snow storms

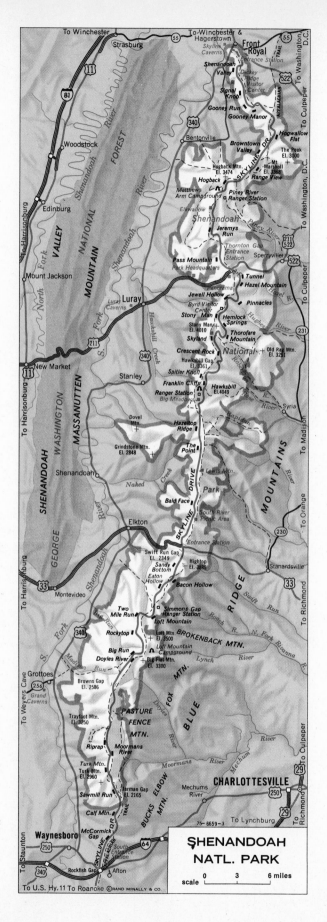

Map labels:
To Winchester — Strasburg — To Winchester & Hagerstown — 55 — To Washington, D.C. — 55 — Front Royal — Skyline Caverns — Entrance Station — Dickey Ridge Visitor Center — 522 — To Culpeper — 11 — 81 — Shenandoah Valley — Signal Knob — Gooney Run — Gooney Manor — Hogwallow Flat — Woodstock — Bentonville — Browntown Valley — The Peak El. 3000 — Mt. Marshall El. 3368 — Hogback Mtn. El. 3474 — Hogback — Range View — Matthews Arm Campground — Piney River Ranger Station — Edinburg — To Harrisonburg — Elkwallow — Shenandoah — Jeremys Run — Piney River — Mount Jackson — Pass Mountain — Thornton Gap Entrance Station — Sperryville — 211 — 522 — To Culpeper — Park Headquarters — Tunnel — Hazel Mountain — Luray Caverns — Luray — Jewell Hollow — Pinnacles — Byrd Visitor Center — Hughes R. — 231 — Stony Man El. 4010 — Hemlock Springs — Thorofare Mountain — Skyland — North Fork — Shenandoah River — New Market — 340 — 211 — Stanley — Crescent Rock — Hawksbill Gap El. 3361 — Spitler Knoll — Franklin Cliffs — Ranger Station — Big Meadows — Hawksbill El. 4049 — National — Old Rag Mtn. El. 3291 — Syria — Dovel Mtn. — Shenandoah — Hazeltop Ridge — Robinson R. — Grindstone Mtn. El. 2848 — The Point — Naked Creek — Lewis Mtn. — Park — To Madison — Elkton — Bald Face — South River Picnic Area — Entrance Station — Blue Ridge Mountains — 230 — To Orange — Stanardsville — 33 — Swift Run Gap El. 2349 — Sandy Bottom — Hightop El. 3585 — Eaton Hollow — Bacon Hollow — To Harrisonburg — 33 — Montevideo — Swift Run — S. Fork Shenandoah River — Two Mile Run — Simmons Gap Ranger Station — Left Mountain — Rockytop — Left Mtn. El. 3500 — Brokenback Mtn. — N. Fork Rivanna River — Big Run — Left Mountain Campground — Lynch River — Doyles River — Big Flat Mtn. El. 3300 — Madison Run — Grottoes — Browns Gap El. 2586 — 256 — Grand Caverns — To Weyers Cave — Trayfoot Mtn. El. 3250 — Pasture Fence Mtn. — Fox Mtn. — Blue — Riprap — Moormans River — Turk Mtn. — Turk Mtn. El. 2960 — Moormans River — Jarman Gap El. 2165 — Bucks Elbow Mtn. — Ridge — Mechum River — Charlottesville — Sawmill Run — Calf Mtn. — Mechums River — 250 — 29 — To Lynchburg — Waynesboro — McCormick Gap — To Staunton — 250 — South Entrance Station — 64 — Skyline Dr. — To Richmond — 29 — To Culpeper — 340 — Rockfish Gap — Afton — To U.S. Hy. 11 To Roanoke — © Rand McNally & Co.

75-6659-3

SHENANDOAH NATL. PARK

scale 0   3   6 miles

close Skyline Drive for short periods. The beauty of winter in the highlands offers a special treat. On cold, crisp days evergreens stand out boldly against the snowy white mountain background. Icicles cascade over the cliffs, presenting opportunities for unusual photography. Winter walkers should stay on the designated trails, wear adequate clothing, and not push their physical endurance while walking through snow. Motorists should carry a good set of chains and have adequate ventilation while the car motor is running. The park remains cool until June, though spring flowers and budding trees begin their show in late March with hepatica, red maple, and bloodroot. In mid-April the magenta flush of redbud floods the valleys, followed by the creamy white of dogwood. In succession come azalea and black locust, then the pink and white mountain laurel—a profusion of flowers during most of June. In summer, temperatures are a comfortable 15 degrees lower than in the valley below. You can usually count on mid-80s by day; mid-40s at night. This is the peak period for visitors, though crowds are fairly light in midweek. By mid-September, foliage begins its autumn color change, gradually flowing downward from the mountain tops to coves and hollows. There are several "color-peaks," the most luxurious displays among non-oak species usually occurring between October 10 and 20. Yet there is still new blossom, of yarrow, asters, and witch hazel. In spring and fall naturalists present illustrated evening talks at the Byrd Visitor Center at Big Meadows.

Nearby. Both the Piedmont and Shenandoah Valley are rich in Civil War battle sites. **Lexington,** in particular, is associated with Robert E. Lee, who served as president of Washington and Lee University, and Stonewall Jackson, who left for the war from the faculty of Virginia Military Institute. **New Market Battlefield Park,** a surprising and outstanding area, depicts Jackson's valley campaign and the role of VMI cadets. The national park is flanked by **George Washington National Forest.** Its largest recreation area, **Sherando Lake,** 14 miles south of Waynesboro, provides campground, sand beach, bathhouse, and naturalist program. An unusually interesting area, **Elizabeth Furnace,** in the Massanutten Mountains near Front Royal, has camping and a nature trail winding through an old iron furnace community.

For further information write Superintendent, Shenandoah National Park, Luray, Virginia 22835.

VIRGIN ISLANDS

Authorized as a national park, 1956

In the fragile underwater forest, coral of many hues rise like trees, mountains, and spires. Schools of brilliant fish rest lazily on stony branches or swim through clear, sunlit waters. Lacy purple sea fans sway in a gentle current, and delicate anemones carpet the reef like flowering shrubbery in full aquatic bloom.

Such waters, significant for the biological treasures they possess, are the offshore pride of the Virgin Islands National Park. This small, priceless fragment of America, 14,470 acres, occupies two-thirds of the island of St. John, which measures but 9 miles long and 5 miles wide. The park was established in 1956, none too soon, considering that the past few years have seen the unending discovery and commercial development of one "unspoiled" West Indies beach after another, in the same pattern that has swept up and down the Atlantic Coast of continental United States. In time, St. John may be one of the few left to show sparkling beaches, tropical forest, Danish ruins, and these coral reefs in their untouched state.

The course of its history began more than 100 million years ago, when volcanoes erupted deep in the ocean and the buckling crust of the earth raised rock islands above the surface of the sea. Ever since then, the beaches of St. John have been a zone of arriving life, with ocean currents and each new tide delivering animals and plants, insects, eggs, seeds, and seedlings to form new colonies here. Meanwhile, the coral reefs have formed a world of flowers that are not plants but tiny animals of the subtropic seas. The coral gardens derive their varied and vivid colors from the myriads of tiny organisms living within them.

At night the reef comes alive with animated bloom. From every branch and tower and domed facade, the coral animals thrust out their tentacled heads to filter food from the surging streams of underwater life.

The pattern of life changes upward from the sea. The pale strand is shaded here and there by a sea-grape tree, its large leaves tinged with red, and with small purple fruit. But in traveling about the island to the rainy mountaintops, one observes a swift transition in vegetation; few areas anywhere of such small geographic dimensions span so wide a range, from underwater coral to lush, broad-leaf evergreens. Land birds are abundant, with a few water birds along the shores.

Men have lived in the Virgin Islands several thousand years. Among the earliest were the Ciboneys and Arawaks, who farmed peaceably near the beaches. Then came the Caribs, a hungry band of aborigines who were not above cooking their enemies for dinner. Christopher Columbus touched St. Croix, the largest island, on his second voyage, but it was the Danes who shaped the colonial culture. They acquired the Virgin Islands in the 1700s, established sugar plantations, imported slaves, and built their estate houses on high breezy hills. They prospered until the mid-19th century, when sugar prices fell, the slaves were freed, and the old plantations were left to become shadowy ruins of history. The United States bought the islands in 1917 solely to keep them out of German hands; now, with the advent of jet airplanes and luxury boat travel they have become a choice vacation spot.

THE PRACTICAL GUIDE

The Virgin Islands are only four hours from New York, less from Miami. Flights go directly to St. Croix, the largest island, or to St. Thomas, the capital, which is closest to St. John (20 minutes by ferry). Many flights, however, go to San Juan, Puerto Rico, making connections for Charlotte Amalie, St. Thomas. If you plan to stay at St. Thomas, there are excellent one-day package tours, including the ferry trip, guided jeep tours, swimming and snorkeling in the clear waters, and lunch. Sailboats and other small craft can be rented on both St. Thomas and St. John. If you come over independently on the ferry to the park entrance at Cruz Bay, taxis with guides offer worthwhile tours. For jeep rentals on your own write At Your Service Travel Agency, Cruz Bay, St. John, Virgin Islands 00830.

Visitor Center. The park Visitor Center has information, maps, and exhibits of park features. Orientation talks are given at 11:15 a.m. Sunday and Monday and at 10:15 a.m. Tuesday through Saturday. Check here for the schedule of naturalist-conducted historic and nature walks and the evening programs at Caneel Bay Plantation and Cinnamon Bay.

Centerline Road, the main road of St. John, climbs over the heights to the harbor of Coral Bay on the east. The road winds up past buildings of the 1700s, including the Moravian Bethany Church. From a distance the wooded hills resemble the New England countryside, but there are fruit trees like the soursop and mango; little plants and vines bearing local botanical names such as clashie melashi, eye bright, and better man better; and exotic trees like the gnarled, strangely shaped silk cotton, which produces kapok in its seed pod. Avoid eating strange wild fruits—some are poisonous. From the overlook near **Maney Peak,** elevation 1,147 feet, islands of the American and British Virgin Islands spread over the brilliant, calm blue sea around Coral Bay. In 1595 Sir Francis Drake put in at Coral Bay before sailing to attack Puerto Rico.

Reef Bay Trail, of special interest to the visitor who wants to hike, or find subjects for sketching and/or photography. From the top of Centerline Road, the 2½-mile trail winds down (a descent of about 800 feet) on an old Danish carriage road, through a moist, then dry, forest. A short side trip leads to undeciphered petroglyphs dating from Arawak and Carib days at the base of a waterfall. Another side trail leads to the Reef Bay estate house, once center of a flourishing plantation. The trail ends on the sand beach, a delightful place for a swim after the

hike. In this area are the ruins of an 18th century sugar mill. Every two weeks during the winter season a park naturalist leads a trip this way. Instead of hiking back up the hill, arrangements can be made (for a reasonable fee) to be picked up by boat.

Snorkeling is to the Virgin Islands what hiking is to Shenandoah: the means of gaining intimate contact with marvels of the park. Anybody who can swim can snorkel, and equipment can be rented at the Cinnamon Bay Commissary, or at St. Thomas. If you're a beginner, start right. Never snorkel alone. Test the snorkel in shallow water. If it leaks, don't use it. Respect submerged features—the coral, the rock, and other underwater formations; leave them for others to enjoy.

Trunk Bay Beach. The snorkeling is excellent at one of the island's loveliest beaches. This is the scene of the world's first **underwater self-guiding trail,** started in 1960. The trail is not quite for everyone, since it reaches a depth of ten feet, but experts can read the labels etched on submerged glass plates while they rub shoulders with trumpet fish and yellow-specked French angel fish.

Swimming, with or without snorkel, is one of the pleasures of the park, but the safest places to swim are where lifeguards are on duty (Hawksnest Beach, Trunk Bay, Cinnamon Bay).

Fishing. Saltwater fishing is equally good in all seasons. Three bonefish flats are near St. John. Tackle may be rented from Cinnamon Bay Camp, while charter boats are available in Cruz Bay and St. Thomas for offshore marlin, tuna, sailfish, wahoo, and others. Spear-fishing in waters of the park is prohibited.

Annaberg Ruins. A self-guiding trail helps you to recapture the story of the sugar estates at these ruins on the North Shore, which the Park Service has stabilized as a protection against further weathering. Cane grown on surrounding hillsides was transported by mules or oxen to the factory to be crushed in the windmill or on the grinding platform.

Accommodations. The largest guest facility on St. John outside the park is **Caneel Bay Plantation,** operated by Rockresorts, Inc., for the Rockefeller Foundation, that purchased the parkland for the government. It is one of the finest resorts in the Caribbean; though high-priced during the winter peak, rates are fairly reasonable, and Caneel Bay is a good vacation buy the rest of the year, particularly with package plans in effect May 1–November 1. Write Caneel Bay Plantation, P.O. Box 4930, St. John, Virgin Islands. A few housekeeping cottages are located at Cruz and Coral bays.

There is a wide choice of lodgings on St. Thomas.

Make a reservation one day for breakfast, luncheon, or dinner at Caneel Bay, where nothing but the best is served, and served beautifully. Or go to Estate Beth Cruz for meat and fish and an inspiring sunset; to Oscar's for fish or goat stew, or Meada's Restaurant in Cruz Bay. At Trunk Bay a small restaurant perched on the hillside has sandwiches and hot luncheons Tuesday through Sunday.

Facilities are necessarily limited on St. John in order to protect natural features. Inside the park, Cinnamon Bay Camp provides unique, modest beach cottages (furnished with cots, bedding, linen, cook-

ing utensils). For cottage reservations (or to rent tent equipment) write well in advance to Cinnamon Bay Camp.

Camping. Cinnamon Bay Camp has become, with recent improvements, probably the finest campground in the Caribbean. The camping limit is 14 days per year. The camp sells essential groceries and supplies.

More varied foods and laundry facilities are available at the tiny port village of Cruz Bay.

Seasons. Peak periods of use for campsites and beach cottages are November to March and June to August. Peak popularity of the Virgin Islands in general, as a refuge from winter cold, ex-

tends from December to March. April and May are very attractive months. The climate is equable year-round, with the average annual temperature 79 degrees. The lowest recorded temperature is 61 degrees, the highest 98 degrees. Temperature of the water is delightful for swimming, neither cold enough to give a shock nor warm enough to be enervating. Rains fall mostly in brief showers at night.

Nearby. Both St. Thomas and St. Croix are popular Caribbean resorts, landscaped with bright hibiscus, oleander, and bougainvillea. At Charlotte Amalie, the capital city, visited by many cruise liners, the 25 shops between Queen's Street and Waterfront Promenade feature merchandise

from all over the world—because St. Thomas is a duty-free port. St. Croix, 40 miles south, clings to its colonial architecture and history, but Danish, rather than American. **Christiansted National Historic Site,** along three waterfront blocks of the main city, comprises the old fort and public buildings. **Buck Island Reef National Monument,** a mile and a half off the coast of St. Croix, is regarded as one of the finest marine gardens in the Caribbean; it is visited on boat cruises from St. Croix and provides snorkelers with an underwater nature trail.

For further information write Superintendent, Virgin Islands National Park, Box 806, St. Thomas, Virgin Islands 00801.

VOYAGEURS

Authorized as a national park, 1971

The first national park in Minnesota embraces a choice portion of the forested lake country on the northern border, once the setting of an epic chapter in American history. For a century and a half, French-Canadian voyageurs plied this network of lakes and streams in sturdy canoes; transporting explorers, missionaries, and soldiers to the West; returning to Montreal with vast quantities of furs.

Sentiment for preserving this area had been felt and expressed in Minnesota for many years. As early as 1891 the Minnesota legislature petitioned Congress to establish a national park on the Kabetogama Peninsula. A National Park Service study in 1938 (renewed in 1960), undertaken cooperatively with Minnesota, indicated the potential of the Rainy Lake-Kabetogama area as a major park site. In the '60s the campaign reached major proportions. In 1962, Governor Elmer L. Andersen and state officials toured the area in company with major landowners and representatives of the National Park Service; they issued a joint memorandum recommending field studies as soon as possible. In 1965, Andersen's successor, Governor Karl Rolvaag, and 5,000 fellow Minnesotans signed a petition at the State Fair urging establishment of Voyageurs National Park. And in 1967, a third governor, Harold LeVander committed the "full force" of his administration to establishment of the park, including the Crane Lake area, administered by the Forest Service. During the same year the National Park Service reaffirmed its choice of Kabetogama as "the outstanding remaining opportunity for a national park in the northern lake country of the United States." The entire Minnesota delegation, led by Representative John Blatnik and Senator Walter Mondale, then introduced legislation in Congress, which acted favorably in late 1971. The bill authorizing the new park was signed by the president in January, 1971.

Sigurd Olson—author, naturalist, and a living Minnesota legend—played a major role in the park movement, making countless presentations in his home state and Washington. Voyageurs Park Association, headed first by Judge Edwin P. Chapman, labored toward making Minnesota's first national park a reality.

The park, though not yet operational, will encompass 219,000 acres of which about 80,000 are water. A portion of the area, at Crane Lake, was formerly administered as part of Superior National Forest, while another portion was held by the State of Minnesota. The largest tracts, almost 79,000 acres, are to be acquired from private owners, principally lumber and pulpwood companies.

The timber forts and other physical traces of the *coureurs du bois* and voyageurs have long since vanished, but the land and waters they knew have been little altered. The park has all the wildness and immense scale associated with the northern shield region—a surface shaped by continental glaciation into an endless system of internal waterways. Stands of fir, spruce, pine, aspen, and birch reach to the water's edge, broken here and there by bogs, cliffs, and sand beaches. Wildlife species such as deer, moose, black bear, and possibly timber wolf remain. Beavers thrive among the aspen. Throngs of birds that are indigenous to the area and numerous varieties of waterfowl make their nests and feed in the peninsula's many bays and lagoons.

THE PRACTICAL GUIDE

Lying east of International Falls, the park is irregular in shape, measuring about 40 miles from east to west and varying in width from 3 to 15 miles. It includes numerous islands and more than 50 lakes. The main body of land, Kabetogama Peninsula, covers 75,000 heavily forested acres, relatively undeveloped and accessible principally by water. Surrounding the peninsula are waters ranging from narrows less than 100 feet in width to lakes several miles across, dotted with islands, accented with rocky points. Four lakes dominate the area within the park: **Namakan, Kabetogama, Rainy,** and **Sand Point.** Rainy Lake, the largest, covers 350 square miles. In time, conducted boat trips, nature walks, campfire programs, and self-guiding trails will explain the natural and historic attractions.

The primary access to the park is via US 53, extending from Virginia, Minnesota, north to International Falls.

Crane Lake Gorge, near the eastern edge of the park, is one of the spectacular scenic wonders of Crane Lake, where the Vermillion River tumbles through a narrow chasm between vertical rock walls before it flows into the lake. There are trails on both sides of the canyon and many plants and mosses on the moist forest floor. Wherever you go in the park, observe the variety of mosses, ferns, and lichens covering the rocks as well as the forest floor. Wild rice grows in shallow bays and streams, and cranberry bogs are common.

Historic values are high. Underwater archaeologists have recovered parts of voyageur canoes, muzzle-loading rifles, beads intended for Indian trade, and other artifacts. An existing link to a more recent era is the **Kettle Falls Hotel** at the extreme east end of Rainy Lake. Built in 1913, the hotel served trappers, traders, fishermen, and lumberjacks. It is remarkably well preserved. There was also a brief gold rush in the early 1890s at **Rainy Lake City** following discovery of the Little America vein, but little evidence remains.

Even though the park is not yet established, a wide spectrum of facilities is already available, ranging from camping to houseboats to resorts.

Boating and canoeing. State regulations apply. Boaters not yet familiar with these waters should obtain the services of a guide (through a local resort or hotel) or obtain charts. Large lakes are formidable and can become suddenly rough. Small boats and canoes should prepare to wait out rough water, better yet to plan a course that avoids wide expanses. Boat and canoe services are available; excursion boats operate during summer. Canoeists can put in at several points and paddle for a day, week, or all summer, and never run out of new vistas. Local outfitters rent full equipment.

Fishing is undoubtedly one of the outstanding recreational resources of the park. The three large border lakes—Rainy, Namakan, and Kabetogama—are popular with walleye anglers; they are also rich in northern pike and smallmouth bass. Shoe Pack Lake on the peninsula is known for its muskellunge, while rainbow trout are found in some of the smaller lakes and streams.

Accommodations. At the eastern end is **Crane Lake,** not really a town, but a grouping of resorts, summer homes, and marinas at the south end of Crane Lake. They cover the whole spectrum of outdoor recreation, from water skiing to outfitting canoe trips and arranging flights to remote fishing lakes. Federal campsites are located in the **Namakan-Sand Point** area north of Crane Lake. On Lake Kabetogama there are 33 resorts. Some provide bathing beaches, fishing launches (plus motor and boat rentals), guide service, and grocery stores (for those with housekeeping cabins).

Camping. Boise Cascade Corporation (International Falls, Minnesota 56649) has developed a number of campsites inside the park area available without charge. The State of Minnesota and U.S. Forest Service provide camping in or near the park area. Along both north and south shores of Kabetogama Peninsula are many places with smooth, glaciated rock well suited for camping and picnicking. The interior holds a number of lakes that can be reached only by foot.

Seasons. Summers are cool. Warm clothes and insect repellent are important. September can be a beautiful month when aspen and birch change colors.

Nearby. East of the park lies the renowned **Boundary Waters Canoe Area,** which includes portions of the Superior National Forest and Quetico Provincial Park across the border in Ontario. Main gateways are at Grand Marais, Ely, and Crane Lake. **Fort Frances,** Ontario, linked by bridge with International Falls, was the site of Fort St. Pierre, built by Pierre de la Verendrye, the French explorer, in 1731.

Recommended reading. *The Singing Wilderness* and *Listening Point,* by Sigurd Olson.

For further information write Superintendent, Voyageurs National Park, P.O. Drawer 50, 405 Second Avenue, International Falls, Minnesota 56649.

WIND CAVE

Established as a national park, 1903

A sea of grass ripples in the prairie wind.

The "waves" are formed of short grasses and medium-tall grasses, with a sprinkling of wildflowers—a rich, rolling blending of the Great Plains.

The sleek pronghorn, singly and sometimes in pairs, roves across the hillsides. Small herds of huge, shaggy bison lumber slowly, following ancient pathways. Black-tailed prairie dogs burrow about and build the crater-shaped mounds that form their colonies or "towns."

The animals are remnants of millions that once covered the mid-continent. Here, on the southeastern flank of South Dakota's Black Hills, they are part of the natural vignette of the period before the white man came. The name officially given may be Wind Cave, but this also is a national park of the original prairie grassland.

The park contains 28,059 acres, a relatively small area. Yet it includes not only a prime example of mixed-grass prairie, but a meeting ground of eastern and western flora. Here you can see the stately American elm and bur oak from the east merging with ponderosa pines of the western mountain forests and with yucca, cactus, and cottonwood from the arid southwest.

The geological features embrace a significant chapter in the history of the "Black Hill Uplift." Below the surface, the Wind Cave was formed in one of the thick limestone formations which underlie a large part of the Black Hills. It derives its name from strong currents of air that blow alternately in and out, believed to be caused by changes in atmospheric pressure outside.

The cave was probably known to the Sioux; but the first white man to explore it appears to have been Tom Bingham, an early Black Hills settler, in 1881. Extensive explorations were begun a few years later by Jesse D. McDonald, who managed the property for the South Dakota Mining Company, and his sons, Alvin and Elmer. Alvin, in particular, named rooms and cave formations, and established routes, some of which are still in use. When he died at the early age of 20, from pneumonia and complications, he was buried near the cave entrance. A bronze plaque marks the grave.

Development began in the 1890s with the "Wonderful Wind Cave Improvement Company." Passages were opened and stairways built, leading to galleries decorated with unusual crystal formations, rather than with stalagmites and stalactites. The principal type, "boxwork," is composed of delicately colored crystalline fins arranged in a honeycomb pattern. These were formed when cracks in the ancient limestone were filled with calcium carbonate deposits. "Frostwork" is formed by clusters of tiny white crystals of aragonite and calcite.

In 1902 legislation was introduced to set aside Wind Cave as a national park. It was enacted that year and signed by President Theodore Roosevelt on January 9, 1903. Wind Cave thus became the seventh national park, and the first cave park to be established in the National Park System.

About 10½ miles have been explored to a depth of 326 feet, but much of the underground chambers remain unexplored.

THE PRACTICAL GUIDE

Wind Cave is a lightly visited national park, thus increasing its charm to the visitor who prefers elbow room. It makes for a very pleasant few-hour natural interlude amidst the Black Hills. Conducted tours of the cave, requiring one to one and a half hours, are given April 1 to October 31. From late June to the end of August they leave every 15 minutes, from 7:30 a.m. until 6 p.m.

Visitor Center. A concession-operated lunchroom is located at the Visitor Center.

Cave trips are led by uniformed guides of the National Park Service, using either the walk-in entrance or elevator. Trails are hard-surfaced. Low-heeled, rubber-soled walking shoes are best for comfort. Temperature year-round is 47 degrees; wear a light sweater or jacket. Besides the regular trips, **candlelight tours,** reminiscent of the turn of the century, are held daily during summer (limit, 30 persons per party). **Spelunking tours** are conducted twice weekly with space-crawling into a primitive section of the cave (limit, ten persons, who must register in advance), and a thrice-weekly evening introductory program to the sport and science of spelunking is presented.

Rankin Ridge Nature Trail leads to the highest point in the park (elevation 5,016 feet). The trail is 1¼ miles long and takes about an hour. Binoculars are useful in getting a panoramic view of the Black Hills from the observation tower.

Wildlife is wonderful to watch and photograph, from a respectable distance. Bison are powerful creatures, which children should not be allowed to approach on foot (and neither should adults); even a young bison may turn impulsively and inflict serious injury. There is much to enjoy, but not to disturb. Early morning and evening are good hours for viewing elk and deer. The long list of park birds includes kingbirds, magpies, warblers, woodpeckers, and grouse.

Naturalist program. Activities will keep you on the go from early morning till after dark. At 8 a.m., park personnel lead a daily four-hour hike into interesting canyons. Each evening, about twilight, auto caravans provide an excellent opportunity to view and photograph wildlife in an undisturbed habitat. Campfire programs each evening range in subject from the saga of the buffalo to a review of all the caves in the National Park System.

Camping. One-half mile north of the headquarters area, **Elk Mountain Campground** provides camping and trailer sites on a first-come, first-served basis.

Seasons. The cave is closed November through March; the surface area is open throughout the year, but windy wintry weather discourages much travel. Tourist centers in the Black Hills are jammed in midsummer. Early summer wildflowers and autumn foliage make these attractive seasons.

Nearby. Within easy range are **Mount Rushmore National Memorial,** where Gutzon Borglum directed the carving of the heads of Washington, Jefferson, Lincoln, and Theodore Roosevelt in solid granite; and **Jewel Cave National Monument,** small but beautiful, a series of chambers and limestone galleries with sparkling crystal-lined walls. **Custer State Park,** immediately adjacent to the national park, contains one of the world's largest bison herds. Fishing on hundreds of miles of streams, riding, hiking, boating, and swimming are among other recreational activities in the state park.

Campgrounds are located in **Black Hills National Forest** and **Custer State Park.** The state park contains several overnight lodgings including **State Game Lodge,** once the summer residence of President Calvin Coolidge—a good place to have a sizzling buffalo steak, or "buffalo burger." Motels are located in Hot Springs, Custer, and other nearby towns along approach highways to the park.

A word of caution: the Black Hills contain a heavy concentration of commercial tourist attractions advertising "fun for the entire family" and "education" for your youngsters. Choose carefully, particularly if you are on a close budget.

Recommended reading. *The Natural History Story of Wind Cave National Park,* by John A. Tyers.

For further information write Superintendent, Wind Cave National Park, Hot Springs, South Dakota 57747.

YELLOWSTONE

Established as a national park, 1872

Yellowstone, above all other areas, goes to the heart of the national park idea.

As the first national park, it came into being to establish the principle that land is a national treasure.

As the largest of our national parks, covering 2,219,-823 acres, Yellowstone embraces vast distance without factory, factory fumes, or firearms. Its spaciousness is a stronghold for wildlife—the grizzly bear, elk, bighorn, and bison, noble creatures that must have roaming room to live and perpetuate their species; and so too for majestic winged animals of the wilderness: the bald eagle, trumpeter swan, raven, and great gray owl. Its spaciousness is a stronghold for people—where city dwellers can stretch their legs beneath a clear sky and parents can show their kids one tremendous unspoiled section reminiscent of what the continent was like.

Outstanding natural features are throughout the park. Old Faithful, spouting hot water in snowy jets, and the 10,000 other geysers, hot springs, and bubbling mud volcanoes make it the most extensive thermal area in the world—but they are only the beginning of the park's wonders. Here are the Grand Canyon of the Yellowstone River, where brawling waters rush through twisting rock walls, and Yellowstone Lake, famed for its scenic beauty and fighting cutthroat trout, and also the gateway to backcountry rowboating and canoeing. Here are innumerable plants, trees, and wildflowers of stream and lake, sagebrush desert, open meadow, and high forest, reminding one that the whole surface of the earth is rendered beautiful by the vegetation that clothes it.

Millions of years ago this region was submerged beneath a shallow inland sea. During a period of internal upheaval, the earth pushed its crust slowly upward and the water receded. Then followed a sequence of volcanic explosions and lava flows over the Yellowstone plateau. The earth's crust fractured, great faults developed, and mountain ranges arose. In time came falling temperatures and the age of the glaciers, carving valleys and canyons into the shapes we know today.

Glaciers modified the hot-spring basins, which are remnants of volcanism—an expressive link between the ancient age and our own. Cold ground waters, trickling downward, strike vapors rising from seething superhot magmas perhaps a mile down. The waters boil upward, emerging at the surface as steam, causing caverns in soft rock below and terraces above. Ten percent of the hot springs are geysers, intermittently gushing forth water.

Men have lived on the Yellowstone Plateau for a very long time. Ancient campsites and stone articles found in many parts of the mountains and valleys strongly suggest human habitation of some kind for most of the 8,500 years since the last ice age. At the dawn of the historic period, little more than 150 years ago, the only Indians in the Yellowstone country, however, were a mixed group of impoverished Bannock and Shoshone known as the Sheepeaters.

John Colter, who took leave of the Lewis and Clark expedition in 1806 to do some independent exploring, is believed to have been the first white man to see and report on this wondrous place. Among trappers and explorers who followed, Jim Bridger, "Old Gabe," added (with some exaggeration) his version—which became known as "Jim Bridger's lies." In 1859, Bridger guided the first government expedition into the area, under Brigadier General W. F. Reynolds of the Army Corps of Topographical Engineers, with the distinguished F. V. Hayden as geologist. Other expeditions followed, building a picture of the wonders and beauties of Yellowstone.

One group that came to verify the frontier stories was the Washburn-Langford-Doane expedition of 1870, a party of 19 which had been organized by several influential Montana citizens. It was named for Henry D. Washburn, Surveyor-General of Montana; Nathaniel P. Langford; and Lieutenant Gustavus C. Doane, who commanded the small military escort. They spent almost four weeks investigating the area and naming many fea-

tures, including Old Faithful, the most famous of all. Most important, they sat around a campfire one evening to discuss the future of the fantastic place they had explored. According to H. M. Chittenden, the noted historian of Yellowstone, it was Judge Cornelius Hedges who insisted that no part of the region should ever be privately owned, but that it ought to be held by the government for the use of the people. The others (according to this account) concurred and charted the campaign to make Yellowstone a national park.

The writing and lecturing done by members of this expedition resulted in an official exploration in 1871 by the U.S. Geological Survey. The enthusiastic endorsement of F. V. Hayden, the leader, was buttressed by a superb set of photographs taken by William H. Jackson. From that came a recognition of the superlative nature of the Yellowstone "wonders." Representative William Horace Clagett, of Montana, introduced his famous Park Bill before 1871 was out and it succeeded after one of the most formidable, public-interest lobbying campaigns in history.

President Ulysses S. Grant signed the bill into law on March 1, 1872, placing—for the very first time—a parcel of the public domain under protection of the federal government as "a public park or pleasuring ground for the benefit and enjoyment of the people."

N. P. Langford—"National Park" Langford, as he had come to be known during the course of the park crusade—became Yellowstone's first superintendent, serving five years without pay. He was left by Congress without funds to maintain the park and without laws to protect it. The same was true of the four superintendents who followed him. They were plagued with many problems, including vandalism, game poaching, and forest fires, deliberately set. Finally, in 1886, the job of managing the park for the nation was given to the U.S. Army.

That mission was fulfilled by the military until 1917. Public works were directed by officers of the Corps of Engineers. Soldiers stationed at key points, aided by hardy scouts, brought respect for law and order. This system continued until a new organization, the National Park Service, was authorized by Congress on August 26, 1916. The park would henceforth be run by a superintendent, assisted by a corps of rangers with the powers of civilian policemen. This structure has become the model for national parks throughout the United States and the world.

Yellowstone is essentially a high rolling plateau, or series of plateaus, surrounded by great ranges of the Rockies—the Absaroka along the east, the Gallatin on the west, and the Tetons to the south—most of which are contained within national forests. Park and forest complement each other, each providing different activities and facilities.

THE PRACTICAL GUIDE

A trip to Yellowstone deserves forethought and preparation. Pick your time carefully. Some 70 percent of the park's visitors come during July and August, when concessions and park facilities are hard-pressed; if you come during these months have a good idea of overnight accommodations and where you will stay. Study a map of the area. Major park campgrounds can be expected to fill beyond capacity, while excellent U.S. Forest Service campgrounds, reasonably convenient to major park features, are only partially filled.

Allow three to five days to tour the highlights, not simply the one and a half days to do the Grand Loop. The park has five entrances: Gardiner, Montana (north); West Yellowstone, Montana (west); via Grand Teton National Park, Wyoming (south); Cody, Wyoming (east); and Cooke City, Montana (northeast).

Without a car. Airports within range are at Billings and Bozeman, Montana; Jackson and Cody, Wyoming; Pocatello, Idaho; and Salt Lake City, Utah. During summer, Western Airlines serves the airport at West Yellowstone. Trains and buses reach Gardiner, Cody, and West Yellowstone, connecting with Yellowstone Park Company buses. Car rentals are also available at these points.

Grand Loop. It links the best known park features on a 145-mile drive. Before you start, think it through; decide which points interest you the most.

Visitor Center. Get a copy of the **Naturalist Program** so you can allow time for the short guided walks and orientation at the Visitor Centers.

Each Visitor Center interprets a different phase of the Yellowstone story. Mammoth, for instance, contains exhibits on Indians, early park history, and wildlife. Fishing Bridge describes birdlife, fish, and geology of the Yellowstone Lake area. Old Faithful, of course, explains hot spring and geyser activity, with probable erupting times of Old Faithful posted prominently. Plan your trip to include campfire programs, which are given each evening during the summer at the main areas. There are no television or movie shows inside the park, but these illustrated programs by park naturalists are much better, dealing with the wonders you came to enjoy.

You will increase your chances of seeing wildlife if you fit your schedule to theirs: the early and late hours of the day are best. Many a meadow is dotted with elk in those periods, especially around Norris, but empty when the sun beats down and insects grow active. Best chances of finding moose are in Hayden Valley, near Fishing Bridge, Yellowstone Lake Lodge area, and Pelican Creek; bighorn sheep on Mount Washburn or near Soda Butte; bison along Nez Perce Creek south of Madison Junction; pronghorn near the north entrance, and coyote in Lamor Valley and Hayden Valley.

Starting from the north entrance (Gardiner), and going counterclockwise around the Grand Loop, the main features begin at **Mammoth Hot Springs,** near park headquarters. Well-marked trails enable the visitor to view at close range the brimming, terrace-like formations created by limestone deposits. **Norris Geyser Basin,** 21 miles south, is filled with exciting geysers and bubbling springs, including Steamboat, the most powerful geyser in the park. **Madison Junction** is within view of National Park Mountain, at the foot of which the pioneering 1870 expedition camped. Then you drive along the Firehole River, a stream heated by hot springs in its bed. **Old Faithful** and other geysers exhibit a large variety of character and action, a wild but delicate scene of nature at work. Each of the three basins—Upper, Midway, and Lower—should be explored, for each has its own claim to fame. Some of the most beautifully colored pools are found at **Black Sand Basin,** where vivid orange and yellow colors trace colonies of algae, water plants growing at the limits of life in the hot springs. The **Geyser Hill Nature Trail** leads through a wonderland of scalding water and superheated steam, a display of tremendous heat inside the earth. Old Faithful, the emblem of the park, has never missed an eruption during more than 80 years of observation, at intervals averaging about 65 minutes, not quite every hour on the hour.

At **West Thumb,** after the Grand Loop twice crosses the Continental Divide, the gaudy paintpots operate against the backdrop of sparkling Yellowstone Lake. The road winds around the northwest shore of **Yellowstone Lake,** the largest body of water in North America at so high an elevation (7,731 feet). Its blue waters, 300 feet deep, are fed by snow stored in forests above its 100-mile shoreline. From the famous **Fishing Bridge** at the outlet of the lake you may see a variety of birds on the water, including white pelicans, gulls, mallards, and geese. North of Fishing Bridge the road follows the **Grand Canyon of the Yellowstone,** 1,200 feet deep, a breathtaking spectacle from any vantage point along its twisting 24-mile course. The dominant color of the walls is yellow, ranging in shade from pale lemon to brilliant orange. Standing on **Inspiration Point,** which juts almost into the center of the canyon, one seems to be looking vertically down on the roaring Yellowstone River. The most exciting way to see and hear the thundering **Lower Falls,** twice as high as Niagara, is to go by trail down to the brink, a rather strenuous walk. The **Upper Falls** are spectacular, too, and can be viewed without a climb. **Tower Fall,** named by the men of the 1870 expedition, is best seen from the observation platform. Along the canyon walls, one of the most interesting rock formations of basalt, a dark lava, looks as though it had been pressed into columns.

Side roads. Give yourself a pleasant detour off the main loop by traveling a secondary road. The old **Tower Fall Road** presents a flower show, especially in early June. **Fountain Flats Drive,** from Madison Junction to Old Faithful, offers a dramatic view of Midway Geyser Basin and Grand Prismatic Spring.

Tour operators. The Yellowstone Park Company conducts tours of varying lengths, while popular package tours of two and three days start from Yellowstone and Grand Teton, featuring both parks.

Guided hikes. Yellowstone has more than a thousand miles of well-marked, safe, backcountry trails. Some of the finest are explored on rewarding naturalist-conducted hikes. If you have but two hours to spend, try the easy **Storm Point Walk,** any morning from Fishing Bridge, to observe birds and plants along the shore of Yellowstone Lake. The **Clear Lake Walk,** afternoons from the Grand Canyon, explores the life of forest and meadow on the way to picturesque Clear Lake, a leisurely introduction to the wild country. If you're interested in seeing mudpots off the beaten path, join the three-hour hike to Pocket Basin, which leaves three mornings a week from Midway Geyser Basin.

Another excellent hike, an all-day one of 7.2 miles round trip and not too strenuous, leads through forest and flowering alpine meadows on the slopes of Mount Washburn to the snowy 10,243-foot summit, an adventure capped by the breathtaking view of the whole park from the lookout tower. This trip is held three mornings weekly from Canyon Village as soon after July 1 as snow conditions permit. Another rewarding, but rigorous, naturalist hike leads three times weekly from Lamar River Bridge, on the northeast entrance road, to **Specimen Ridge,** the setting of the many-layered fossil forest. The **Absaroka Peaks Hike** takes you above timberline to lofty summits; it leaves Fishing Bridge four times weekly, beginning July 1, or as soon as snow conditions permit.

Backpacking. Trails open the way to hot springs, choice fishing streams, and wildlife summering in the high country. From the Bechler Ranger Station, in the southwest corner of the park (reached by car from Ashton, Idaho), the **Bechler Trail** leads past one waterfall after another. Sandhill cranes, rare trumpeter swans, ducks, and shore birds find an ideal home in meadows and swamps. Diagonally across the park, **Hellroaring Creek Trail** starts at Tower Fall Ranger Station, leading down along Elk Creek and across the Yellowstone River on a high, narrow suspension bridge. Deer, elk, and moose are common. Fishermen consider this a choice area. Study of a U.S. Geological Survey topographic map and a talk with a ranger will reveal the wide variety of trips to appeal to your own interest. Notify the ranger of your backcountry itinerary when you obtain a campfire permit. If you don't have equipment, you can easily rent a lightweight kit (tent, sleeping bag, cooking utensils) and buy food at the Hamilton Stores.

Riding. The Howard Eaton Trail, named for a famous pioneering horseman and guide, parallels the Grand Loop Road. You can take good one-day guided trips from Mammoth Hot Springs, Canyon, and Roosevelt Lodge near Tower Junction. Top outfitters, located around the park in Montana, Idaho, and Wyoming, can arrange trips for a week or a whole summer during which you never cross a motor road or retrace your own tracks.

Boating and fishing. For good fishing and/or nature enjoyment, take a trip to the South Arm or the Southeast Arm of Yellowstone Lake, where no roads reach and no power boats are permitted, but where a series of camps line the shores. Though canoes are not rented, you can hire a good rowboat. Gear, equipment, and a boat can be hauled or towed by boat taxi from Bridge Bay or West Thumb to (and from) Plover Point, the gateway to the South Arm. Deep in the Southeast Arm the Molly Islands are nesting grounds for white pelican, gull, cormorant, and tern. Around Peale Island in the South Arm, the trout fishing is celebrated. Abundant moose may be observed—from a safe distance—munching aquatic plants. Another outstanding experience is the trip from **Lewis Lake to Shoshone Lake,** 7 miles in length but well worth the effort (average time about three hours), especially for backcountry camping. Travel here is restricted to hand-propelled craft. Shoshone, a sanctuary for animal and bird life, abounds in fish, with a geyser basin at the southwest corner. Canoeists and rowboaters must bear in mind that Yellowstone waters are icy cold, and that sudden winds can whip up a violent surf within minutes. This explains the regulation that craft 16 feet or less in length and all canoes stay within one-quarter mile of shore. A boat permit is required for all boats used on park waters.

Boats longer than 32 feet are not allowed in the park. In fact, for sheer powerboating pleasure, better recreation is available on man-made lakes in surrounding Wyoming, Utah, Idaho, and Montana.

Fishing and Yellowstone are synonymous, though the best waters are in the backcountry. Heart, Riddle, Grebe, and Shoshone lakes are recommended for combined hiking, camping, and fishing trips. Firehole River is a choice dry-fly trout stream, due to abundant aquatic insect life and the tempering influence of warm springs. Consider engaging a guide at one of the popular tackle shops near the park. You are now required to obtain a fishing permit (free) to show you understand the regulations. Opening dates and

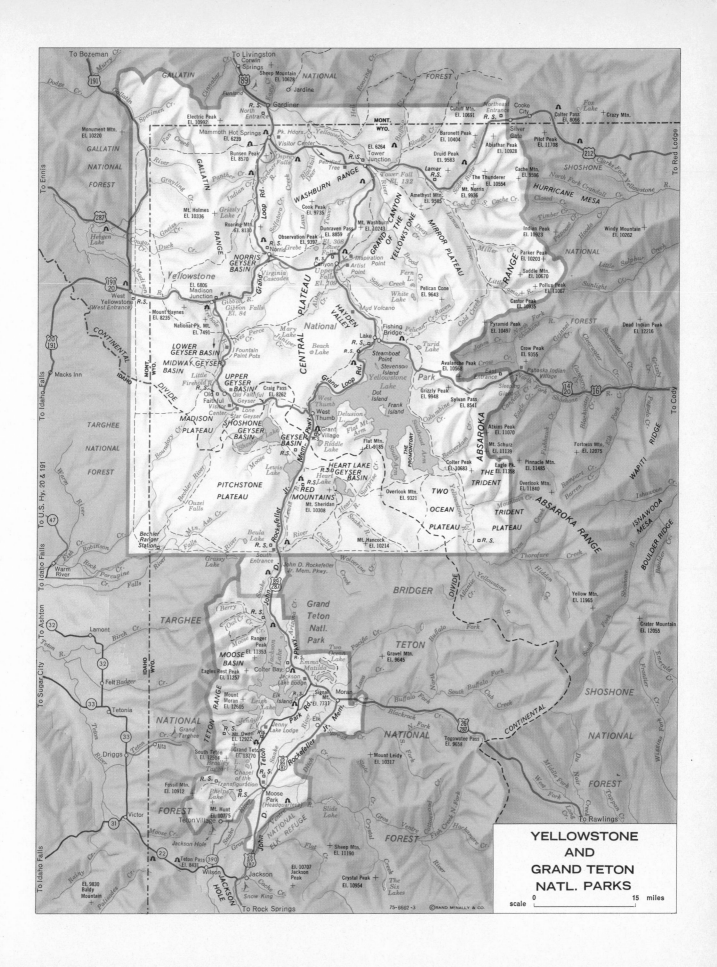

YELLOWSTONE
AND
GRAND TETON
NATL. PARKS

scale 0 15 miles

catch limits vary throughout the park. "Fishing-for-fun" is encouraged.

To maintain native species despite a steady increase in fishing, the Yellowstone, Lamar, and lower Lewis rivers within park boundaries are on "catch-and-release" regulations. Fishing is no longer allowed on the famous Fishing Bridge near the outlet of Yellowstone Lake. A two-fish limit is in effect, but five fish may be taken in a few brook trout streams in the northern part of the park.

Photography. Use fast shutter speed to photograph geysers. Hot pools are best on warm days, when steam does not obscure the subjects. Clean your camera lens with a soft, lintless cloth after leaving each area, since silica residues stick to the surface once they dry. If you need film or questions answered, Haynes Photo Shops throughout the park are well equipped.

Accommodations. Three concession-operated hotels, built many years ago, are located along the Grand Loop. These are Mammoth Hot Springs Hotel, Old Faithful Inn, and Lake Hotel. Old Faithful Inn is a good spot for lunch or dinner, where you can have dessert in time to rush out and see the big show. A fourth unit is the motel-type Canyon Village Lodge. All have dining rooms. In addition, there are cottages with and without bath, and simple camper's cabins, furnished and partially furnished, at several locations, with access to cafeterias. For rates and reservations write Reservations Department, Yellowstone Park Company, Yellowstone National Park, Wyoming 82190. Accommodations also are available outside the park at Cooke City, Gardiner, and West Yellowstone, Montana; along US 191, the Island Park section of Idaho; and Cody, Wyoming; some visitors use facilities in Grand Teton as their base for touring both parks.

Camping. Consider staying in smaller campsites in or outside the park. During the summer peak you may expect to find the following major campgrounds filled to capacity: Bridge Bay, Fishing Bridge, Grant village, Madison Junction. Try Lewis Lake, Pelican Creek, or Tower Fall, and ask a ranger for suggestions about other less crowded sites. Trailers are permitted, but there are no electrical or plumbing hookups. A concession-operated **trailer village** at **Fishing Bridge,** with utilities, coin laundry, and showers, is the best base for trailerites. For reservations write Hamilton Stores, Inc., West Yellowstone, Montana 59758. Scenic Forest Service campgrounds around the park perimeter include **Snake River,** near the south entrance; **Pahaska** and **Three Mile,** east entrance; **Chief Joseph** and **Colter,** near

Cooke City; **Bakers Hole** and **South Fork,** west entrance.

Seasons. Lodgings and stores gradually start to open in May; all are in business from about June 20 to mid-September; some remain open through October, and one facility even in winter. Accommodations are always available in nearby communities. The northern portion of the park is open all year through the Gardiner entrance, affording excellent opportunities to view and photograph elk, deer, bighorn, and pronghorn around thermal features.

Flowers are in full bloom in the lowlands around Mammoth Hot Springs in late May when Yellowstone is covered with ice and much of the park is still snowbound. Flowers continue up the slopes, reaching Mount Washburn in mid-July. The best periods to see animals and birds are May–June and September–October. With the onset of summer, animals spread over the high country summer range, while some birds move north and others become secretive around their nests. In autumn, snows on high ridges nudge animals to sites nearer the roads and birds start moving south. The most memorable hour of any September visit involves the sound (and sometimes sight) of bull elk bugling their challenge. Flies can be troublesome in June. Summer days are filled with sunshine; temperatures average in the 70s, though nights are cool, with temperatures dropping to the 30s before sunrise. September is frequently as pleasant, though a little cooler. Sometimes light snows fall, discomforting campers, though adding beauty to the scene. Naturalist programs continue on a limited basis.

Winter is a newly popular visitor season. The concession-operated Motor Inn at Mammoth, near the north entrance, is open and is the starting point for tours in heated snowmobiles to various parts of the park. The spectacular winter panorama is well worth the trip.

Park manners constitute a serious problem. No preaching, or even efforts at policing, can really solve it, but parents should encourage children to: stay on wooden walks in geyser basins; refrain from throwing litter in thermal pools (or anywhere else); catch fish only to be eaten rather than discarded as waste; admire the black bear from a respectable distance, without feeding, teasing, or inviting injury.

Nearby. Due east through Sylvan Pass, the Buffalo Bill Highway (US 14/20) leads through **Shoshone National Forest,** the country's oldest forest reserve, a scenic region of lakes, glaciers, and camping areas, to Cody, location of the outstand-

ing **Whitney Gallery of Western Art.** Northeast through Silvergate and Cooke City, the Beartooth Highway (US 212) winds around snow-clad Granite Peak, the highest point in Montana (12,850 feet), and through Red Lodge to spectacular Beartooth Pass in **Custer National Forest** en route to Billings. **Madison River Canyon Earthquake Area,** north of West Yellowstone, scene of the 1959 earthquake, is interpreted in displays and by personnel of the **Gallatin National Forest.** South of West Yellowstone, the **Island Park** region of **Targhee National Forest** in Idaho has beautiful scenery, with streams and reservoirs for boating and fishing. Due south of Yellowstone lie the mighty **Grand Tetons,** a worthy companion park to Yellowstone.

Recommended reading. Write to Yellowstone Library and Museum Association, Yellowstone National Park, Wyoming 82190, for its complete price list of literature. Publications especially worth having: *Haynes Guide; Yellowstone National Park,* H. M. Chittenden; *Yellowstone Back Country,* W. S. Chapman; and *U.S. Geological Survey Topographic Map of Yellowstone.*

For further information write Superintendent, Yellowstone National Park, Wyoming 82190.

YOSEMITE

Established as a national park, 1890

The Sierra Nevadas, a high mountain chain virtually unbroken for 250 miles, are filled with scenic riches that reach crystallization in Yosemite. John Muir, who came into what is now the park in 1868, fell in love with the country while listening to "the most songful streams in the world"; and so does every visitor of this day while walking among what Muir called "the noblest forests, the loftiest granite domes, the deepest ice-sculptured canyons, and snowy mountains soaring into the sky."

Yosemite is the embodiment of grandeur in nature, and also of its gracefulness. The towering waterfalls sound at close range like roaring volcanoes, but from a distance appear like strands of silver. The granite spires and domes rising massively from the floor of Yosemite Valley are softened by subtle shadows and the conifers growing beneath them. The giant sequoias are impressive as towering monarchs, but observe one closely and you'll appreciate its intimate beauty. The bark is colored a soft reddish brown, in younger trees tinged with purple; and in late winter tiny bright yellow flowers burst forth from the limbs in a delicate golden spray.

Few areas of this size (761,096 acres) have a wider variety of native plants and animals. From the warm foothills below Arch Rock, at 2,000 feet above sea level, to the windy summit of 13,114-foot Mount Lyell, five of the seven continental life zones are represented. They range from the Upper Sonoran where trees begin to crowd out brushy chaparral at Arch Rock to the Arctic-Alpine above treeline at Mount Lyell. Between these two limits, bear, deer, and about 75 other species of mammals make their homes. Observers have noted about 220 kinds of birds, 25 kinds of reptiles, and a dozen kinds of amphibians. There are over 1,300 species of flowering plants and many species of trees, including magnificent stands of pine and fir and enormous incense cedars, whose red bark leads some visitors to mistake them for giant sequoias.

The natural history of Yosemite spans many million years, starting from the ancient age when a warm, shallow sea spread across what is now the Sierra Nevada and Great Valley of California. After a long sequence of earth upheavals followed by erosion, glaciers gouged Yosemite Valley into a U-shaped trough. The first of at least three glaciers extended down the Merced River as far as El Portal, while the last left a moraine of rock debris damming the Merced back into Yosemite Valley. Sediments that subsequently filled the lake form the level valley floor of today. It was glacial action that rounded and polished domes like Liberty Cap in Little Yosemite Valley and Lembert Dome in Tuolumne Meadows. Other domes, however, like Sentinel and Half Dome, are the result of a geologic process called *exfoliation,* a steady weathering, chipping, and crumbling of rock layers that shape angular monoliths into rounded contours on their way toward ultimate dissolution.

Indians dwelled in Yosemite for centuries and many resided there as late as the mid-19th century. A party of trappers crossing the Yosemite upland region in 1833 were probably the first whites to see the area, but the awesome Yosemite Valley was not then discovered. In 1851 the Indians living there were ordered to attend a reservation agreement meeting and when they refused the governor of California dispatched a group of soldiers (called the Mariposa Battalion) to bring them out of their mountain stronghold. The soldiers destroyed the "U-zu-ma-ti" tribe, but at least bestowed the Indians' name on the valley. The accounts of this party attracted others, and within a decade the valley was well established as a tourist attraction, complete with trails and hotels.

In the early 1860s Dr. Josiah Dwight Whitney, in charge of the newly established California State Geological Survey, made expeditions into the area, pioneering the first geological interpretations. In this same period Galen Clark, recognizing the wealth of unique features, encouraged its preservation.

Public interest in its preservation led Congress to enact a law, which Abraham Lincoln signed June 30,

1864, granting Yosemite Valley and the Mariposa Grove of Giant Sequoias to California to be held "inalienable for all time." Thus was created the first "state park" in America. Galen Clark was assigned the position of guardian.

Yosemite's immortal, John Muir, made his first trip in 1868, opening 40 historic years of adventuring, exploring, interpreting, and alerting the public to its wonders. Concerned that the high country meadows, which had not been included in the state grant, were endangered by overgrazing of stock, he launched a campaign for their protection. This led to the establishment in 1890 of Yosemite as a national park. In 1892, Muir also organized the Sierra Club, now an influential national organization, to aid in the effort to secure federal administration of the entire Yosemite region. Fourteen years later, in 1906, California re-ceded the Valley and the Grove.

In 1903 President Theodore Roosevelt spent three days in the park with Muir. The first night they bedded down in fir boughs among giant trunks of the sequoias, listening to the hermit thrush and the waterfalls tumbling down the sheer cliffs. "It was like lying in a great solemn cathedral," wrote the president, "far vaster and more beautiful than any built by the hand of man."

(and from Merced all year) to Yosemite Valley; the company also runs bus service from Lake Tahoe via Tioga Pass in summer. Once in the park you can use the comfortable free shuttle buses that travel to all of the major points of interest.

Visitor Center. Yosemite Valley Visitor Center has outstanding paintings, photographs, and exhibits about the valley. During summer, demonstrations of Indian basketry are presented outdoors. Naturalists provide information on over 700 miles of trails and answer a thousand questions a day about wildflowers in bloom and guided hikes, and still enjoy their work.

A focal point of the **naturalist programs,** which began in 1920 as the first in any national park, is the Happy Isles Nature Center at the upper end of Yosemite Valley, with exhibits on animals, fish, and backpacking. Here also children 8 to 12 are invited to meetings and guided walks of the unique Junior Rangers. Interpretive facilities vary throughout the park. At Wawona the Pioneer Yosemite History Center displays old structures and conveyances associated with the early days of the area, and a collection of the works of several artists, including Thomas Moran and Chris Jorgensen. Illustrated evening campfires are conducted during the summer in Yosemite Valley, at Glacier Point, Tuolumne Meadows, Wawona, and Bridalveil Creek campgrounds.

Yosemite Valley. Filled with inspirational sights, the mile-wide valley is flanked with granite walls, domes, and peaks rising 2,000 to over 4,000 feet, and lovely waterfalls streaming down to feed the Merced River. Instead of driving your own car, try the free shuttle bus system that moves visitors on two loops in the eastern half of the valley—you'll enjoy the park more and be helping to pollute it less. At the head of the valley from the west, the massive buttress of **El Capitan,** a geological wonder, has scarcely a fracture in its entire perpendicular wall. Other imposing formations are the **Three Brothers** (named for sons of Chief Tenaya, whose tribe lived in the mountains), **Sentinel Rock, Cathedral Spires,** and, at the opposite end of the valley, mighty **Half Dome.** From high "hanging valleys," carved by glaciers, the famed waterfalls include **Upper Yosemite Fall,** dropping 1,430 feet, a height equal to nine Niagaras, and **Lower Yosemite Fall,** immediately below, dropping another 320 feet, as well as celebrated **Bridalveil, Ribbon, Vernal, Nevada,** and **Illilouette.**

Glacier Point. From the stone lookout you get a sweeping bird's-eye panorama, from the crest of the Sierra Nevada down into Yosemite Valley. Hiking trails start here, including Four Mile Trail, leading to

THE PRACTICAL GUIDE

Though some people mistakenly regard Yosemite Valley as the whole park, the valley actually occupies only 7 of the total 1,189 square miles. More than 1,100 square miles lie in the vast High Sierra region, an exciting stretch of mountain wilderness.

Plan two days here if you're on a tour of the West; allow one week for a good backcountry trip. The park has four entrances. Three are open all year: Arch Rock entrance (67 miles from Merced via El Portal); south entrance (59 miles from Fresno), connecting with Wawona Road; north entrance on Big Oak Flat Road (71 miles from Oakdale). Tioga Pass Road, the only entrance from the east, traverses the park from the high country to a junction with Big Oak Flat Road, but is open only from about June 15 to October 1.

Without a car. Airlines, railroads, and bus lines from Los Angeles and San Francisco serve Merced and Fresno, where rental cars are available. The Yosemite Transportation System (a unit of Yosemite Park and Curry Company) operates daily during summer from both cities

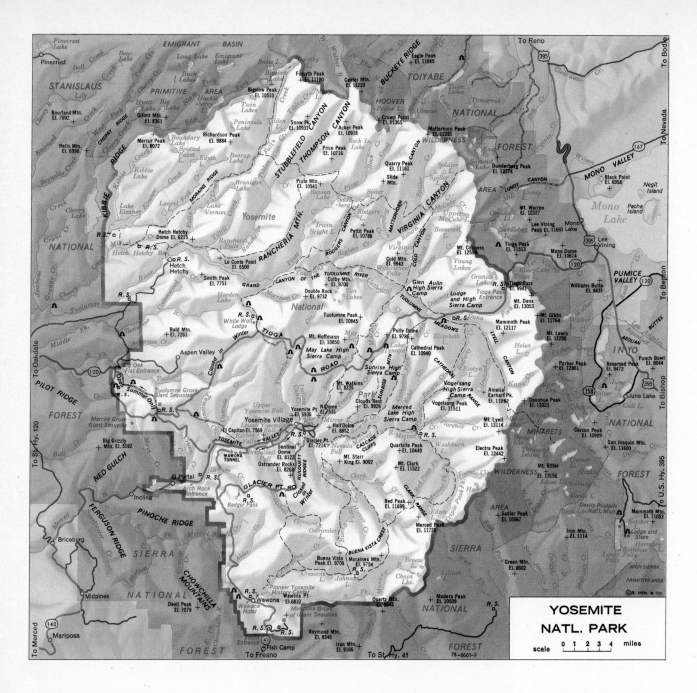

YOSEMITE
NATL. PARK

scale 0 1 2 3 4 miles

the valley 3,254 feet below.

Giant sequoias. Yosemite has three major groves of the *Sequoia gigantea,* a near relative of the coastal redwood, *Sequoia sempervirens.* The largest stand in the park, the **Mariposa Grove** near the south entrance, contains more than 200 trees, each at least ten feet in diameter, and thousands of young trees. The oldest, the Grizzly Giant, is estimated to be over 3,000 years of age and stands 209 feet tall. Visitors now park their cars in a designated area at the edge of the Mariposa Grove and ride through Muir's "Columns of Heaven" on a free tour bus. Better yet, combine a walking and riding

tour through the grove. The **Tuolumne Grove,** a group of 25 fine specimens, covers about 20 acres near the Big Oak Flat entrance. Four miles south, the **Merced Grove** contains 20 large trees. In this same region is the **"Rockefeller Tract,"** one of the finest stands of sugar pine in the world, whose purchase price was contributed by John D. Rockefeller, Jr. Though overshadowed by the giant sequoias, this stand adds to the importance of Big Oak Flat as a natural forest laboratory.

Tuolumne Meadows. This is the center of the high country, an ideal camping place and starting point for fishing, hik-

ing, and climbing trips across meadows flecked with wildflowers, tumbling streams, and along blue lakes in the shadow of glacial cliffs. It is the only one of the six permanent trail camps accessible by automobile. From this favorite region of John Muir, the **John Muir Trail** starts at Happy Isles, traverses Tuolumne, then winds its spectacular way along the Sierra Crest to Mount Whitney, 188 miles southeast, in Sequoia National Park.

Trips may be taken on foot or horseback to aptly named Waterwheel Falls, as well as to Glen Aulin, Muir Gorge, Tenaya Lake, and Soda Springs (where you can drink real soda water). During the summer the park conducts a full-scale naturalist program, including nature walks and hikes.

High Sierra by muleback. Saddle trips of six days start three times a week from Yosemite Valley, making a loop into the mountains. Overnight stops are made at the permanent trail camps, each set in an area of scenic beauty about 9 miles apart. For instance, **Glen Aulin,** the most restful of the campsites, is located at the foot of the White Cascade of the Tuolumne River, in the outer fringe of one of the finest stands of graceful mountain hemlock. Nearby is the spectacular series of falls made by the river in its drop to the Grand Canyon of the Tuolumne. **Merced Lake Camp,** at the head of one of the largest lakes bordering the western Sierra slopes, lies 13 miles from Yosemite Valley over a thrilling stretch of trail. The camps provide hot showers, wholly adequate tent accommodations, and wholesome food served camp-style. Mules are really not stubborn, just surefooted and mountain-wise. Besides the group trips, you can arrange for a guided saddle-horse-pack trip, or hire a pack burro to haul your gear while you hike. For rates and reservations write Yosemite Park and Curry Company, Yosemite National Park, California 95389.

Hiking the loop. The Yosemite Park and Curry Company also conducts seven-day trips afoot, beginning each Monday from Tuolumne Meadows, which enable you to see the mountains while tramping light. A ranger-naturalist leads the way for a maximum 15 persons in a party so that everyone gets a good understanding of trailside flora, fauna, and geology. Individuals and family groups of all ages take such trips, though anyone under 18 must be accompanied by an adult. Backpacking is also popular in Yosemite. From early June through mid-September use of the park's backcountry is regulated, with a limit of 4,000 visitors in the area at any one time. Permits are issued on a first-come, first-served basis, free of charge. Considering elevations range up to 10,000 feet, hikers are advised to spend at least a day at Tuolumne Meadows in order to acclimate to the rarefied air.

Fishing and boating. Eastern brook, rainbow, brown and, at high elevations, the sporting California golden make Yosemite a trout fishermen's park. The Tuolumne and Merced rivers, and tributary streams and lakes, remarkably clear, offer many possibilities for dry fly and a variety of lures. A California fishing license is required. Boats (but without motors) are permitted on only a few lakes; you can rent a boat at Merced Lake.

Photography. Many of the unusual rock formations are as striking in black and white as in color, as Ansel Adams, master photographer of nature, has been demonstrating for years. Ask at Best's Studio about his summer Yosemite Photography Workshop.

Accommodations. The most celebrated and expensive lodging house is the **Ahwahnee Hotel,** a work of art of another day that has not quite gone out of style. Even if you don't stay there, stop by for a drink in the El Dorado Room and a meal in the splendid dining room (dinner reservations advisable in summer). Vastly renovated and improved is **Yosemite Lodge,** with motel-type units among the pines near the foot of Yosemite Falls. The largest facility, **Camp Curry,** consists of 600 units in wood and tent cabins. The most welcome addition is the **Housekeeping Camp** along the Merced River, consisting of tent cabins rented unfurnished except for cots and stove; the visiting family can either bring or rent as much gear as needed. Besides these facilities in Yosemite Valley, other lodgings are located in beautiful Wawona Basin, Mariposa Grove, and at Glacier Point—plus the tented Tuolumne Meadows Lodge and High Sierra Camps. For rates and reservations (advisable well in advance and in all seasons), write Yosemite Park and Curry Company, Yosemite National Park, California 95389.

Yosemite Valley is a busy spot. On some summer nights as many as 10,000 people sleep there in tents, cottages, hotel rooms.

Camping. Campsites are assigned on a first-come, first-served basis, with 14-day limit (10 days in the valley). When campgrounds in the valley are full you may be sent to others at Bridalveil Creek, White Wolf, and Tuolumne Meadows, with equal conveniences and more elbowroom. Showers are available in the valley and Tuolumne Meadows; a coin laundry is open summers in the valley. Trailers are accommodated in most campgrounds, but only one trailer court, on private property at Wawona, has utility connections. There are smaller, secluded campgrounds at Yosemite Creek, Porcupine Flat, and Tenaya Lake.

Seasons. Yosemite Lodge is open all year. The Ahwahnee closes only briefly in late autumn. The Wawona Hotel and other hotels run mid-May to mid-September. One campground in Yosemite Valley and one at Wawona are open all year, but others in the park during summer only. Between April and May, when snows are melting, the great falls are at their thunderous best; mariposa lilies and other wildflowers spread carpets of color across the lower meadows. By July the upper meadows are bright with flowers and the short High Sierra season begins; by late summer, many of the falls practically disappear. To many, autumn is the finest time to see Yosemite Valley, particularly for the vista from Glacier Point, overlooking the coloring of oaks, willows, and cottonwoods. By the end of October, Big Oak Flat and Wawona roads are often in riotous display. In winter the high passes are snowed in, but the towering granite walls shelter the valley. Winter sports facilities include a large outdoor skating rink near Camp Curry, ski slopes and school at Badger Pass, 20 miles away, and ski touring trails to the hut at Ostrander Lake. The sight of forests and mountains laden with a thick blanket of white makes a winter visit worthwhile.

Nearby. An interesting approach to the park from the northwest is via California 49 and 120, through the **Mother Lode Country** and old gold mining communities like Amador City, Angels Camp, and Columbia. On the east side of the park, near Lee Vining, **Mono Lake** at 6,400 feet elevation contains a protected sea gull rookery, with boat launching and campsites on the shore. **Devils Postpile National Monument,** in a magnificent lake and forest country southeast of the park, features an extraordinary formation of colored basalt columns, some rising more than 60 feet and fitting together like the pipes of a great organ. Flanking the park are three national forests, **Inyo,** on the east; **Stanislaus,** on the northwest; and **Sierra,** on the south, all with fishing, swimming, and camping.

Recommended reading. *Gentle Wilderness—the Sierra Nevada,* text by John Muir, pictures by Richard Kauffman.

For further information write Superintendent, Yosemite National Park, California 95389.

ZION

Established as a national park, 1919

In Southern Utah, the "Land of the Rainbow Canyons," Zion presents a rich concentration of bold multicolored features. The park appeals equally to the color photographer, landscape artist, geologist (amateur or professional), trail rider, and hiker, with a special challenge awaiting the tested backcountry explorer in the aptly named "Narrows" of the Virgin River.

Through this strange land of high plateaus, deep canyons, and broad mesas, the Virgin River has cut its valley. The vertical walls of red sandstone gradually merge upward into white, while beneath them shales of purple, pink, orange, and yellow are among the most brilliantly colored rocks in the world.

These rocks reveal that at times Zion was covered with water, oceans moving in and out as the region continued to rise and then subside. At other times broad, raging rivers traversed its surface. Most of the rocks were laid as gravel, sand, mud, and limy ooze, which then consolidated and cemented. Across its six geologic epochs were periods of deserts with moving sand dunes, and of tropical lowlands with cycad and tree-fern forests. Embedded in the rocks are fossilized seashells, fish, trees, and the bones and tracks of land animals. Thus it is known that immense reptiles and dinosaurs once wallowed in marshes and bayous.

Zion Canyon, central feature of the 146,570-acre park, bespeaks the middle, or Mesozoic, period of geological history. It begins where the ancient record of the Grand Canyon leaves off, and it ends where the later history of Bryce Canyon begins. In these three parks, one can journey through a thousand million years of time, unfolding the story of this continent from one logical sequence to the next. Geologic forces, the water, wind, and ice—even the plants and animals—that shaped this narrow canyon in the Markagunt Plateau are still at play.

During spring runoffs and after a sudden summer storm, the Virgin River, an important erosion force, may become a raging torrent depositing debris at every turn—logs, rocks, and other materials from many miles distant.

Zion's "hanging gardens" in the cliffs are beautiful during spring and summer, with a cover of columbine, shooting-star, and cardinal flowers. The park's most interesting blossom, however, the "Zion moonflower," grows on the canyon floor, reaching heights of two feet and more, its large, white, trumpet-shaped flowers opening in the evening and wilting beneath the sun's rays in the morning. In contrast to the desert vegetation and water-loving plants crowding the river bottoms are the deep-green forests of pine, Douglas fir, and white fir along the cool upper ledges and at the rim of the plateau.

Human history in Zion, traced through crumbling ruins, reaches back to the Basketmakers, the earliest inhabitants of the Southwest, followed by the Pueblos, followed by the Paiutes, a peaceful people who claimed this region when the Spaniards arrived at the time of the American Revolution. It was the Mormons of the succeeding century who named it Zion, interpreted as the "heavenly city of God." The whole region was called "Dixie Land" in the hope that cotton planting would become the chief industry. It was a strange era in the Virgin Valley. Notice the frequency of religious names given to natural temples in the canyon, most of which have been retained from early Mormon days.

THE PRACTICAL GUIDE

You can see enough to make a visit of even two hours worthwhile, for many scenic attractions of Zion Canyon are visible from the roadway, but you can also take wonderful trips of two days or more into the backcountry on foot or horseback.

Zion-Mt. Carmel Highway, the approach from US 89 and the east gate (elevation 5,725 feet), ranks among the spectacular drives of the country. In descending 11 miles and 1,800 feet from the entrance, the highway passes through mile-long Zion Tunnel, where windowlike galleries gouged in the rock enable travelers to view at close range the panorama of the canyon and scenic wonders like East Temple and the Great Arch. Then it zigzags over six huge switchbacks, dropping 800 feet in less than 4 miles. The **Kolob Canyons Road** is a 5.2-mile spur leading into the northeast corner of the park from I-15.

Visitor Center. The attractive low building near the south entrance (from I-15), should be your first stop. Besides observing the museum displays, you can check the schedule of naturalist-guided walks conducted several times each day during the summer. Illustrated evening programs are presented by the naturalists nightly at park campgrounds and at Zion Lodge.

Zion Canyon Scenic Drive, a round trip of 12 miles, provides a constantly changing vista of varicolored cliffs rising above the valley floor. The dominant feature, beyond Twin Brothers, Mountain of the Sun, and Red Arch, is the towering 2,400-foot monolith called **Great White Throne.** The throne ranges in color from deep red at the base up through pale pink and gray to white at the top. North of the throne the road and river make a wide swing past a splintered crimson formation called the Organ, with Angels Landing rising 1,500 feet behind it. As the canyon steadily narrows, the roadway reaches its end at the **Temple of Sinawava,** a huge natural amphitheater, with two large stone pillars, the "altar" and "pulpit," in the center.

Weeping Rock Trail is one of two easy self-guiding nature trails. It takes only 45 minutes from the parking area at the foot of Cable Mountain climbing gradually to the Weeping Rock, with a display of wildflowers along the way. The abundant vegetation is due to water-resistant qualities in the shale; downward percolation from the highlands is interrupted, so the water streams down the rock face and seemingly "weeps." The other self-guiding trail, **Canyon Overlook,** begins at the upper end of Zion Tunnel, following the rock ledges above Clear Creek and Pine Creek Canyon through pinyon pine, juniper, yucca, and cactuses to a point directly above the Great Arch.

Narrows Trail is an easy, popular trip (of two hours or less) starting from the Temple of Sinawava and following the Virgin River up the narrow canyon to a point where there is no longer room for both river and trail—only a few feet separate walls one-quarter mile high. This is a naturalist-guided walk, but you may take it on your own. The high cliffs, springs, and seeps offer a cool, moist environment for a large variety of plants and animals. In the wider parts of the canyon are cottonwood, box elder, and desert ash. Watch for mule deer along the trail, and for tracks of skunk, bobcat, gray fox, and ringtail. You may see the "blue-bellied lizard" and a few choice snakes, including the rare, beautiful, regal ringneck. Well-maintained trails of approximately 155 miles give access to other impressive features. Going to **Angels Landing** requires a fairly strenuous 5-mile round trip to the top, but you'll be rewarded with beautiful views of the canyon. The climb up and down **Lady Mountain** is only 2 miles long, but the average round trip is about five hours. This is Zion's steepest, toughest trail, a challenge to experts.

Kolob Canyons Road (or Taylor Creek Road) leads to the northeast section of the park near Kanarraville, with overlooks commanding spectacular views. This section formerly was known as Zion National Monument. It contains the red sandstone canyons of the Kolob, almost as deep as Zion Canyon itself. Sheer walls form box canyons 1,500 feet deep. Hurricane Fault represents a displacement of rock caused by splitting of the earth's crust. Layers from the time of the Kaibab formation are clearly exposed by the fault.

Backcountry trails. Among several routes, a choice and accessible one is the **West Rim Trail,** 12.3 miles long, good for two days of backpacking, particularly by using the shelter cabin (always open) atop the rim as a base. The West Rim country, formed of deep and beautiful canyons and high forested plateaus, is rich in wildlife, with even a few cougars and such birds as swallows, nuthatches, bluebirds, and warblers. Hawks and golden eagles nest in the higher pinnacles. The Great West Canyon is about the size of Zion Canyon and as inspiring, but without automobile traffic. **Kolob Trail** affords an opportunity to view the high rugged wilderness at its best, with an excellent backpacking and horseback route and good campsites along LaVerkin Creek. The trail can be approached from several directions on the west side, but a U.S. Geological Survey topographic map should be a part of your equipment. A highlight of the trail is the side trip to the Kolob Arch, 120 feet thick and 390 feet high, even higher than the famed Rainbow Bridge. The Kolob Canyons constitute some of southern Utah's most scenic country. Several trails, starting on the headwaters of the Virgin River, north of the park, join the celebrated and unique **Narrows Trail,** which ends at the Temple of Sinawava in Zion Canyon. A three-day trip begins on Deep Creek in Dixie National Forest near Cedar Breaks National Monument. The most popular hike, 12 miles on the North Fork, starting from the vicinity of Chamberlain's Ranch, can be done in one day, but may be better in two. Much of the trip is negotiated by wading between sheer, smooth walls. Sometimes the walls overhang the stream; at other times they widen into amphitheaters of sculptured cliffs where meadows are carpeted with grass and wildflowers. Rocky bars and sandy banks in shoal areas provide campsites. Such was the way of travel of the Paiutes and the early explorers like Jedediah Smith, who named the river for a contemporary, Thomas Virgin. Weather conditions govern the trip season. It is dangerous in spring due to snow runoff from the mountains, and even more so during July and August when flash floods rise in the narrow gorge. The best months are June, September, and early October, but even then hiking parties should notify the chief ranger's office and check for advice.

Tour operator. Horseback trips are conducted by the concessioner, TWA Services, Inc., every day during the summer travel season from Zion Lodge to the East or West Rim, high over the canyon. There also are half-day trips to the Narrows or Angels Landing.

Photography possibilities are unlimited with deep shadows and bright cliffs, but along with recording scenery you can tell the story in pictures of Zion's intriguing geology. Start with the pattern of cross-bedded deposits in Checkerboard Mesa near the east entrance. Shoot the East Rim trail for Navajo sandstone, the East Temple for Carmel limestone, the Chocolate Cliffs or Belted Cliffs of Moenkopi, ancient rocks exposed to view—before long you'll find new meaning in photographs, and in your travels. During summer, midmorning is best to photograph Zion Canyon; midday is best in winter. Photography in the high country is best during morning and late afternoon.

Accommodations. In the center of Zion Canyon, Zion Lodge comprises hotel, rustic cabins, and dining room. For rates and reservations, write TWA Services,

Inc., Box 400, Cedar City, Utah 84720.

Camping. The two campgrounds in the park are the South, near the Inn, and the Watchman, just inside the south entrance station. During summer the camping limit is 14 days.

Seasons. The park is open all year (but accommodations only from May 15 to October 1). Winter is mild and snowfall light in the canyon, though higher trails become impassable. Colored cliffs stand out in contrast to snow-covered terraces and slopes. May is the time for violets, orchids, penstemons and, in shady nooks, columbine and monkey flowers. Summers are hot (up to 100 degrees), except in the high country. Late summer is a blooming time, of asters, paintbrush, and cardinal flowers.

September and October are excellent months in which to visit Zion, with clear skies, light crowds, and mild climate.

Nearby. The North Rim of the **Grand Canyon** lies 125 miles south, while **Bryce Canyon National Park** lies 89 miles northeast—a compact triumvirate of scenic and geological marvels. **Cedar Breaks National Monument,** 86 miles north on the Markagunt Plateau, contains a gigantic, multicolored natural amphitheater, the Pink Cliffs, a part of the Wasatch formation, at elevations as high as 10,700 feet. In surrounding **Dixie National Forest,** Navajo Lake is a favored vacation spot with fishing, lodge, and choice campgrounds. **Strawberry Point,** southeast of the lake, affords panoramic views across the Zion Canyon country. **St. George,** just above the state line on the road to Lake Mead and Las Vegas, is the site of the first Mormon temple in Utah; nearby **Dixie State Park** contains Snow Canyon, with walls of red and yellow sandstone.

Several motels are located at Springdale, just outside the park, as well as in nearby Cedar City, Glendale, Kanab, and St. George.

For further information write Superintendent, Zion National Park, Springdale, Utah 84767.

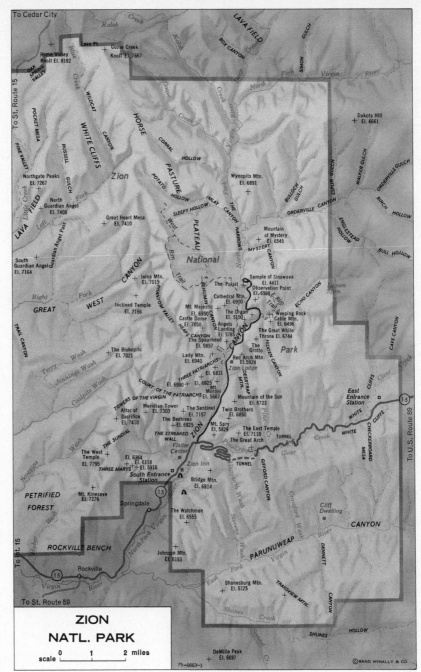

ZION
NATL. PARK

scale 0   1   2 miles

© RAND McNALLY & CO.

Enjoying the Other Parklands

The national parks and other public lands are more than places that can be identified by dots on a map. They are a *way of travel*. The national parks, monuments, recreation areas, seashores, and historic sites constitute a gallery of American treasures; treasures that inspire, instruct, and stimulate spiritual well-being —that not only enable visitors to see the U.S.A., but to understand it and all its creatures and to absorb the national heritage.

Visiting the national parks is truly an art, requiring time, training, patience. Walking through a gallery, the man who has learned how to look at pictures perceives deeper than eye level. He absorbs with his mind and senses. So too should it be with national parks.

Proper Planning. Preparing to explore the parks can be almost as important as the trip itself. The largest single reason for disappointing travel experiences is the failure to plan properly. Some people set forth without the foggiest notion of available overnight accommodations (let alone reservations), or of the location of campgrounds. Others are determined to visit a dozen national parks in the course of a week, little realizing the distances between them. By driving day and night, they may indeed pass through half a dozen parks and monuments, but they have little chance to see, and no chance to understand, the very places that attracted them.

Start by choosing the season carefully. Summer has been accepted for years as virtually the only period to visit the parks. Yet this is the very time when highways, motels, campgrounds, and restaurants are congested (and when air conditioning and community swimming pools now make life more livable at home).

More national parks are open throughout the year than most people realize. Autumn is superb. The leaves turn color; skies are clear; the sun is bright. Campgrounds may be chilly in September and October, but you can easily find space. Even in the northern parks, roads and some overnight lodgings are open until late October. Best of all, the scene is natural. Far more wildlife—deer, bison, moose, coyotes and antelope—is in evidence than during the summer peak. The animals are relatively undisturbed, the way all visitors hope to see them.

At least three national parks (Everglades, Big Bend, Virgin Islands) are at their peak of attractiveness in winter. One of the best to visit in winter is the mighty Grand Canyon, where the South Rim remains open all year. Though summers are crowded and advance reservations for lodgings are imperative, all other months are pleasant and congestion-free.

Even families that feel they must travel in summer, when children are out of school, can choose their own part of summer. The parks reach their peak of attendance from about July 10 to August 15. This is the "rush hour" that wise travelers endeavor to avoid, either by going early or waiting until the end of the season, when the crowds are turning homeward.

Exploring all the public lands. While the 38 national parks are the core of a many-sided system, they are by no means all of it. Almost 300 areas are administered by the National Park Service and all of them are included in this guide. Each of these units possesses outstanding qualities. Although the areas were established under differing laws and statutes, they are endowed with nationally significant scenic, natural, scientific, historic, or recreational features, or perhaps some combination of them.

Even in the case of national recreation areas—which are usually centered on large federally operated reservoirs and designed to emphasize water-based recreation—preeminent features of scenery, history, and wildlife (such as rare and endangered species) are protected and interpreted. For example, Lake Mead National Recreation Area, the largest unit of its type, provides extensive water sports in the Southwest. But within its nearly two million acres are far-reaching tawny deserts, deep canyons, and lofty plateaus, characteristic of the vanishing natural scene of this region. Glen Canyon National Recreation Area, another major water playground, covers more than 1,200,000 acres, much of it filled with superlative scenic beauty, with rich historical and archaeological associations.

The point is to look for uncrowded quarters in lesser-known monuments and recreation areas. The art of sophisticated travel involves choosing wisely for yourself, rather than following the beaten path. Why not discover an out-of-the-way treasure, know it intimately, and think of it as your special place? This was the way of the early park travelers, in the era when hundreds walked the trails now pounded by millions.

The rest of this guide will introduce you to the many other areas and units of the National Park System. They are grouped under four headings: "In and Around Washington, D.C." (pages 132–135), "Archaeological Areas" (pages 136–139), "Historical Areas" (pages 140–163), and "Natural and Recreational Areas" (pages 164–186). On pages 187–202 is an introduction to "The Environment of the National Parks," which can help the reader-explorer to understand the land forms, geology, and ecosystems of the park areas.

National forests and other areas. Camping and fishing, good outdoor sports, sometimes can be pursued on other lands at least as well as in the national parks, which basically are sanctuaries of nature. Instead of jamming into overstrained park campgrounds or hotels, it sometimes proves more practical to stay elsewhere.

National forests, administered by the Department of Agriculture, have thousands of well-spaced campsites in their recreation areas. The Bureau of Land Management (BLM), a sister agency of the National Park Service in the Department of the Interior, has developed hundreds of new campsites and recreation areas on the vast "public domain" that still remains in 11 western states and Alaska. The Indian people have done the same on their reservations. The traveler can set up headquarters in one of these areas, then go hiking and touring inside nearby parks.

Consider also the facilities in state parks, recreational areas administered by the Army Corps of Engineers at major public reservoirs, and private campgrounds. Campsite reservations now can be made in state parks in Vermont, Virginia, Florida, California, and several regions of New York. Lakes impounded by the Corps of Engineers, whether small flood-control reservoirs or large multipurpose projects, provide an ideal opportunity for outdoor recreation. They usually furnish campsites (with use up to 14 consecutive days), picnic areas, swimming beaches, and boat launching ramps. Fishing is available to all with valid licenses.

Wherever you go, time your trip according to climatic conditions. In the southwestern mountains, conditions usually are favorable from mid-June to early October. The desert wilderness shows its spectacular blossoms in late winter and early spring. In the parks of the northern Rockies, the best time for a wilderness trip is between July 15 and September 15. If you go into the high country too early, snow may interfere with travel, streams tend to be high and difficult to ford, trout fishing may be poor, and meadows and trails are apt to be too soft for horses. August and early September provide good weather, and the mosquitoes of early summer have gone. In the eastern national parks, autumn is an outstanding time for backcountry hiking.

Join a group. A novice does well to join an outdoors or hiking club, in which he can benefit from trips in association with experts. Some groups conduct tours, which are especially attractive for beginners. The Sierra Club (220 Bush Street, San Francisco, California 94104) has conducted a program for many years that now includes national parks in Hawaii, Alaska, and throughout the West. For families with small children, unusual burro trips of one and two weeks are held in national parks of California.

The Wilderness Society (Trip Department, 4260 East Evans Avenue, Denver, Colorado 80222) features trips by horseback, backpack, and canoe, and hiking with pack animals. Family participation is encouraged. Generally, three-fourths of the days are spent on the trail, the balance in layovers, with access to fishing streams and high meadows abloom with alpine flowers. Horses, guides, packers, canoes, food, and tents are furnished —usually everything necessary except sleeping bags.

Above all, wherever and however you may go, remember that travel to outdoor areas is at its best as the antithesis of haste. Those who spend their energies to see "all the parks" usually end up in a state of frustrated exhaustion without knowing any place well. Consider your trip to the parks, monuments, and historic places as something more than two weeks or a month away from the normal pattern of things. It's really the sum total of years past and years ahead, a fabric of enlarged vistas that span an entire lifetime.

In and Around Washington, D.C.

Includes selected parts of the National Capital Parks and other memorials and monuments in the Washington, D.C. area.

National Capital Parks in and around Washington, D.C., constitute a different kind of recreation area. Within the boundaries of the District of Columbia there are 364 park reservations, comprising 46,000 acres, including almost all the major monuments and shrines and nearly everything green in the city, from the Mall to the Civil War fortifications that once protected the capital. Now, in a period of vast urban development, the National Capital Parks provide activities and facilities from concerts, nature walks, pools, and picnic areas to jogging and bicycle trails and countless scheduled events for youngsters. Kiosks, or information booths, staffed during summer with Park Service personnel to assist visitors, can be found at these locations: Jefferson Memorial; Lincoln Memorial; Ellipse, south of the White House; the Mall, near the Smithsonian Institution; Grant Memorial, at the foot of the Capitol; and near the Washington Monument (open all year).

"Summer in the Parks" offers a season-long program of free concerts, arts and crafts programs, puppet shows, National Symphony Orchestra concerts, and numerous other diversified activities. For a daily schedule, visitors can check with Dial-A-Park at 426-6975 or call National Capital Parks at 426-6700.

For details or further information on any of these areas, write National Capital Parks, NPS, 1100 Ohio Drive, S.W., Washington, D.C. 20242.

ARLINGTON HOUSE, THE ROBERT E. LEE MEMORIAL

Virginia. George Washington Parke Custis, the adopted son of George Washington, built this splendid mansion on a bluff overlooking the Potomac and called it Arlington House. Robert E. Lee married Custis's daughter and lived here until he left for the Civil War. The house was occupied by Union troops, and at the war's close the surrounding estate was transformed into a cemetery. The stately mansion, now beautifully restored with original furnishings, faces the national capital as the frontispiece of Arlington National Cemetery, with the grave of John F. Kennedy on the knoll below.

CATOCTIN MOUNTAIN PARK

Near Thurmont, Maryland, 65 miles north of Washington. A mountain retreat of 6,000 acres. Park Central, the main park road, begins at the Visitor Center off Maryland 77, winds through the park for 4.6 miles to its junction with the Foxville-Deerfield Road. Twelve miles of well-marked trails traverse the park, leading to outstanding views and natural features. The Owens Creek Campground is available from mid-April through October for family camping. Modern rest rooms, tables, and fireplaces are provided. Camping is limited to five consecutive days and 14 days per season; a nominal fee is charged. Due to the terrain, trailers more than 22 feet in length are not permitted. A full program of interpretive services such as guided walks, talks, and campfire programs is offered; a schedule is available at the Visitor Center, which houses a small museum. The two organized camps you will pass along Park Central Road—Greentop and Misty Mount—were constructed during the early days of the recreational demonstration area to provide an outdoor experience for underprivileged children. They are now used primarily for Environmental Education and are not open to visitors. Camp David, the presidential retreat, is closed to the public, too, but you can share the beautiful natural setting.

CHESAPEAKE AND OHIO CANAL
NATIONAL HISTORICAL PARK

District of Columbia-Maryland-West Virginia. Many canals were built in the age of westward movement, but this remains one of the longest and least altered. The canal was begun with enthusiasm in 1828, designed to link Georgetown, in the District of Columbia, with Pittsburgh, on the Ohio River. However, endless difficulty and adversity slowed things down so that by 1850 it extended only as far as Cumberland, in western Maryland, and by then the railroad obviously was becoming the dominant means of transportation. The canal lingered on until 1924, principally as a carrier of coal from Cumberland to the eastern market.

At its peak, during the 1870s, about 500 boats navigated

the 185 miles from Georgetown to Cumberland, loaded with coal, flour, grains, and lumber. Each was pulled by two or three mules and raised and lowered through 75 locks along the way. All told, almost 500 structures—dams, lift locks, and lockhouses—have been left to represent the skills of the canal era.

The historic canal was placed under the National Park Service in 1938, then proclaimed a national monument in 1961; through congressional action the park was significantly enlarged in 1971 and given historical park status. Unfortunately, the following year a severe hurricane caused $50 million worth of damage, ripping 26 breaches in the canal wall, tearing 200-foot gashes in the towpath, demolishing stone locks, and washing out bridges. The hurricane weakened the 140-year-old stone aqueducts, which carried the canal over Potomac River tributaries, and two have since collapsed.

As part of the extensive repair program, the towpath was resurfaced and is back in use for its full length, open to bikers and campers as before the hurricane. All canal breaches, except one, were closed by mid-1974. The six-mile stretch from Georgetown to Lock 5 was completely restored. Rewatering of the 22-mile Georgetown-Seneca section and resumption of the popular mule-drawn barge trip is expected by 1976, possibly late in 1975. Further west, the Old Town Level area is open for fishing.

Along the towpath the National Park Service has installed a series of simple campsites, nicknamed "Hiker-Biker Overnighters," 10 miles apart, from Dam 3, opposite Harpers Ferry, to Cumberland. Antietam Creek campground is the largest one, providing access to the towpath and to fishing (for bass, catfish, and sunfish) in the nearby Potomac.

FORD'S THEATRE
Washington, where Abraham Lincoln was fatally shot by John Wilkes Booth on April 14, 1865, has been authentically restored to its appearance of that period. Plays are presented from September through May, Tuesday through Sunday evenings, and Saturday and Sunday afternoons. Some, but not all, are historic in nature. *Godspell,* the biblical rock musical, was featured for 14 months. Prices are high for the average

family. The **Lincoln Museum** in the basement houses valuable exhibits associated with the fallen president's life. A sound and light program depicting events in the assassination is presented daily, without charge.

The **House Where Lincoln Died,** directly across the street, is restored to its original appearance. Here Secretary of War Stanton uttered his memorable words, "Now he belongs to the ages."

FORT WASHINGTON
Faces Mount Vernon from the Maryland side of the Potomac River. This is an imposing bastion of another age. The first fort was built in 1809, designed by Pierre Charles L'Enfant (who laid out the city of Washington). It was destroyed by the British during the War of 1812, then subsequently rebuilt as an outer defense of the Capital. Open 7:30 a.m. to dark.

FREDERICK DOUGLASS HOME
Washington. The former slave who became a prominent statesman as well as America's leading Negro spokesman lived in this attractive 14-room home, which he named "Cedar Hill," from 1877 until his death in 1895. Its rich furnishings have been saved by organizations which protected the property through the years. The home and grounds are newly restored, overlooking Anacostia in southeastern Washington, with a view of the United States Capitol.

GEORGE WASHINGTON MEMORIAL PARKWAY
Virginia-Maryland. Landscaped with native plants, the 23-mile completed section of the parkway extends from the Capital Beltway (I-495) on the Virginia side of the Potomac River to the country's foremost mansion, George Washington's home at Mount Vernon. Since it opened in 1932, the parkway has become a well-traveled route from the nation's capital to the shrine. Many walk the paths along the Potomac, some fish, others watch birds. Picnic tables are popular.

The parkway includes important shrines and recreation areas. **Great Falls** offers spectacular views of the Potomac River gorge and falls on both sides of the river. On the Virginia side are picnic areas and remnants of an old canal

Mount Vernon

started by George Washington; on the Maryland side, the old Great Falls Tavern, C & O Canal locks, and conducted walks during summer months. At the U.S. Marine Corps War Memorial, popularly called the **Iwo Jima Memorial,** the American flag flies 24 hours a day; weekly sunset reviews are given by Marines during the summer. Nearby, the **Netherlands Carillon** represents an expression of appreciation from a small nation for help during World War II; carillon concerts are given Sundays spring to fall, and on holidays. **Arlington House** (formerly Custis Lee Mansion) is the frontispiece of Arlington Cemetery (see page 132) facing Washington. **Theodore Roosevelt Island,** reached by bridge, is an 88-acre preserve in the Potomac River with forest and swamp trails (see page 135).

At the south end of the parkway the great reward is to stroll the grounds of Mount Vernon (administered by the Mount Vernon Ladies Association) and gaze over the Potomac to the opposite shore, where some parts are preserved today much as they looked years ago. Nearby points of interest associated with Washington's family and friends include Woodlawn Plantation, Gunston Hall, and Pohick Church.

When completed, the parkway will also extend along the Maryland shore to historic Fort Washington, part of the early defense system around the national capital.

HOUSE WHERE LINCOLN DIED. See Ford's Theatre, page 133.

JEFFERSON MEMORIAL. See Thomas Jefferson National Memorial, page 135.

Jefferson Memorial

JOHN F. KENNEDY CENTER FOR THE PERFORMING ARTS
Washington. The Concert Hall, Opera Hall, Eisenhower Theater, Film Institute, and other facilities comprise a national cultural center in this overpowering structure adjacent to the Watergate Apartments on the banks of the Potomac River between Key and Memorial bridges. It opened in September 1971, and was dedicated as a memorial to the late President Kennedy. The Park Service is responsible principally for maintenance and protection. It is one of the most heavily visited buildings in Washington, handsomely furnished with gifts of other nations.

KENILWORTH AQUATIC GARDENS
Washington. Located in Anacostia Park, reached via Kenilworth Avenue, N. E., the gardens were started by a government employee as a hobby 80 years ago. Now they contain more than 100,000 water plants, including rare exotic species

Lincoln Memorial

with immense leaves up to six feet in diameter. Best time to visit is mid-June, when thousands of plants are in bloom. Late July and August are good, too, to see the tropical water lilies open. Many flowers close in the heat of day, so visit in the mornings.

LINCOLN MEMORIAL
Washington. The classical structure of dignity and beauty at the approach to Arlington Memorial Bridge is bordered by 36 columns, one for each state in the Union at the time of Lincoln's death. Within the chamber, the 19-foot marble statue of the emancipator, by Daniel Chester French, occupies the place of honor, while on flanking walls the Gettysburg Address and Second Inaugural Address are inscribed. On the wall behind the statue are these words: "In this temple as in the hearts of the people for whom he saved the Union, the memory of Abraham Lincoln is enshrined forever." Open 9 a.m. to 9 p.m.

LINCOLN MUSEUM. See Ford's Theatre, page 133.

OXON HILL CHILDREN'S FARM
Overlooking the Potomac River, a few miles south of Washington on the Maryland shore. The farm includes pens and pastures with common farm animals. Hay barn, feed room, equipment shed, and workroom are open; machinery and equipment are displayed and demonstrated.

PISCATAWAY PARK
Maryland. Seven miles of riverfront across the Potomac River from Mount Vernon will be utilized to preserve the scenic character of the lands. The historic landscape of marshes, streams, forests, and open fields enhance simple pursuits like fishing and picnicking.

PRINCE WILLIAM FOREST PARK
At Triangle, Virginia, located about 35 miles south of Washington. A forested parkland, it is an excellent place to camp on a visit to the Washington area. Approximately 35 miles of trails and fire roads afford access to the wilder regions of the park. Parking areas along park roads provide convenient starting points for many hikes. Self-guiding nature trails begin and end at each picnic area and campground. There are also bike trails in the park and rental bicycles available. Oak Ridge Campground has 120 family sites, each with a paved slip, available on a first-come, first-served basis. Turkey Run Ridge

Campground has 12 group tent sites, for which reservations are required. Travel Trailer Village, operated by a concessioner, has 64 sites—29 with connections for electricity, water, and sewage; the remainder with electricity only.

ROCK CREEK PARK
This natural woodland following winding Rock Creek through the heart of the northwest district of Washington has many flowering trees and shrubs, small mammals and birds, nature trails and bridle paths. Regular programs are conducted at the Rock Creek Nature Center. Fort Dupont and Fort Stevens played important roles during the Civil War; at the latter, President Lincoln stood on the parapet under enemy fire. West Potomac Park is the setting for the Lincoln, Jefferson, and other memorials, the Tidal Basin, and celebrated Japanese cherry trees; here one can see games of cricket and soccer. East Potomac Park offers other sports and views of the Potomac.

THEODORE ROOSEVELT MEMORIAL ISLAND
Washington. This island of plants and animals in a wild state is a living memorial to Theodore Roosevelt, who, while in the White House (1901–09), did more than any other president to preserve the nation's natural resources through establishment of the national forests and wildlife refuges. Even in Washington he loved to explore the outdoors. Roosevelt Island, one mile long and a half mile wide, lies south of Key Bridge in the Potomac. The woods and waters provide the habitat for raccoons, muskrats, and other small animals; you may see or hear a variety of birds from kingfishers to woodpeckers and wood thrushes. Interpretive programs are given frequently. The island is now accessible by footbridge from the Virginia shore. The bridge crossing its southern tip was constructed in the 1960s, despite bitter objection from Theodore Roosevelt's admirers and members of his family.

THOMAS JEFFERSON NATIONAL MEMORIAL
Washington. Reflections of the circular colonnaded structure in the waters of Washington's Tidal Basin enhance its beauty, especially in early spring when Japanese cherry trees are in blossom. Jefferson's immortal words, "I have sworn upon the altar of God eternal hostility against every form of tyranny over the mind of man," are inscribed in the memorial above the 19-foot bronze statue of the man who wrote the Declaration of Independence and served as third president of the United States. Open daily 8 a.m. to midnight.

WASHINGTON MONUMENT
Washington. A fitting monument to the father of his country, the granite shaft rises 555 feet from ground to apex. The elevator ride to the 500-foot-high observation room takes one minute. The observation windows afford the finest orientation view of the capital—on a clear day you can see everything within 20 miles. Open 9 to 5; summer, 8 a.m. to midnight.

WHITE HOUSE
Washington. The grounds of the nation's foremost residence and office are administered by the National Park Service. Many of the trees are of historic interest; every president since James Madison has planted a tree on this national estate. The White House is open to visitors Tuesday through Saturday from 10 a.m. to noon; in summer, Saturday to 2 p.m.

WOLF TRAP FARM PARK FOR THE PERFORMING ARTS
Near Vienna, Virginia, 14 miles from Washington. It has been under development since 1966. The park has become a show-

Washington Monument

case for the performing arts, ranging from opera, jazz, modern dance, ballet, and symphony concerts to lectures, folk dances, and rock. These performances in the Filene Center are held throughout the summer and on special holidays, but the park's 100 acres of lovely rolling woodland are open throughout the year, with walking paths and picnic areas available to visitors. The only park for the performing arts in the National Park System, and a unique cooperative venture between public and private funding, Wolf Trap represents an effort to make parks more relevant to the needs of the fast-growing urban population.

White House

Archaeological Areas

Many of the archaeological ruins of the Southwest were observed by the early Spanish explorers. Father Kino is believed to have discovered the Casa Grande ruin, in the Gila River Valley of Arizona, as early as 1694. Escalante, the Franciscan missionary, reported on finding extensive cliff dwellings and pueblos along his route. In 1805 the Spaniards massacred Navajos in Canyon del Muerto, a part of what is now Canyon de Chelly National Monument.

For the most part, the ruins were left as they had been lived in long before the dawn of recorded history on this continent. The aboriginal Indians had abandoned their dwellings in good condition, presumably driven out by a long period of drought in the 13th century. The Spaniards saw no promise of gold in these cities in the rock and caused little disturbance to them.

By the end of the 19th century, however, it was another story. The surge of migration from the East into the Southwest brought with it a wave of uncontrolled vandalism. Wholesale commercial looting was conducted by "pot hunters" to meet increasing demands for artifacts. Probably no cliff dwelling in the Southwest was more thoroughly dug over in search of pottery and other objects for commercial purposes than Cliff Palace,

in what is now Mesa Verde National Park. Parties of "curio seekers" camped on the ruins for several winters. Some of the treasures they carried out are now in museums, others are lost forever to science. Perhaps even worse, in the process of digging they blew out walls with powder, mutilated buried kivas, and used beams for firewood so that not a single roof was left.

In 1906, at last, Congress adopted the Act for the Preservation of American Antiquities, or the Antiquities Act, which made it a federal offense to injure, damage, or destroy antiquities on federal lands. It also provided for the establishment of national monuments by presidential proclamation. National monuments now can be established either by such proclamation or by congressional action, so long as they have national significance worth preserving—scientific, historic, or natural. All of the archaeological areas are national monuments.

Most of the archaeological national monuments administered by the National Park Service are in the Southwest, but not all of them. Others are protected by state and local communities. The most important in all parts of the country are covered in *America's Ancient Treasures,* the Rand McNally Travel Guide to Archeological Sites and Museums of Indian Lore, by Franklin Folsom.

ALIBATES FLINT QUARRIES AND TEXAS PANHANDLE PUEBLO CULTURE

Texas. On this site, 35 miles northeast of Amarillo, the Alibates mines were found and used by ancient man over 12,000 years ago—7,000 years before the pyramids were built in Egypt. The brightly colored flint was quarried for making tools and weapons. Use of Alibates flint continued into the modern period by the Plains Indians, until metal was obtained from the white man. Tours are conducted by a historian during the summer. The monument adjoins the Bates Canyon portion of Lake Meredith National Recreation Area. Traces of pre-Pueblo culture have also been found at Palo Duro Canyon State Park (noted especially for the exposure of 200 million years of geological formations). The Panhandle-Plains Historical Museum, at Canyon, presents the panorama of life in the area

from ancient to frontier times. Address: c/o Lake Meredith National Recreation Area, Box 325, Sanford, Texas 79078.

AZTEC RUINS

New Mexico. Near Farmington and the Navajo Reservation in the Four Corners country, the monument preserves the stabilized ruins of a major prehistoric Indian town built of masonry and timber in the 12th century. A giant ceremonial building, the Great Kiva, is the only restoration of its kind in North America. Pottery, weapons, and jewelry are on display at the Visitor Center. Address: Box U, Aztec, New Mexico 87410.

BANDELIER

New Mexico. This beautiful canyon country 46 miles west of Santa Fe contains many cliff and open-pueblo ruins of the late prehistoric period. The most accessible features are the ruins in Frijoles Canyon, houses of masonry one to three stories high with many cave rooms gouged out of the soft pumice stone of the cliff. The Frijoles inhabitants grew corn, beans, and squash in their oasis in the dry country. They used cotton cloth and operated a type of loom; they made glazed, decorated pottery. The story of these people, where they came from and where they went, is gradually being brought to light through research. The monument was named to honor Adolph F. A. Bandelier, who carried on an extensive survey of prehistoric ruins and Pueblo Indians in the 1880s, and who pictured early life in Frijoles Canyon in a novel, *The Delight Makers*.

The monument has an excellent museum in the Visitor Center. A self-guiding walking tour of the principal ruins takes about an hour; evening campfire programs are given in summer. Approximately 90 percent of its 29,661 acres is back-country, accessible by 60 miles of trail leading through forests and steep-walled gorges. These trails unfold the geologic, as well as archaeological, interest in the Pajarito Plateau, formed largely of tuff and basaltic lava ejected millions of years ago by a great volcano. The caldera created by the collapsed summit is among the world's largest.

The monument is open all year. Weather is favorable and relative humidity generally low. During the summer travel season, overnight accommodations and a snack bar are provided by concession facilities that blend in with the environment. A campground is situated on the mesa above the canyon. Areas of interest nearby include: Los Alamos, the atomic city; Indian pueblos along the Rio Grande; Spanish-American settlements in the Sangre de Cristo Mountains; and the cultural centers of Santa Fe and Taos. For further information write Superintendent, Bandelier National Monument, Los Alamos, New Mexico 87544.

CANYON DE CHELLY
Arizona. About 300 Navajos have their summer hogans on the floor of the 27-mile-long canyon, while they pasture cattle between sheer red sandstone walls rising 100 to 1,000 feet. Canyon de Chelly itself is joined by Canyon del Muerto, 35 miles long. Pictographs on walls of cliffs and caves date to early prehistoric occupation. Cliff-dweller ruins and natural formations like 800-foot Spider Rock make Canyon de Chelly one of the finest adventures in the Southwest. Campground and self-guiding trail. Except for the self-guiding trail (from White House Overlook to the White House Ruin), all visitors must travel with a park ranger or authorized guide—for safety reasons. Personnel from Thunderbird Lodge, near monument headquarters, conduct jeep trips daily, mid-May to mid-October. Navajo guides and rental horses are also available. The Visitor Center is open daily 8 a.m. to 5 p.m., to 6 during summer. The 83,000-acre monument lies one mile east of Chinle in the Navajo Reservation, and is reached either north from Gallup, New Mexico; south from Monument Valley; or from Holbrook, near Petrified Forest. Address: Box 8, Chinle, Arizona 86503.

CASA GRANDE RUINS
Arizona, between Phoenix and Tucson at the edge of the Pima Indian Reservation. In 1694 the Spanish missionary, Father Kino, discovered the ruins, a classic of Indian construction, and described them as "a four-story building as large as a castle." Guided ranger trips of 45 minutes; museum devoted to Arizona archaeology and ethnology. The monument lies 9 miles west of Florence. You can reach it via Arizona 87 at Coolidge or from the Coolidge exit of I-10. Address: Box 518, Coolidge, Arizona 85228.

Bandelier National Monument

Chaco Canyon

Reservation, you can see vestiges of this old system and learn how it worked. The Gila River Indian Community Council holds beneficial interest acquisition rights to the monument lands. Address: c/o Casa Grande Ruins National Monument, Box 518, Coolidge, Arizona 85228.

HOVENWEEP
Utah-Colorado. In the Four Corners region west of Mesa Verde National Park, seven clusters of prehistoric towers, pueblos, and cliff dwellings (four in Colorado, two in Utah) are reached only via dirt road. They represent the northern, or Mesa Verde, branch of the prehistoric San Juan Anasazi Culture that occupied this arid land 700 years ago. Camping facilities, but carry wood and water. Address: c/o Mesa Verde National Park, Colorado 81330.

MONTEZUMA CASTLE
Arizona. In the scenic Verde Valley, the five-story, 20-room "castle," built in a limestone cliff during the 13th and 14th centuries, is still 90 percent intact. It was a perfect natural fortress, reached only by ladders from above or below. A self-guiding trail offers views of the castle and other pueblos, but tours are not taken into the castle itself because of dangers of collapse. The monument also includes Montezuma Well, 7 miles northeast, a large limestone sinkhole rimmed with pueblos and cave houses. Visitor Center; no camping permitted. Address: Box 218, Camp Verde, Arizona 86322.

MOUND CITY GROUP
Ohio. In the Scioto Valley of southern Ohio, the prehistoric Hopewell Indians reached their cultural zenith from about 500 B.C. to A.D. 500. They are best known for artistic achievements and for erecting burial mounds. From the extraordinary

CHACO CANYON
New Mexico. Though remote and reached only by unpaved roads (New Mexico 57 north from I-40 near Gallup or 57 south from New Mexico 44 near Farmington), it contains the finest collection of prehistoric ruins representing the highest stage of Pueblo culture. To archaeology enthusiasts it's worth all the effort. Visitor Center and campground are maintained, but other lodgings and food are not to be found in the vicinity. Address: Box 156, Bloomfield, New Mexico 87413.

EFFIGY MOUNDS
Iowa. Extending for 3 miles along the bluffs of the Mississippi River near Marquette, the mounds are the remains of an Indian society of a thousand years ago. Some are in the shape of animals and birds. Self-guiding trail and Visitor Center. Address: Box K, McGregor, Iowa 52157.

GILA CLIFF DWELLINGS
New Mexico. In rugged country 45 miles north of Silver City on New Mexico 15, these small but interesting cliff dwellings are well preserved in natural cavities in the face of an overhanging volcanic cliff. Address: Route 11, Box 100, Silver City, New Mexico 88061.

GRAN QUIVIRA
New Mexico. South of Mountainair (off US 60), it contains 21 Pueblo house mounds as well as the ruins of a 17th century Spanish mission and convent. Guided tours; archaeological and historical displays at Visitor Center. Address: Route 1, Mountainair, New Mexico 87036.

HOHOKAM-PIMA
Arizona. A prehistoric people known as the Hohokam left the most valuable record of their culture at this desert location, 20 miles south of Phoenix and 80 miles northwest of Tucson. Congress designated the 1,555-acre site as a national monument in 1972 in order to preserve its "significant archaeological values, including irrigation systems in the valleys of central Arizona developed by the Hohokam and Pima Indians and their descendants." Using a well-developed system of irrigation as early as 300 B.C., the Hohokam culture endured in the harsh desert country for more than a thousand years. At the Snaketown archaeological site on the Gila River Indian

wealth of ornaments, pottery, and other items found in the mounds, archaeologists have learned a great deal about these people. An observation deck and marked trails provide a close view of the group of 24 mounds; the Visitor Center displays the fine Hopewell handiwork. Lodging and camping facilities in Chillicothe, 3 miles south, and in nearby state parks. Southern Ohio is rich in prehistoric Indian sites, including several state memorials. Address: Box 327, Chillicothe, Ohio 45601.

NAVAJO

Arizona. Three of the largest, most elaborate of known cliff dwellings are preserved in rugged country 41 miles west of Kayenta and 63 miles northeast of Tuba City, completely surrounded by the Navajo Reservation. The most accessible, 700-year-old Betatakin, or "Hillside House," once had almost 150 rooms. Displays and a slide show at the Visitor Center provide a helpful introduction to the Anasazi. In summer there are evening campfire programs. The trip to the ruin should be planned carefully; it makes a good excursion from Goulding's in Monument Valley. Campgrounds are located in the monument; trading posts and lodgings in Kayenta, Tuba City, and Shonto. Address: Tonalea, Arizona 86044.

OCMULGEE

Georgia. Substantial remains of mounds and prehistoric towns at the eastern edge of Macon trace the cultural evolution of Indian lifeways from the Wandering Hunters of about 8000 B.C. to the Creeks of the 18th century. A large reconstructed earth-covered lodge graphically depicts the mound-builder life of 900 years ago. Address: Box 4186, Macon, Georgia 31208.

PECOS

New Mexico. The remains of two ancient Indian villages and a large Spanish colonial mission are located 26 miles southeast of Santa Fe. The earliest village was inhabited during the 13th century. When the Spaniards arrived in 1540, they found a five-story communal house with 2,500 inhabitants; the following year Coronado left from here on his expedition into the Great Plains. The mission was established in the early 1600s by the Franciscans, though little more than crumbling walls remain. Museum. Address: P.O. Drawer 11, Pecos, New Mexico 87552.

PIPESTONE

Minnesota. This was a sacred place known to tribesmen of a large part of the continent. "It is not too much to say that the great Pipestone Quarry," wrote John Wesley Powell, founder of the Bureau of American Ethnology, "was the most important single location in aboriginal geography and lore." The monument now conserves the remainder of the unusual red stone from which the Indians for at least three centuries fashioned their prized calumets, or ceremonial pipes. The material is now called catlinite, in honor of the artist-explorer, George Catlin, who entered the quarries in 1836 and then gave the first published description. The Visitor Center and self-guiding trail interpret the geology and history of the area. Attractive pipes and other stone products made by local Indians are on sale. The monument lies near the town of Pipestone, in southwest Minnesota, near Sioux Falls, South Dakota. Address: Box 727, Pipestone, Minnesota 56164.

RUSSELL CAVE

Alabama. Excavated only as recently as 1953, the cave contains tools, weapons, and other evidence showing a record of life from at least 6000 B.C. to about A.D. 1650. It lies near the town of Bridgeport, close to Chattanooga, Tennessee. Visitor Center and archaeology exhibit. Address: Route 1, Box 175, Bridgeport, Alabama 35740.

TONTO

Arizona. Reached via the thrilling Apache Trail above Roosevelt Lake, the well-preserved Pueblo cliff dwellings were occupied in the 14th century by Indians farming the Salt River Valley. Small museum and steep trail. Address: Box 1088, Roosevelt, Arizona 85545.

TUZIGOOT

Arizona. In the Verde Valley near Clarkdale, the excavated ruins include a rambling pueblo which housed approximately 200 persons, with each unit individually designed—an outstanding example of late prehistoric pueblos (about A.D. 1400). Museum contains pottery, basketry, stone implements, and turquoise jewelry. Address: Box 68, Clarkdale, Arizona 86324.

Tuzigoot

WALNUT CANYON

Arizona. Cliff dwellings in shallow caves at the edge of Flagstaff were inhabited by Pueblo Indians about 800 years ago. Utilizing projecting limestone ledges as foundations, the houses apparently were built for separate families. Museum, observation building, and self-guiding trails. Address: Route 1, Box 790, Flagstaff, Arizona 86001.

WUPATKI

Arizona. Red sandstone prehistoric pueblos about 45 miles northeast of Flagstaff were occupied from about A.D. 1100 to 1225 by farming Indians, from whom the Hopi are believed to be partly descended. After the late 11th century eruption of nearby Sunset Crater made farming productive, this became one of the most densely populated sections of northern Arizona, until winds eventually removed or drifted the water-retaining cover of ash and cinders. Among the most impressive of more than 800 ruins are Wupatki, the "Tall House," and the Citadel, built at the edge of a limestone sinkhole. There also are earth lodges on the mesa tops and isolated field houses of one and two rooms, used by the Indians while tending crops. Self-guiding trail through Wupatki and Citadel ruins. Address: Tuba Star Route, Flagstaff, Arizona 86001.

Historical Areas

More than one-half of all areas of the National Park System relate directly to the aspirations, inspirations, struggles, and achievements of humankind on the American soil. These include the principal landmarks to be commemorated in the American Revolution Bicentennial in 1976.

Besides the national historical monuments, there are the national historical parks, national military parks, national battlefield parks, national historic sites, national battlefield sites, national memorials, national cemeteries, and one national memorial park. The differences in nomenclature have to do more with size and legal origin than with purpose. Most battlefields, for instance, had been administered by the War Department until transferred in 1933 to the National Park Service. Two years later Congress adopted the Historic Sites Act, directing the Park Service "to preserve for public use historic sites, buildings, and objects of national significance."

In many of these areas natural history and human history are intertwined—as they always have been in the unfolding story of the world and its people striving to find harmony with their surroundings.

ABRAHAM LINCOLN BIRTHPLACE NATIONAL HISTORIC SITE

Kentucky. A granite memorial building encloses a log cabin believed to be the one in which Abraham Lincoln was born at Hodgenville. The grounds include 116 acres of his father's farm. Address: R.F.D. 1, Hodgenville, Kentucky 42748. While in Kentucky, visit his father's boyhood home, Lincoln Homestead State Park, at Springfield.

ADAMS NATIONAL HISTORIC SITE

Massachusetts. The home at Quincy of the distinguished Adams family for four generations, beginning with the second president of the United States, is one of the finest historic houses of New England, if not the entire country. The beautiful garden was started by Mrs. John Adams. Address: 135 Adams Street, Quincy, Massachusetts 02169.

ALLEGHENY PORTAGE RAILROAD NATIONAL HISTORIC SITE AND JOHNSTOWN FLOOD NATIONAL MEMORIAL

Pennsylvania. These twin parks are being developed to interpret periods in the growth of western Pennsylvania. The Portage Railroad, built between 1831 and 1834, crossed a forested mountain divide to link the Eastern Seaboard with the Ohio Valley; the great flood of 1889 gave the nation an enduring legend. An important mission is to safeguard surviving earthworks, structures, and buildings at five locations. Address: Box 216, Johnstown, Pennsylvania 15907.

ANDERSONVILLE NATIONAL HISTORIC SITE

Georgia. In the quiet country above Americus, about 27 miles west of I-75, more than 49,000 Union soldiers were once imprisoned, 13,700 of whom died of hunger, thirst, and disease. You can walk into the stockade, outlined by stone posts, and look into the deep holes where prisoners dug with their hands, hoping to reach water, and see the beginnings of long tunnels through which they sought escape. Most of the few who got away were tracked down by bloodhounds. A quarter-mile north, at the National Cemetery (which is still open for burials), the Union soldiers are buried among giant magnolias, oaks, and arborvitae. In dramatic isolation from the rest are the graves of the six notorious Raiders, sentenced to death by the prisoners themselves. The cemetery and prison park have been well maintained by the Army. Address: Andersonville, Georgia 31711.

ANDREW JOHNSON NATIONAL HISTORIC SITE

Tennessee. The tailor shop where Johnson started his modest business in Greeneville in 1831, his attractive home, and his grave memorialize Lincoln's successor to the presidency. He would have been impeached but for one Senate vote, then achieved election to the Senate himself following the presidency. Address: Greeneville, Tennessee 37743.

ANSLEY WILCOX HOUSE NATIONAL HISTORIC SITE

New York. It was here at 641 Delaware Avenue, Buffalo, that Theodore Roosevelt took the oath of office as president of the

United States on September 14, 1901, within hours after the death of President McKinley. Roosevelt had been sidetracked into the vice-presidency by the political bosses, but once he assumed command he became the "Apostle of Energy" in the domestic and foreign policies of the nation. The site will be operated and maintained by a local group, but is not yet open to the public. Address: Regional Director, NPS, 150 Causeway Street, Boston, Massachusetts 02114.

ANTIETAM NATIONAL BATTLEFIELD SITE
Maryland. The scene of the bloody battle on September 17, 1862, between 87,000 Union troops and 41,000 Confederates, that brought to an end Lee's first northern invasion, is marked by monuments, battlefield exhibits, and Visitor Center. Cannons denote the places where six generals lost their lives. Civil War burials in the National Cemetery number more than 5,000. Address: Box 158, Sharpsburg, Maryland 21782.

APPOMATTOX COURT HOUSE
NATIONAL HISTORICAL PARK
Virginia. The village where General Lee surrendered the Confederate Army to General Grant on April 9, 1865, bringing the Civil War to an end, has been restored to present a moving and impressive picture of that day. When Grant told Lee, in the McLean House, that Confederate soldiers could keep their horses and mules to work their farms, his old foe replied, "It will be very gratifying and will do much toward conciliating our people." Address: Box 218, Appomattox, Virginia 24522.

ARKANSAS POST NATIONAL MEMORIAL
Arkansas. The site of the first European settlement in the lower Mississippi Valley and Louisiana Territory, established in 1686 by Henri de Tonti, the French "Father of Arkansas," is located 7 miles south of Gillett, 20 miles northeast of Dumas.

Five flags have flown over the oldest settlement in Arkansas. Picnicking facilities and interpretive markers. Address: Gillett, Arkansas 72055.

ARLINGTON HOUSE. See page 132.

BENJAMIN FRANKLIN NATIONAL MEMORIAL
Pennsylvania. "The American people feel a deep debt of gratitude to Benjamin Franklin for his outstanding services to the Nation as a statesman and for his achievements as a scientist and inventor," Congress declared in designating this memorial in 1972. The Benjamin Franklin Institute, which observed its 150th anniversary in 1974, has been a leader in scientific progress since its founding in 1824. The main institute building contains James Earle Frazer's 20-foot, 10½-inch marble statue of Franklin. When Franklin Memorial Hall was dedicated in 1938, delegates from 57 nations heard the message sent by President Franklin Roosevelt. The action of Congress has now conferred national recognition on the hall. Address: The Franklin Institute, 20th and Benjamin Franklin Parkway, Philadelphia, Pennsylvania 19103.

BENT'S OLD FORT NATIONAL HISTORIC SITE
Colorado. A principal outpost of civilization on the southern plains, this fort on the banks of the Arkansas River, 8 miles from La Junta, was a rendezvous for Indians, trappers, traders, and troops. It played a key role in shaping the destiny of the Southwest between 1833 and 1849. Address: Box 581, La Junta, Colorado 81050.

BIG HOLE NATIONAL BATTLEFIELD
Montana. Remains of shallow, grass-grown trenches and battle-scarred trees in a remote but scenic setting recall the fierce two-day battle in August 1877, when Indian women and

Appomattox Court House

children were slain, along with their warriors, by U.S. troops. Led by valiant Chief Joseph, the Nez Perce were making their epic retreat from Idaho when they were trapped here. The Visitor Center occupies a dramatic viewpoint high above the scene. It displays authentic relics of the battle, and garments that belonged to Chief Joseph. Markers tell how, despite defeat in the Bitterroot Valley, the Indians pressed on through Yellowstone, only to be captured 5 miles from Canada and freedom. Address: c/o Yellowstone National Park, Wyoming 83020.

BOOKER T. WASHINGTON NATIONAL MONUMENT

Virginia. In a humble, dirt-floor slave cabin, the founder of Tuskegee Institute was born. From these backcountry beginnings, he achieved respect and fame as author, educator, and orator. The 218-acre monument, comprising the original plantation and a replica of a cabin similar to his birthplace, is the only one in the park system that interprets life under slavery. The monument is a Living History Farm with farm animals and period crops cultivated with period implements. Costumed interpreters make soap, cook, and perform other plantation crafts and chores on summer Sundays. Catalpa and juniper trees that were growing when Washington was a boy still stand today. It is located at Rocky Mount, east of Roanoke. Address: Route 1, Box 195, Hardy, Virginia 24101.

BRICES CROSS ROADS NATIONAL BATTLEFIELD SITE

Mississippi. General Nathan Bedford Forrest led his cavalrymen in a brilliant tactical victory near Tupelo over a large Union force on June 10, 1864. Sherman was so impressed that he ordered his commander in the field to "go out and follow Forrest to the death, if it costs ten thousand lives and breaks the Treasury." From the high ground of the one-acre site, a large part of the scene of action is within view, identified by marker and maps. Address: c/o Natchez Trace Parkway, R.R. 5, N.T. 143, Tupelo, Mississippi 38801.

CABRILLO NATIONAL MONUMENT

California. The discovery of the coast of California by Juan Rodriguez Cabrillo in 1542 is commemorated at the scene of his landfall on Point Loma in San Diego Bay. At the southern

Cabrillo National Monument

tip, the famous old lighthouse served from 1855 to 1891. The view from its tower embraces the ocean, bays, islands, and the foothills and mountains rising beyond San Diego. Especially popular mid-December to mid-February as an observation point for watching gray whales offshore heading to Baja California from the Arctic. Address: Box 6175, San Diego, California 92106.

CARL SANDBURG HOME NATIONAL HISTORIC SITE

North Carolina. Connemara, in the highland foothills near Flat Rock, where the noted writer and poet lived the last 22 years of his life, until his death in 1967, is preserved in the 247-acre national historic site. The unpretentious white colonial-style house, with its hewn timbers and floor-to-ceiling bookshelves in every room, was built in 1838 as a summer residence for Christopher G. Menninger, secretary of the Treasury of the Confederacy. While at Connemara, Sandburg wrote many literary works, including his autobiography, *Always the Young Strangers.* The house and grounds, extensively renovated, were opened to the public in 1974. Work continues on other improvements, including trails to the quarry, pond, and mountain area where Sandburg strolled. All this helps to interpret Sandburg the man, poet, historian, and bearer of American traditions. Address: P.O. Box 395, Flat Rock, North Carolina 28731.

CASTILLO DE SAN MARCOS NATIONAL MONUMENT

Florida. Construction of the masonry fort on Matanzas Bay was started by the Spanish in 1672 in order to protect St. Augustine, northernmost outpost of their vast New World empire. Construction continued almost 25 years, using native shellstone, called coquina, and mortar made from shell lime. The white plastered walls of the symmetrical, four-bastioned structure were 30 feet high and up to 12 feet thick—a grim symbol of conquest and power. Over the years it was the target of death-dealing raids by pirates, Indians, and Englishmen. It endured major attacks and sieges in 1702 and 1740, the latter by General James Oglethorpe of Georgia, but it was never conquered. During its stormy history the fort served under four flags (Spain, Britain, Confederacy, U.S.A.) and was a military prison through much of the 19th century. Today the massive, well-preserved fort is the finest structure in St. Augustine, the oldest city in the United States. Guides lead visitors through the garrison, guardrooms, and to the gun deck. An old smoothbore gun is fired at regular intervals, adding a touch of realism. Address: 1 Castillo Drive, St. Augustine, Florida 32084.

CASTLE CLINTON NATIONAL MONUMENT

New York. Built in 1808 as a fort at the tip of Lower Manhattan, it served variously as civic garden festooned with shrubs and flowers; setting of fireworks, gala concerts, and an occasional balloon ascent; receiving depot for more than seven million immigrants following the Civil War; and, from 1896 to 1941, as a fabulous aquarium. It was rescued from destruction after World War II when Congress voted to establish the old castle-in-the-round as a national monument. Address: c/o New York City NPS Group, 26 Wall Street, New York, New York 10005.

CHALMETTE NATIONAL HISTORICAL PARK

Louisiana. At dawn on January 8, 1815, the last major land battle of the War of 1812 was fought on the Chalmette plantation, 6 miles from the heart of New Orleans. The decisive victory by the raw Americans over crack British troops had profound effects upon history. It preserved the U.S. claim to the Louisiana Territory. General Andrew Jackson emerged from the smoke of the Battle of New Orleans as a national hero, and later won the presidency. The Visitor Center and battle museum are aptly located in the historic Beauregard House, starting place for touring the battlefield. Walk to the levee for a view of the winding Mississippi. Address: Box 125, Arabi, Louisiana 70032.

CHAMIZAL NATIONAL MEMORIAL

Texas. A section of Cordova Island in the Rio Grande River at El Paso has been chosen to commemorate friendship between the United States and Mexico and the peaceful settlement of an old boundary dispute. *Chamizal* is the Spanish name for the plants which once covered the area. The national memorial, dedicated in November 1973, features a cultural pavilion, managed by a bilingual staff, designed as a center for the exchange of Mexican and American cultural programs. The 500-seat auditorium and outdoor amphitheater are both being utilized for musical and dramatic events in both Spanish and English. The Mexicans have constructed a matching memorial building in a landscaped park across the Rio Grande in Cuidad Juarez, Mexico. Address: 814 Southwest Center, 300 East Main Drive, El Paso, Texas 79901.

CHESAPEAKE AND OHIO CANAL. See page 132.

CHICAGO PORTAGE NATIONAL HISTORIC SITE

Illinois. A portion of the famous portage discovered by Marquette and Joliet and used by the pioneers to link the waters of the Great Lakes with those of the Mississippi is preserved in the nation's second largest city. Address: c/o Cook County Forest Preserve District, 536 North Harlem Avenue, River Forest, Illinois 60305.

CHICKAMAUGA AND CHATTANOOGA NATIONAL MILITARY PARK

Georgia-Tennessee. These engrossing battlefields, scenes of some of the hardest fighting during the Civil War, comprise the oldest and largest (8,113 acres) national military park. Over 2,000 markers and monuments are along the battle lines of both sides, and historical tablets tell the story of every brigade and division. From **Point Park,** on the northern tip of Lookout Mountain, there is a sweeping view of the whole area and the Moccasin Bend of the Tennessee River; while the Ochs Museum depicts both the siege and battle of Chattanooga. Chickamauga Battlefield, 7 miles south of Chattanooga, includes almost the entire scene of the first battle, with the Visitor Center a focal point for orientation and information. Here you learn that in September 1863, General Braxton Bragg with 66,000 men attacked 58,000 battle-toughened Federals under General William Rosecrans. The prize was Chattanooga, key rail center and gateway to the heart of the Confederacy. Bragg drove the Federals from the field, but his losses in killed, wounded, and missing totaled over 18,000 (compared with 16,000 Union casualties), and he failed to pursue his routed enemy, who retreated into Chattanooga. In the face of a Confederate siege, starvation seemed inevitable for the Federal soldiers; 10,000 horses and mules were killed or died. Drive to **Missionary Ridge,** where the reinforced Union army under U. S. Grant engaged the Confederates in November in an effort to break their stronghold; and to **Orchard Knob,** where Grant had his headquarters. The action was fierce in the three-day Battle of Chattanooga, which ended with a strategic Confederate withdrawal into Georgia. The siege lines were broken, and the next spring Chattanooga became the springboard for Sherman's march. Address: Box 2126, Fort Oglethorpe, Georgia 30741.

Chimney Rock

CHIMNEY ROCK NATIONAL HISTORIC SITE

Nebraska. Towering 500 feet above the North Platte River Valley, this strange rocky spire of solitary grandeur was a celebrated prairie landmark on the Oregon Trail. Many passersby swam the river to climb "this great natural curiosity," and probably to look ahead toward Scotts Bluff, 23 miles west. Chimney Rock lies southwest of Bayard, reached in the pioneer style only, afoot. Address: c/o Scotts Bluff National Monument, Box 427, Gering, Nebraska 69341.

CHRISTIANSTED NATIONAL HISTORIC SITE

St. Croix, Virgin Islands. Three city blocks on the Christiansted waterfront preserve the colonial aura when "sugar was king" and St. Croix exemplified Danish plantation society in the New World. In this stimulating environment, Alexander Hamilton lived his youthful years. Fine architectural taste was reflected in buildings like the Customhouse, Steeple Building, and Government House. Tours daily from Fort Christiansvaern. Address: Box 160, Christiansted, Virgin Islands 00820.

CITY OF REFUGE NATIONAL HISTORICAL PARK

Hawaii. On the "Big Island," the ancient place of refuge on a 20-acre lava shelf dipping into the ocean at the village of Honaunau, was a guaranteed sanctuary to vanquished war-

Jamestown, Colonial National Park

riors and taboo breakers. Here you can see prehistoric house sites, royal fish ponds, coconut groves, and spectacular shore scenery along the coves, cliffs, and tidal pools. Address: Honaunau, Kona, Hawaii 96726.

COLONIAL NATIONAL HISTORICAL PARK

Virginia. On the Virginia Peninsula, three famous places between the York and James rivers—Jamestown, Williamsburg, and Yorktown—form a triangle only 14 miles at the base, linked today by the Colonial Parkway. Each has a thrilling story of its own, starting from **Jamestown,** the first permanent English settlement in the New World, established in 1607. Jamestown Island in its entirety is a national memorial, jointly preserved by the Park Service and the Association for the Preservation of Virginia Antiquities. From the Visitor Center, a walking tour extends over the town site, along old streets and paths to the ivy-covered church where Pocahontas was married, and the ruins of early houses, taverns, and shops. A motor road loops the wildwood section of the island, while Glasshouse Point, scene of the reconstructed Jamestown glassworks of 1608, lies on the tip of the mainland across the isthmus. Adjacent to the point, a state park features a reproduction of the early "James Fort" and reconstructions of the three ships that landed here from England. **Williamsburg,** capital of the Virginia colony after the decline of Jamestown, has been restored to its 18th century appearance through the interest of the late John D. Rockefeller, Jr. More than 400 buildings stand in their colonial form; over half are original structures and the rest, faithful reproductions on original sites. From Williamsburg the parkway passes early plantation sites while following the York River to the final battleground of the American Revolution at **Yorktown.** The Siege Line Lookout on the roof deck of the Visitor Center affords a panoramic view over the strategic areas of the famous battle when Washington scored his great victory over Lord Cornwallis in 1781. A self-guiding motor drive circles the battlefield, encampment areas, and the old town. Along the tour are the famous redoubts, with cannons in place; the Moore House, where terms of surrender were drawn; and the site of Washington's headquarters. Address: Box 210, Yorktown, Virginia 23490.

CORONADO NATIONAL MEMORIAL

Arizona. Commemorating the first significant explorations by Europeans into the Southwest, the 2,834-acre memorial lies on the international boundary with Mexico, within sight of the valley through which Francisco Vasquez de Coronado and his

City of Refuge

expedition entered the present United States in 1540. From the parking area at Montezuma Pass, 30 miles west of Bisbee, a well-marked foot trail leads to Coronado Peak, and a view of San Pedro Valley and the stark country through which the bold expedition marched. Another trail, about 3 miles long, follows Smugglers' Ridge to a picnic area. Coronado failed to find the golden cities, but he brought back knowledge of vast lands, paving the way for Spanish colonization. Address: Star Route, Hereford, Arizona 85615.

COWPENS NATIONAL BATTLEFIELD SITE

South Carolina. General Daniel Morgan, despised and feared by British commanders, won a brilliant victory with backwoods militia in January 1781, raising patriot hopes. This engagement, held near the town of Gaffney, served as a link in the chain that led toward the final decision at Yorktown. Address: c/o Kings Mountain National Military Park, Box 31, Kings Mountain, North Carolina 28086.

CUMBERLAND GAP NATIONAL HISTORICAL PARK

Kentucky-Tennessee-Virginia. 20,177 acres in scenic hills where three states meet, memorializes the westward adventure of Daniel Boone and his 30 axmen who blazed the "Wilderness Road" into Kentucky, and of throngs of pioneers who followed their paths in the trans-Allegheny migration.

For almost 150 years after the European settlement of Virginia, the forbidding Allegheny ridge had kept the English colonists from Kentucky, a magic land teeming with buffalo, deer, and smaller game; a paradise for Indian hunters. Then, in 1750, Dr. Thomas Walker, surveyor for a land company, discovered the mountain pass and probed eastern Kentucky. The intrepid Boone followed on a series of hazardous explorations, culminating in the trailblazing adventure of 1775, when he and his men reached the Kentucky River and erected a fort named Boonesborough. Others came, first in a trickle, then a stream, and then a flood tide, before the final defeat of the Indians opened other routes. During the Civil War the Gap was strategically important to both sides, and changed hands several times until secured by Union troops.

The **Visitor Center,** near the Middlesboro entrance, houses paintings, pioneer tools, and weapons. Naturalist-historians answer questions and explain recreation facilities.

Pinnacle Mountain Overlook, 3,000 feet above sea level, reached on an easy 4-mile scenic drive from the Visitor Center, affords a view of the historic notch in the mountain far below; the Tri-State Peak, where Kentucky, Virginia, and Tennessee meet; and a panorama of forested mountain and valley. **Hensley,** America's "last pioneer settlement," straddling the hilly Kentucky-Virginia line like an Inca fortress, is an isolated pioneer village of 28 buildings, restored as part of a recent Job Corps project. The mountaintop village, the home of one family, the Hensleys, reached a population of about 120 in 1925; when the land was acquired for the national historical park after World War II, one lone dweller remained. You can see cabins made with hand-hewn logs, stone and wooden hinges, gun racks, plows, bee gums, possum boards for drying skins, and remains of a moonshine still. It is a good hike up the Cumberland Mountain to Hensley, but it is worth it.

Mischa Mokwa Adventure Trail, developed by the Boy Scouts and Elks of Middlesboro, offers one of the finest backcountry experiences in the East. The 21-mile trail lies in the mountains, without crossing or nearing a highway from its beginning at Wilderness Road Campground, 4 miles east of the Visitor Center, to Ewing, Virginia. It leads upward through the cool Appalachian forest to the **Goose Nest,** a limestone sink surrounded by tall virgin timbers, then continues to **Indian**

Rock Shelter, a vast area littered with flint and stone chipped by the Cherokee and Shawnee. An overnight shelter is located at **Chadwells Gap,** where natural springs and a cabin stand as they have for generations. Five miles beyond lies **Sand Cave,** with an entrance 80 feet high leading into a chamber with sand of seven different colors.

Cumberland Iron Furnace, reached on a remaining portion of the Wilderness Trail from the Gap, is one of many cold-blast, charcoal-burning furnaces of pre-industrial America.

Accommodations. Motels are available in Cumberland Gap, Tennessee, and Middlesboro, Kentucky. Modern lodge and cottages at Pine Mountain State Park, Kentucky, 15 miles away, provide an excellent base. Wilderness Road Campground, a mountaintop site inside the national historical park, is bordered on one side by sheer cliffs with a panoramic view of the valley from the opposite side. Open May 1 to October 31, with naturalist campfire programs in summer. Tent and trailer camping at Pine Mountain, with utilities.

Nearby. Less than a mile north of the Gap, **Cudjo's Cave** contains stalagmite, stalactite, and solid onyx formations. **Lincoln Memorial University** in Harrogate, Tennessee, 4 miles from the park, has a distinguished collection of Lincolniana, including books, paintings, and sculpture. At **Big Stone Gap,** Virginia, visit the restored June Tolliver House, where the heroine of John Fox's *Trail of the Lonesome Pine* actually lived, and the Southwest Virginia Museum. In Kentucky, **Middlesboro** holds interest as the scene in the 1880s of a multimillion dollar industrial scheme by an English syndicate, with an early golf course still in use; **Pine Mountain State Park** is the setting of the outdoor summer drama, *Book of Job.* **Dr. Thomas Walker State Park,** near Barbourville, contains a replica of the one-room log cabin which Dr. Walker built in 1750.

For further information write Superintendent, Cumberland Gap National Historical Park, Box 840, Middlesboro, Kentucky 40965.

CUSTER BATTLEFIELD NATIONAL MONUMENT

Montana. The Sioux and Cheyenne, in the Battle of the Little Bighorn, destroyed the flamboyant Lt. Col. George A. Custer and his troopers of the Seventh Cavalry during two hot days in June, 1876, but it was the final victory in their defense of an independent way of life. The field of "Custer's Last Stand" is in southeastern Montana, near Hardin, on the route between the Black Hills and Yellowstone. Start at the Visitor Center to see maps and dioramas of the battle, then drive the loop road over the frontier ridges where Custer and his troopers earned an immortality that victory could never have achieved. Address: Box 116, Crow Agency, Montana 59022.

DE SOTO NATIONAL MEMORIAL

Florida. On May 30, 1539, Don Hernando de Soto, Knight of Santiago, set foot on the west coast of Florida about 5 miles west of downtown Bradenton. The approximate site on the shore of Tampa Bay is commemorated by a De Soto Trail marker and the preservation of 25 surrounding breeze-swept acres. The Visitor Center offers exhibits of 16th century arms and armor and a historical documentary film on De Soto. A living history camp, complete with costumed conquistadores and crossbow demonstrations, gives the visitor an insight into the daily lives of Spanish soldiers. The half-mile interpretive trail winding around Shaws Point calls attention to plants and wildlife that De Soto probably encountered during his march. From here De Soto and his conquistadores crossed 4,000 miles of wilderness to the north and west. Address: Box 1377, Bradenton, Florida 33506.

DORCHESTER HEIGHTS NATIONAL HISTORIC SITE

Massachusetts. A memorial tower and greensward mark the location of American batteries which threatened the British in Boston leading to their evacuation of the city on March 17, 1776. It was here the Americans achieved their first real stroke of military success in the Revolution. This came about when George Washington fortified Dorchester Heights with cannon brought by Colonel Henry Knox on sleds from Fort Ticonderoga. With these strong batteries in place, the position of the British became untenable and they departed Boston; it was declared a nonfederally owned national historic site on March 17, 1951, the 175th anniversary of the British evacuation. Address: c/o Park and Recreation Department, 33 Beacon Street, Boston, Massachusetts 02108.

DOUGLASS, FREDERICK, HOME. See page 133.

EDISON NATIONAL HISTORIC SITE

New Jersey. The laboratories where Thomas A. Edison and his coworkers spent 44 years in technological investigation and development of electric generators, incandescent lamps, and the famous tinfoil phonograph of 1878 form the nucleus of this site of recent history in West Orange. The "Black Maria," a reconstruction of the master's motion picture studio, shows old films Tuesday through Saturday. His 23-room house, completely furnished as when he and his family lived in it, is laden with mementos from important visitors. Address: Box 126, Orange, New Jersey 07051.

EISENHOWER NATIONAL HISTORIC SITE

Pennsylvania. The late President Dwight D. Eisenhower donated his 230-acre Gettysburg Farm to the United States on November 27, 1967. The area will not be open to the public for some time. However, it adjoins Gettysburg National Military Park and enhances the pastoral environs of that area. Address: c/o Gettysburg National Military Park, Gettysburg, Pennsylvania 17325.

EL MORRO NATIONAL MONUMENT

New Mexico. Located 53 miles from Gallup and 42 miles from Grants (en route to Zuni Reservation). Principal feature is "Inscription Rock," a sandstone monolith bearing Indian petroglyphs, as well as inscriptions left by Spanish explorers and early western settlers. Guide service during summer; small picnic ground. Address: Ramah, New Mexico 87321.

FEDERAL HALL NATIONAL MEMORIAL

New York. On the corner of Wall and Nassau streets in downtown Manhattan, site of the present Federal Sub-Treasury Building, momentous events in American history took place. Here stood Federal Hall, where the first Congress met under the Constitution and where George Washington was inaugurated the first president. The stone on which he stood to take the oath of office is preserved in the rotunda, and one exhibit hall is set aside as a memorial to Peter Zenger, whose trial here marked a milestone in freedom of the press. Address: c/o New York City NPS Group, 26 Wall Street, New York, New York 10005.

FORD'S THEATRE. See page 133.

FORT BOWIE NATIONAL HISTORIC SITE

Arizona. Created as a military post in 1862 commanding Apache Pass at the end of the Chiricahua Mountains, the fort was the center of operations during the bloody campaign against Cochise, the famed Apache chief, and the taming of the Southwest. Many of the walls of the fort still stand. The new area also includes sections of the Butterfield Overland Trail and Stage Route, one of the oldest in the West. Address: c/o Chiricahua National Monument, Dos Cabezas Star Route, Willcox, Arizona 85643.

FORT CAROLINE NATIONAL MEMORIAL

Florida. About 10 miles east of Jacksonville along the St. Johns River, the reconstructed walls of Fort Caroline and the Visitor Center recall the French colony of 1564. It was the first European colony in North America this side of Mexico, but the following year the Spanish newcomers of St. Augustine destroyed the settlement, starting two centuries of colonial rivalry. The Spanish considered it a threat to their vast New World claims, and especially to their treasure fleets which had to sail past the Florida coast en route to the motherland. Presently they established a strong base at St. Augustine and proceeded to wipe out what they called "a pirates' nest" on their land. They also trapped and killed more than 300 of the French colonists who had sailed south and been shipwrecked near St. Augustine, at the present Fort Matanzas National Monument. The massacre finished the French in Florida.

On approaching the memorial you come first to the Visitor Center area. The Spanish-moss-draped trees bordering the entrance road, and the forest surrounding a clearing where the museum is located, inspire a feeling of stillness and isolation. The beautiful museum building, backgrounded by tall trees, stands on the ridge topping St. Johns Bluff with a spectacular view of the river here, and of the flat tidal marshes beyond.

The arch over the gate at reconstructed Fort Caroline bears the French arms and those of Gaspard de Coligny, Admiral of France, the sponsor of the colonizing enterprise. The blue French flag with golden fleurs-de-lis flies over a bastion. Four reproductions of 16th century French field cannons are placed at embrasures in the parapet.

A half-mile farther east on the road is the Ribault Column overlook, named for the Huguenot leader of the colony. From the overlook, the highest point on St. Johns Bluff, you can obtain the most commanding view of the river and also see the ocean in the distance as the French settlers did. Address: 12713 Fort Caroline Road, Jacksonville, Florida 32225.

FORT CLATSOP NATIONAL MEMORIAL

Oregon. Lewis and Clark enthusiasts will find a replica of the log fort in which the explorers spent the winter of 1805–06, after their epochal journey to the Pacific Coast. Trails from the Visitor Center, corresponding to those used by the pioneers, lead to the canoe landing and to the camp spring. Address: Route 3, Box 604FC, Astoria, Oregon 97103.

FORT DAVIS NATIONAL HISTORIC SITE

Texas. A key post in the defense system of West Texas from 1854 to 1891, Fort Davis guarded immigrants, freighters, and stages from Comanches on the San Antonio-El Paso run. The stone and adobe remains, including officers row, barracks, and hospital, are the most impressive of any Southwestern fort. It makes a worthwhile stop en route from Carlsbad Caverns to Big Bend. One unit of the officers' quarters has been furnished in period; in the summer women guides in costume are on duty to explain it. During this season a living history program includes demonstrations of adobe making, frontier cooking, and horse currying. Any day of the year you can enjoy the recording of a sundown dress parade, complete with martial music and the sounds of a mounted review. You may also want to hike the trail to the ridge crest for another perspective of the fort. Adjacent is scenic Davis Mountain State Park (lodge, camping, hiking trails). Address: Box 785, Fort Davis, Texas 79734.

FORT DONELSON NATIONAL MILITARY PARK
Tennessee. The well-preserved fort, rifle pits, and batteries, along with many markers and tablets, trace the course of action near Dover in early 1862, when General U. S. Grant made bold use of the Tennessee River. He moved 17,000 men on transports, then marched them across a watershed between the Tennessee and Cumberland, and attacked. After intensive action Grant's demand for "unconditional surrender" resulted in the capture of 14,000 Confederate troops and opened a river route into the heart of the Confederacy. Visitor Center contains exhibits and slides. Almost 800 war dead are buried in the national cemetery, with a heart-shaped arrangement of headstones over Union graves. Address: Box F, Dover, Tennessee 37058.

FORT FREDERICA NATIONAL MONUMENT
Georgia. The ruins of the fort on St. Simons Island symbolize Great Britain's struggle to hold southeastern coastal lands against the Spaniards. In its day this was the largest, most costly British fort in America, built of "tabby"—a mixture of oystershell, sand, and lime. In 1742 the Spanish fleet and army attacked, but James Oglethorpe, founder of the Georgia colony, scored a decisive victory in the aptly named Battle of Bloody Marsh fought nearby. The excellent Visitor Center and markers unfold the story in a tranquil setting beneath moss-draped live oaks. Address: Box 816, St. Simons Island, Georgia 31522.

FORT JEFFERSON NATIONAL MONUMENT
Florida. Work on the largest all-masonry fortification in the Western world began in 1846 in the Dry Tortugas, 70 miles west of Key West, as part of the chain of seacoast defenses strung from Maine to Texas. Though construction continued 30 years, it was never really finished and never saw action, but served as a Federal military prison during and after the Civil War. The monument may be even more important today as a natural area, with reefs of coral and "forests" of marine plants providing refuge for the myriad forms of animal life in nature's aquarium. Between May and September terns land by the thousands for their nesting season, while frigate birds glide on thermal drafts above the fort. This is an isolated wilderness, to which visitors make their own way via seaplane or boat. Address: c/o Everglades National Park, Box 279, Homestead, Florida 33030.

FORT LARAMIE NATIONAL HISTORIC SITE
Wyoming. Nestled in the narrow valley of the Laramie River near its junction with the North Platte, Fort Laramie was a frontier center for trade, diplomacy, and warfare from 1834 to 1890. Over the years it was associated with Kit Carson, Jim Bridger, Buffalo Bill, General John C. Fremont, and countless wagon trains heading west. Today 11 original structures, including "Old Bedlam" (post headquarters) and the Sutler's Store, have been restored, surrounded by eloquent ruins of others. The commissary serves as Visitor Center; guided tours during summer. Address: Fort Laramie, Wyoming 82212.

FORT LARNED NATIONAL HISTORIC SITE
Kansas. As a key frontier post established in 1859, this fort guarded the eastern part of the Santa Fe Trail and served as a base of operations against the Plains Indians. Nine of its original sandstone buildings still stand at the quadrangle. The

enlisted men's barracks were probably begun in 1866 and, except for the addition of roofs, are basically unchanged. The west barracks serves as the Visitor Center. Exhibits are also located in the west end of the old commissary. Fort Larned is located 6 miles west of the city of Larned. Address: Route 3, Larned, Kansas 67550.

FORT McHENRY NATIONAL MONUMENT
Maryland. From a vessel offshore in the Patapsco River, Francis Scott Key, who had gone to secure the release of a friend from the British fleet, witnessed the 25-hour bombardment of this fort at the entrance to Baltimore's inner harbor. A barrage of 1,500 to 1,800 bombs, rockets, and shells was fired until after midnight. In the morning, when he saw the Stars and Stripes still waving, he began his immortal lines on the back of a letter. So the National Anthem was born. The Visitor Center contains exhibits on the history of the fort and its place in the War of 1812. Address: Baltimore, Maryland 21230.

FORT MATANZAS NATIONAL MONUMENT
Florida. On the southern tip of Anastasia Island in 1565, a Spanish commander put to death two bands of French prisoners and eliminated the threat of continued French settlement in Florida. Later, in 1742, the Spaniards built Fort Matanzas on nearby Rattlesnake Island to protect St. Augustine's south entrance from Oglethorpe's attack—and it worked. Visitors may view the fort from the dock on Anastasia Island on Florida A1A, or take a ferry to Rattlesnake Island (daily all year). Address: c/o Castillo de San Marcos National Monument, 1 Castillo Drive, St. Augustine, Florida 32084.

FORT NECESSITY NATIONAL BATTLEFIELD
Pennsylvania. The little stockaded fort near Uniontown where George Washington engaged in his first major battle—which signaled the opening of the French and Indian War—has been reconstructed for the benefit of new generations. The battle took place July 3, 1754, when Washington, a young lieutenant colonel heading a Virginia force, was surrounded by 600 French and 100 Indians.

After sporadic fighting, the colonials negotiated their withdrawal. But this sparked the power conflict between England and France in the New World, a reverberation of the Seven Years' War then taking place in Europe. It ended in 1763 with the expulsion of French power from North America and India. Details of the fort (which the French burned after the surrender) were unknown for nearly 200 years. Finally a document was discovered describing it as a circular enclosure. Archaeological research then revealed the exact location, shape, and size, making possible the present replica of the fort, entrenchments, earthworks, and log cabin.

Three nearby areas should be included in your visit. Jumonville Glen, about 6 miles away, was the scene of a wild preliminary skirmish after Washington had led a striking force of 40 men on an all-night march. Braddock's Grave, 1 mile from the fort, marks the site where Major General Edward Braddock, commander of all British soldiers in the American colonies, was buried in 1755 after being mortally wounded in the Battle of Monongahela. (His aide-de-camp, George Washington, had two horses shot from under him.) Mount Washington Tavern, overlooking Fort Necessity, typifies the sturdy stage stations built during the 1820s on the Old National Pike, when it was a mainstream of travel to the West. It is now a museum of the early pioneer period. Address: c/o Allegheny Portage Railroad National Historic Site, Box 216, Johnstown, Pennsylvania 15907.

FORT POINT NATIONAL HISTORIC SITE

California. Preserved here, in the Presidio near the south end of the Golden Gate Bridge is the massive brick fortification built by the Army between 1854 and 1861 to guard the entrance to San Francisco Bay.

Forts in America are somewhat similar to castles in Europe—relatively numerous and obsolete for all practical purposes. Of the few of truly outstanding architecture, Fort Point is one, incorporating most of the technical refinements into the masterwork of the Pacific Coast. It was used over a wide span of military history, from the Civil War down through the Indian Wars and the Spanish American War. Address: Box 9163, San Francisco, California 94129.

FORT PULASKI NATIONAL MONUMENT

Georgia. Built in the 19th century with 25 million bricks and walls 11 feet thick, it took 18 years to complete the massive structure on Cockspur Island commanding the mouth of the Savannah River, 17 miles east of Savannah. In the long casemated galleries are examples of some of the finest brick-arch masonry in America. Surrounded by a moat, Pulaski was declared impregnable at a time when smoothbore guns would do little damage beyond 1,000 yards. And then came the Civil War.

The fort was taken first by the Confederates, but in 1862 Union forces on Tybee Island, a mile distant, unleashed a bombardment with a new weapon, the rifled gun. Within 30 hours the fort surrendered, and the era of the moated medieval fortress was done. As you make your tour, notice the solid walls and the amazing detail of the brickwork; each brick was hand-cut and trimmed. Cross the parade ground, where Robert E. Lee stood and declared the fort invulnerable, and climb the parapet where the Confederate flag was lowered after the walls had been pocked with Yankee shells, many of which are still embedded. History aside, Fort Pulaski lies in a natural setting bordered by marsh and woodland; its moat, though a military failure, serves successfully as a rendezvous for semitropical plants and for birds like the heron, crane, and egret. The best time for Pulaski is spring, and the ideal base is Savannah, distinguished by palmetto-shaded squares, really small parks, and block after block of restored buildings. On the drive out, across tidal marshes and winding rivers, visit Bonaventure Cemetery, originally a colonial plantation, where weathered tombstones are brightened by camellias, wisteria, and azalea, yet shaded by live oak. For further information write Superintendent, Fort Pulaski National Monument, Box 98, Savannah Beach, Georgia 31328.

FORT RALEIGH NATIONAL HISTORIC SITE

North Carolina. The restored fort occupies the site of the legendary "Lost Colony," the first attempted English settlement within the bounds of the present United States. The 150 men, women, and children sent by Sir Walter Raleigh arrived at Roanoke Island on the Outer Banks in July 1587. One month later the first child of English parentage in the New World, Virginia Dare, was born. But when Governor John White went to England and then returned to Roanoke Island in August 1590, he found the colony had disappeared. The only clue he found was the word "CROATOAN" carved on a tree. The mystery of the "Lost Colony" has never been solved. Illustrated talks are given in the Visitor Center, which houses excavated artifacts. The center is the starting place of the scenic Thomas Hariot Trail, named for the eminent natural scientist of the 1587 expedition. Vegetation along the way is like that seen by the first settlers—plants used by the Indians and early settlers.

The Elizabethan Garden, adjacent to the national historic site, was created by interested local citizens as a memorial to the first settlers. In a setting of carefully planned and tended flowers, shrubs, and trees, such as a homesick colonist might have cultivated, subjects of exceptional interest include the gatehouse, wrought-iron gates, an armillary sundial, and a fountain of Pompeian stone. Overlooking Roanoke Sound is Waterside Theatre, the scene of an impressive outdoor drama, the *Lost Colony,* given on summer evenings.

Spring and fall are choice times. In April the dogwoods bloom with large, white flowers. In the fall, these same trees have bright red leaves and berries. The island hardwoods offer beautiful coloration in October and November. Good sunny days are prevalent from April through November. After this, cloudy and rainy days are common, but they, too, enhance the historical scene.

The nearby Outer Banks stretch 120 miles along the coast, forming a barrier between the Atlantic Ocean and the interior sounds and constantly undergoing changes caused by wind and wave. Cape Hatteras National Seashore and the Wright Brothers National Memorial should be visited. Address: c/o Cape Hatteras National Seashore, Box 457, Manteo, North Carolina 27954.

FORT SCOTT HISTORIC AREA

Kansas. Through cooperative activity with the state and local governments, vestiges of pre-Civil War conflicts typical of the "Bloody Kansas" period are to be preserved. These include old Fort Scott, which the city of that name will operate and display, and the sites of at least three battles between Free-Staters and pro-slave forces—Osawatomie, Mine Creek, and the Marais de Cygnes Massacre. Address: c/o Fort Larned National Historic Site, P.O. Box 49, Larned, Kansas 67550.

FORT SMITH NATIONAL HISTORIC SITE

Arkansas. Although one of the first U.S. military posts in the Louisiana Territory, two decades—the 1870s and 1880s—represent Fort Smith's period of greatest fame. During that period it sheltered a famous tribunal, the court of Isaac C. Parker, the "Hanging Judge," who sentenced 151 men to the gallows while spreading law to the raw frontier. The site preserves the remains of two forts and Judge Parker's court. Address: Box 1406, Fort Smith, Arkansas 72902.

FORT STANWIX NATIONAL MONUMENT

New York. The British built this fort in 1758 to protect a major Mohawk River portage in the French and Indian War. The 18-acre site is now in the center of the city of Rome, New York. Though the fort no longer stands, its outlines remain and it is being completely reconstructed as it was, in time for the 1976 Bicentennial. The fort was the scene in 1768 of the Indian Treaty of Fort Stanwix, in which the Iroquois ceded to the British a vast area east of the Ohio River. When the British attacked the colonies from Canada in August 1777, during the Revolution, the fort withstood siege. Six miles away, General Nicholas Herkimer defeated British Colonel Barry St. Leger in the Battle of Oriskany, the bloodiest battle of the Revolution, on August 4, 1777. The British eventually gave up their attempt to invade the colonies down the Mohawk Valley. Address: c/o New York City NPS Group, 26 Wall Street, New York, New York 10005.

FORT SUMTER NATIONAL MONUMENT

South Carolina. The five-sided fort, built on a small island in Charleston harbor as part of the chain of coastal fortifications, gained a place in history on April 12, 1861, when Confederate

troops fired the opening shots of the Civil War at the small Federal garrison striving to hold it. For 34 hours the fort was defended until, as the commanding officer reported, "the quarters were entirely burned, the main gates destroyed by fire, the gorge walls seriously injured, the magazines surrounded by flames." After the Confederates occupied the fort, it became a symbol. For nearly two years Federal forces were held at bay, despite siege and bombardment, until the Confederates made their evacuation in February 1865. Today the fort is reached on regular two-hour boat tours from the Municipal Yacht Basin in the harbor. The visitor should not overlook Fort Moultrie, a part of the national monument accessible by car on Sullivans Island, the scene of the first decisive victory of the American Revolution in 1776, and the burial place of the valiant Indian chief Osceola. It is destined for new recognition as part of the 1976 Bicentennial celebration. Address: Drawer R, Sullivans Island, South Carolina 29482.

FORT UNION NATIONAL MONUMENT

New Mexico. Located on the route of the Santa Fe Trail, 26 miles north of Las Vegas (New Mexico), where the mountains meet the plains, this fort was the largest military post guarding the 19th century Southwestern frontier. Kit Carson and Phil Sheridan were two of the lustrous figures who served here. Only adobe walls and chimneys rising starkly from the plains remain today, but a self-guiding trail leads through the ruins, while displays at the Visitor Center recall the drama and adventure of yesterday's Southwest. Address: Watrous, New Mexico 87753.

FORT UNION TRADING POST NATIONAL HISTORIC SITE

North Dakota-Montana. As the principal fur-trading center on the upper Missouri River for four decades, Fort Union became a stopping place for every important trailblazer, trapper, soldier, and traveler, from Jim Bridger to John J. Audubon and George Catlin. Remains of the fort, located south of Williston, include masonry bastions and earth-mound outlines. Address: c/o Theodore Roosevelt National Memorial Park, Medora, North Dakota 58645.

FORT VANCOUVER NATIONAL HISTORIC SITE

Washington. Founded by the Hudson's Bay Company in 1825, stockaded Fort Vancouver became the hub of all trading activity, as well as the political, social, cultural, and military center for the vast Pacific Northwest. The original stockade and buildings are outlined on the site, adjacent to the still-active post now called Vancouver Barracks, where Grant, Custer, Sheridan, and George C. Marshall served. Address: Vancouver, Washington 98661.

FRANKLIN, BENJAMIN, NATIONAL MEMORIAL. See Benjamin Franklin National Memorial, page 141.

FREDERICKSBURG AND SPOTSYLVANIA COUNTY BATTLEFIELDS MEMORIAL NATIONAL MILITARY PARK

Virginia. No other area of comparable size on the American continent has witnessed such heavy and continuous fighting as this setting of four major Civil War battles within a 17-mile radius. The Visitor Centers near the southern edge of Fredericksburg and at Chancellorsville feature dioramas, pictorial displays, and maps, while narrative markers and monuments interpret the field of action with miles of original, well-preserved trench remains and gun pits. Fredericksburg, midway between the two capitals of Washington and Richmond, became the scene of fierce action in December 1862. You can see where Longstreet's men fired point-blank from Marye's Heights at charging Federals along the Sunken Road and forced them to retreat over the Rappahannock. One year later the Confederates won another signal victory at Chancellorsville, but Stonewall Jackson was accidentally wounded by his own men and died at Guiney Station (now Stonewall Jackson Memorial Shrine). At battles of the Wilderness and Spotsylvania Court House, in March and May, 1865, a determined Union army under Grant began the final drive that sealed the

Confederacy. Bitter fighting led to a savage hand-to-hand struggle of almost 24 hours' duration at the point known as the Bloody Angle. Over 15,000 dead are buried in the National Cemetery here, including 12,000 unidentified of both sides. Address: Box 679, Fredericksburg, Virginia 22401.

GENERAL GRANT NATIONAL MEMORIAL

New York. On a bluff overlooking the Hudson River in Manhattan, the gray granite memorial to the great soldier who commanded the Union armies contains the sarcophagi of General Grant and his wife. To the rear are two trophy rooms displaying battle flags and mural maps. Address: c/o New York City NPS Group, 26 Wall Street, New York, New York 10005.

GEORGE ROGERS CLARK NATIONAL HISTORICAL PARK

Indiana. In the oldest city of the state, Vincennes, the imposing circular, domed memorial to George Rogers Clark celebrates his heroism in the winning of the Northwest. The 22 acres of formally landscaped grounds surrounding the stately memorial occupy part of the site of Fort Sackville, with the Wabash River flowing by and forming the western boundary. As early as 1732 the French built the first fort here, but lost it in time to the English.

Within the memorial rotunda a bronze statue of Clark, the fiery young Virginian, is flanked by seven large murals, each depicting a dramatic scene in his expedition of 1778–79, when his little army swept the British out of the Northwest frontier.

Near the memorial other historic structures are well worth visiting. The white-spired St. Francis Xavier Church, built in 1826 on the site of the first log church, is a prominent reminder of French Catholic religious roots in the beginnings of the American nation. In front of it lies the old French Cemetery. At the other end of town are important points of interest, including Grouseland, the home of William Henry Harrison while he was the first governor of the Indiana Territory; the two-story frame building that served as first capitol of the territory; and the adjacent Printing Office, where the pioneer newspaper of the territory appeared in 1804.

In summer a "Trailblazer" train operated by Vincennes University tours these and other sites. Address: 115 Dubois Street, Vincennes, Indiana 47591.

GEORGE WASHINGTON BIRTHPLACE NATIONAL MONUMENT

Virginia. A pastoral setting on the bank of Pope's Creek, about 38 miles east of Fredericksburg, marks the ancestral plantation where George Washington was born; even sheep graze in the meadows. The original house burned; the present structure, designed to represent a typical planter's quarters, is carefully furnished in the period of Washington's boyhood. On the grounds of the estate, the family burial plot contains the remains of his father, grandfather, and great-grandfather. Important additions have been made in recent years, including a colonial "living farm," complete with Morgan horses and a colonial garden. A few miles south along the Potomac is Stratford Hall, the ancestral estate of the Lees of Virginia and birthplace of Robert E. Lee. Address: c/o Fredericksburg National Military Park, Box 679, Fredericksburg, Virginia 22401.

GEORGE WASHINGTON CARVER NATIONAL MONUMENT

Missouri. Birthplace of a slave who rose to fame as botanist, agronomist, and pioneer conservationist, the monument is located a few miles southeast of Joplin. The Visitor Center traces Carver's career and mighty achievements, including his developing new uses for Alabama clay, peanuts, sweet potatoes, and cotton. A self-guiding trail winds along the stream and through the same woods and fields he knew as a boy. Address: Box 38, Diamond, Missouri 64840.

GETTYSBURG NATIONAL MILITARY PARK

Pennsylvania. Of more than 2,000 land engagements during the Civil War, Gettysburg ranks first in the memory of a nation. On the three days of July 1, 2, and 3, 1863, more men died than in any other battle ever fought on the soil of North America. Under terrible strains and sacrifices, the Confederate Army of 75,000 under Lee reached its high-water mark, but met its match in 97,000 Union troops under Meade and was turned back. Then, four months later, a portion of the battleground was dedicated as a burial ground by President Lincoln in a speech of 296 immortal words. When you come to Gettysburg, you will find many entertaining commercial diversions. If you have come for an absorbing historical experience and are traveling on a careful budget, choose carefully. Your starting point should be the handsome modern **Visitor Center** of the National Park Service. It houses exhibits, an auditorium with a slide orientation, and the mammoth circular painting called the *Cyclorama,* depicting Pickett's Charge, the thrust of 15,000 heroic Confederates in dressed ranks across the mile-wide open fields, the supreme effort that failed. Take your youngsters to the **Campfire Program** at the amphitheater in Pitzer's Woods nightly at dusk during June, July, and August, where they can hear a talk on the Civil War soldier and see a Hollywood film, "The Battle of Gettysburg." From the Visitor Center, take the **one-hour walking tour** or the **two-hour auto tour** over the battlefield—the routes are well marked, and monuments and memorials are more eloquent than spoken words. You will see the **High Water Mark,** the climax of Gettysburg, where Pickett's Charge was halted; the **Pennsylvania Monument,** with statues of officers and the names of 35,000 Pennsylvanians who fought in the ranks; the **Virginia Memorial,** surmounted by a statue of General Robert E. Lee on his horse, Traveller; the spirited monuments of other states, possibly including your own; the **Eternal Light Peace Memorial,** dedicated to "peace eternal in a nation united"; and the **National Cemetery,** where Lincoln rose to his full height on November 19, 1863, and transformed the word Gettysburg from memorial to the dead into inspiration for the living. Address: Box 70, Gettysburg, Pennsylvania 17325.

Gettysburg Battlefield

GOLDEN SPIKE NATIONAL HISTORIC SITE
Utah. The ceremony on May 10, 1869, when the Union Pacific from the East met the Central Pacific from the West, is commemorated on seven historic acres. Thirty miles west of Brigham City the first complete rail link across the country was forged. The site includes about 15 miles of the old right-of-way. Address: 623 South Main Street, Box 639, Brigham City, Utah 84302.

GRAND PORTAGE NATIONAL MONUMENT
Minnesota. On the site of the old North West Company depot, bordering serene Grand Portage Bay, a newly reconstructed stockade (replacing an earlier one that burned) recalls the adventurous age when voyageurs, seeking a treasure in furs, transferred supplies and trade goods from Lake Superior to the border lakes canoe route. The "great depot," established in 1778 near the Canadian boundary, was the first white settlement in Minnesota, a vital link in the 3,000-mile waterway extending from Montreal to Western Canada. Much of the charm of the 770-acre monument today is in the centuries-old trail—the 9-mile portage, with its lichen-covered rocks, reindeer moss, and thundering Pigeon Falls, one of several obstacles to canoe travel that made the portage necessary. During summer, a naturalist-historian is on duty at the fort; excursion boats operate from Grand Portage to Isle Royale National Park, 25 miles away in Lake Superior. Address: Box 666, Grand Marais, Minnesota 55604.

GRANT-KOHRS RANCH NATIONAL HISTORIC SITE
Montana. Located in the Deer Lodge Valley, north of Yellowstone, the headquarters of a 19th century cattle kingdom—one of the giant "spreads" of the Old West—still preserves early log buildings and main ranch house. Saddles, tools, wagons, buggies and other artifacts have been donated to complete the cattleman's saga. Address: c/o Yellowstone National Park, Wyoming 83020.

GUILFORD COURTHOUSE NATIONAL MILITARY PARK
North Carolina. In gentle rolling country near Greensboro, the battle fought here in March 1781 was part of the British campaign to subdue the southern colonies one by one while advancing north. Though the strategy had already backfired at Kings Mountain and Cowpens, Cornwallis won this battle over General Nathanael Greene's poorly equipped colonials. But he lost 25 percent of his troops, and when he advanced into Virginia, it was to the ultimate defeat at Yorktown. Graphic, colorful exhibits at the Visitor Center tell the story of the Southern campaign, while memorials are located at various points on the battlefield. Address: Box 9334, Plaza Station, Greensboro, North Carolina 27408.

HAMILTON GRANGE NATIONAL MEMORIAL
New York. The only home ever owned by Alexander Hamilton, a principal figure in shaping the Republic, and one of the few Federal period structures surviving in New York City, The Grange was safeguarded by the American Scenic & Historic Preservation Society until its recent transfer to the federal government. Address: c/o New York City NPS Group, 26 Wall Street, New York, New York 10005.

HAMPTON NATIONAL HISTORIC SITE
Maryland. A distinguished Georgian mansion built with formal charm and elegance during the latter part of the 18th century lies on a 48-acre tract near Towson, north of Baltimore. Formal gardens, tearoom, and antique shop. Open Tuesday through Saturday, 11 a.m. to 5 p.m., Sunday, 1 p.m. to 5 p.m. Address: c/o Fort McHenry National Monument, Baltimore, Maryland 21230.

Harpers Ferry, an early painting

HARPERS FERRY NATIONAL HISTORICAL PARK
West Virginia-Maryland. In the shadow of the Blue Ridge Mountains, where the Shenandoah and Potomac rivers meet, the reddish-gray hillside town became the scene of John Brown's ill-fated abolitionist raid in 1859, which forced the nation to realize the slavery issue was inescapable. The Visitor Center and museum are located in the paymaster's headquarters of the old arsenal that was the target of Brown's little band in its effort to arm the slaves and establish a free state in the mountains. Gun buffs will appreciate the breech-loading Hall rifles on display. Though Brown's men captured the arsenal, within two days they were driven to refuge in the little engine house known as "John Brown's Fort" and forced to surrender. It is located at what is now the Stephen T. Mather Center of the National Park Academy. When the Civil War broke out two years after Brown's raid, the town was almost a continual battleground and finally was left in ruins. Follow the marked half-mile walking tour (about one hour) past restored old houses, and to the heights of Jefferson Rock, for a view of the rivers favored by Thomas Jefferson. May and June are especially attractive months in this area, when redbud, dogwood, and wildflowers bloom; October coloring on the three heights above the rivers is spectacular. Address: Box 117, Harpers Ferry, West Virginia 25425.

HERBERT HOOVER NATIONAL HISTORIC SITE

Iowa. At West Branch, the 31st president of the United States was born August 10, 1874, in a simple two-room cottage that still stands and forms the nucleus of this attractive, landscaped area. Here, too, are the grave, where he was buried in 1964 while 75,000 mourners stood in silent tribute, and the gleaming limestone Hoover Presidential Library, a museum full of mementos of a life of humanitarianism and public service. Address: P.O. Box B, West Branch, Iowa 52358.

HOME OF FRANKLIN D. ROOSEVELT NATIONAL HISTORIC SITE

New York. The house at the edge of a gently rolling plateau overlooking the Hudson River where the "Squire of Hyde Park" was born and reared was ample for the large family, but scarcely reflects elegance or opulence. The mood is set by the surrounding woodlands he loved and helped to plant, and by the burial place where he and his wife lie beneath a plain white marble monument within a garden where roses bloom. Oil portraits, gifts of crystal, gold, and brocade, tokens sent by emperors and little people—these are housed with 30,000 volumes and vast correspondence in the adjacent Franklin D. Roosevelt Library, a source of learning for scholars and schoolchildren for generations to come. Closed Monday, except June 15 to Labor Day. Visiting hours 9 a.m. to 5 p.m., but arrive early during summer and on weekends to ensure admittance. Address: Hyde Park, Dutchess County, New York 12538.

HOMESTEAD NATIONAL MONUMENT

Nebraska. A T-shaped quarter section of prairie and woodland, 160 acres, near Beatrice (due south of Lincoln), is on the site of the claim of one Daniel Freeman, an Illinois farmer, who became one of the first to file for free land under the Homestead Act. This law, signed by Abraham Lincoln in 1862, was an epochal advance in democracy, enabling over one million citizens to become landholders. The Visitor Center displays trace development of the Homestead movement. The adjacent cabin is furnished to the finest details with remnants of the belongings of the people who once called it home. In a covered, yet open-air display behind the Center are farm implements and carriages. History touches everything, even to

Homestead National Monument

the mile-long nature trail. The path winds through native prairie and densely wooded areas, reaching its high point at the graves of Freeman and his wife Agnes, high on a windswept hill. The monument was recently expanded to include the Freeman School, built with brick from the homesteader's kiln in 1871. It will be restored as funds become available. Address: Beatrice, Nebraska 68310.

HOPEWELL VILLAGE NATIONAL HISTORIC SITE

Pennsylvania. A surviving ironworks symbolizes the industrial skills of the 1700s and early 1800s, and represents the charcoal-furnace villages that were a way of life. Many of the structures beyond the Visitor Center are the originals—the "Big House," or Ironmaster's Mansion, blacksmith shop, charcoal house, furnace, and tenant homes. Others like the waterwheel, bridge house, barn, and store have been handsomely restored to complete the walk into America's yesterday. Besides the national historic site near Reading, early ironmaking is depicted also at Cornwall Furnace, near Lebanon. Address: R.D. 1, Elverson, Pennsylvania 19520.

HORSESHOE BEND NATIONAL MILITARY PARK

Alabama. Along the shore of the Tallapoosa River near Dadeville (90 miles southeast of Birmingham), in March 1814, a military force under Andrew Jackson broke the power of the Upper Creek Indians, strong allies of the British. Jackson was aided by heroic Cherokee Indians. The battle is interpreted at the museum. Address: Daviston, Alabama 36256.

HUBBELL TRADING POST NATIONAL HISTORIC SITE

Arizona. His name was John Lorenzo Hubbell, but he was known as "Don Lorenzo," champion of Indians, and especially of Indian craftsmen. His was the first trading post operated without direct military protection. The sprawling adobe home appears as it did at the turn of the century, displaying his valuable collection of Indian crafts and paintings. It recalls the time when nearly everyone who passed through northeast Arizona stopped in, including President Theodore Roosevelt, General Lew Wallace, Mary Roberts Rinehart, scientists, archaeologists, and artists. The trading post is open to all as a living remnant of the old days and old ways.

The rug room has been famous for decades. Mr. Hubbell influenced the Navajo women to produce well-made rugs with native patterns and natural dyes, products that would find ready acceptance by tourists who passed through Ganado. Today stacks of beautiful rugs are available for inspection and sale. Collections of firearms, books, and other memorabilia further enhance the Southwestern atmosphere of the room.

In the dining room a massive carved oak table, chairs, and sideboard—all brought to Arizona from the East—tell of family dinners and of those attended by many visitors through the decades. Comfortable living in the midst of a collection of Southwestern treasures is perhaps difficult for the modern American to comprehend, but a visit through the Hubbell home will convince the skeptical.

The Park Service intends to maintain the live atmosphere of the home just as in the operation of the trading post. There are no cords across doorways to exclude visitors from any of the rooms, and there are no protective covers on the Navajo rugs—a type of textile that absolutely defies wear. Visitors are not admitted to the home except during tours conducted by Park Service personnel.

The large wareroom adjacent to the store also will continue in use. At sheep-shearing time, visitors will see purchased wool being bagged in the wareroom as in Don Lorenzo's day. Plans are to reactivate the outdoor bake oven, and fresh loaves of bread made of grain raised on the premises will be available for purchase by visitors.

The trading post is located one mile west of Ganado within the boundaries of the Navajo Reservation, and 55 miles from Gallup, New Mexico. From the east it is on the way to Grand Canyon National Park, Canyon de Chelly National Monument, and the Hopi mesas. Address: Box 38, Ganado, Arizona 86505.

INDEPENDENCE NATIONAL HISTORICAL PARK
Pennsylvania. The principles of self-government by men and self-determination by nations are memorialized in the heart of Philadelphia, in an area properly called "the most historic square mile in America." This compact corner is the focal point of the oncoming Bicentennial, the 200th birthday of the United States, to be celebrated in 1976. Here lie the scenes where the Continental Congress met and governed the colonies during the bitter, trying days of the American Revolution, where the Declaration of Independence and Constitution were conceived and adopted, and where, starting in 1790, Congress and the Supreme Court conducted their affairs for ten years before moving to the new capital city, Washington.

You will also find in Independence Square the most extensive and complex restoration ever undertaken by government in the United States, a combined federal, state, and city effort. In block after block, the visitor can see historic and architectural monuments that figured in the flowering of America's independence.

Once this was a tiny Swedish hamlet in the wilderness. It became William Penn's "green countrie towne," the gateway to Pennsylvania, or Penn's Woods. Then it grew into the metropolis of English America, a fitting birthplace of the Republic in 1776.

The place to begin is the modern Visitor Center, which provides orientation to the park through displays and a new film shown in twin 300-seat cinemas. The development of the 20-acre historical park has involved demolishing 100 worn and faded structures, including one ten-story building, and replacing them with greensward, trees, walks, walls, and gates, such as those that stood here long ago. This restoration tells a story of Philadelphia as well as the nation. The city stepped in to rescue the hall and square in 1818, when it was proposed to parcel out land for building lots, and it continues to hold title to them.

The main building to visit, of course, is Independence Hall. Once, as the capitol of Pennsylvania, it was the most impressive building in the colonies; now it is being pieced together anew after precarious years when ceilings sagged and walls neared collapse.

In the interior, the hall has been returned to its appearance of 1793. Toward this end skilled technicians performed patient, minute work, taking apart brick walls and wood paneling, studying them piece by piece; historians examined 4 million manuscripts in this country and in the British Museum. The Assembly room has been refurnished with authentic period items and originals, and it appears substantially the same as the day when delegates adopted the Declaration of Independence. The Liberty Bell, originally ordered in 1751 as a memorial to William Penn's "Charter of Privileges," but which became in time a worldwide symbol of liberty, has long been located on this floor. The 2,000-pound bell is being moved to the new state mall across the street. Congress Hall next door is again open, looking the way John Adams found it for his inauguration, and as Congress knew it when it adopted the Bill of Rights. Other buildings in this cluster harmonious in style are Philosophical Hall, headquarters of

The Liberty Bell

America's oldest learned society, founded by Benjamin Franklin; Library Hall, a reconstruction of the original; and Carpenters' Hall, meeting place of the First Continental Congress.

Components of the national historical park which have undergone restoration or reconstruction for the Bicentennial are the Second Bank of the United States, a Greek revival temple of the 1820s, containing an intriguing gallery of 185 life portraits of leading Americans at the time of the Revolution and early Federal period, mostly painted by Charles Willson Peale and James Sharples; Old City Hall, first meeting place of the Supreme Court; the Graff House, where Thomas Jefferson stayed while writing the Declaration of Independence; and City Tavern, a rendezvous of delegates to the Continental Congress. At Franklin Court, at the site of his home, you can learn of Benjamin Franklin's life and times, his ideas and influence.

Among other notable buildings in the park are: Christ Church, where Franklin, Washington, and other statesmen worshiped; Gloria Dei Church, among the oldest churches in Pennsylvania; and the house where Dolley Todd Madison lived with her first husband. You can walk to Mikveh Israel Cemetery, ancient Jewish burial ground, where Haym Salomon, patriot of the Revolution, is interred. A lovely nearby area, Society Hill, consists of block after block of small restored brick houses. Strolling here is a pleasure. Address: 313 Walnut Street, Philadelphia, Pennsylvania 19106.

JEFFERSON MEMORIAL. See Thomas Jefferson National Memorial, page 135.

JEFFERSON NATIONAL EXPANSION MEMORIAL

Missouri. Commemorating the territorial growth of the United States, this national historic site covers 91 acres at the "Gateway to the West," the original site of St. Louis. The newest and dominant feature, a 630-foot-high stainless steel arch designed by Eero Saarinen on the shore of the Mississippi River, contains an elevator system—really a five-passenger train—enabling the visitor to reach a lofty observatory. At the base of the arch, a Museum of Westward Expansion depicts adventures in shaping the western heritage. The Old Courthouse, high above the river, is also part of the memorial. Dating from 1839, it served as setting of the famous Dred Scott case. The Old Cathedral, begun in 1831, has also been preserved and included in the park. Address: 11 North Fourth Street, St. Louis, Missouri 63102.

JOHN FITZGERALD KENNEDY NATIONAL HISTORIC SITE

Massachusetts. At 83 Beale Street, Brookline, the late president of the United States was born on May 29, 1917. The family lived here until 1921. Mrs. Rose Kennedy, the late president's mother, supervised restoration and refurnishing of the two-story house. Address: Box 160, Concord, Massachusetts 01742.

JOHN MUIR NATIONAL HISTORIC SITE

California. The apostle of national parks lived in this rambling house in Martinez from 1890 to 1914, while writing some of his most important works. During this period he founded the Sierra Club, a great conservation organization which carries on in his tradition throughout the country. Interpretive services and tours are provided while restoration is underway. Address: 4202 Alhambra Avenue, Martinez, California 94553.

JOHNSON, LYNDON B., NATIONAL HISTORIC SITE. See Lyndon B. Johnson National Historic Site, page 155.

JOHNSTOWN FLOOD NATIONAL MEMORIAL. See Allegheny Portage Railroad, page 140.

KENNESAW MOUNTAIN NATIONAL BATTLEFIELD PARK

Georgia. A major engagement of the Atlanta campaign of 1864 was fought on the bluffs northwest of Marietta between the superior invading Union forces of William Tecumseh Sherman and the Confederates under General Joseph E. Johnston. From the top of Big Kennesaw you have a sweeping view of the well-preserved battlefield. After two costly frontal attacks, Sherman outflanked the Confederates, forcing them back toward Atlanta. Exhibits at the Visitor Center interpret the entire campaign; walking tours afford close-up views of the battle lines. Address: Box 1167, Marietta, Georgia 30060.

KINGS MOUNTAIN NATIONAL MILITARY PARK

South Carolina. On a quiet, stony crest in the foothills just below North Carolina, visitors can walk in the footsteps of back-country men of Appalachia who struck an overwhelming blow against British forces on October 7, 1780, during the darkest period of the Revolutionary War in the South. The 900 men, unsoldierly and roughly dressed, advanced with their long rifles against the steel bayonets and disciplined ranks of British troops and Tories who held the mountaintop. They screamed and hooted, charging through tangled brush and wooded ravines, stirring autumn leaves and driving birds to flight. "Face to the hill!" shouted Major William Chronicle when his troops wavered; they moved ahead, even as he was struck and killed, destroying the Tory force of 1,100. At the Visitor Center and along the trails lined with memorial stones, you will learn how the tide was turned at Kings Mountain into the advance toward victory at Yorktown.

At the summit you will find the grave of Major Patrick Ferguson, an experienced, capable British officer who misjudged the temper of the American frontiersmen and paid with his life. Kings Mountain is a beauty spot of the southern highlands in any season. Since the battle occurred during October, autumn is especially appropriate for photography, both for historical significance and fall color. While here, also visit Cowpens National Battlefield Site, 30 miles away. Address: Box 31, Kings Mountain, North Carolina 28086.

KOSCIUSKO, THADDEUS, NATIONAL MEMORIAL. See Thaddeus Kosciusko National Memorial, page 161.

LINCOLN, ABRAHAM, BIRTHPLACE. See Abraham Lincoln Birthplace, page 141.

LINCOLN BOYHOOD NATIONAL MEMORIAL

Indiana. Lincoln's boyhood home and the burial site of his mother are preserved near two memorial buildings of native limestone connected by a semicircular cloistered walk. Lake with picnic facilities at nearby Lincoln State Park. Address: Lincoln City, Indiana 47552.

LINCOLN HOME NATIONAL HISTORIC SITE

Illinois. To Abraham Lincoln, Springfield was home. Here he moved his family into the only house he ever owned, where he lived from 1844 to 1860, the period that saw the major part of his growth. It was from here that he went to Washington to become president. Though State-owned and protected since 1887, deterioration of the neighborhood and land use incompatible with such a shrine stimulated effort to preserve and improve the home's environment. Address: c/o Lincoln Boyhood National Memorial, Lincoln City, Indiana 47552.

LINCOLN MEMORIAL. See page 134.

LINCOLN MUSEUM. See Ford's Theatre, page 133.

LONGFELLOW NATIONAL HISTORIC SITE

Massachusetts. Henry Wadsworth Longfellow wrote "Evangeline," "Hiawatha," and other literary works here. It is one of the newest areas in the National Park System, designated by Congress in 1972. The mansion at 105 Brattle Street in Cambridge, Massachusetts, was the poet's residence from his appointment as a professor of modern languages at Harvard University in 1837 till his death in 1882. Built in 1759 by a wealthy Royalist, the house is a prime example of Georgian architecture. It served as a hospital in the battles of Lexington, Concord, and Bunker Hill. George Washington used it as his headquarters for 10 months in 1775–76. Longfellow rented a room in the house in 1837, and six years later became the owner. On the poet's marriage to Frances Appleton, his father-in-law gave the house to the young couple. The house is furnished with attractive pieces of Longfellow's own period. The property, covering almost two acres, includes a carriage house and formal gardens, all of which were maintained by the Longfellow House Trust since 1913. Address: c/o Boston NPS Group, 150 Causeway Street, Boston, Massachusetts 02114.

LYNDON B. JOHNSON NATIONAL HISTORIC SITE

Texas. The birthplace and boyhood home of the 36th president of the United States are both in the Pedernales River country. The small two-bedroom birthplace is a reconstruction of the original, where the Johnson family lived from 1907 until 1913, when Lyndon was five years old. It is located one-half mile east of the LBJ Ranch, the celebrated Texas White House. The boyhood home, 16 miles north at Johnson City, was Lyndon's home until he married in 1934. Both houses have been refurnished with many items belonging to the Johnson family and with period pieces. The LBJ Ranch is not open to the public, but Lyndon B. Johnson State Park, directly across the Pedernales, features exhibits and programs on the Hill Country and the president's life. Address: P.O. Box 329, Johnson City, Texas 78636.

MANASSAS NATIONAL BATTLEFIELD PARK

Virginia. The opening field battle of the Civil War was fought July 21, 1861, about 26 miles southwest of Washington, the first test of strength between two armies. When you reach Henry House Hill, the most significant site within the park, you will be at the location where General Stonewall Jackson arrived at the crucial hour. Another officer, striving to rally his disorganized men, pointed to Jackson's line and shouted: "There stands Jackson like a stone wall! Rally behind the Virginians!" Jackson had won his immortal name, and before the day was done, the desperate Confederate defense changed into an attack, routing the Union army back to Washington. The following summer, the Second Battle of Manassas (Bull Run, it was called in the North) was fought between 73,000 Union troops and 55,000 Confederates under Robert E. Lee. After two fierce days the Confederates scored a decisive victory, and Lee prepared to invade Maryland. At the Visitor Center, an electric map traces the troop movements. Among many landmarks on the battlefield, the historic Stone House served as a field hospital in both battles. Address: Manassas, Virginia 22110.

MAR-A-LAGO NATIONAL HISTORIC SITE

Florida. This 17-acre Palm Beach estate exemplifies architectural styles and opulence of the 1920s. The 110-room mansion, designed by Marion Sims Wyeth, reflects the influence of Addison Mizener, Palm Beach architect, whose Florida style spread afar. The estate includes furnishings, sculpture and other artwork, landscaped gardens, cabanas, and a dance pavilion. Because it authentically represents a distinctive culture, Mar-A-Lago was designated a national historic site in 1969. In 1972 Congress authorized acceptance of the estate from its owner, Mrs. Marjorie Merriweather Post, who died in 1973. Her bequest provides financing for operation and maintenance of the site for residential use of members of the Executive branch of government and visiting dignitaries, without use of appropriated funds. Mrs. Post retained title during her lifetime and the area is not open to the public. Address: c/o Florida NPS Group, P.O. Box 2764, Tallahassee, Florida 32304.

MCLOUGHLIN HOUSE NATIONAL HISTORIC SITE

Oregon. One of the few remaining pioneer dwellings in the region once known as the "Oregon Country" was built in 1845–46 by Dr. John McLoughlin, who won enduring fame by aiding American settlers in establishing their homes. Federal, state, and private funds have combined to restore and refurnish the house. Address: Oregon City, Oregon 97045.

MINUTE MAN NATIONAL HISTORICAL PARK

Massachusetts. The park was established only in 1959, with the land still to be acquired, but it reclaims from neglect the "Battle Road of the Revolution," embracing portions of the route in Lexington, Lincoln, and Concord, along which armed citizens declared their right to be free. Original stone walls, boulders, and important landmarks are still in place, west of Massachusetts 128. "If they mean to have war, let it begin here," Captain Jonas Parker exhorted his Minutemen at 5 a.m., April 19, 1775, at Lexington Green. Three hours later at Old North Bridge, in Concord, the first British soldier fell and, by Emerson's poetic testimony, "the embattled farmers stood, and fired the shot heard round the world."

Concord and Lexington, spurred by their historical societies, have already saved individual landmarks and protected the general historic character of their communities. Now the new National Historic Park is being developed to present and interpret roadsides and rural landscape. Eventually 750 acres will be returned to their 1775 appearance, but already some of the vital scenes await the visitor.

Lexington Green makes an excellent starting point. The heroic statue of a minuteman represents Captain Parker facing the line of British approach. The Revolutionary monument, on the southwest corner, commemorates the eight Americans killed here; they were the first fatalities of the war. The British continued their march—but would return later in the day in defeat.

From the center of Lexington drive to Fiske Hill, start of the preserved 4-mile section of the Battle Road on which the famous running battle took place. During the afternoon of

MOORES CREEK NATIONAL MILITARY PARK

North Carolina. A brief but intensive battle between Loyalists and Revolutionists was fought about 20 miles northwest of Wilmington, North Carolina, in an opening phase of the Revolution—an engagement often called "the Lexington and Concord of the South." It was on February 27, 1776, when 1,500 Loyalist militia attacked a patriot force of about 1,000 entrenched on Moores Creek. The Revolutionists turned back the assault and captured or dispersed the invaders.

At the Visitor Center, just inside the park entrance, you can learn the full significance of the battle. A loop road leads past monuments to the participants and to the Old State Road Trace, where the focal point is the historic bridge. The flooring, now reconstructed, was removed by the patriots and the girders were greased in order to make the crossing more difficult for the enemy. As the Loyalists stormed over, they were met by withering musket fire, many falling into the water. It was all over in three minutes. The victory discouraged the growth of Loyalist sentiment and spurred Revolutionary fervor throughout the colonies. Although the battle took place in February, April is a good time to observe magnolias, Venus's-flytraps, and spring wildflowers. Address: Currie, North Carolina 28435.

MORRISTOWN NATIONAL HISTORICAL PARK

New Jersey. Barely 30 miles from New York, Americans may experience the richest single source spot of the Revolution. In a little state where over 100 battles and skirmishes were fought, this was the site of Washington's military headquarters and the main encampment of his ragged army during the toughest winters of the war—the times that tried men's souls. Morristown illustrates Washington's personal courage and ability and the unconquerable will of the common soldier to insure the survival of a new nation.

The place to begin is the Historical Museum in the heart of Morristown. Exhibits in this modern structure consist of weapons, military equipment, paintings, old prints, and costumes, including Washington's inaugural costume and sword. Dioramas depict the Revolutionary events. In the winter of 1779 thousands of men, suffering from lack of shoes or stockings or food, were ravaged by smallpox, dysentery, and assorted fevers. Next winter was even worse. The Pennsylvanians, 12 months without pay, short of rations, and without a hogshead of rum in sight, marked New Year's Eve by killing three officers and marching toward Philadelphia to lay their case before Congress; their mutiny nearly destroyed the war effort.

Adjacent to the museum, facing Morris Street, the Ford Mansion served as Washington's headquarters, where he reorganized his weary and depleted forces almost within sight of British lines in New York. It was here that Lafayette brought the welcome word that a French army was on its way to aid in the struggle. On the inside, much of the furniture now displayed was there when Washington occupied it, while the remaining furnishings date from the Revolutionary period or earlier. Few kitchens of the period are so completely furnished with colonial utensils and cooking equipment.

From the south end of Court Street, a road leads upward into the Fort Nonsense area, where you can see a restored earthworks that serves as a key orientation point overlooking Morristown. Jockey Hollow, 4 miles south of Morristown, with rolling woodlands and open fields, closely resembles the setting at the time the main Continental army of 10,000 encamped here during the winter of 1779–80. Many of the campgrounds have remained relatively undisturbed and physical evidence of army occupation can still be seen. You can photograph reconstructed log huts, chinked with clay and held

April 19 this was the scene of some of the heaviest fighting. Visit the Information Station for guidance, then walk the 1-mile, self-guiding trail to the site of the 18th century Fiske Farm, which was looted by the fleeing enemy.

Entering Concord, the Wayside unit of the historical park includes the homes of illustrious literary figures in Concord history. North Bridge over the Concord River is the focal point of interest, surrounded by a variety of photographic subjects. The Concord monument occupies the site of the British position, which they held after searching for and destroying provincial supplies. On the opposite side of the stream, the famous *Minute Man* statue by Daniel Chester French marks the American position, from which they stared at the bright-red coats and then fired. Musket-firing demonstrations are presented by local commemorative minute companies Sunday afternoons June through October between the yellow Buttrick Mansion and the bridge. Buttrick Gardens are in bloom late spring and early summer.

Many outstanding features lie in and around Concord, including the stately First Parish Meeting House, rebuilt on the site of the old church where the Provincial Congress met; and Sleepy Hollow Cemetery, where Hawthorne, Emerson, Thoreau, and the Alcotts are buried. Here too one can trace the life of Henry David Thoreau, champion of man and wilderness, from the ancestral homes to Walden Pond, the source of his classic work *Walden.* Address: Box 160, Concord, Massachusetts 01742.

together with nails and wooden pegs; the originals were built to hold 10 to 12 soldiers each. The Wick House, standing along the road to Menham, represents an architectural complement to the Ford Mansion, one typifying the elegance of town life, the other the solid qualities of the colonial rural scene. During the war the farm home served as the military headquarters of Major General Arthur St. Clair, then commander of the Pennsylvania line. Here Tempe Wick, youngest daughter of the Wick family, supposedly hid her horse in her bedroom in order to prevent its seizure by the Pennsylvania mutineers.

The kitchen garden of the Wick House is a feature in itself, with its herbs and rows of quince, gooseberry, and currant shrubs before the background of fruit trees, the whole ensemble recreating an 18th century scene. Nature, both cultivated and wild, is much a part of this park. More than 100 species of birds, some 20 species of mammals, and over 300 species of shrubs, trees, and wildflowers have been identified in Jockey Hollow. A walk over the Primrose Brook Nature Trail affords the opportunity to see many such elements of the park landscape.

Morristown is a park of all seasons. Spring brings dogwood, flowers, and new foliage. Autumn is a blaze of color with brilliant reds and yellows and skies as clear as they can be in the metropolitan area. Winter is the time to see the bare trees and white carpet before the Ford Mansion and the snow nestling in the chinks of the little log huts, and to feel the chill breeze that swept over the encampment. Address: c/o Morristown-Edison NPS Group, Box 1136R, Morristown, New Jersey 07960.

MOUNT RUSHMORE NATIONAL MEMORIAL

South Dakota. On the solid granite face of 6,000-foot Mount Rushmore, about 25 miles from Rapid City in the Black Hills, colossal carved figures represent the heads of four great presidents—Washington, Jefferson, Lincoln, and Theodore Roosevelt. Work began under the direction of Gutzon Borglum

Mount Rushmore National Memorial

in 1927 and was completed in 1941. The figures are best seen under morning light; they are also visible by floodlight on evenings June 1 to Labor Day, when programs are presented each night at 8 p.m. Visitor Center open all year. Food service mid-April to mid-October. Camping in nearby Black Hills National Forest. Address: Keystone, South Dakota 57751.

NEZ PERCE NATIONAL HISTORICAL PARK

Idaho. Scattered over 12,000 square miles, 23 sites interpreting history and culture of the Nez Perce Indians and early white pioneers are joined together to form a new kind of historical park, a cooperative venture of private organizations, state and federal agencies, and the Nez Perce tribe. The loop tour of the new park begins at historic Lewiston on the Snake River. Numerous campgrounds are located in Clearwater and Nez Perce national forests, which cover more than half this region. The last of the marked stops is at Lolo Trail and Pass, where Lewis and Clark breached the Bitterroot Range on their way west. It was used again by the peaceable Nez Perce Indians in 1877 when they fled the U.S. Army. National Park Service visitor centers will be located at Spalding, East Kamiah, and Whitebird Battlefield. Address: Spalding, Idaho 83551.

PEA RIDGE NATIONAL MILITARY PARK

Arkansas. A hard-fought battle of the Civil War took place 30 miles northeast of Fayetteville in March 1862. Displays at the Visitor Center and along the self-guiding auto battlefield tour explain the action and how the Federal victory saved Missouri for the Union. Address: Pea Ridge, Arkansas 72751.

PERRY'S VICTORY AND
INTERNATIONAL PEACE MEMORIAL

Ohio. "We have met the enemy and they are ours," reported Oliver Hazard Perry after his dramatic victory in the Battle of Lake Erie during the War of 1812. The imposing pink granite memorial, commemorating that victory and the enduring peace between the United States and Canada, is located at Put-in-Bay on South Bass Island, 4 miles from the mainland. It is served during summer by car ferries from Catawba Point and Port Clinton and by plane both summer and winter from Port Clinton. From the observation deck, near the top of the 352-foot-high memorial, you can see the battle scene between the shorelines of both Canada and the United States. Address: Box 78, Put-in-Bay, Ohio 43456.

PETERSBURG NATIONAL BATTLEFIELD

Virginia. Due south of Richmond—the main objective that never quite fell—Petersburg was the scene of ten months of grim siege and warfare, beginning in the summer of 1864 and ending with the Confederate retreat toward surrender at Appomattox in April 1865. The most engrossing part of this battlefield surrounds the Visitor Center in the section called the Crater. Here Union troops from Pennsylvania, who had been coal miners, dug a tunnel under Confederate lines and exploded four tons of powder on July 30, 1864. The explosion killed 278 men and created an immense crater. In fighting that followed, the Confederates recaptured the crater, while the Union Army lost 4,000 men—killed, wounded, or captured. The Crater is the start of the 27-mile auto tour to many points of interest, including Fort Stedman, the site of Lee's "Last Grand Offensive"; Battery 9, with a trail leading to Meade's Station, which Lincoln visited during the fighting; and Battery 5, from which Grant shelled Petersburg with "The Dictator," a 17,000-pound seacoast mortar. The graves of about 6,000 Union soldiers and 36 Confederates are in Poplar Grove National Cemetery, on the old camping ground of the 50th New York Engineers. Address: Box 594, Petersburg, Virginia 23804.

PIPE SPRING NATIONAL MONUMENT

Arizona. The well-preserved Mormon fort, nestled at the base of the colorful Vermillion cliffs near Fredonia in northwestern Arizona, was settled by the hardy followers of Brigham Young, who were determined to make their way in a harsh land. Within sturdy high sandstone walls and heavy gates, two houses face each other, sharing the benefits of a spring. Two mirrorlike pools of water and large shade trees enhance the area. A recently developed feature is the "living ranch," with working cattle, branding, baking of bread, spinning, and weaving. Even newer is the Kaibab-Paiute Cultural Building, where you can learn about the native Indians of the region. Craft items are available for purchase. There is food service here, too. Address: c/o Zion National Park, Springdale, Utah 84767.

PUUKOHOLA HEIAU NATIONAL HISTORIC SITE

Hawaii. The fourth unit of the National Park System on the "Big Island" will protect the famous temple built by Kamehameha the Great and closely associated with the founding of the Kingdom of Hawaii, as well as remnants of the home site of John Young, English advisor to the king. It is located at Kawaihae Bay on the beautiful northwestern shore. Address: c/o City of Refuge National Historical Park, Honaunau, Kona, Hawaii 96726.

RICHMOND NATIONAL BATTLEFIELD PARK

Virginia. Of seven thrusts against the capital of the Confederacy, only two approached success. All attacks were resisted until Grant's siege of Petersburg finally forced abandonment of Richmond. This park links the scenes of battles in defense of the city. Markers, maps, and parts of the fields of combat bring to life the Battle of Seven Pines, the Seven Days' Battles culminating at Malvern Hill, and Cold Harbor, which proved to be Lee's last major victory. Visitor centers in Chimborazo Park and Fort Harrison. Address: 3215 East Broad Street, Richmond, Virginia 23223.

ROGER WILLIAMS NATIONAL MEMORIAL

Rhode Island. At the site of the old town spring in the heart of Providence, this memorial will commemorate the large and lasting contributions of Roger Williams to civil and religious liberty. The old spring lies within an urban renewal program and it is not known when development of the Memorial can take place. Address: c/o Regional Director, National Park Service, 143 South Third Street, Philadelphia, Pennsylvania 19106.

ROOSEVELT CAMPOBELLO INTERNATIONAL PARK

New Brunswick, Canada. Jointly owned and administered by the United States and Canada, this unique memorial covering 2,600 acres was established in 1964. It lies 80 miles north of Bangor, Maine, just across the Canadian border. The Franklin D. Roosevelt Memorial Bridge links Campobello Island, part of the little archipelago clustered about the mouth of Passamaquoddy Bay, with Lubec, Maine. It was here Franklin D. Roosevelt spent all his summers from age one until stricken with polio in 1921. He described it as a place of "rest, refreshment, and freedom from care." The focal point of the park is the 34-room Dutch colonial summer home, the center of a 10½-acre landscaped estate, with its rooms restored and furnished as they were in the 1920s, when FDR lived here. The park is open mid-May to mid-October seven days a week,

9 a.m. to 5 p.m., to 6 p.m. during July and August. Also on the island (but not in the park) are the Campobello Library and St. Anne's Anglican Church, where Roosevelt prayed and his pew is marked. Campobello offers fine beaches and fishing. Three motels are located on Highway 774 at Wilsons Beach. Camping facilities are at Herring Cove Park. Crossing the Canadian border presents no difficulty, but be sure to carry identifying papers or proof of citizenship, just in case. Address: Welshpool, Campobello, New Brunswick.

ROOSEVELT, HOME OF FRANKLIN D.

See Home of Franklin D. Roosevelt National Historic Site, page 152.

ROOSEVELT, THEODORE, BIRTHPLACE.

See Theodore Roosevelt Birthplace National Historic Site, page 161.

ROOSEVELT, THEODORE, NATIONAL MEMORIAL PARK.

See Theodore Roosevelt National Memorial Park, page 161.

SAGAMORE HILL NATIONAL HISTORIC SITE

New York. The home of Theodore Roosevelt from 1885 until his death in 1919 lies at the end of Cove Neck Road in historic Oyster Bay, Long Island. The rambling Victorian structure, the summer White House for eight years, is furnished with original Roosevelt pieces. Trophies of a crowded life pack the North Room. His gun collection is on the top floor. On every hand are crowded bookshelves, reflecting his wide interests. Closed Tuesday; 10 to 5 other days. Address: c/o New York City NPS Group, 26 Wall Street, New York, New York 10005.

ST. CROIX ISLAND NATIONAL MONUMENT

Maine. On this island in the St. Croix River, which forms the boundary between Maine and New Brunswick, Canada, the French attempted to found a permanent settlement in 1604; from here Champlain continued his journey to the coast and the area of present-day Acadia National Park. Address: c/o Acadia National Park, Box 388, Bar Harbor, Maine 04609.

SAINT-GAUDENS NATIONAL HISTORIC SITE

New Hampshire. The home, studio, and gardens of the celebrated sculptor Augustus Saint-Gaudens are preserved, with

Lincoln, by Augustus Saint-Gaudens

many of his portraits, busts, and casts on view, at Cornish, 2 miles from the Windsor, Vermont, covered bridge. Each summer the Saint-Gaudens Memorial sponsors concerts and art exhibitions. Address: c/o Saratoga National Historical Park, R.F.D. 1, Box 113C, Stillwater, New York 12170.

ST. PAUL'S CHURCH NATIONAL HISTORIC SITE
New York. The 18th century church of Renaissance revival architecture in Mount Vernon was intimately connected with events leading to the trial by Peter Zenger for a free press. It served as Hessian troop quarters in the Revolution. Address: 859 South Columbus Avenue, Mount Vernon, New York 10550.

ST. THOMAS NATIONAL HISTORIC SITE
Virgin Islands. Fort Christian, the oldest standing structure in the Virgin Islands (completed 1680) stands essentially as when it served as hub of the early Danish settlement; now it houses the police department and municipal offices. Address: c/o Government of the Virgin Islands National Park, Charlotte Amalie, St. Thomas, V.I. 00801.

SALEM MARITIME NATIONAL HISTORIC SITE
Massachusetts. The long Derby Street wharf is used now only by a small naval reserve unit, but in its day, when Salem skippers mapped the distant oceans, it was crowded with vessels laden with silk from India, tea from China, coffee from Arabia. In 1796 the first elephant seen in the United States arrived here from Bengal. Just east of the wharf, the brick Derby House, built in 1762, represents the beginning of Salem's tenure as mistress of the seas. It was owned by Elias "King" Derby, the coastal magnate called "America's first millionaire," and contains some of the most elegantly carved woodwork found anywhere. Adjacent to it stands the largest vestige of Salem's seaport glory, the Custom House, erected in 1819, where Nathaniel Hawthorne worked as a bookkeeper in 1846. He described the scene and mood of the wharf, as viewed through his office window, in *The Scarlet Letter.*

The Rum Shop, a building probably erected in 1800 or soon after, stands on the corner east of the Derby House. The Hawkes House, just west of it, was originally designed about 1780 as a sumptuous mansion for Elias Hasket Derby by Samuel McIntire, Salem's great architect. In fact, you would do well to study and photograph some of the other houses in Salem, such as the beautiful Peirce-Nichols House on Federal Street and the Pingree House on Essex Street, which he designed. McIntire was a self-taught genius, a carver as well as architect. When Salem was at its height, he and others designed fine houses—square, three stories tall, with high ornamental porches and doorheads. A large number of these fine houses are still in use and lend charm to Salem.

Other points of interest in the city should not be overlooked. The Peabody Museum, for example, was established in 1799 by a group of Salem captains, who contributed objects from the four corners of the earth and examples of their own carvers' work—ship models, mouldings, and figureheads. The legendary **House of the Seven Gables,** named from Hawthorne's story, and the **Witch House,** where "witches" were quizzed, are two of several buildings dating from the 17th century. Address: Custom House, Derby Street, Salem, Massachusetts 01970.

SAN JOSE MISSION NATIONAL HISTORIC SITE
Texas. Admired as one of the finest Spanish missions in North America, San Jose y San Miguel de Aguayo Mission was founded in 1720 at the southern edge of the present city of San Antonio. It still serves the community as a church.

A visiting priest 60 years later recorded that it was inhabited by some 350 Indians, all proficient in some art, as evidenced by their carvings on the facade and paintings on the walls of the church. They spoke Spanish fluently, played various musical instruments, sang and danced the Spanish dances.

During the 19th century the mission fell into disuse and disrepair. The church dome and roof caved in. But during the 1930s, after an absence of more than 100 years, the Franciscan fathers returned to San Jose and the mission church is again active. Through cooperative efforts of federal, state, and local agencies, and the loving care of the San Antonio Conservation Society, the mission was restored.

The mission is laid out as a self-contained community, with a trail connecting all the significant structures. The most impressive is the church, with its beautiful facade and rose window, considered the finest Spanish colonial ornamentation sculptured in America. The winding stairway leading to the choir loft and belfry is made of live oak logs, hand hewn into shape and assembled into place over 200 years ago. Adjoining the church, the Convento served as the living quarters and offices for the clergy. The cloisters have been purposely left in their ruined state because of the structural beauty of more than 60 Roman and Gothic arches.

The most renowned mission in San Antonio, of course, is the Alamo, the low, gray chapel where in 1836 a rugged band under William Travis, James Bowie, and Davy Crockett died fighting off Santa Anna's army. You will also want to visit the Spanish governor's palace, restored and furnished by the Conservation Society as an example of an aristocratic European mansion on the Southwest frontier. Address: 6539 San Jose Drive, San Antonio, Texas 78214.

SAN JUAN ISLAND NATIONAL HISTORICAL PARK
Washington. Historic sites of American and English camps on San Juan Island, the second largest island in Puget Sound, associated with the Oregon Territory boundary dispute, are protected in this new park. Both camps were fortified in the so-called "Pig War" of 1859, but there was no fighting before the final settlement by arbitration in 1872 sustained the American claim to the San Juan and the last British flag was lowered within territorial United States. The island is reached on a pleasant trip by ferry from Anacortes, Washington, or Sidney, British Columbia. Address: P.O. Box 549, Friday Harbor, Washington 98250.

SAN JUAN NATIONAL HISTORIC SITE
Puerto Rico. The massive masonry fortifications, the oldest within the territorial limits of the United States, were begun by the Spanish in the 16th century to protect a strategic harbor guarding the sea lanes to the New World. El Morro, at the northwest tip of the city, was enlarged continually between attacks by the English, French, and Dutch. San Cristóbal, the largest castle in the San Juan defensive system, was completed about 1773, protecting the approaches by land.

The fortifications of San Juan have had a colorful history, associated with attacks of Elizabethan Sea Dogs, Dutch merchants, and the contrabandists. In 1595, Sir Francis Drake led an invasion fleet of 23 ships and 3,000 men but was driven off with heavy casualties. Three years later the Earl of Cumberland marched on the city from the land side and captured El Morro, but dysentery forced him to leave. The walls and gun decks were continually enlarged between attacks during the 17th and 18th centuries. Spaniards used El Morro during the war between the United States and Spain in 1898. U.S. armed forces manned the fortifications until the late 1960s, when all of these defenses were transferred to the National Park Service.

Today the face of colonial Spain can still be seen in the streets of San Juan. But the city's most impressive features are the old castles and fortifications, embodying functional military architecture and the legends of history. The national historic site embraces most of the city walls and the Spanish forts of El Morro, San Cristóbal, El Cañuelo, and Casa Blanca.

You will also want to examine the city wall, standing around much of the old town, including the harbor front between El Morro and La Fortaleza, the home of the governor, which dates from 1533. Walking along the old narrow streets, you will find the whitewashed arches and garden patios, the pastel-colored buildings and overhanging balconies with freshly-painted grilles. At night old Spanish wrought-iron lamps cast a soft glow on the cobblestones. Address: Box 712, San Juan, Puerto Rico 00902.

SARATOGA NATIONAL HISTORICAL PARK
New York. Thirty miles north of Albany, where the Hudson River narrows to flow through wild forest and field, a ragtag rebel army dug in behind entrenchments designed by the Polish general, Kosciuszko. The British came from Canada in September 1777, intending to trim them to proper size and to cut off New England from the rest of the country. From the Visitor Center on Fraser Hill, the highest point in the park, you can see the battleground where Burgoyne's Redcoats were greeted by the fire of Colonel Dan Morgan's long rifles of Virginia. This was one of the most decisive battles in world history, the victory here earning support for the rebels from France, Holland, and Spain.

The park is extremely well laid out. It is best to enter from New York 32, where your first stop is at the Visitor Center, overlooking the battlefield from the highest hill in the park. On a clear day the visibility is sufficient to allow one to see into Vermont and Massachusetts. Battle maps, dioramas, and displays chart the entire course of action.

The automobile route, which begins at the Visitor Center, has nine marked stops that place you in the heart of the action. Stop 3, the American River Fortifications, provides the same good views of the Hudson that American infantry and cannon batteries enjoyed. This powerful position was the key to strategy, since it closed off the Hudson Valley route to Albany. Stop 7, the Breymann Redoubt, has special appeal in the uniquely designed monument to Benedict Arnold, called the "Boot Monument." Arnold played a key role in the American attack on the British position here. At the moment of charging into the log breastworks from the rear, he was shot in the leg. It has often been noted that had he died at Saratoga, Benedict Arnold would have been immortalized as an American hero.

The first two weeks of October coincide with the dates of the battle and find fall color at its peak. During the second weekend in October the National Park Service presents a Tactical Weapons Demonstration, utilizing "troops" from the brigade of the American Revolution. This is not a reenactment, but an unrehearsed and spontaneous tactical exercise; it provides a preview of the large-scale presentation scheduled for the Bicentennial in 1976.

During the summer season park employees, both men and women, in period dress, are stationed at various stops along the tour road. They engage in such 18th century crafts as dipping and moulding candles, baking waffles and cookies, dressmaking, and weapons demonstrations of rifles, muskets, swivel guns, and mortars.

Eight miles north of the park, at Schuylerville, New York,

the General Philip Schuyler House is a separate portion of the park. The fine country house, the third on the site, was built in late 1777 to replace one the British burned. The restored house and 25 acres are a gentle reminder of country life in upper New York. Address: R.D. 1, Box 113-C, Stillwater, New York 12170.

SAUGUS IRON WORKS NATIONAL HISTORIC SITE
Massachusetts. A meticulous reconstruction of America's first well-sustained iron works came into being in 1954 as the result of six years of work by historians, architects, archaeologists, and builders financed by the American Iron and Steel Institute. Excavations produced over five tons of artifacts left by the original works, which operated from 1648 to about 1670. The old ironmaster's house stands as built in 1636, except for small repairs, complete with ten-foot fireplaces and original hand-hewn beams. The ironworks contain the reconstructed blast furnace, forge, and rolling and slitting mill. Daily demonstrations of early methods of iron working have been conducted by the First Iron Works Association, Inc., for several years. The property has been given to the United States, and the Park Service will continue these demonstrations. Six of the seven waterwheels operate each day during late spring, summer, and early fall; the splash of the water and the movement of the wheels add the right amount of action for movie photography. The Wharehouse and Wharf will help you to imagine the scene when iron and iron products were shipped to colonies along the coast and to overseas customers. Address: Box 160, Concord, Massachusetts 01742.

SCOTTS BLUFF NATIONAL MONUMENT
Nebraska. The rocky promontory, rising 800 feet above the North Platte Valley, served as landmark and favored camping area for thousands crossing the treeless plains in the westward migrations between 1843 and 1869 over the Oregon and Mormon trails, and the trails to gold in California. The Visitor Center tells the story of early fur traders, the wagon trains, and pony express, and displays paintings by William Henry Jackson, the pioneer photographer-artist. A paved road and foot trail lead to the summit of the bluff. Address: Box 427, Gering, Nebraska 69341.

SHILOH NATIONAL MILITARY PARK
Tennessee. In the first major battle of the western campaign, General U. S. Grant opened the wedge to control of the Mississippi River, which he completed the following year at Vicksburg. From the park Visitor Center, where battle relics, exhibits, and maps are displayed, the 10-mile self-guiding auto tour begins. At Pittsburg Landing, Grant's 40,000 troops established their base after steaming up the Tennessee River from Fort Donelson. At the Reconnoitering Road and Fraley Field, the two-day battle began April 6, 1862, when Confederate scouts of General Albert Johnston attacked the Union forces. The Hornet's Nest was the site of deadly fighting the first day around a natural fortress of dense woods, and at the Bloody Pond soldiers of both sides came to drink and bathe their wounds. At the National Cemetery, 3,700 men of both sides are buried. Address: Shiloh, Tennessee 38376.

SITKA NATIONAL HISTORICAL PARK
Alaska. Adjoining the town of Sitka in southeastern Alaska, the park centers around 18 totem poles of the finest native craftsmanship in a setting of spruce and hemlock and also takes in the area in which the Tlingit Indians made their last stand against the Russians in 1804. The site of the Indian fort is marked, and the newly enlarged park includes the forested

grounds where the battle took place. The Visitor Center here is one of the finest historical showcases in Alaska. Address: c/o Alaska NPS Group, 334 W. Fifth Avenue, Anchorage, Alaska 99501.

STATUE OF LIBERTY NATIONAL MONUMENT

New York-New Jersey. The colossal copper statue on Liberty Island, New York harbor, is a universal symbol of freedom and democracy. "The New Colossus," as Emma Lazarus called it in her celebrated poem, was the work of Frederic Bartholdi, and a gift of the French people in 1884, commemorating the alliance of France and America during the American Revolution. The monument is reached by ferry, a delightful trip starting from the slip at the Battery next to Castle Clinton (every hour on the hour, every half-hour in summer). This trip has been called "the shortest cruise in the world"—it takes 25 minutes. Within the statue an elevator runs to the balcony level, and a spiral stairway leads to the observation platform in the lady's head, affording thrilling views of ships and shoreline. The new American Museum of Immigration in the base of the statue has been dedicated as a memorial to the millions who chose to start a new life in this country. Displays, posters, dioramas, restored photographs—all tell the dramatic story of the life and times of the immigrant, beginning as far back as the arrival of the first Indians. One early poster proclaims the arrival of indentured laborers who can be "bought" to work for their sponsors until the cost of their passage has been met. Another, issued in the spring of 1792, offers "Irish servants just arrived from Dublin—healthy, indentured men and women servants, a variety of tradesmen and some good farmers and laborers." Short-order food service is available. Address: c/o New York City NPS Group, 26 Wall Street, New York, New York 10005.

STONES RIVER NATIONAL BATTLEFIELD

Tennessee. A stubbornly fought three-day midwinter battle which started December 31, 1862, a short distance from Murfreesboro, began the Federal offensive to split the Confederacy in three parts. The Hazen Brigade Monument, erected in 1863, is believed to be the oldest memorial of the Civil War. The decisive turn of events came the second day with a 58-gun concentration of Union artillery roaring out more than 100 rounds a minute on advancing Confederates. In a matter of minutes, 1,800 Confederates fell—killed or wounded. Under the pall of disaster, General Braxton Bragg ordered the withdrawal of his army. The national battlefield contains about 6,400 burials, over one-third unidentified. Address: Box 1039, Murfreesboro, Tennessee 37130.

TAFT, WILLIAM HOWARD, NATIONAL HISTORIC SITE. See
William Howard Taft National Historic Site, page 000.

THADDEUS KOSCIUSZKO NATIONAL MEMORIAL

Pennsylvania. This small row house at 301 Pine Street, Philadelphia, is the country's only surviving residence of General Thaddeus Kosciuszko, Polish patriot and hero of the American Revolution. While living here in 1797–98, Kosciuszko was visited frequently by Vice President Thomas Jefferson, who asked him to serve as a peace emissary to France. An old friend, Jefferson had described Kosciuszko during the Revolution: "as pure a son of liberty as I have ever known." Kosciuszko wrote his will in this house and gave it to Jefferson, bequeathing his fortune to the cause of freedom of slaves. Educated in military science in Poland, France, Germany, and Italy and in naval fortifications and tactics in France, Kosciuszko volunteered his services to the colonies in 1776. He

quickly won recognition for his plans to fortify the Delaware River approaches to Philadelphia, and was commissioned a colonel of engineers in the Continental Army. He prepared fortifications at Fort Ticonderoga, Saratoga, and West Point, and is credited with much of the success of the decisive Battle of Saratoga. He was appointed chief engineer of the Army in the South, where his logistical planning was instrumental in the campaign's success. For his six years of skilled service, Congress bestowed American citizenship on Kosciuszko and commissioned him a brigadier general. A Philadelphia businessman, Edward J. Piszek, bought the three-story brick memorial house a few years ago when it appeared in danger of being razed. Piszek offered to give the house, built in 1775, to the nation. Congress authorized acceptance in 1972, plus $592,000 for its restoration. Address: c/o Independence National Historical Park, 313 Walnut Street, Philadelphia, Pennsylvania 19106.

THEODORE ROOSEVELT BIRTHPLACE
NATIONAL HISTORIC SITE

New York. In the four-story brownstone at 28 East 20th Street, Manhattan, currently amid an area of low-cost residences, the 26th president was born in 1858. He lived his formative years here—until he was 15—beset by asthma and ailments. Furnished in period style, with two museum rooms. Address: c/o New York City NPS Group, 26 Wall Street, New York, New York 10005.

THEODORE ROOSEVELT NATIONAL MEMORIAL PARK

North Dakota. 70,436 acres, primarily interprets the period of the 1880s when young Theodore Roosevelt lived a rancher's life in the Badlands. The natural history of this strange region of buttes, gorges, and canyons carved by the Little Missouri River has a special appeal. You can wake in the morning at Cottonwood Campground and hear a coyote howl, then visit prairie dog towns and watch herds of bison roaming freely as they did before the white man came.

Roosevelt owned cattle ranches in the area from 1883 to the turn of the century. He rode the range with his buckaroos, organized a local stockmen's association, and spread the gospel of responsible government on a near-lawless frontier. As a result of a bitter winter, when cattle perished by the thousands, Roosevelt lost more money than he made in ranching—but he learned the need for protecting natural resources from indiscriminate use, and later became the "Conservationist President."

The park is divided into three separate units, which may be linked in time by a scenic road. One is near Medora; another near Watford City; and the third, the site of Roosevelt's Elkhorn Ranch, is midway between them on the Little Missouri and difficult to reach. The units are all within the Badlands, but each is distinctively different.

Maltese Cross Cabin, Roosevelt's first home in the Badlands, restored with furnishings of the mid-1880s, stands adjacent to the Visitor Center in the south unit; guided tours conducted throughout the year. Visitor Center exhibits cover the early cattle industry and Roosevelt's life. Ask for a bird checklist; the park is rich in birdlife.

South Unit. Drive the scenic loop road to the **burning coal bed,** where lightning or other causes have ignited lignite veins producing the type of rock known as "scoria." **Wind Canyon,** probably the best example of Badlands erosion accelerated by the force of wind, affords a spectacular vista of weird and brilliantly colored tablelands, buttes, and other formations. **Buck Hill Overlook,** highest formation in the Painted Canyon, gives the broadest panoramic view. **Nature trails** in both units of the park, lined with wildflowers in early summer, explain ever-changing landforms and the erosion caused by the many creeks and streams. **Petrified Forest,** an area of ancient conifer stumps (which may have been a species of Giant Sequoia), with diameters of six and eight feet, is reached on a 10-mile round trip by foot or horseback.

North Unit. Take the drive of about 13 miles for breathtaking views of bluish bentonitic clay and the weird erosional patterns carved by the meandering Little Missouri. Note that cottonwoods are first to grow in newly deposited sediment along the river's edge, stabilizing the soil and providing shade. This creates an environment for less hardy trees like ash and elm, which eventually crowd out the cottonwoods. If you meet a herd of bison crossing the road, yield the right-of-way and stay in your car for your own safety.

Accommodations. Two excellent campgrounds are located in the park (limit 14 days). Sites cannot be reserved, but arrive by early afternoon and you will probably find an attractive location. The Forest Service and the State of North Dakota maintain other campgrounds in the immediate vicinity. In Medora the Rough Riders Hotel, where Roosevelt stayed, is refurnished and open for business, along with modern log-cabin motels patterned after the Maltese Cross ranch cabin.

Nearby. The little town of Medora is linked intimately with the park. The **Chateau de Mores,** a lavish two-story mansion, was built by the founder of Medora, the Marquis de Mores, a contemporary of Roosevelt, who spent a fortune trying to develop a meat-packing center in the range country. The adventures of these two colorful figures are related each summer evening in *Old Four Eyes,* an excellent outdoor drama. In recent years Medora has taken on new life as a result of the major restoration of old buildings undertaken by Harold Schafer, a patriotic Dakotan. For further information write Superintendent, Theodore Roosevelt National Memorial Park, Medora, North Dakota 58645.

TOURO SYNAGOGUE NATIONAL HISTORIC SITE

Rhode Island. The most significant and most exquisitely designed building in Newport is the oldest house of Jewish worship in the United States, founded by 15 families responding to Roger Williams' declaration of religious liberty. The plans were made by Peter Harrison, known as America's first professional architect, who is also responsible for great Boston churches. Among features of the restored synagogue are Windsor benches, massive bronze candelabrum, fine examples of 18th century silversmithing—and the memory of George Washington's appearance in 1790, pledging that the government would yield "to bigotry no sanction, to persecution no assistance." The synagogue continues as the place of worship for Congregation Jeshuat Israel, while the Society of Friends of Touro Synagogue conducts efforts toward fulfilling the 18th century appearance.

From the synagogue it is only a short walk to the old burial ground, a small plot which served as inspiration for Longfellow's poem, "The Jewish Cemetery at Newport." Among those interred are Aaron Lopez, Moses Seixas, and Judah Touro, prominent men of their day.

As for Harrison, he was a native Newporter who began life as a ship's steward and went on to a versatile career as captain, shipbuilder, woodcarver, and architect of great churches, including King's Chapel in Boston and Christ Church, Cambridge. His earliest design, Newport's 1748 Redwood Library, still serves its original purpose; it is filled with valuable books and a gallery of historic portraits. His Brick Market, near the waterfront, is also still in use. Address: 85 Touro Street, Newport, Rhode Island 02840.

Touro Synagogue

TUMACACORI NATIONAL MONUMENT

Arizona. The northern outpost of a mission chain built by Franciscan priests in the late 1700s, Tumacacori has the charm of culture planted in the desert. Though courtyard structures long ago fell almost entirely into ruin, the Park Service has conserved the stately church in which you may study interesting structural elements of the baroque architecture and the faded but original colors which Indian workmen applied. Patio garden and fountain; the museum contains dioramas, drawings, and maps that bring the frontier mission age to life. Address: Box 67, Tumacacori, Arizona 85640.

TUPELO NATIONAL BATTLEFIELD

Mississippi. A granite marker serving as a memorial to soldiers of both armies and interpretive maps are within a one-acre tract in the city of Tupelo where Federal forces fought in July 1864, to protect Sherman's supply line while he was moving on Atlanta. Address: c/o Natchez Trace Parkway, R.R. 5, NT 143, Tupelo, Mississippi 38801.

VANDERBILT MANSION NATIONAL HISTORIC SITE

New York. The 54-room country home was built at Hyde Park in 1898 by Frederick W. Vanderbilt, grandson of Cornelius Vanderbilt, "the Commodore." This "monument to an era," complete with Italian marble, Flemish tapestry, a 300-year-old Persian carpet, Swiss wood carvings, and French Renaissance furniture, contrasts greatly with the nearby more sober, Victorian home of Franklin D. Roosevelt. Address: c/o Franklin D. Roosevelt National Historic Site, Hyde Park, Dutchess County, New York 12538.

VICKSBURG NATIONAL MILITARY PARK

Mississippi. General U. S. Grant, striving to split the Confederacy with daring, large-scale movements across the heartland of America, moved against Vicksburg in the spring of 1863. On May 18, one of Grant's three corps launched an attack. It was repulsed. Three days later his whole army moved. When Union officers set their watches to start the forward movement at 10 a.m. it marked the first battle on the American continent started by watches instead of the usual signal gun. Failure to capture the heavily defended city, despite bloody fighting, compelled Grant to start siege operations, aided by the Union navy, to cut off communications and blast the city from the river. After 47 days of tightening the grip from three sides, Grant took Vicksburg and control of the Mississippi. You can see the whole length of the defensive fortifications (along Confederate Avenue) and the main part of the investment line (along Union Avenue) in the semicircular park around the city. About 1,600 monuments, memorials, and tablets have been erected to mark positions of the armies. The equestrian statue of General Grant stands in the area where the general maintained his headquarters. The national cemetery, at the north end of the park, contains the graves of 18,000 Union soldiers, including many who died in other actions nearby. The Confederate dead are buried in the city cemetery.

The Visitor Center, adjacent to the entrance near US 80 (Clay Street) contains life-size exhibits. An 18-minute film relates the events of the siege. Displays include a scale model of the gunboat U.S.S. *Cairo.*

While in Vicksburg, see the old Court House Museum, with an exhibit of relics from the siege. Address: Box 349, Vicksburg, Mississippi 39180.

WASHINGTON, BOOKER T., NATIONAL MONUMENT. See Booker T. Washington National Monument, page 142.

WASHINGTON, GEORGE, BIRTHPLACE. See George Washington Birthplace, page 150.

WASHINGTON MONUMENT. See page 135.

WHITE HOUSE. See page 135.

WHITMAN MISSION NATIONAL HISTORIC SITE
Washington. Near Walla Walla, Marcus and Narcissus Whitman established a mission for the Cayuse Indians and a haven for travelers on the Oregon Trail, which they operated from 1836 until they were slain by superstitious Indians in 1847. A Visitor Center, housing artifacts uncovered by archaeologists, tells the story of the mission, while an easy trail leads past foundation ruins of mission buildings that were burned by the Indians after the massacre. Address: Route 2, Walla Walla, Washington 99362.

WILCOX, ANSLEY, HOUSE NATIONAL HISTORIC SITE. See Ansley Wilcox House National Historic Site, page 140.

WILLIAM HOWARD TAFT NATIONAL HISTORIC SITE
Ohio. The 27th president was born in September 1857 in this two-story brick home on Auburn Avenue in Cincinnati. His father had been Secretary of War and Attorney General under President U. S. Grant, but this did not prevent young William and his four brothers from enjoying a typical boyhood and active neighborhood life, including swimming, skating, and baseball. After studying at Yale, he returned home in 1878 to complete his studies at Cincinnati Law School. Then he began his advance on the national scene, reaching the double pinnacle, as President (1909–1913) and Chief Justice (1921–1930). The expansive house passed through various owners until 1961, when it was acquired by the Taft Memorial Association. Congress established the national historic site in 1969 and the National Park Service since then has been undertaking restoration of the home. Address: Box 19072, Cincinnati, Ohio 45219.

WILLIAMS, ROGER, MEMORIAL. See Roger Williams Memorial, page 158.

WILSON'S CREEK NATIONAL BATTLEFIELD PARK
Missouri. At a site 10 miles southwest of Springfield, Union and Confederate forces engaged in a bitter struggle during the first year of the Civil War (August 10, 1861) for control of Missouri. Though the Southerners won the battle of Wilson's Creek, they were too badly crippled to follow through in pursuit. Thus, Missouri was secured for the Union. Exhibits in the information trailer, a self-guiding loop drive, and an audiovisual program help in understanding the battle and its significance. Address: c/o George Washington Carver National Monument, Box 38, Diamond, Missouri 64840.

WRIGHT BROTHERS NATIONAL MEMORIAL
North Carolina. The site of the first sustained flight by a heavier-than-air machine, made by Wilbur and Orville Wright at Kill Devil Hills in December 1903, is marked by a granite pylon monument in the dunes. The Visitor Center contains a replica of their famous plane, *Kitty Hawk.* Address: Box 457, Manteo, North Carolina 27954.

The *Kitty Hawk*

Natural and Recreational Areas

All of the natural and recreation areas administered by the National Park Service offer unlimited opportunities for education, recreation, and travel enjoyment. Whether called national parkways; national seashores, lakeshores, or riverways; national monuments; or national recreation areas—they are all national treasures.

National monuments are the oldest type of category in this section. Devils Tower, Wyoming, was established as a national monument by presidential proclamation in 1906, and since that time more than 80 have been added to the Park System. National monuments span prehistoric cliff dwellings, caverns, an underwater marine garden, fortresses, landmarks of early settlement, spectacular canyons and desert wilderness, virgin stands of redwood and cactus. National monuments devoted to nature are described in this section of the guide. (Monuments relating to archaeology are described in Archaeology Areas, pages 136 to 139; monuments of historical significance are included in Historical Areas, pages 140 to 163.)

National seashores (eight in number), national lakeshores (four), and national riverways (four), on the other hand, are among the newest categories in the system. All have been established since 1953. The concept of these areas is one of the federal government's finest achievements of this recent period. For many years the nation has protected representative portions of other natural environments, such as virgin forest, glacial wilderness, and inland marsh. We have been concerned with rescuing endangered species of wildlife—the alligator, grizzly bear, and whooping crane. Now it can be said that the nation has recognized the value of the native seashores and lakeshores and rivers. The seashore has been with us forever, which may explain why we have taken it so much for granted and despoiled it generously and thoughtlessly. Now, however, it has been determined that it shall not become an extinct species of earth form. Our rapidly eroding lakeshores are finally receiving attention, and the paths of our most scenic rivers are being recognized also as gifts of nature that must be preserved.

In this section you will read about some of the largest units of the National Park System (the National Recreation Areas) and the most heavily visited (National Parkways). Parkways are distinctive parks in their own right, in which the roadway is designed exclusively for pleasure travel by private car, rather than as a means of transportation from one point to another. The bordering right-of-way includes areas expressing the best of nature and recreation.

The natural and recreation areas offer an infinite variety of outdoor experiences; each one is worth a visit.

AGATE FOSSIL BEDS NATIONAL MONUMENT

Nebraska. On two isolated grass-covered hills of western Nebraska rich concentrations of fossil remains of mammals tell the story of life 15 million years ago. For many years the area has played an important role in scientific research. Plans are to expose representative fossil remains so that visitors will be able to see the skeletons where they were buried. It will also be possible to observe scientists reconstructing some of the skeletons and reliefing certain deposits in place. For the present, however, it is impossible to see exposed fossils at the principal quarries; a temporary Visitor Center offers exhibits on the fossil story and a view of hills across Niobrara River.

The monument is 20 miles north of Harrison, 34 miles south of Mitchell. Address: c/o Scotts Bluff National Monument, Box 427, Gering, Nebraska 69341.

AMISTAD NATIONAL RECREATION AREA

Texas. A joint project of the United States and Mexico, this major new recreational facility in the warm, dry Southwest comprises nearly 63,000 acres of land and water, approximately 12 miles west of Del Rio, 155 miles west of San Antonio, and 400 miles east of El Paso. Behind a huge dam more than six miles long, a 138-square-mile reservoir is filling up along the Rio Grande, Devils, and Pecos rivers. Construction was started in 1963, completed in 1969.

Already two marinas, Diablo East and Rough Canyon, are in operation; houseboats, fishing boats, and guides are available at both. The 40-room Amistad Lodge occupies an ideal site with sweeping view of the lake. Lakeview Lodge and Anglers Lodge are nearby.

Water sports are the main activity through most of the year, but lands bordering the reservoir can be used for picnicking and nature study. The tawny desert and scrubby grassland above the Rio Grande have a charm all their own.

Mammals in the area include coyote, whitetail deer, peccary, raccoon, ringtail, squirrel, and jackrabbit. Some unusual animals include Mexican opossum, coati, ocelot, tropical indigo snake, alligator lizard, and golden-fronted woodpecker.

Even while traveling by boat, you can see cave pictographs and murals representing thousands of years of human occupation. These galleries in Seminole Canyon, Rattlesnake Canyon, Eagle Cave, and other sites, combining color, form, and composition in a highly developed art style, have been compared to the famous cave paintings of Europe.

Many islands at various reservoir levels lend themselves to use by boating parties, while fishing for largemouth bass, white bass, and white crappie should be excellent for the first few years of operation, with channel catfish thereafter. The shoreline especially is a bass angler's delight, with hundreds of pockets, caves, and canyons branching off the main bodies of water. There is no reciprocal license arrangement with Mexico; a license must be obtained before fishing its portion of the lake. One may be purchased in Ciudad Acuna, Del Rio's sister city across the Rio Grande before 1 p.m. weekdays or at El Mirador Motel on the Mexican side near the dam. A Texas license is required for the U.S. side. Hunting should be an important activity, particularly for whitetail deer, mourning dove, and waterfowl. Address: Box 1463, Del Rio, Texas 78840.

APOSTLE ISLANDS NATIONAL LAKESHORE

Wisconsin. They were thought to number only 12 by the early missionaries who named them, but the cluster of islands off the Bayfield Peninsula in Lake Superior actually number 22, ranging in size from tiny islets to one of 14,000 acres. Some of the earliest fur traders and French explorers came this way.

Established as the core of a new national lakeshore in 1970, the breezy Apostles are among the delights of the Great Lakes region. Some are inhabited only by deer, bear, and birds.

The national lakeshore will consist of 42,000 acres, and virtually all will be protected in primitive, natural condition. Following pending approval of the Wisconsin legislature transferring title of three islands, nearly 60 percent will be under federal administration. The 16,000-acre transfer includes Stock, Oak, and most of Basswood islands. A Park Service information center is at Bayfield. Camping permits for York and Michigan islands may be obtained at Bayfield and Little Sand Bay.

Bayfield, the gateway town, has an attractive boat basin shared by commercial and sport fishermen. It faces a thousand miles of blue-water sailing and cruising among the Apostles. From here campers can travel by regular ferry service to Stockton Island, which has been safeguarded as a state forest. They can locate at Isle Point or Quarry Bay (named for quarries that yielded materials for the brownstones of New York), then proceed to explore agate beaches, a large lake, caves and rock outcrops, and old commercial fishing camps. Sightseeing cruises from 10 a.m. to 4 p.m. are conducted aboard the *Chippewa* from June to early September. They pass forested Michigan Island, purchased by the Izaak Walton League for conveyance to the federal government, and include views of sandstone caves and the lighthouse on Devils Island. The cruise stops for lunch and passengers can walk ashore at Rocky Island, "Wisconsin's most northern eating place," 18 miles from the mainland. There is also a two-hour cruise aboard another boat, adequate for most visitors.

Madeline Island, the largest of the Apostles (though not included in the national lakeshore), is reached from Bayfield on a 30-minute ferry ride. It has a long history dating from the era of the Chippewas down through the first French exploration and the beaver trade. At the historical museum opposite the dock you can learn about the activities of John Jacob Astor's American Fur Company, which once had headquarters at La Pointe, the only town on the island. Fifty miles of road lead to small resorts, white beaches, and rock caves. The Pub is a popular dining spot, featuring pheasant and wild rice. At Big Bay, which is partly state-owned, the primitive camper is welcome to pitch his tent and watch the gulls, terns, and sandpipers.

A mainland unit of the lakeshore adjoins the Red Cliff Indian Reservation, with secluded sand and pebble beaches and vistas of rock cliffs. Address: 1972 Centennial Drive, Bayfield, Wisconsin 54814.

ARBUCKLE NATIONAL RECREATION AREA

Oklahoma. About eight miles from Platt National Park, near Sulphur in the rolling Osage plains of south-central Oklahoma, the new Arbuckle Reservoir provides fishing, boating, and swimming, while three areas around the lake are being developed for land activity. Stream fishing and hiking are features of Upper Rock Creek. Camping and picnicking are also available. So are nature trails through a woodland of oaks, persimmon, osage-orange, hickory, walnut, and juniper; and shrubs such as sumac, elder, plum, and redbud.

Students have come from great distances to study the unusual geology of the ancient Arbuckle Mountains, which have been uplifted, deformed, and worn down to their roots. Within a few miles of the reservoir are unusual outcrops, rugged slopes and gorges, an outstanding fossil-bearing site, waterfalls, and a dramatic geologic array (along US 77) known locally as the "gravestones." Oklahoma City is 75 miles away and Dallas-Fort Worth 130 miles. Address: Box 201, Sulphur, Oklahoma 73086.

ASSATEAGUE ISLAND NATIONAL SEASHORE

Maryland-Virginia. Named by Indians, roamed by the legendary Chincoteague ponies, Assateague is a low barrier island, 35 miles long, with 19,000 acres of land stretching along the Atlantic Ocean. It is connected by bridges to the mainland at both the northern and southern ends and lies about 150 miles from Baltimore or Washington, D.C., 140 miles from Philadelphia, and 90 miles from Norfolk, Virginia. Regular conventional two-wheel drive vehicles can presently travel on the island a distance of 3½ miles from the Maryland bridge and approximately 4 miles from the Assateague Island bridge in Virginia. There are no communities on the island, which is the largest undeveloped seashore between Massachusetts and North Carolina.

Assateague and the other national seashores are different from the usual public beaches. Their purpose is to protect and restore coastal wilderness, not to provide beachfront playgrounds; they afford the chance to explore scenes formed by nature, rather than by men.

Bird and wildlife watching. Birds flock to the area, which is on the Atlantic flyway, to occupy varying habitats of sea, beach, pine woods and thicket, marsh, and bay. More than 275 kinds of birds have been identified, and each season has its own coterie of species. Approximately 10 miles of the southern part of the island form the Chincoteague National Wildlife Refuge, where large flocks of ducks, geese, and swans are at home all winter, and where enormous flocks of shore birds are seen in migration during April and May. The Chincoteague ponies, whose ancestors came here centuries ago from some mysterious source, roam wild, living off the marsh grass. The last week in July is "Pony Penning Week," time of the annual sale of the year's colts following the traditional roundup.

The exotic small Sika deer (released on the island by a Boy Scout troop in 1923) can be glimpsed occasionally, along with foxes, raccoons, muskrats, and otters. Hunting in fall and winter is permitted in designated areas and from numbered blinds in Maryland.

Fishing, boating, crabbing, swimming, beachcombing are popular activities. Surf fishing for blues, striped bass, weakfish, drumfish, and channel bass is excellent and can be enjoyed at both ends. Water temperatures are comfortable for ocean swimming during summer and early fall. The offshore slope is gentle; miles of clean white sand beaches make for excellent sunbathing. The national seashore provides lifeguard service at two beaches, one in Maryland and one in Virginia. A bathhouse and a small restaurant can be found at the seaside in the Virginia portion; future development will bring these and additional facilities to the Maryland end of the island. Light, cartop boats can be launched and used in most of the shallow bay, though heavier boats are restricted to bay channels or to the ocean. Marinas are available in nearby

Assateague Island

Bighorn Canyon

towns of Chincoteague, Virginia, and Ocean City, Maryland. Approximately 30 miles of beach can be traversed by foot (19 miles by four-wheel-drive vehicles), providing for excellent beachcombing during winter; summer beachcombing is rarely good except near the two inlets at either end, or after a heavy storm. The shallow bay offers many places to dig for hard-shell clams and to crab for blue crabs, for which this country is famous.

Primitive camping is presently available in the Maryland portion of the seashore, where bare essentials (water, toilets, trash cans, and tables) are provided. Maryland's Assateague State Park, at the end of the bridge, has 350 campsites on hardtop loop roads.

National Park Service Visitor Centers at both ends will help visitors to understand the ecology of a true barrier beach. Address: Route 2, Box 111, Berlin, Maryland 21811.

BADLANDS NATIONAL MONUMENT

South Dakota. Fantasy and beauty characterize the ridges, low hills, and cliffs between the White and Cheyenne rivers in southwestern South Dakota. The national monument, recently enlarged, covers more than 243,000 acres, with an endless array of varicolored formations resembling spires, towers, and pinnacles—all created by the erosion of layers of sedimentary deposits. These contain great numbers of prehistoric animal fossils. When vegetation was plentiful the titanothere (a prehistoric grass-eater), three-toed horse, saber-toothed tiger, oreodon, and early ancestors of the hog, camel, and rhinoceros existed here. The region was then a marshy plain, but climatic changes caused the present appearance, a landscape of sudden, unexpected shapes. The geology and wild-life of the area are interpreted through attractive displays and a brief film at the Visitor Center, conducted nature walks,

marked foot trails along the park road, and summer evening programs. The monument has two campgrounds (one primitive) and overnight and meal facilities at Cedar Pass Lodge (open mid-May to mid-October). Coming from the east turn off I-90 to US 16A; the road makes an arc through the monument, returning to the Interstate at the town of Wall. A visit to the Badlands is easily linked with a trip to Wind Cave, Jewel Cave, Mount Rushmore, and other attractions in the Black Hills. Address: Box 72, Interior, South Dakota 57750.

BIGHORN CANYON NATIONAL RECREATION AREA

Wyoming-Montana. With completion in 1966 of the 525-foot-high concrete Yellowtail Dam near the mouth of spectacular Bighorn Canyon and the 71-mile reservoir behind it, this new area southeast of Billings, Montana, became a reality. The dam, a tall, thin arch with symmetrical double curvature, is the highest in the Missouri Basin. Just upstream, spectacular cliffs almost one-half mile high rise up from the Bighorn River. Their exposed rocks span more than half a billion years of geological history. Both Wyoming and Montana have planted millions of fish, principally trout and walleye. Already available at Horseshoe Bend site (17 miles from Lovell, Wyoming) are 125 camping units, boat ramp, and docks. Other launching ramps are located at Afterbay and Barry's Landing in Montana, and Kane Bridge (on the road from Sheridan) in Wyoming. Docking and fuel supplies are available at Frozen Leg Bay. Deer, elk, game birds, and waterfowl are within the area, which is open to hunting in season.

The canyon is rich in archaeological and historical interest, with remains of ancient settlements and military action. Crow Indians, from whom parts of the land for the recreation area and powersite were purchased, were among the earliest peoples in the Bighorn country. With respect for the environ-

167

ment, they called the area Food Valley because of the numerous buffalo. With the discovery of gold in western Montana the famous Bozeman Trail became a means of supply and access—traces still can be seen along the river 3 miles below the damsite.

West of the national recreation area lies the Pryor Mountain Wild Horse Lands, a sanctuary recently designated by the Bureau of Land Management, an agency of the Department of the Interior. In the late 1800s a few horses strayed from the Crow Reservation into this small but colorful mountain range named after Sergeant Pryor of the Lewis and Clark Expedition. In the 1930s, a rancher was licensed to graze 20 horses on the south slopes. From this stock the herd grew to about 200 animals. They can be seen by traveling on a rough road suitable for four-wheel vehicles and for hikers. East of the Bighorn Canyon, 15 miles south of Hardin, Montana, Custer Battlefield National Monument lies in the heart of the Crow Reservation. This region can easily be visited while traveling between the Black Hills of South Dakota and Yellowstone National Park. Address: Box 458 YRS, Hardin, Montana 59035.

BISCAYNE NATIONAL MONUMENT

Florida. This unusual natural area, encompassing about 4,200 acres of land on the Upper Florida Keys and 92,000 acres of submerged lands and shallow waters in Biscayne Bay and the Atlantic Ocean, is located north of Pennekamp Coral Reef State Park. The extensive coral reef, located on the Atlantic side of the Keys, protects many types of corals, sponges, sea grasses, shellfish, crabs, starfish, and various types of reef fish. Presently you can get there only in your own boat or a boat hired from one of the many marinas along the mainland and in the Upper Florida Keys. On Elliott Key are a marina, primitive campground, restrooms, and showers. Bring your own fresh water. Address: Box 1369, Homestead, Florida 33030.

BLACK CANYON OF THE GUNNISON
NATIONAL MONUMENT

Colorado. Sunlight sparkles on dark-colored ancient rock, opened to view in the narrow gorge cut by the Gunnison River east of Montrose to a maximum depth of 2,425 feet. The narrowest width at the top is 1,300 feet, but at one point in the bottom the river channel narrows to only 40 feet. Descent into the canyon is arduous and hazardous, but on each rim a 4-mile highway leads to spectacular observation points over the shadowed depths. Campgrounds on both rims are open June to October. Address: c/o Curecanti National Recreation Area, Montrose, Colorado 81401.

BLUE RIDGE PARKWAY, the most popular unit of the entire National Park System, attracts over 12 million visitors a year and sends them home as satisfied customers. It is the finest, longest scenic drive in the world, providing quiet, leisurely travel, free of commercial congestion, for 469 miles through the forested mountains of Virginia and North Carolina. It is much more than a road: it is a *garden* of flowering trees, shrubs and herbs; a *park* with nature trails, picnic grounds, and camping; a *museum* of the southern highlands culture, expressed at restored mills, weathered cabins, and farms bordered by split-rail fences; a *wildlife sanctuary* for deer, bear, bobcat, skunk, and more than 100 species of birds; and a *center of mountain handicrafts* that evokes the true pride of Appalachia.

In some sections the parkway runs along the very crest of the mountains. Breathtaking vistas unfold from overlooks 2,000 to 6,000 feet high. Many miles of excellent hiking trails are available, from short leg-stretchers to steep climbs. The

Appalachian Trail roughly parallels the parkway north of Roanoke. High spots in the Virginia portion include: **Humpback Rocks,** near Waynesboro, the northern end of the parkway, where the self-guiding trail weaves among a cluster of log buildings of pioneer days. **James River Overlook,** high above one of America's historic rivers. Exhibits and a restored lock tell the story of the Kanawha Canal, once a waterway to the West. **Peaks of Otter,** near Roanoke, a high valley sheltered by the towering twin peaks, popular as a mountain retreat since Jefferson's day. Visitors who take to the trails early may be treated to the rare sight of handsome grayish brown elk (part of a herd restored to the hills) feeding in the meadows. **Mabry Mill,** where you can see a genuine water-powered gristmill in operation, grinding cornmeal and buckwheat flour with crude iron gears and shafts.

Across the border in North Carolina: **Brinegar Cabin** offers weaving demonstrations on an old mountain loom. **Linville Falls,** a wilderness beauty spot around a mighty gorge, presented to the Park System by John D. Rockefeller, Jr. **Museum of North Carolina Minerals,** near Spruce Pine, a special delight to rockhounds with a display of gem stones and metals found nearby. **Mount Mitchell** (6,680 feet), in a state park bordering the parkway, the highest mountain in the East. **Devils Courthouse,** a rocky summit affording a 360° view across the mountains of the Carolinas, Tennessee, and Georgia. **Waterrock Knob,** looking straight into the Great Smoky Mountains from over 6,000 feet elevation.

Shoppers Guide. Craft demonstrations at key points and the finest souvenir shops in the entire National Park System help visitors to appreciate native skills and to purchase worthwhile travel mementos. **Northwest Trading Post,** near West Jefferson, North Carolina, features everything from homemade cheeses and jellies to five-string banjos of curly maple. At **Parkway Craft Center,** near Boone, members of the Southern Highlands Handicraft Guild are seen making rugs, baskets, gem-cutting, and weaving. These are skills handed down through generations.

Seasons and Accommodations. In early spring migrant birds, including many warblers, grace forests and fields. Dogwood and wildflowers open the flowering season late in April. Flame azalea blazes in the hills from mid-May, reaching a peak in the high mountains west of Asheville in mid-June. Craggy Gardens, northeast of Asheville, is a magnificent sight with purple rhododendron about mid-June. Mountain laurel and snowy-white rhododendron continue the flower show until late July. Autumn brings a new set of colors from late September to late October. Three excellent lodges on the parkway are open May 1 to November 1: Peaks of Otter Lodge (Box 121, Bedford, Virginia); Bluffs Lodge (Laurel Springs, North Carolina), and Pisgah Inn (Route 2, Box 375 A, Canton, North Carolina). Advance reservations are desirable. Resorts are found in surrounding communities. Nine parkway campgrounds, all well designed in wooded settings, are open May through October. Other campgrounds are located nearby in George Washington and Jefferson national forests, Virginia; Pisgah National Forest, North Carolina; Fairy Stone and Claytor Lake state parks, Virginia; and Mount Mitchell State Park, North Carolina. From late June to early September two exceptional outdoor dramas are presented nightly (except Mondays) in adjacent communities: *Horn in the West,* Boone, North Carolina, and *Unto These Hills,* Cherokee, North Carolina. From July 4 to Labor Day, park naturalists and historians present guided walks and evening campfire programs at principal areas. The parkway is open all year, but some sections are closed in icy or snowy weather. Address: Box 7606, Asheville, North Carolina 28807.

BUCK ISLAND REEF NATIONAL MONUMENT

Virgin Islands. Off the northeast coast of St. Croix, the prime attraction of this uninhabited island is the coral reef—a marine garden of coral, grottoes, sea fans, gorgonias, and myriad tropical fish. Here the Park Service has established the underwater Buck Island Reef nature trail, complete with arrow markers and numbered signs on the ocean floor to guide snorkelers. You can swim the trail—an outstanding snorkeling opportunity—in about 30 minutes. Day trips in small boats are conducted by captains operating from St. Croix. They furnish snorkeling equipment and some refreshments. There is also ample time to walk the nature trail through the tropical vegetation covering the island. You may get the chance to see the rookery of frigate birds and pelicans. The island is also the habitat of green turtles. Address: c/o Virgin Islands National Park, Box 806, St. Thomas, V.I. 00801.

BUFFALO NATIONAL RIVER

Arkansas. Massive bluffs and deeply entrenched valleys give the Buffalo River a striking setting as it winds 132 miles through the Ozarks of northwest Arkansas to its mouth on the White River at the hamlet called Buffalo City. The Buffalo is undoubtedly one of America's most beautiful streams, with countless rapids, cliffs, caves, hills, mountains, and scenic side canyons, many with waterfalls and sinkholes, along its course. Bordering lands support 1,500 varieties of plants and many types of small animals. Eventually the park may include 95,730 acres for fishing, hiking, boating, hunting, camping, and nature study. One highlight, Hemmed-in Hollow (reached only by foot), contains the largest free-leaping waterfall between the southern Appalachians and the Rockies. The former Buffalo River State Park, 20 miles south of Yellville, reached via Arkansas 14 and 268, is now administered by the National Park Service. Facilities include 90 campsites, 14 housekeeping cottages, dining room, picnic areas, and canoe rentals. Along the river, camps are made on innumerable gravel bars edging the stream. **Nearby.** The Ozark Folk Center, at Mountain View, is a living museum for the area's musicians and craftsmen. Blanchard Springs Caverns is a great underworld experience. Address: Box 1172, Harrison, Arkansas 72601.

CAPE COD NATIONAL SEASHORE

Massachusetts. The slender bent arm of land thrust 70 miles into the ocean from the mainland was settled within two decades after Plymouth, to be lived on by fishermen, sea captains, and whaling men. For generations it was a remote place of heath, marsh, pine forest, and lakes, and its principal visitors, millions of birds, en route between Canada and the South. Then it became vacation country, building slowly, with increasing numbers attracted by the aura of the sea, soft summer weather, and graciousness of the towns.

The national seashore was established in 1961, preserving the old heritage on 44,600 acres. Thus was rescued from development a 40-mile ribbon, where the life community of the land—plants like milkwort, sandwort, and seaside goldenrod—can still steal to the ocean's edge to meet incoming jellyfish, kelp, clam, and rockweed.

Four areas of the national seashore have been readied for visitor use. **Province Lands.** Some of the most spectacular dunes along the Atlantic Coast are at the tip of the Cape in a 4,400-acre area set aside ever since 1670, when the "Plimoth Colony" undertook an early conservation action. The lookout platform atop the Province Lands Visitor Center commands a panoramic view of the Atlantic and the shore. Swimming beaches (lifeguards on duty) at Race Point and Herring Cove are open 10 a.m.–6 p.m. Guided walks are conducted through

the beech forest and marshland. Behind the "hook of the cape," the visitor looks at Provincetown on Cape Cod Bay, where the *Mayflower* made its first landfall.

Pilgrim Heights. Self-guiding trails lead along heath-covered slopes bordering the Atlantic and to a spring where the Pilgrims may have found their first fresh drinking water after leaving England. Picnic tables, guarded swimming at Head-of-the-Meadow Beach, Truro.

Marconi Station. Overlooking the ocean from high, sandy bluffs near the village of Wellfleet, a shelter house stands near the site of the first wireless station in the United States, and contains a scale model of the original from which Guglielmo Marconi successfully transmitted a message to England in 1903. The views are spectacular, particularly of the Great Beach, which was given its name by Thoreau. ("A man may stand there and put all America behind him," he wrote.) Guided walks. Cape Cod National Seashore headquarters is located here. A swimming beach is available at Marconi.

Coast Guard Beach. Guided walks are conducted through the Nauset Marsh area in summer, and illustrated talks are given nightly in the amphitheater. Guarded swimming at Coast Guard Beach; surf fishing for striped bass at Great Beach.

Accommodations and Seasons. Resort accommodations ranging from simple cottages to deluxe hotels and motels are located in towns adjoining the seashore. Privately operated campgrounds are within the authorized boundaries, and several are nearby. For complete listings, write the Cape Cod Chamber of Commerce, Hyannis, Massachusetts 02601. Advance reservations, for rooms and campsites, should be made for the summer months. Little America Youth Hostel, 10 miles south of Provincetown, is located in a former Coast Guard station 200 yards from Ballston Beach on the ocean. You must write in advance (North Pamet Road, Truro, Massachusetts 02666) and send $2.50 deposit with self-addressed envelope for confirmation; you must also be a member of American Youth Hostels. The hostel is open June 15–September 15. Summer is the year's crowded season for vacationers who crave sun and surf. But if your urge is to feel the precious timelessness of the cape, then heed Thoreau: "A storm in the fall or winter is the best time to visit it."

Nearby. Wellfleet Bay Sanctuary of the Massachusetts Audubon Society complements the seashore. It conducts a year-round program, including September camp-out, Christmas bird count, summer natural history day camp for juniors, and jeep tours along the beach. (Address: Box 171, South Wellfleet, Massachusetts 02663.) Another beauty spot on the Cape, the little town of Sandwich, mirrors 60 years of famous Sandwich glass in its Glass Museum. Address: Box 428, Eastham, Massachusetts 02642.

CAPE HATTERAS NATIONAL SEASHORE

North Carolina. A 70-mile slender strand, never more than 1½ miles at its widest, lies between foaming ocean surf and broad, shallow sounds. One should not come here anticipating the usual seaside vacation, but rather a *different* experience, where the main activities are apt to be watching thousands of snow geese, or the bottle-nose dolphin rolling and playing offshore, or vivid sunsets over the sea and sand.

This is the first of the national seashores, established in 1953. It covers 28,500 acres from Nags Head, on Bodie Island, southward to include Hatteras and Ocracoke islands, now connected by bridge and ferry. An asphalt road leads through villages like Rodanthe, Salvo, and Buxton, which date to Colonial days. From parking turnouts visitors can walk to the beach to fish, swim, or explore the wreckage of ships that ran aground in the "Graveyard of the Atlantic." These storied

Cape Hatteras

Outer Banks, where the English first tried to establish colonies in 1585, and where Blackbeard was tracked down and killed, are no longer isolated—but they offer a spirit of isolation.

Bodie Island Visitor Center is the best place to start; exhibits and slide film preview the seashore, its attractions, and facilities. Other visitor centers are at Cape Hatteras and Ocracoke. From mid-June to Labor Day guided walks along the beach and illustrated evening talks are held.

Pea Island National Wildlife Refuge, at the north end of Hatteras Island, is a key way station on the Atlantic flyway, and it helps to make the national seashore a birder's delight. Throngs of snow geese winter here, as do large numbers of whistling swans, Canada geese, and ducks. About 300 species of birds have been recorded.

Cape Hatteras Lighthouse, the best known of three lighthouses in the area, overlooks the treacherous Diamond Shoals. Built in 1870, it is the tallest lighthouse in the country, with 265 winding steps leading to a lofty view over shifting dunes, coastal wilderness, and rolling surf.

Ocracoke Village is well worth a visit, though it lies at the southern tip of the national seashore. The small fishing fleet at harbor, gnarled live oaks, the oldest lighthouse of the Outer Banks, sandy lanes, and Teach's Hole, where Blackbeard may have met his end, are among its attractions.

Besides the free ferry across Hatteras Inlet, Ocracoke can be reached by the Cedar Island ferry from the mainland (it makes several round trips daily) via the town of Atlantic on North Carolina 70.

Sport fishing is celebrated: surf casting from the ocean beach; trolling from boats in the inland sounds and bays and in the deep waters of the Gulf Stream 20 miles offshore. Best periods for channel bass are April 15 to June 15 and September 20 to November 20; cobia, June and July; blues and mackerels, July and August. However, fish may be caught every month. Charter boats available.

Swimming is best at Coquina Beach, Cape Point, Salvo, and Ocracoke Oceanside campgrounds, where lifeguard service is provided in summer. Strong currents make swimming at unguarded beaches hazardous.

Accommodations and Seasons. Hotels, motels, and cottages in Nags Head and other communities just north of the seashore; villages within the boundaries, including Hatteras and Ocracoke, and Manteo, on Roanoke Island. For a complete list, write Dare County Tourist Bureau, Manteo, North Carolina 27954. Five campgrounds for tents and trailers (no utility connections) are located in the seashore park, generally on flat, shadeless areas; awnings and long tent stakes are advised. No reservations; limit 14 days. Facilities are crowded in summer. Ocracoke Oceanside, Oregon Inlet, and Cape Point campgrounds are open all year.

Autumn and even winter can be pleasant, and are always interesting—the time for birding and fishing.

Nearby. Fort Raleigh National Historic Site, scene of the "Lost Colony," and Wright Brothers National Memorial. Address: Box 457, Manteo, North Carolina 27954.

CAPE LOOKOUT NATIONAL SEASHORE
North Carolina. This national seashore established in 1966 encompasses 58 miles of ocean shore on Portsmouth Island, Core Banks, and Shackleford Banks south of Ocracoke Inlet. The combination of Hatteras and Lookout gives North Carolina the greatest length of continuous protected shoreline. Present use includes sport fishing and waterfowl hunting. Commercial fisheries harvest shellfish and finfish from the adjacent waters. Dolphins are often seen breaking water close inshore. Beach areas, campgrounds, Visitor Center, and marina are planned, but no public facilities are available yet. Address: Box 690, Beaufort, North Carolina 28516.

CAPULIN MOUNTAIN NATIONAL MONUMENT
New Mexico. Motorists spiral up a 2-mile winding road around a symmetrical cinder cone to the rim of a crater formed by volcanic action only 7,000 years ago. Trails lead around the rim and down into the crater. It lies near Raton, in the northeast corner of the state. Visitor Center and picnic ground. Address: Capulin, New Mexico 88414.

CATOCTIN MOUNTAIN PARK. See page 132.

CEDAR BREAKS NATIONAL MONUMENT
Utah. A huge natural coliseum, eroded into the Pink Cliffs, lies between Zion and Bryce national parks. The rim of the amphitheater, whose amazing colors change with the sun's rays, averages over 10,000 feet in elevation. Mule deer often graze meadows and slopes in morning and evening. Campground and Visitor Center; lodge open mid-June to mid-September,

with recreation facilities in surrounding Dixie National Forest. Address: c/o Zion National Park, Springdale, Utah 84767.

CHANNEL ISLANDS NATIONAL MONUMENT

California. Lying 27 miles off the coast from Santa Barbara, the monument includes Anacapa Island, a surviving nesting ground for brown pelicans and Farallon cormorants; and Santa Barbara Island, a large, key rookery of sea lions. One of the most conspicuous and striking island plants is the giant coreopsis, a treelike sunflower, found here in the largest known stand in the world. The islands have received few visitors (though they have had serious poaching problems). Camping permitted on Anacapa, but you must bring water and arrange private transportation. Address: Box 6175, San Diego, California 92106.

CHIRICAHUA NATIONAL MONUMENT

Arizona. A wilderness of unusual rock shapes, gigantic monoliths eroded by wind and water, with strata telling the story of nearly a billion years of the earth's forces, lies high in the Chiricahua Mountains, the old stronghold of Cochise and his Apache braves. The "wonderland of rocks" lies between Willcox on I-10 and Douglas on the Mexican border. A paved road leads to an overlook, with horseback and foot trails reaching all parts of the monument. Visitor Center and campgrounds; lodgings in guest ranch and cabins. Address: Dos Cabezas Star Route, Willcox, Arizona 85643.

COLORADO NATIONAL MONUMENT

Colorado. Sheer walled canyons, towering monoliths, and weird formations have been hewed by erosion near Grand

Colorado National Monument

Junction. Rim Rock Drive follows the canyon rims, with parking overlooks facing Independence Rock, the Coke Ovens, and other formations. Wildflowers flourish among juniper and pinyon pine in spring and summer. Campgrounds; lodgings in Grand Junction. Address: c/o Curecanti National Recreation Area, Montrose, Colorado 81401.

COULEE DAM NATIONAL RECREATION AREA

Washington. The area centers on Franklin D. Roosevelt Lake, a reservoir in eastern Washington, extending 151 miles along the Columbia River from Grand Coulee Dam north to the Canadian border. It offers many outdoor activities: fishing, water skiing, swimming, boating, and camping in quiet coves. In addition, it holds interest in the immense dam, rolling hills, varied plants, and wildlife. On the north and west shores are Indian lands, the dwelling place of a dozen tribes, including the descendants of Chief Joseph's Nez Perce, who made their valiant, futile struggle for freedom in 1877.

The best place to gain an impression of the lake's dimensions is the high lookout point at the west end of the dam. The dam was built by the U.S. Bureau of Reclamation to provide irrigation water for the Columbia River Basin. The powerhouse is open to visitors during summer; at night colored floodlights illuminate water cascading down the face of the dam. The lake has 660 miles of shoreline, with 13 developed beaches and 25 recreation areas providing camping, boat launching, picnicking, and bathhouses. Camping sites range from highly organized to primitive.

The travel season extends from May to November. Water in the reservoir reaches maximum level in late June or early July, and remains full all summer. Illustrated programs are presented at major campgrounds to interpret geology, and plant and animal life, as well as human history, of the Columbia River Valley. A choice attraction is the boat trip from Coulee Dam through the beautiful Arrow Lakes of Canada, a distance of 300 miles. A popular scenic drive leads from Coulee Dam east to Fort Spokane, then north along the shore to Kettle Falls.

Hunting is permitted within the recreation area and on the adjacent Colville and Spokane Indian lands, subject to state and reservation regulations. Upland birds are common, and chukars have been introduced. Address: Box 37, Coulee Dam, Washington 99116.

CRATERS OF THE MOON NATIONAL MONUMENT

Idaho. This is an astonishing landscape of vast lava fields studded with cinder cones. Although the last eruptions occurred about 2,000 years ago, volcanic activity in the area dates back over a million years. The repeated floods of massive rivers of liquid rock destroyed all vegetation in their paths. Barren and sterile, the surface presented a harsh environment which at first only the hardiest plants could invade; but in time 200 species of plants and many animals have successfully established themselves in this seemingly desolate area that resembles the craters on the moon as seen through a telescope.

The national monument covers 53,545 acres. Many features are readily accessible by car and trail. Start at the Visitor Center, which contains exhibits explaining the volcanic formations, plants, animals, and history. Then take the 7-mile loop drive and side trips leading from it. Look for "bombs" scattered about the cinder slopes, curious objects formed from ejected blobs of frothy lava that hardened into globular shape while in the air. Lava tunnels and caves are other remarkable features. Two are over 30 feet in diameter and several hundred feet long, with red and blue formations.

In spring, wildflower displays are spectacular in the cinder gardens. You can see them closely on one of the several trails that range from a 20-minute walk in the formation called Devils Orchard to a two-hour hike to the Tree Molds. For the veteran explorer, who checks first with a ranger, a vast lava wilderness lies waiting in the southern section. During summer a one-hour auto caravan is scheduled several times daily with stops along the way for the naturalist to explain the story of volcanism. Each evening an illustrated program is presented at the campground (open about April 15 to October 15).

The national monument lies 20 miles west of Arco, which provides the nearest facilities for gas or food. A visit can easily be tied in with a trip to Sun Valley or the Salmon River country. For further information write Superintendent, Craters of the Moon National Monument, Box 29, Arco, Idaho 83213.

CUMBERLAND ISLAND NATIONAL SEASHORE

Georgia. It will be mid-1977 before this new national seashore, with its Spanish moss-draped forests and 18 miles of golden beach, is open to the public. There is one small guest facility, called Greyfield, on the island now that can be reached by plane or ferry. Field, forest, and unpolluted beach are rich in natural growth, and the National Park Service intends to keep them unimpaired throughout the 40,000-acre island. Visitor access will be solely by ferryboat and personal watercraft. The only vehicles allowed on the island for visitor use, aside from bicycles, will be minibuses or jitneys to convey visitors from the ferry landing to the three beach areas for swimming and fishing, or to trailheads of the biking, hiking, horseback riding, and nature trail system. The island is the southernmost of the Golden Isles, which have been inhabited continuously for 10,000 years. The live oak-palmetto and long-leaf-slash pine forests add a rare dimension to the National Park System's plant communities, including many species heretofore not represented. The Golden Isle marshes inspired the poet Sidney Lanier to write "The Marshes of Glynn." Deer, raccoon, a rare pocket gopher, numerous birds, and nesting loggerhead turtles dwell on the island. A grant from the Andrew W. Mellon Foundation a few years ago permitted acquisition of 8,250 acres by the National Park Foundation, which then turned the land over to the National Park Service. Industrialist Thomas Carnegie, brother of Andrew Carnegie, once owned 80 percent of Cumberland Island. Address: c/o Fort Frederica National Monument, Box 816, St. Simons Island, Georgia 31522.

CURECANTI NATIONAL RECREATION AREA

Colorado. In the heart of Colorado's western slope—an area of rugged high country, open mesas, and rushing mountain streams—a chain of three dams and reservoirs form the Curecanti Unit of the Colorado River Storage Project. Blue Mesa Dam, completed in 1965, backs up the largest body of water in Colorado, 20-mile-long Blue Mesa Lake, the major storage feature of the Curecanti Unit. It is already popular for fishing, boating, swimming, and water skiing. Work is underway on Morrow Point Dam, 12 miles from Blue Mesa Dam. Crystal Dam will be built later.

Millions of trout and kokanee salmon have been planted in Blue Mesa. The National Park Service has constructed an access road, parking facilities, and launching ramp at Iola, just off Colorado 149, and an access road, parking facilities, launching ramp, and campground at Elk Creek, off US 50, which parallels the length of the lake. The surrounding high mountain country of the Gunnison and San Isabel national forests to the north and east and the San Juan Mountains to

Death Valley

the south and southwest add a greater dimension to the enjoyment of this recreation area. The Black Canyon of the Gunnison National Monument, adjacent on the west, is one of the scenic highlights of western Colorado. Address: 334 South Tenth Street, Montrose, Colorado 81401.

DEATH VALLEY NATIONAL MONUMENT
California-Nevada. The vast desert, covering almost two million acres, is one of the world's most colorful places, a classic area where every geologic age, and most of the periods, are to be found. It also includes the lowest point in the western hemisphere, 282 feet below sea level.

More than 650 different species of plants live in Death Valley, ranging from the pickleweed growing at Badwater, well below sea level, to bristlecone pines thousands of years old on Telescope Peak, above 10,000 feet. No less than 21 species of plants are endemic to the valley, while four, possibly five, species of fish also are found only here—these being relic populations of fish descended from ancestors that lived in lakes that existed in this country during the Pleistocene age. There are innumerable insects and other invertebrate animals, including many not found elsewhere. Among larger mammals, the Desert Bighorn sheep is the most spectacular; small

bands make their homes in the mountains surrounding the valley. Deer are found in the higher mountains, and cougars, foxes, coyotes, badgers, and other mammals are found in the monument.

Death Valley is one of the driest areas of the country; despite low average rainfall (1.66 inches per year) and high temperatures, some streams run year-round. There are springs large enough to support two large resort areas, a date grove, and an 18-hole golf course. One spring forms a lake and marsh area of more than 15 acres. In these water areas many migratory birds come through and stop for a short time—not desert birds, but Canada geese, snow geese, many kinds of ducks, egrets and other herons, ibis, and sandhill cranes; even a flamingo has been seen.

Death Valley is famous in western history. Records of Indians go back thousands of years. It first gained its name as an obstacle to the '49ers in the California gold rush. Roads were built in the 1880s for "Twenty Mule Teams" hauling borax from desert mines, and later "Death Valley Scotty" constructed his celebrated castle at the northern boundary.

Outstanding views accessible by road include Titus Canyon, the Salt Pools, Badwater, Dante's View, Devil's Golf Course, and Zabriskie Point in the rugged Black Mountains. A

7-mile trail leads from Mahogany Flat to Telescope Peak. Though in sight of the cool Sierras, Death Valley is one of the world's hottest places. The travel season runs from about mid-October to the first of May, definitely does not extend to summer. Campgrounds are popular. Centers of activity are at Furnace Creek and Stove Pipe Wells Village. Furnace Creek Inn provides resort accommodations; Furnace Creek Ranch, motel-type units, cottages, general store, gas station. Stove Pipe Wells Village has modern motel units, dining room, general store, snack bar, gas station. Visitor Center programs include hourly slide shows and evening talks. Address: Death Valley, California 92328.

DELAWARE WATER GAP NATIONAL RECREATION AREA

Pennsylvania-New Jersey. The famous gap—a break in the Kittatinny Range of the Blue Ridge Mountains, threaded by the Delaware River—is a forested canyon and a real beauty spot astride the Pennsylvania-New Jersey border near Strouds-burg, Pennsylvania. Interstate 80 and US 611 now pass through the gap, but it was rather remote until recent years, for all its proximity to the eastern megalopolis. The national recreation area was originally conceived as part of the pro-

posed Tocks Island dam and reservoir project. In the face of strong citizen opposition, the dam may never be built and the recreation area never developed.

Points of interest presently available for visitor use and enjoyment are located principally in and around the gap itself, which the Park Service has pledged to maintain in its natural, wild character. Activities in the vicinity range from fishing, swimming, and canoeing, to hiking, camping, hunting, and scenic driving.

From the overlook near the Kittatinny Point Information Station, between Interstate 80 and the Delaware, you get a wonderful view of the river flowing between the rocky walls of the gap. Hiking trails leading from here join the Appalachian Trail and glacial Sunfish Pond, a mountain lake rescued from desecration by a local power company. It lies atop Kittatinny Ridge on the New Jersey side, which remained unchanged down through the time of the Indians, who came into the valley 10,000 years ago, and the Dutch, who began settling here even before William Penn founded Philadelphia.

Accommodations of wide variety are found in resort centers such as Stroudsburg, East Stroudsburg, and the Poconos. Public campgrounds are located in Worthington State

Devils Postpile

Dinosaur National Monument

Forest, Stokes State Forest, and High Point State Park, on the New Jersey side, and in G. W. Childs State Park, on the Pennsylvania side. Old Mine Road Youth Hostel, at Hainesville, New Jersey, and Rising Waters Youth Hostel, at Bushkill, Pennsylvania, provide low-cost lodgings to young people and family groups in rooms and bunks. Address: Highway I-80, Columbia, New Jersey 07832.

DEVILS POSTPILE NATIONAL MONUMENT

California. In the eastern part of the Sierra Nevada, near Yosemite National Park, symmetrical blue-gray columns rise as high as 60 feet, fitting closely together, a remnant of a basaltic lava flow. Trails lead to the top and to the Rainbow Fall on the Middle Fork of the San Joaquin River. Situated at an elevation of 7,600 feet, the monument is open approximately July to October. Campgrounds at the northern end and in surrounding Inyo National Forest. Address: c/o Superintendent, Sequoia-Kings Canyon National Park, Three Rivers, California 93271.

DEVILS TOWER NATIONAL MONUMENT

Wyoming. The first national monument, established in 1906,

centers around the most conspicuous landmark in northeast Wyoming, an 865-foot tower of columnar rock, the remains of a molten formation born of volcanic activity. The sides are symmetrical, almost perpendicular, while the small top, high above the Belle Fourche River, has a growth of sagebrush and grass. A prairie-dog colony is located near the monument entrance. A marked trail from the Visitor Center encircles the monument; there are nightly summer programs at the campground. A good stop en route from the Black Hills to Yellowstone. Address: Devils Tower, Wyoming 82714.

DINOSAUR NATIONAL MONUMENT

Utah-Colorado. This monument is an ancient burial ground, with the world's greatest known deposit of petrified skeletons of dinosaurs, crocodiles, and turtles. In addition, the folded and tilted rock layers show the results of tremendous forces of earth movement; weird and fascinating contours of the land tell the story of wind and rain erosion; the deep canyons of the Green and Yampa rivers have a haunting wilderness beauty about them. Dinosaur is a large area of 206,234 acres; the place to begin is the Visitor Center in the Dinosaur Quarry. One wall is formed of the quarry face, enabling you to watch

175

workmen with jackhammer and chisel cutting away barren rock to expose fossil bones. From this quarry, 26 dinosaur skeletons have been removed for display in museums. Only a small part of the monument is developed, so you need go only a short distance from the Visitor Center to feel detached from everything that is man-made. From viewpoints above the confluence of the Green and Yampa rivers, you can watch the stream swirl and plunge, almost 3,000 feet below, past the base of Harpers Corner, through Whirlpool Canyon, Island Park, and Split Mountain Gorge. The area called Echo Park became the focus of nationwide attention when reclamation engineers proposed to construct a dam; the resulting controversy reached culmination in the 1950s when Congress upheld the principle of park values. Regularly scheduled float trips of one to six days are conducted through the wilderness of cliff-bordered rapids. The one-day trip, designed for those with limited time, travels through Split Mountain Gorge. A longer trip, of five days, begins at Lily, Colorado, near the head of the Yampa, and allows time for swimming, fishing, camping on sandbar beaches, exploring side canyons and ancient Indian caves. Write Western Rivers Expeditions, Inc., 1699 E. 3350 South, Salt Lake City, Utah 84106. Monument campgrounds are at Split Mountain Gorge and Echo Park. If you're not camping, make your motel headquarters at nearby Vernal, Utah, gateway to Flaming Gorge and the Uinta Mountains. Visit the Field Museum (open till 9 p.m. in summer) inspired by the late Arthur Nord as a great showcase of "Dinosaurland." Address: Box 101, Artesia, Colorado 81610.

FIRE ISLAND NATIONAL SEASHORE

New York. Located within 60 miles of Manhattan, this national seashore protects the largest remaining barrier beach off the south shore of Long Island, extending 32 miles, with a changing tableau of high thickets and forests, salt marshes, grassy wetlands, and rolling swales.

Fishing and wildlife watching. On the ocean side, along the Great South Beach, you can catch striped bass, bluefish, mackerel, weakfish, and fluke; in the shallow bay, bluefish, fluke, winter flounder, and blowfish. From October to March, the sheltered waters are alive with waterfowl. Small populations of ducks and geese remain to breed. Night herons nest in the bayside forests. Deer are best seen along the eastern portion of the national seashore. **Swimming** at protected beaches is available at the new Watch Hill recreational site (which also provides marina, picnic area, and campground) and at Sailor's Haven (marina, snack bar, picnic area, and groceries). **Nature walks** and illustrated talks are given during the summer seasons. You will find a growing network of walking and bicycle trails—a relief from motorways. One of the highlights of any visit is a walk through the Sunken Forest, adjacent to Sailor's Haven, a secluded woodland with gnarled American holly, black gum, and serviceberry. Bear in mind that some land within the authorized boundary of the seashore is still privately owned and should be respected.

By automobile, you can reach the island near its eastern end over William Floyd Parkway and Smith Point Bridge; then check with the ranger at Smith Point West. Several mainland ferry lines operate from Bayshore, Sayville, and Patchogue to various points of the island. Eight state parks are located within 40 miles. Address: Box 229, Patchogue, Long Island, New York 11772.

FLORISSANT FOSSIL BEDS NATIONAL MONUMENT

Colorado. The area contains geologic remains of some 40 million years ago. Within the ancient mudflows are sequoia stumps as large as 10 feet in diameter and 14 feet tall, and

well-preserved insect and leaf fossils. These beds have been the subject of scientific study since their discovery in 1877. Developments are planned but not imminent. Address: c/o Rocky Mountain National Park, Estes Park, Colorado 80517.

FOSSIL BUTTE NATIONAL MONUMENT

Wyoming. Fish that were swimming in western Wyoming waters 40 to 65 million years ago are visible in fossil form in this 8,178-acre area set aside by Congress in 1972. Fossil Butte contains some of the world's best known and most significant aquatic fossils of the Paleocene and Eocene epochs. Fossilized marine life is rare. "No other fossil-bearing formation in North America," says paleontologist Curtis Julian Hesse, "has produced so many and such characteristic fossils as this great series of lakebeds." Perch, paddlefish, garpike, stingray, and herring which once plied the waters of Fossil Butte are preserved here by the thousands. In no other National Park System area is this important chapter in the history of life represented. The monument also contains outstanding examples of lake, shoreline, and tributary river floodplain deposits. The fine-bedded layers of the Green River formation make up much of the rugged landscape. The richest fossil deposits are in limestone layers three feet thick and 30 to 300 feet below the butte surface. The Green River formation also contains well-preserved fossils of insects and of about 12 species of other invertebrates such as snails, clams, and ostracods, along with fragments of a few birds and bats. Plant remains—from fossil palm and fern leaves to pollen—are also numerous. Address: c/o Director, Midwest Region, NPS, 1709 Jackson Street, Omaha, Nebraska 68102.

GATEWAY NATIONAL RECREATION AREA

New York-New Jersey. The first units of this 26,172-acre area to operate under the National Park Service are expected to open to the public in the summer of 1974. Several miles of ocean beaches are among the shorefronts scheduled to open in **Jacob Riis Park** on Rockaway Peninsula and **Sandy Hook** in New Jersey, contingent—as this is written—upon favorable action of the New York State legislature. **Jamaica Bay,** a wildlife haven of more than 9,000 acres, may also open this year. Other park units, such as **Breezy Point** on Rockaway, will open later. **Floyd Bennett Field** in Brooklyn is another major unit. Gateway was authorized by Congress in 1972, but the park requires an abundance of federal, state, and local cooperation for full visitor enjoyment and for fast, safe transportation by sea, river, subway, and surface mass transit. Sandy Hook, with 7 miles of sandy beach, reaches from the Jersey shore within 7 miles of Breezy Point. Long a military area containing old Fort Hancock and New Jersey's most popular state park—on lease from the Defense Department—Sandy Hook is ideal for swimming, surfing, and surf fishing. Jamaica Bay contains a 6,000-acre saltwater marsh and a wildlife refuge protecting at least 200 species of birds, including 29 species of waterfowl. Miles of nature trails will be a major attraction. Address: c/o New York District, NPS, 26 Wall Street, New York, New York 10005.

GLACIER BAY NATIONAL MONUMENT

Alaska. The adventure begins at Bartlett Cove, no longer remote as once it was when John Muir made his way into the heart of a distant, dazzling glacial world. That was 1889; in 1966 the first overnight lodgings were completed for visitors impelled to share an exciting natural drama. From Glacier Bay Lodge, 30 minutes by plane from Juneau and a little less than a thousand miles from Seattle, the concession-operated cruise boat departs on its probing day-long voyage

through the largest unit (2,803,611 acres) of the National Park System. The bay itself is about 50 miles long and from 2½ to 10 miles wide, its waters flecked with icebergs, and dotted with islands and rocks teeming with bird colonies, from eagles to cormorants and puffins. Along the waterfront you can see glaciers in every stage of development, from actively moving ice masses to those nearly stagnant and slowly dying, recalling that as recently as 250 years ago the entire bay was covered with an ice cap 3,000 feet thick. The changing coastline, visible from the cruise boat, is forested by varieties of vegetation ranging from spruce-hemlock rain forests to small alpine plants claiming a foothold in recently exposed glacial slopes. You may catch a glimpse of mountain goats on the high crags, for the monument is rich in wildlife, especially in bears, including the Blue Glacier, Alaska Brown, grizzly, and black. Still higher, the summits of snow-clad peaks, where the glaciers begin their journey, rise 12,000 to 15,000 feet above sea level. The glaciers reach the water's edge at narrow, fjordlike inlets, with ice cliffs at least 100 feet high, and some up to 200 feet, causing huge waves when icy blocks crash into the sea. On this trip you are almost certain to see hundreds of seals, occasionally sea lions, possibly whales, and porpoises. Bartlett Cove, the site of the modern lodge, is located in relatively mild climate, the summer temperature ranging from 55 to 75 degrees. It serves as an excellent base for fishing, with panoramic views of Lower Glacier Bay, the Beardslee Islands, and the Fairweather Range, which culminates in 15,320-foot Mount Fairweather. The cove is easy to reach by Alaska Airline and charter float planes from Juneau. The travel season extends from about mid-May to the end of September. Address: Box 1089, Juneau, Alaska 99801. For reservations on the tour boat and at the lodge, write Glacier Bay Lodge, Inc., Gustavus, Alaska 99826.

GLEN CANYON NATIONAL RECREATION AREA

Arizona-Utah. This is more than a water playground astride the desert boundary of Arizona and Utah; it is an immense area covering over 1,200,000 acres, much of it superlative in scenic beauty. Lake Powell, formed behind Glen Canyon Dam, extends 186 miles, with 1,900 miles of shoreline, including vividly colored fjordlike side canyons.

Glen Canyon Dam, a major engineering achievement built across the Colorado River by the Bureau of Reclamation, rises 580 feet above the riverbed. The graceful Glen Canyon Steel Arch Bridge, even higher, supports US 89 as a link between Flagstaff (and the South Rim of the Grand Canyon) and Kanab, southern gateway to Utah's national parks. Adjacent to the dam are many scenic viewpoints, an impressive lakeshore drive, and the extensive development at Wahweap. Here the National Park Service provides complete camping facilities, guarded swimming beach, concession-operated Wahweap Lodge, and a large marina, offering boat rentals and guided boat tours of the lake. One outstanding destination by water (an all-day tour) is Rainbow Bridge National Monument, containing the largest known natural stone arch. Another is Hole-in-the-Rocks, the famous and seemingly impossible crossing of the Colorado River used by Mormons in 1879–80. A party of 236 men, women, and children drove several hundred cows, sheep, and 80 wagons to Hole-in-the-Rock, then blasted a gap in the slim, impassable crevice that blocked their path. They lowered the wagons by rope, built a boat on the shore, and crossed the river to what is now called Register Rock. Facilities are also available at **Hite Crossing, Halls Crossing,** and **Bullfrog Basin**—good road access to Bullfrog is now available on Utah 95 and Utah 276. A boat ride on the river above Lees Ferry is a delightful cruise between towering, rust-colored sandstone walls. The twisting channel, now flowing with cold crystal-clear water, is a trout fisherman's paradise. Access to this area, about 55 miles by road from Wahweap, is from US 89A at Marble Canyon, Arizona.

Fishing for bass rates with the best in the West. Lake

Great Sand Dunes National Monument

Powell is currently undergoing the period of a "blossoming" new reservoir when fish population multiplies. In addition, warm weather of late spring and early fall combine with hot summer weather to produce a long growing period. Choice fishing occurs on the Escalante River from late September through October, when fish migrate into canyons and coves in search of shallower layers of water.

Boating and swimming can be enjoyed even in the hottest weather, but anyone in an open boat needs protection from the sun. Between mid-June and early September days are hot, and physical activity for most people is limited. (Temperatures at Wahweap sometimes reach 106°.) Nevertheless, hiking or walking in the early morning or twilight hours can be delightful. Many interesting plants can be studied, including several species of cactus and bayonet-tipped yuccas. Because most desert animals are nocturnal travelers and feeders, footprints and tracks become as intriguing as the sight of animals themselves. Look for rounded pad marks of bobcat, doglike tracks of coyote, sharp-pointed tracks of mule deer at drinking places.

Indian ruins dot the lakeshore in several places to attract the attention of hiker, explorer, and photographer. Two of the most interesting are located in **Iceberg Canyon** and **off the Escalante River.** These dwellings, remnants of the Anasazi people, are protected from the elements by huge cliff overhangs which prevent all but the most direct wind and rain from reaching the ruins.

Seasons. Winters are relatively short and suited for hardy souls with campers or trailers. Spring arrives early, with many March days enjoyable. Autumn is mild up to mid-November. You can fish year-round for trout and bass. Hunting is permitted during fall.

Nearby. The town of Page, which served as construction headquarters for the dam, is part of the overall recreation center, with airport, modern motels, and nine-hole golf course overlooking the dam. The Navajo Reservation, forming the southern boundary of the national recreation area, provides visitor facilities in its recently developed parks. Address: Box 1507, Page, Arizona 86040.

GOLDEN GATE NATIONAL RECREATION AREA
California. Golden Gate and Gateway National Recreation areas were brought into the National Park System at the same time in 1972. "Gateway West" embraces the 34,202-acre

178

scenic coastline north and south of San Francisco's Golden Gate Bridge. The area extends from Olema in Marin County southward, paralleling Point Reyes National Seashore, to Bolinas Lagoon and then approximately 22 miles along the Pacific Ocean to the north end of the Golden Gate Bridge. To the south and across the bridge, it will extend from the **San Francisco Maritime State Historic Park,** adjacent to Fisherman's Wharf on the east, to **Fort Point** on the west, and then from Fort Point westward and southward along the Pacific Ocean about 9 miles terminating at and including **Fort Funston.** In San Francisco Bay, **Angel Island State Park** and **Alcatraz** comprise the third major component of the National Recreation Area.

Included within the Golden Gate National Recreation Area are **Fort Point** National Historic Site and **Muir Woods** National Monument, but they will be administered as separate entities of the National Park System and managed to complement the interpretive themes and recreational opportunities of the total recreation area. The numerous coastal fortifications throughout the recreation area offer an opportunity to relate the history of coastal defense from 1776, when the Presidio was established, to the present defensive missile installations. Fort Point will provide the focal point for this interpretation.

The Maritime State Historic Park and the San Francisco Maritime Museum together tell the story of the maritime history of San Francisco Bay and the Pacific Coast.

The transition from military to recreational use of the property adjacent to Golden Gate takes into account the essential nature of some existing military activities, and makes space available for public use.

State-owned lands within the recreation area will be managed by the State of California in a manner compatible with federal administration of adjoining areas. Should the state donate any of these park lands to the federal government they will be administered by the Secretary of the Interior. City-owned park lands in San Francisco are to be donated to the federal government and administered as a part of the recreation area. Address: c/o Director, Western Regional Office, NPS, 450 Golden Gate Avenue, Box 36036, San Francisco, California 94102.

GRAND CANYON NATIONAL MONUMENT
Arizona. Adjoining Grand Canyon National Park on the west, the monument offers exceptional views of the inner gorge of the canyon from Toroweap Point, including geologically recent lava flows. The monument is large, almost 200,000 acres, but remote and reached only via unimproved road from Fredonia. Limited water available at Tuweep Ranger Station; anyone making the trip must plan carefully and be well equipped. Address: c/o Grand Canyon National Park, Box 129, Grand Canyon, Arizona 86023.

GREAT SAND DUNES NATIONAL MONUMENT
Colorado. Deposited over thousands of years by southwesterly winds, towering sand dunes rise to heights of 600 feet on the western slope of the lofty Sangre de Cristo Mountains, 36 miles from Alamosa. Medano Creek disappears in the dunes, rising again 5 miles away as an immense spring. Campground. Address: Box 60, Alamosa, Colorado 81101.

GULF ISLANDS NATIONAL SEASHORE
Florida-Mississippi. President Nixon signed the bill creating the seventh national seashore on January 8, 1971, at a critical time when coastal islands and their marshes were falling more rapidly than any other land type before the bulldozers

of ''progress.'' The seashore will include a series of history-rich offshore islands and keys stretching 150 miles from Gulfport, Mississippi, to Destin, Florida. The outstanding recreation resources consist of 52 miles of sparkling white sand beaches, primitive camping areas, and facilities for fishing, swimming, and bird watching.

The seashore contains 20,430 acres. The Mississippi section includes about 7,737 acres, mostly in three islands. Ship Island, the key island in the barrier chain, was held at various times by France, Britain, Spain, and the Confederacy. It was later used as a prison for captured Confederate soldiers, and old Fort Massachusetts still stands in remarkably good condition. Daily excursions are available from Biloxi and Gulfport, as they have been for years. Portions of the other two Mississippi islands, Horn and Petit Bois, formerly were part of Gulf Islands National Wildlife Refuge. Their brackish inland ponds, lagoons, and marshes provide ideal habitat for wintering migratory waterfowl and nesting places for permanently residing shorebirds. Horn Island is believed to support the largest nesting population of ospreys on the Gulf Coast, as well as a sizeable population of alligators and ocean turtles, which lay their eggs on the beaches.

The Florida section of the seashore embraces Santa Rosa Island, part of Perdido Key, the old Naval Live Oaks Reservation, and the historic forts and lighthouse located on the Pensacola Naval Air Station. History and military buffs will find this section especially appealing. Santa Rosa offers Fort Pickens, on which construction was begun in 1828, as well as coastal defense structures of later periods up to World War II. The Live Oaks Reservation was set aside in 1828 to assure the Navy of timber for its sailing vessels—probably the first federal conservation measure. Pensacola's forts include Fort San Carlos, built by the Spanish, and two later American additions, Fort Barrancas and Fort Redoubt. Most of the Florida section is accessible by automobile. Address: Box 100, Gulf Breeze, Florida 32561 or Drawer T, Ocean Springs, Mississippi 39564.

ICE AGE NATIONAL SCIENTIFIC RESERVE
Wisconsin. One of the great natural history sagas of North America, the Ice Age of the Pleistocene Epoch, is recorded in areas of Wisconsin which will be preserved and interpreted as a cooperative venture of federal, state, and county governments. This story of continental glaciation that ended 10,000 years ago is inscribed in the landscape of Kettle Moraine State Forest with peculiar ''pop-up'' hills and depressions known as ''kettles.'' Kettle Moraine and three other units— Devil's Lake State Park, Mill Bluff State Park, and Interstate Park—were opened to the public in 1973. The other five units in the reserve—Campbellsport Drumlins, Sheboygan Marsh, Two Creeks Buried Forest, Cross Plains Terminal Moraine, and Bloomer Wilderness Area—should be ready for opening within the next year or two. Address: Wisconsin Department of Natural Resources, Box 450, Madison, Wisconsin 53701.

INDIANA DUNES NATIONAL LAKESHORE
Indiana. Along the southern shore of Lake Michigan, between Gary and Michigan City, the clean sandy beaches backed by huge sand dunes, some covered with trees and shrubs, have long attracted interest and attention. A national park was proposed here as early as 1917. Finally authorized 50 years later through the untiring efforts of the Save-the-Dunes Council, the national lakeshore will preserve some of the remaining dunes, bogs, and marshes, and provide recreational opportunities. Facilities at Indiana Dunes State Park include swimming, bathhouse, pavilion, and naturalist tours. Cowles Bog,

near the state park, and Pinhook Bog, six miles south of Michigan City, are of special interest for their variety of plants and animals. Additional buildings and utilities are being constructed, and work has begun on roads and trails. Coronado Lodge Youth Hostel, at Porter, operating under National Park Service permit, furnishes low-cost lodgings in rooms and bunks; open year-round. Address: RR 2, Box 139A, Chesterton, Indiana 46304.

JEWEL CAVE NATIONAL MONUMENT

South Dakota. This beautiful cave in the Black Hills, 14 miles west of Custer, is particularly noted for its lining of sparkling calcite crystal. In 1972, the 64-year-old monument opened a new Visitor Center with all new surface facilities, new underground facilities, and a new cave route featuring subterranean formations of major importance. All this resulted from the effort hardy cave-explorers started 15 years ago to find new passageways, hoping to connect two dead-end tour routes.

A local couple, Herbert and Jan Conn, explored over 42 miles of passage, a bewildering maze that made Jewel Cave the fourth longest cave in the world. Many spectacular cave formations were discovered, including several of a type found in Jewel Cave and nowhere else. In some locations cementations of quartz and calcite—called scintillite—cover walls or floors with deep red encrustation of sparkling jewels. At other locations, hoary gypsum "beards," grow over a foot long from limestone walls, fragile beauty swaying in the cave breeze. Jewel Cave had been a national monument of limited significance, but the new scenic and geological values are unquestioned. Guided tours are conducted daily June through Labor Day. Address: c/o Wind Cave National Park, Hot Springs, South Dakota 57747.

JOHN D. ROCKEFELLER, JR., MEMORIAL PARKWAY

Wyoming. Named in honor of the philanthropist whose gifts of land and money were instrumental in establishment of sev-

Joshua Tree National Monument

eral national parks, the parkway extends the full length of Grand Teton National Park to West Thumb in Yellowstone National Park, a distance of 82 miles. It includes a section between the two parks formerly administered by the Forest Service. The existing Snake River campground and concessions at Flagg Ranch and Huckleberry Hot Springs will be continued. Address: c/o Grand Teton National Park, Moose, Wyoming 83012.

JOSHUA TREE NATIONAL MONUMENT
California. A choice parcel of the steadily diminishing Southern California desert, the monument abounds in varieties of flora growing among striking granite formations, and provides refuge to desert wildlife, including bighorn sheep, bobcat, badger, and coyote. The Joshua tree, *Yucca brevifolia,* is found only in the arid lands of California, western Arizona, Nevada, and southern Utah. Varying in height from 10 to 40 feet, with densely clustered, sharp-pointed leaves, the long greenish-white blossoms of the tree are at their best from March through May. Nearly 40 percent of all visitors come during these three months. The Jumbo Rocks and Hidden Valley areas offer exceptional scenery. From Salton View Point, you can look down over the panoramic Coachella Valley, including Indio, Palm Springs, and the Salton Sea. This is a large area, covering over half a million acres. Stop at the Visitor Center at Twentynine Palms, and chart your course from here into the northern and western sections, where you'll find the largest stands of Joshua trees and the rock formations of monzonite. It is quite cold from late December to early April. Ten campgrounds are located at scenic areas; accommodations are plentiful in the nearby communities. Address: Box 875, Twentynine Palms, California 92277.

KATMAI NATIONAL MONUMENT
Alaska. The second largest area of the National Park System (2,792,090 acres), Katmai was the scene of a violent eruption in 1912 which turned a nameless green valley on the southern shore of the Alaska Peninsula into the Valley of Ten Thousand Smokes. For months afterward the sun was dimmed with dust, and in 1916 the vast, mountain-circled valley was found to contain millions of steam jets, some rising more than 1,000 feet. Less than a dozen large fumaroles remain active in the valley, but the monument is noted also for superlative scenery and some of the finest lake and stream fishing in Alaska. Of many lakes, one of jade-green color fills the crater of Mount Katmai, above a coniferous forest at the edge of the Arctic. The monument is home to the world's largest land carnivore, the Alaska brown bear, weighing from 600 to 1,300 pounds, as well as moose, wolf, and a host of smaller mammals, and birds. Commercial airlines serve King Salmon, 35 miles away, on a spectacular flight from Anchorage, passing great volcanoes and glaciers. Then you transfer to a Wein Consolidated amphibian for the short flight to Brooks River Lodge in the monument. Wein Consolidated operates an outstanding three-day package, which includes a scenic bus tour to the Valley of Ten Thousand Smokes, and plenty of time for trout and salmon fishing in the fabulous Brooks River. The travel season is from about June 1 to mid-September. Address: Box 2252, NPS, Anchorage, Alaska 99501.

LAKE CHELAN NATIONAL RECREATION AREA. See North Cascades National Park, page 79.

LAKE MEAD NATIONAL RECREATION AREA
Arizona-Nevada. Nearly 2,000,000 rugged acres of far-reaching tawny deserts, deep canyons, and lofty plateaus, spread across Arizona and Nevada from Grand Canyon National Monument almost to the edge of lively Las Vegas and southward past Davis Dam. Within these boundaries Lake Mead and Lake Mohave, vast reservoirs, provide water sports centers in the midst of cactus country.

Hoover Dam spans the Colorado River, its crescent top serving as a highway. You can park at either side and join a tour of the power plant in the heart of the dam, descending by elevator 528 feet—the equivalent of a 44-story building. The power plant alone, with its turbines and generators, equals the height of a 20-story building. Nearby Boulder Beach is the most developed of five main recreation centers around Lake Mead's 550-mile shoreline. It has a modern lodge, marina, and swimming pool. One-hour boat trips operate daily to Hoover Dam, the colorful Paint Pots, and Fortification Hill. Boulder Beach has a swimming beach; all centers have launching ramps, camping facilities, boat rentals, lodgings, restaurants, and trailer courts; Las Vegas Bay, however, does not have lodgings. Evening illustrated programs, covering history, geology, and biology of the area, are presented throughout the year at Boulder Beach and seasonally at Temple Bar, 55 miles from Boulder City on the south side of the lake.

The most developed of four recreation areas on Lake Mohave, a long, narrow lake extending 67.5 miles south from Hoover Dam, is at Katherine, near Davis Dam (35 miles west of Kingman). Naturalist programs are given in the new amphitheater here, too. Fishing is popular on both lakes all year, rainbow trout and bass are the chief catches in Lake Mohave; bass, crappie, and catfish in Lake Mead.

Although water is the focal point for outdoor sports, the region is rich in natural, historical, and archaeological resources which should not be overlooked. About 60 species of mammals have been identified, including wild burros along the lakeshores, desert bighorn, coyotes, cougars, and bobcats. Over 200 miles of secondary road lead into the backcountry, where fossilized bones of mammoths, camels, ground sloths, and giant beavers in soft silt of ancient lake basins are part of the patterns of geology. Two roads are of special interest. One leads from Las Vegas to Callville Bay, Echo Bay, and Overton Beach, on the north shore of Lake Mead, with access to Valley of Fire State Park, a fantastic desert area with ancient petroglyphs left by primitive Americans amid brilliant sandstone formations. The other cuts across the desert from US 466 along the Grand Wash Cliffs and through a forest of Joshua trees to Pierce Ferry, at the western edge of the Grand Canyon—93 miles of which are part of this mighty national recreation land. Address: 601 Nevada Highway, Boulder City, Nevada 89005.

LAKE MEREDITH NATIONAL RECREATION AREA
Texas. This scenic lake, surrounded by grasslands and steep canyons, answered a long-felt need in the High Plains of the Texas Panhandle near Amarillo. It was created behind Sanford Dam, the principal structure in the Canadian River reclamation project, and is bordered by seven developed areas providing boating, fishing, picnicking, semi-improved and primitive campsites, and access to hunting. Fish include bass, crappie, walleye, and catfish. Among the animals of the Canadian River country are deer, pronghorn, coyotes, turkeys, and quail, with throngs of ducks, geese, and beautiful sandhill cranes in winter. The uplands vegetation typifies the High Plains, with mixed grasses, mesquite, and yucca, while bottomland trees include cottonwoods, hackberries, and salt cedar (or tamarisk). On the south side of the lake, the Alibates

Flint Quarries and Texas Panhandle Pueblo Culture National Monument contains quarries used by prehistoric man 12,000 years ago. Address: Box 325, Sanford, Texas 79078.

LAVA BEDS NATIONAL MONUMENT

California. Great cinder cones, deep chasms, and over 200 caves spreading across rugged terrain below the Oregon border, midway between Crater Lake and Lassen national parks, are the remnants of flaming volcanoes which spewed masses of molton lava centuries ago. Some caves of the 46,239-acre monument, like Merrill Cave, contain rivers of solid ice. In contrast, Fern Cave is carpeted by a garden of ferns and mosses, and bears Indian pictographs on its walls. In a detached northeast section, petroglyphs are carved on the bluffs near Tule Lake, where the national wildlife refuge attracts throngs of ducks, geese, and other birds during spring and fall migration. The lava beds served as principal theater of the Modoc Indian War of 1872–73, when the Indians entrenched themselves in the natural lava fortifications. Campgrounds near park headquarters; lodgings at the community of Tulelake and in Klamath Falls and Merrill, Oregon. Address: Box 867, Tulelake, California 96134.

LEHMAN CAVES NATIONAL MONUMENT

Nevada. On the eastern flank of towering Wheeler Peak, one of the highest mountains of the Great Basin (13,063 feet), the illuminated limestone cave has a variety of colorful and curious formations, including columns 30 feet high and others shaped like shields or palettes. Guided tours (1½ hours) are conducted throughout the year. Above ground, the square-mile monument is carpeted with wildflowers in spring and early summer. The Visitor Center contains geology displays, and meal service from April to October. Picnic grounds; campgrounds 3 miles from the monument in Humboldt National Forest. Address: Baker, Nevada 89311.

LOWER ST. CROIX NATIONAL SCENIC RIVER

Wisconsin-Minnesota. Congress amended the Wild and Scenic Rivers Act in 1972 to designate the Lower St. Croix River as a component of the National Wild and Scenic Rivers System. The Lower St. Croix Act places under Department of Interior protection the upper 27 miles, containing 7,845 acres, of this river segment. The Lower St. Croix, a 90-minute drive from the Twin Cities, is one of the last unspoiled recreational rivers in the United States located near a major metropolitan center. It affords boating, fishing, and camping in a primeval Midwest setting. The act provides that the lower 25 miles shall be designated by the secretary of the Interior after his approval of an application by the Minnesota and Wisconsin governors. Address: c/o St. Croix National Scenic Riverway, P.O. Box 579, St. Croix Falls, Wisconsin 54024.

MARBLE CANYON NATIONAL MONUMENT

Arizona. Extending 50 miles upstream from Grand Canyon National Park, this monument, established in 1969, protects rapids of the Colorado River and 3,000-foot canyon walls.

Marble Canyon links historic Lees Ferry, the boat access point in Glen Canyon National Recreation Area, with Grand Canyon National Park and Grand Canyon National Monument downriver, thus completing protection of a 300-mile free-flowing water route available to those who enjoy running the rapids in wild canyons. Address: c/o Grand Canyon National Park, Box 129, Grand Canyon, Arizona 86023.

MUIR WOODS NATIONAL MONUMENT

California. In a mountain valley just north of San Francisco, at the foot of Mount Tamalpais, the cathedral-like grove of redwoods was given in 1908 by Congressman William Kent and his wife, in honor of John Muir.

The area covers less than one square mile near San Francisco along a beautiful forested canyon, where redwoods grow in full splendor. The main trail winds among these giant trees, interspersed with other trees of the western forest—Douglas fir, bigleaf maple, California buckeye, tanbark oak, and madrona. The last named is a beautiful broadleaf evergreen related to eastern rhododendron; its bright orange-colored bark and shiny leaves make it seem, as John Muir wrote, "like some lost wanderer from the magnolia groves in the South." This was the only area in the park system containing coastal redwoods until establishment of Redwood National Park. The 503-acre monument is reached easily via the Golden Gate Bridge. Address: Mill Valley, California 94943.

NATCHEZ TRACE PARKWAY runs diagonally across Tennessee, Alabama, and Mississippi to commemorate the storied Indian and pioneer trail between Nashville and Natchez called the Natchez Trace. Along the roadside the forest, meadows, and fields present a continually changing landscape, with many flowering plants and lush semitropical vegetation of the Deep South. It is pleasantly free of commercialism.

A number of recreation areas and vestiges of the old trace lend interest to the trip. Near Hohenwald, in middle Tennessee, **Meriwether Lewis Park** marks the spot where the great trailblazer died. Nearby **Metal Ford** and **Napier Mine** offer a look at iron mining and smelting of the early 1800s, when the trace was the most heavily traveled road in the Old Southwest, linking the Union with the remote lower Mississippi Valley. In Alabama, contrast between old and new is provided at Muscle Shoals, rapids that once provided sport for Indians and, later, strenuous work and danger for frontier rivermen. Today it is part of a vast hydroelectric complex, where visitors can see Wilson Dam, first in the TVA system, and enjoy recreation facilities around it.

In Mississippi you can motor over the longest completed section of the parkway, 164 miles between Tupelo and Jackson. Stop at the **Visitor Center** at park headquarters north of Tupelo to see the film and exhibits that explain how the ancient trail evolved into a post road and highway. Beginning about 1785, farmers from as far up as the Ohio River floated crops down to Natchez or New Orleans, then hiked homeward along the Trace. It was used by boatmen, bandits, settlers, and soldiers until the steamboat and better-roads era of the 1830s. Markers, trails, and exhibits like those at **Chickasaw Village** and **Bynum Mounds** remind you that this was the land of the Choctaw, Chickasaw, and prehistoric Indians. **Emerald Mound,** an ancient ceremonial earthwork covering eight acres, is among features on the southernmost section leading past Port Gibson to Natchez. Here **Mount Locust** has been restored to its appearance when it was a lodging house accommodating travelers coming to the new Mississippi Territory. And the terminal of the parkway is Connelly's Tavern, one of the earliest and most outstanding buildings in Natchez, built when Spain still ruled the lower valley; the tavern is now the headquarters of the Natchez Garden Club.

Seasons and Accommodations. In spring nature trails are at their best in areas like the Tupelo-Bald Cypress Swamp. Camellias and azaleas bloom in March in parkway communities like Natchez and Vicksburg, where garden pilgrimages are held. An interesting campground is located on the Trace at **Jeff Busby Park,** a high wooded area near French Camp, Mississippi; rangers present campfire programs Saturday evenings during summer. Another splendid campground is located at **Rocky Springs Park,** northeast of Port Gibson. Both operate on a first-come, first-served basis. Address: R.R. 5, NT 143, Tupelo, Mississippi 38801.

NATURAL BRIDGES NATIONAL MONUMENT
Utah. In a land of brilliantly colored cliffs, tortuous box canyons, sandstone pinnacles and arches, the three major natural bridges of this monument are outstanding for both their proportions and height. The largest, Sipapu, rises 220 feet above the stream bed, with a span of 268 feet and width of 31 feet. Thousands of Indian ruins stud the surrounding canyons and mesas. The setting is little changed from the time when Zane Grey wrote his famous story, ''The Rainbow Trail.'' Facilities have been much improved, the result of developments completed in 1966, including an 11-mile paved loop road linking the three major bridges, a new Visitor Center, and campground-picnic area. The monument lies 45 miles west of Blanding and can easily be visited on an itinerary that includes Arches, Canyonlands, Monument Valley, and Lake Powell. Address: c/o Canyonlands National Park, Moab, Utah 84532.

OREGON CAVES NATIONAL MONUMENT
Oregon. Joaquin Miller, celebrated poet of the Sierra, did much to attract attention to this area in the Siskiyou Mountains, 20 miles from Cave Junction, by calling the cave the ''Marble Halls of Oregon.'' Pillars, stalactites, and canopies of limestone formation line passageways and hang from vaulted domes. Guided tours, with nursery for small children. Oregon Caves Chateau and cottages (open summer) at monument entrance; campgrounds in adjacent Siskiyou National Forest. Address: Box 377, Cave Junction, Oregon 97523.

ORGAN PIPE CACTUS NATIONAL MONUMENT
Arizona. A segment of the Sonoran desert, complete with stark mountains, sweeping *bajadas,* or outwash plains, rocky canyons, flats, and dry washes, is preserved within the 330,874-acre monument in southwestern Arizona at the Mexican border. The desert reveals itself as a fascinating life community of plants and animals. Some 30 species of cactus have been identified within the monument, notably the organpipe, this country's second largest cactus, which produces a cluster of stems some of which reach a height of 20 feet. Desert ironwood, giant saguaro, palo verde, and ocotillo are among other interesting plants that have solved the problem of survival in an arid region. Animals, too, have adapted to the harsh environment, including the famous Gila monster— the only poisonous lizard native to the United States—desert bighorn sheep, pronghorn, coyote, and a variety of birds. The life of the desert is interpreted at the Visitor Center, the starting point for two graded scenic loop drives (one of two hours, the other half a day), and short foot trails. Campgrounds; accommodations in nearby towns of Ajo and Gila Bend. A good stop during spring while heading south for Mexico via Phoenix and Tucson. Address: Box 38, Ajo, Arizona 85321.

OZARK NATIONAL SCENIC RIVERWAYS
Missouri. In the heart of the steep, wooded hills south of Rolla, are preserved about 140 miles of the unpolluted, natural, free-flowing Current River and its tributary, the Jacks Fork, both noted for fine fishing and camping on gravel bars. Local outfitters provide canoe and guide service in skiffs or johnboats. The headwaters of the Current are formed at an immense spring in Montauk State Park, adjoining the north end of the riverways. Three state parks are within the boundaries: Big Spring near Van Buren; Alley Spring near Eminence; and Round Spring, 13 miles north of Eminence and 30 miles south of Salem. All these, and Montauk, have campsites available. Summers on the Ozark rivers are hot; spring and fall are ideal seasons. Address: Box 448, Van Buren, Missouri 63965.

PADRE ISLAND NATIONAL SEASHORE
Texas. An offshore barrier dune island paralleling the south Texas coast in the Gulf of Mexico and separated from the mainland by the Laguna Madre, a shallow, 10-mile-wide part of the Intracoastal Waterway.

Oregon Caves National Monument

The 113-mile-long island has an endless sweep of broad beaches, grass-topped dunes, and windswept sand formations. It is developed for several miles at both ends, but the boundaries of the national seashore embrace 69 miles of the middle section (up to 3 miles in width).

There are two approaches from the north; one leads from Corpus Christi over a toll causeway to Nueces County Park at the tip of the island; the other leads from Port Aransas, historic and scenic seaport, down Mustang Island via Park Road 53. The south end of the island is reached by causeway from Port Isabel to Cameron County Park.

Padre Island National Seashore is a biological showcase. Over 600 species of plants grow here and over 300 species of birds are either permanent residents, part-time residents, or pass through on migration. The national seashore contains the only nesting colony of white pelicans on the east coast of the United States. Commonly seen birds include herons, egrets, ibis, gulls, terns, and more than 30 species of shorebirds. Ducks and geese are abundant in fall and winter, attracting hunters to Laguna Madre. Coyotes are heard at night and occasionally seen in the daytime, but most mammals spend the daylight hours underground to avoid the hot sun, coming out to forage for food in the cool of evening.

Shelling is a popular pastime. The shell beaches abound with marine snails, clams, and other mollusks. The struggle and survival of humble plants and grasses in the dunes are a marvel of their own.

Swimming and surf fishing are year-round activities. Redfish, sea trout, and black drum are the most commonly caught fish. A Texas fishing license is required. Guides and boats for deep-sea fishing are available in Port Aransas.

Seasons and Accommodations. Winters are generally mild; however cold snaps ("northers") sometimes drop temperatures to uncomfortable levels for short periods. Summers can be hot and windy. The humidity is high year-round. There are no overnight accommodations in the national seashore. The closest motels are in the Corpus Christi area, approximately 12 miles north of the northern boundary. For information on motels and hotels at or near Corpus Christi, write to the Chamber of Commerce, Box 640, Corpus Christi, Texas 78403, or the Corpus Christi Tourist Bureau, 403 N. Shoreline, Corpus Christi, Texas 78403. For information on accommodations on the southern end of Padre Island, write to the Chamber of Commerce, Port Isabel, Texas 78578.

A 150-site campground is located within the national seashore at Malaquite Beach, near the northern entrance. Chemical toilets, water, and a trailer dump station are provided. Primitive camping is also permitted on the beach on the seaward side of the sand dunes. Chemical toilets are provided during the summer months. There is a 14-day limit on camping.

Nueces County Parks on North Padre Island and at Port Aransas provide trailer facilities. For information on rates and facilities, write to Nueces County Parks, 10901 S. Padre Island Drive, Corpus Christi, Texas 78418. For information on camping on South Padre Island, write to Cameron County Parks, Box 666, Port Isabel, Texas 78578.

Nearby. Aransas National Wildlife Refuge, winter home of the rare whooping cranes, can be seen November through March from a charter boat sailing daily from Rockport. Address: Box 8560, Corpus Christi, Texas 78412.

PICTURED ROCKS NATIONAL LAKESHORE

Michigan. Between Munising and Grand Marais on Michigan's Upper Peninsula, the multicolored sandstone cliffs called the pictured rocks, rising perpendicularly to heights of 200 feet, stretch approximately 15 miles along the shore of Lake Superior, the largest freshwater lake in the world. These are the nucleus of the national lakeshore, which also includes 5-mile-long Pine Bluff Beach and the towering Grand Sable Dunes, plus inland lakes, ponds, and waterfalls. Munising Falls, which drops 50 feet over the sandstone bluff, is a high point of interest—especially since visitors can walk along a natural cavity behind the falls without getting wet. A great variety of birds, fish, and mammals inhabit the area. Visitors are requested to respect the rights of private landowners within the proposed boundaries. Camping is now limited to primitive sites, although developed campgrounds are available in nearby Hiawatha National Forest and Grand Sable State Forest. Cruises leave daily in summer from Munising, following the arches, caves, and other formations carved in the cliffs. Address: c/o Isle Royale National Park, 87 N. Ripley Street, Houghton, Michigan 49931.

PINNACLES NATIONAL MONUMENT

California. The last remnants of an ancient volcano, carved by erosion into spectacular pinnacles and spires, many over 1,000 feet high, contrast strikingly with smooth contours of surrounding country of west-central California between Hollister and King City. Mantling these rugged slopes, the dense, brushy plant cover is considered the finest example of chaparral in the National Park System, and is the habitat of an interesting association of plants and animals. Hiking is popular over 15 miles of trails, especially in spring when wildflowers carpet the hills. Visitor Center, with evening talks on summer weekends; campground. Address: Paicines, California 95043.

PISCATAWAY PARK. See page 134.

POINT REYES NATIONAL SEASHORE

California. A peninsula noted for its long beaches, sand dunes, and lagoons, backed by tall cliffs, forested ridges, grassland, and brushy slopes, lies barely 35 miles northwest of San Francisco. Somehow it escaped private development, perhaps because most of the peninsula was in use as cattle and dairy ranch land, or because the promontory itself experiences more wind and fog than any other part of the California coast.

The national seashore was authorized in 1962. Almost half of its 64,546 acres will remain in private ownership as a pastoral zone. The other portions are being purchased and developed judiciously for public use in balance with the natural values.

Hiking trails start from the Visitor Center at Bear Valley, 1 mile west of Olema on famous US 1, the Coastal Highway, and from the Palomarin Trailhead, near the Point Reyes Bird Observatory, off Mesa Road. Pick up a copy of the leaflet titled "Point Reyes Trails," which will get you started. The trail system, including old ranch roads, covers more than 40 miles of backcountry, but if you're bicycling, the Bear Valley and Coast trails are the only ones suitable. You can rent bikes at Olema. Traveling on foot, you can take the Sky Trail to the summit of Mount Wittenberg (1,407 feet), 5 miles round-trip, or continue on the Ridge Trail to Drake's Bay on the coast. Those with time should take the 11-mile complete loop, with a hike through the Bear Valley area, a choice bit of unspoiled country. It cuts through a natural break in the Inverness Ridge covered with Douglas fir, resembling the forests growing farther north. The floral mantle is rich and diversified with groves of broadleaf trees and a profusion of shrubs. Little pocket beaches at the base of cliffs along Drake's Bay are reached only by trail.

Birdwatching and wildlife watching are outstanding, with over 300 species of birds ranging from sea voyagers to dwellers of the dense forest. A 1965 Christmas count listed 186 species. Limantour Estero and its mudflats are famous for concentrations of shorebirds. Abbott's Lagoon is an important wintering ground for waterfowl. Both offer unusual opportunities to observe birds from screened blinds. Point Reyes also provides sanctuary to a living fossil, the mountain beaver.

Sir Francis Drake Highway leads through Tomales Bay State Park and across the pastoral zone of canyons and arroyos, freshwater lakes, and grassy lowlands, with access roads to Pacific beaches. Some views are not unlike those that greeted Sir Francis Drake in 1579, when he presumably stopped here on his global voyage, and the 19th century traders, whalers, and fur hunters who frequented Drake's Bay.

Point Reyes Beach is a beautiful coastal wilderness, a beachcomber's paradise, but it receives the full brunt of the Pacific—prepare for fog and high wind. **Drake's Beach,** on the sheltered side, has new facilities for day use (no camping) and lifeguards on duty in summer. **McClure's Beach,** near the north end of the peninsula off Drake Highway, has 4 miles of foot trail.

Camping. Hikes to four backpacking campgrounds along the trail system—Sky, Coast, Glen, and Wildcat—go from 3 to 8 miles. These are in great demand and should be reserved at Bear Valley Visitor Center. Other camping facilities are at Samuel P. Taylor State Park, 6 miles from park headquarters on the road to San Rafael. Motel accommodations are at Inverness, on Tomales Bay. Address: Point Reyes, Cal. 94956.

PRINCE WILLIAM FOREST PARK. See page 134.

RAINBOW BRIDGE NATIONAL MONUMENT
Utah. In the semidesert just north of the Arizona-Utah border, the monument embraces the greatest known natural bridge in the world. With a 278-foot span, the symmetrical arch of salmon-pink sandstone curves gracefully upward to a height of 309 feet. You can reach it by special boating trips on Lake Powell to the Bridge Canyon landing, then walking one mile, or by horse trail from Rainbow Lodge (14 miles), or Navajo Mountain Trading Post (24 miles). No facilities within the monument. The nearest town, Page, Arizona, is near Glen Canyon Dam, 60 miles away. Address: c/o Glen Canyon National Recreation Area, Box 1507, Page, Arizona 86040.

ROCKEFELLER, JOHN D., MEMORIAL PARKWAY. See page 181.

ROOSEVELT, THEODORE, ISLAND. See page 135.

ROSS LAKE RECREATION AREA. See North Cascades National Park, page 79.

SAGUARO NATIONAL MONUMENT
Arizona. A forest of giants dominates the Sonoran desert at the edge of Tucson. Studding this country are thousands of stately saguaros, *Cereus giganteus,* kings of the cactus world, which sometimes live over 200 years and reach heights of 25 to 35 feet, occasionally higher. The saguaros produce beautiful creamy-white flowers, which are most profuse in late May. You can also see how the plant, unique to southern Arizona and Mexico, serves as a nesting site for flickers, wrens, and other birds. Exceptional Visitor Center

with huge picture windows facing the desert and mountains above; 9-mile loop drive and nature trails. The Tucson Mountain section, added to the monument in 1961, adjoins the famed Arizona-Sonora Desert Museum. Address: Box 17210, Tucson, Arizona 85710.

ST. CROIX NATIONAL SCENIC RIVERWAY
Minnesota-Wisconsin. For 50 years the Northern States Power Company owned most of the land on both sides of the St. Croix and kept it open to the public, though recently it was no longer needed as a hydropower site. The scenic riverway was designated in early 1970, following establishment by Congress of the National Wild and Scenic Rivers System. Access routes, campsites, and boat-launching areas are well developed. Fishing (for trout, muskie, and smallmouth bass) is excellent along many stretches of the river. Rapids provide canoeing adventure, though canoeists should exercise extra care during spring and other high-water periods. Canoe rentals and light outfitting plus put-in and take-out service are available at several communities along the river. Interstate State Park, at Taylors Falls and St. Croix Falls, on the Wisconsin side, lies along the Dalles, a scenic gorge with lava cliffs rising 200 feet high. Launch trips are offered from Taylors Falls daily June through October. Address: Box 579, St. Croix Falls, Wisconsin 54024.

SHADOW MOUNTAIN NATIONAL RECREATION AREA
Colorado. The area borders the southwest corner of Rocky Mountain National Park in Colorado. Lake Granby and Shadow Mountain Lake are man-made reservoirs, part of the Colorado-Big Thompson Project which diverts water from the Colorado River Valley on the western slope of the Continental Divide to the Big Thompson River drainage on the eastern slope. This water flows beneath the great peaks in the heart of the national park. Granby and Shadow Mountain are linked by channel to Grand Lake, Colorado's largest natural body of water.

The visitor may launch his own boat or rent one at over 15 privately owned docks. Hiking and horseback riding are popular. Campgrounds are located near the lakeshores, and the areas of Grand Lake and Granby offer a wide variety of overnight accommodations. Address: c/o Rocky Mountain National Park, Box 1080, Estes Park, Colorado 80517.

SLEEPING BEAR DUNES NATIONAL LAKESHORE
Michigan. This newly established area protects 31.5 miles of shoreline on Lake Michigan on the northwest section of Michigan's lower peninsula, together with the two Manitou islands, bearing sand dunes, forests, and inland lakes of their own. The most prominent feature of the lakeshore is a towering mass of sand that looks from a distance like the profile of a bear at rest. The dunes are fed by sands from wind-eroded headlands and stretch in a shifting pattern across great plateaus. The vegetation within the lakeshore varies, ranging from beachgrass and bunchgrass near the shore up through heath, pine, and hemlock, to birch and beech-maple forests, interspersed with luxuriant bogs. Substantial portions of the area have been maintained as two state parks, where a popular activity is climbing the dunes. Traverse City, the center of the cherry-growing and the summer resort belt, lies 25 miles to the east. Address: Box B, Frankfort, Michigan 49635.

SUNSET CRATER NATIONAL MONUMENT
Arizona. Nearly 900 years ago the last of a long series of eruptions occurred amid the peaks of the San Francisco

Mountains north of Flagstaff. The massive, 1,000-foot-high volcanic cinder cone of Sunset Crater, whose crater-pocked summit is tinted with reddish-orange hues, probably appears much as it did after the eruption. Remains of hot springs, spatter cones, and other traces of volcanism look as if they have barely had time to cool. Trails lead to the crater rim and over the lava flow. Easy to visit while driving north to Grand Canyon (with a stop also at nearby Wupatki National Monument), but usually closed by snow in winter. Address: c/o Wupatki National Monument, Tuba Star Route, Flagstaff, Arizona 86003.

TIMPANOGOS CAVE NATIONAL MONUMENT
Utah. A series of small underground limestone chambers, ornamented with beautiful mineral deposits, is situated on the slope of snowcapped Mount Timpanogos, easily reached between Salt Lake City and Provo. Much of the cave interior is covered by a filigree of pink and white translucent crystals. It is noted especially for its helictite formations. Open May 1 to October 31; guided tours. Address: R.F.D. 1, Box 200, American Fork, Utah 84003.

WHITE SANDS NATIONAL MONUMENT
New Mexico. In the wide Tularosa Basin, a glistening sea of sand has been drifted by the wind into huge wavelike dunes almost bare of vegetation except along the fringes, creating intriguing patterns of light and shadow. Displays at the Visitor Center explain how runoff water carries tons of gypsum, in solution, from the mountains into Lake Lucero, and how evaporation transforms the solution into crystals for ever-changing dunes. A scenic loop drive (16 miles) leads through the heart of the vast dunes; a section of the road is on pure, hard-packed gypsum. Feel free to climb the dunes for an exhilarating view and choice picture taking. Picnic area; lodgings and meals in nearby Las Cruces and Alamogordo. Address: Box 458, Alamogordo, New Mexico 88310.

WHISKEYTOWN-SHASTA-TRINITY NATIONAL RECREATION AREA
High in the mountains of northern California, the area is located near Redding, within one day's drive of San Francisco, Sacramento, and Portland, Oregon. It is a three-unit area, with the 43,000-acre Whiskeytown unit being administered by the National Park Service, and the Shasta unit and the Clair Engle-Lewiston unit under the jurisdiction of the Forest Service. Whiskeytown Reservoir, with 5 miles of open water, extensive shoreline, and numerous coves, was formed by the Whiskeytown Dam, dedicated by President John F. Kennedy in 1963 as a part of the Central Valley Project of the Bureau of Reclamation. It is an excellent area for boating, water-skiing, scuba diving, and swimming. The shallows begin to warm by late May or early June, although deeper waters are always cold.

Fishing is permitted March 1 through November 30, in autumn or early spring. The California Department of Fish and Game and the U.S. Fish and Wildlife Service stock the lake with trout, bass, and kokanee salmon. Hunting is permitted during autumn in compliance with California regulations; principal game animal is the black-tailed deer, but there also are seasons on pigeon, quail, rabbit, squirrel, and bear.

Campgrounds, picnic areas, marinas, and boat ramps have been constructed and are available for use.

Shasta Bally, the most prominent landmark within the recreation area, rises 6,209 feet in the midst of rolling woodlands and clear streams. Below Whiskeytown Dam, Clear Creek winds through gorges and rocky hills. Address: Box 188, Whiskeytown, California 96095.

The Environment of the National Parks

When the National Park Service was established in 1916, Congress assigned to it the responsibility of conserving scenery, natural objects, historic objects, and wildlife for the "enjoyment" of the people and by such means as to perpetuate these resources "for the enjoyment of future generations."

This goal doubtless seemed logical then; there were fewer Americans and lots more elbow room. While certain species of wildlife were threatened with extinction, as yet none of the landforms were, with the exception of certain types of forests. Today, by contrast, however, everything is threatened—the marshes, deserts, prairies, the few remaining virgin forests, San Francisco Bay, the Great Lakes, and all the living creatures dependent upon them, including humankind.

Is there adequate realization of the dangers facing the human race through destruction of its supporting environment?

"Modern man seems to believe he can get everything he needs from the corner drugstore," observes explorer Thor Heyerdahl. "He doesn't understand that everything has a source in the land or sea, and that he must respect these sources. If the indiscriminate pollution continues, we will be sawing off the branch we are sitting on."

Every time you sit down to a meal, every time you turn on the water spigot, you are consuming something that had its beginning in Nature. There is no other way. Living things use the products of life over and over again. No new substances come into our world from beyond. Man is a creature of Nature, wholly dependent on it for physical well-being and for psychic and spiritual advancement.

In the national parks every man can be his own ecologist. By walking only a short distance away from the main paths, one can find solitude and can meet the flowers, trees, birds, minerals, and other parts of the life-community. It's astonishing how one can train his eyes to note things which most people ignore. Looking at scenery can be a passive experience, but when the visitor starts to explore with the eye and mind, to discover the patterns in which we all live, he begins to understand that he is part of the grand design.

The most important lesson to learn from the national parks is that man does not stand alone and that all living things are subject to environmental conditions, even to the conditions of seemingly unimportant elements within the natural environment. Sound conservation practices are based on this knowledge.

When certain species of birds, animals, or plants become extinct, the danger flag flies for all. The endless cutting of forests, draining of marshes, widespread use of chemical poisons, and the pollution of air and water are issues of grave concern for the future of mankind.

The untamed ecosystems of the national parks afford the opportunities to learn and appreciate the genius of landforms and life-forms and the need for respecting and preserving them, wherever they may be.

The Edge of the Sea

The seashore is the meeting place of two worlds, land and water. It is a place to swim and lie in the sun, a rocky coast from which to watch the pounding surf and feel the spray of sea wind, a hunting ground for shell collectors.

But there is more to it. The rim of the sea is a place to unravel the puzzles of energy being transferred from one life-form to another and to learn to understand the relationships that bind plants and animals together. Little of the American seashore remains in its native state, but we know it constitutes one of man's greatest and most beneficial resources.

Life at the shore contends with water always in motion, often with great force, bringing food and oxygen to the land, carrying eggs, larvae, spores, and waste into the sea. Many sea and shoreline creatures follow the tidal changes on built-in biological clocks. For example, at Cabrillo National Monument, in Southern California, on the second, third, and fourth nights after the highest tides of each lunar month from April to August, the beaches swarm with thousands of small fish known as grunion. They wiggle onto the wet sand and lay pods of eggs several inches below the surface, protected from gulls and predators, then return to the water. For two weeks the embryos grow within the eggs and then hatch—but only if washed by high tides of the next dark moon. If not, they wait another two weeks for the next high tide.

Sea birds show us the implicit unity of the planet. The North Pacific and Bering Sea regions bordering Katmai National Monument and the Aleutian Islands National Wildlife Refuge are a fantastic aerial crossroads and a staff of survival for many species. Millions of shearwaters assemble in Unimak Pass during the summer, between long journeys to nesting grounds in Australia and New Zealand. Arctic terns breed on far north islands and coasts, then fly far south to the equator to winter. And at least half the world's population of emperor geese winter in the misty Aleutians, feeding on kelp and sea lettuce and on the plentiful berries of the tundra. The eelgrass-dense tidal lagoons of Izembek National Wildlife Range support the entire continental black brant population for two to three months each autumn—the area is essential to the survival of this small beautiful sea goose.

At the edge of the sea one learns respect for the humblest forms of life as the basis for all. Shorebirds and mammals prey on inhabitants of the beach community, such as crustaceans, mussels, oysters, and clams. During the retreat of the tide, numerous snails, which in time will furnish food to others, slowly make their way while pasturing on minute algae. In all natural waters, algae are the primary producers of organic matter. In fact, of all the world's gardens, the largest and most productive are found growing in water. Most of the plants are microscopic, yet each cell is an independent green plant. Plankton, the algal "grass of the sea," grows in incredible quantity while it converts the energy of the sun into the basic food of nearly all marine life, passing it along to fish, which pass it on to birds. It is the first link in almost every food chain of the sea; without it, billions of animals would starve.

Algae are primitive life-forms. Some, the giant seaweeds, grow as long as 200 feet. The fronds absorb minerals from the water and trap energy from the sun. The most common seaweed, eelgrass, grows on muddy bottoms in protected waters, its swaying blades providing food and shelter for eels, flounder, and smaller creatures. Its seeds are used as food by marine birds and fish. The interdependence of life-forms became plain after a serious disease struck and devastated the eelgrass in the early 1930s. The whole superstructure of the submarine forests collapsed. Scallops perished; so did starfish, clams, worms, jellyfish, snails, and numerous small fish. The brant lost its feeding grounds and declined. The sea began to wash away beaches formerly stabilized by eelgrass roots. The eelgrass beds have since recovered their luxuriance, but the whole experience underscored the importance of this plant in the successful existence of fish and birds.

The importance of algae to man is increasingly recognized as man begins to realize the value of the aquatic environment and to cope with the effects of its use and abuse. No longer is dilution an acceptable solution to pollution, for the ocean is not infinite. Natural recovery processes in bodies of water, partly dependent on the algae they contain, are neither sufficiently rapid nor sufficiently complete to keep up with man's capacity for damaging change.

There is no telling where lack of care or knowledge in dealing with the marine ecosystem may lead. When hydrogen bombs were first tested over the western Pacific atolls of the Marshall Islands, soon after World War II, radioactive materials entered the sea as fallout. Clams and other creatures concentrated it in their tissues. They passed it on to others that fed on them, and even now, after many years, marine creatures of the area are still unsafe for human consumption. This should be a warning, for at present sealed containers of radioactive and other wastes are being dumped into the sea. Should any containers develop leaks and the waste escape, the primary consumers will likely concentrate it in their tissues and pass it along to mankind.

Life at sea is linked with life on land. Destructiveness far inland can result in disaster for marine life. Erosion results in floods that carry quantities of sediment down to the sea, cutting down the light in previously clear water and preventing plant production. Floods of fresh water flow in great sheets over salt water of bays and shallow seas, killing marine organisms living a foot or more below low tide. When bottom populations perish, their anchoring effect is lost. And when channels are dredged and inlets cut through, sand drifts to new locations. Some regions build up while others are depleted of sand—thus whole beaches disappear.

Much of the shoreline has vanished forever under the development of resorts and cities. There is nothing left but the sand of the large barrier island now occu-pied by Miami Beach. Fine sand dunes on the wild Atlantic have been bulldozed out of existence.

Still, we can see and learn a great deal from the parts of the edge of the sea that survive. The shore teems with life, even though hardiness is required to endure the onrushing waves. Limpets and other snails hold fast by suction, barnacles and oysters cement their shells to the rocks, while mussels anchor themselves with clusters of taut threads. On the drier side, ghost crabs, with color matching the sand, run sideways with eight legs, shifting easily into forward, reverse, and sideway gear, feeding on dead beach hoppers and mole crabs, then disappearing into their burrows like ghosts. Terns, skimmers, sandpipers, and plovers sleep quietly in marshes or on the dunes. Gulls float in protected bay waters or rest at water's edge. Skunks, rats, mink, and raccoons forage among the exposed mussels, oysters, fish, and the many varieties of crustaceans.

Perhaps nowhere else in nature, either in the sea or on dry land, have so much beauty and variety of life

been crowded into so small an area as the coral reef community of the Florida Keys and parts of the Caribbean. Coral flourishes in warm, shallow, well-lighted waters, making the reef world easy to enter and enjoy. One of the finest reef areas is John Pennekamp Coral Reef State Park, extending out from Key Largo. Another is Buck Island Reef National Monument, an hour's pleasant boat ride from St. Croix in the Virgin Islands. It has an underwater nature trail, which even the inexperienced swimmer can follow in safety.

The long fertile coast bordering the Atlantic slopes off gently to the continental shelf; the Pacific shore is largely a series of great cliffs rising out of the sea, with the deep water only a short distance offshore. At Point Reyes National Seashore, cliffs 600 feet high meet the waves, which pound grottoes hundreds of feet long. The California waters bear remnants of the sea otters, marine mammals once found in great numbers from Baja California to the Aleutians. For decades they were hunted mercilessly, to the verge of extinction, for their fur. In 1938, a tiny colony was discovered off Monterey County, and now the otters can be seen again as far south as central California.

Farther south, one finds another rare species along the edge of the sea, this one a tree. The Torrey pine occupies the smallest range of any pine in the United States, a narrow strip of coast just north of San Diego and on Santa Rosa Island, off the coast a few miles southwest of Santa Barbara. This botanical rarity grows where other trees cannot make it, on the thin-soiled highlands facing the sea and on the sides of deep ravines and washes leading to the coast. It is hardly a tree to tempt the timberman as much as the artist or poet—being low, crooked, bent, and sprawling. Nevertheless, the Torrey pine forests have been decimated by uncontrolled encroachments until only the two native stands remain—the last of these trees remaining in the world.

Approximately 6,000 trees are in the mainland forest, half under protection of the Torrey Pines State Reserve, where visitors have the opportunity to view the gnarled, stunted sentinels, then to descend to the beaches below the steeply rising cliffs. The balance of the Torrey pine forest, located outside the reserve, is covered with fine stands, with abundant wildflowers, birds, and small animals. However, it is unprotected and could easily be obliterated in the galloping environmental decay called progress. Therefore, several years ago a band of Californians organized as the Citizens Committee for the Extension of the Torrey Pines Reserve and launched a large-scale campaign to acquire this tract. They have received aid from the State of California and organizations ranging from the Daughters of the American Revolution to the San Diego Junior Chamber of Commerce and the Sierra Club.

The seashore has always been with us, which may explain why it has been taken for granted and thoughtlessly despoiled. At last, efforts to undo yesterday's mistakes are making headway. Not only are some sections being preserved in their native state, but others are being restored.

It is never too late to begin.

Estuaries and Other Wetlands

When the first European settlers came to America this country contained approximately 127 million acres of wetland. The Indians had appreciated the natural role of these wet places as sources of wood and wildlife and had left the land essentially unchanged.

Not so the settlers. They saw the wetlands as wastelands. In 1728, Colonel William Byrd II led a band of surveyors to run a dividing line between the disputing colonies of Virginia and North Carolina. They entered a vast swamp covering 1,500 square miles; it was a natural body that had taken millions of years to form. Byrd saw dense forests, including gnarled, mossy cypress trees hundreds of years old growing in the water, hollies loaded with berries, pale blue hepatica, Virginia bluebell, crepe myrtle, oleander, and altheas—luxuriant and exotic plants rising from rich, humid soil. He saw animals darting through the woods; it was a hunter's paradise, with no end of deer, bears, bobcats, raccoons, muskrats, and quail. But Colonel Byrd, lost and out of food, attacked by yellow flies, chiggers, and ticks, considered this land a "filthy bogg." He gave it the uncomplimentary name of Great Dismal Swamp.

Into the same region a young adventurer, surveyor, and land promoter named George Washington made his first of seven trips in 1763. In contrast to Byrd, he described it as a "glorious paradise, abounding in wild fowls and game," but he and others organized a lumber and land firm called the "Adventurers for Draining the Great Dismal Swamp." The company dug drainage ditches and built a canal as an outlet for timber. These were considered the things to do in order to make the land "useful."

Thus the pattern emerged—draining, dredging, and filling of wetlands have been pursued in all sections of the country without restraint. The original 127 million acres have been reduced by more than 50 million acres. The Great Dismal Swamp is less than half its early size. Along the Atlantic Coast, from Maine to Virginia, ditches for mosquito control and for production of salt-marsh hay have affected 90 percent of the original tidewater marshland. In the South, much drainage has been a direct result of the construction of logging roads to gain access to valuable timber sites. In the northern prairie states, almost half the marshland used by waterfowl has been destroyed by drainage, accomplished with technical and financial assistance of the federal government —yet some counties where drainage was done later had to ask for drought relief.

"Wetlands" refers to low land covered with shallow, sometimes temporary or intermittent, waters, fluctuating in depth from a few inches to 15 or more feet. They have variously been called marshes, swamps, bogs, wet meadows, potholes, sloughs, swashes, and ponds, and are found in most parts of the country. Even in Utah and Nevada, salt marshes are remnants of salty inland seas and support plants typical of the coastal areas.

The estuarine zone—the life-community where river currents merge with the sea—has been particularly attacked. Thousands of miles have been destroyed along the Atlantic and Gulf coasts, while California has lost two-thirds of its estuary habitat.

Estuaries, however, are immensely productive. They mix freshwater with mineral-rich seawater and organic products of underwater decay. The fertility of the estuarine zone is evident in its large population of wildlife: songbirds, shorebirds, waterfowl, and mammals—even deer. In addition, many saltwater fish spend at least part of their lives in the estuaries, feeding on insects, mollusks, and crustaceans. They are dependent on the coastal bays, lagoons, and tidal rivers for spawning and feeding or temporary shelter in their rhythmic migrations to the sea. A properly protected estuary continually produces economic returns without cost of maintenance—it never runs down; this productivity is of direct importance to man.

One of the main reasons for the decline in Long Island oysters in recent years undoubtedly is the increased filling and dredging, which deprives the bivalves of the steady bath of nutrients from the marshlands. San Francisco, as recently as the early 1930s, ranked as the most important commercial fishing port on the West Coast. Since then an estimated 83 percent of the estuarine area has been destroyed in San Francisco Bay. The oysters, clams, and other links in the food chain are gone.

The environment around estuaries and other wetlands affects its plant and animal life. Some industries pipe in bay water for cooling purposes, then release it. While the water may not be polluted, the rise in tem-

perature is apt to have a critical bearing on the settling of larvae and migration of young fish. Many of the crustaceans have been killed by pesticides intended to eliminate insects.

Another sort of environmental damage has been done to Everglades National Park, one of the most fascinating wetlands in the world. Since 1948 programs of water diversion around the park for the benefit of large-scale agriculture and real estate have severely disturbed the natural balance so that the Everglades is in danger of drying up. The reduced water flow has lowered the number of fish and, in turn, the number of tropical birds for which the park is noted. Economic values are at stake, too, for the shrimp which are harvested in the Dry Tortugas spend part of their lives in the Everglades.

Many trees in the wetlands, such as the tupelo of the South, thrive on a natural abundance of water. But artificial drainage decelerates growth; if the drainage permanently lowers the water tables, the older trees will die. Prolonged droughts cause mortality and induce insect attack. Both tupelos and bald cypresses regenerate well where their seedbeds are moist, but if this moisture is removed they die and are replaced by less valuable species.

Wetlands are the headwaters for countless streams and lakes, watersheds serving as recharge areas for huge groundwater reserves. Near coastal areas they provide a freshwater buffer against intrusion of salt-water into supplies for human use.

Anyone canoeing through a southern marsh at an early morning hour will find himself gliding beneath a canopy of tall trees festooned with Spanish moss. The rush of flapping wings, warming for the morning flight, stirs the calm, for marshes are alive with herons, egrets, and redwing blackbirds. In salt marshes, the reedy call of the marsh hen can be heard day and night. One hears also the loud hoot of the barred owl, the raucous scream of the red-shouldered hawk, the deafening chorus of frogs and, in contrast, the bubbling of air from sandy soil when water rises with the tide. Now and then you can see strong bills poking into mudflats after fiddler crabs, which in turn have been feeding on tiny organisms. Wetlands teem with prolific life-forms, and the smaller the organism the less space and food it requires.

Small frogs diet mostly on insects. Bullfrogs, their tongues unfolding and thrusting out rapidly to full length, capture small fish, snakes, mice, and ducklings and other young birds. Snakes are normally abundant in wetlands; they eat small fish such as perch, chub, and sunfish, controlling competition for food with other species, such as bass and pickerel, which are more attractive to fishermen. Snakes also serve man by destroying millions of rats and mice.

The king of the swamp, the alligator, is an energetic environmentalist. Working tirelessly and endlessly, the gator roots out dense stands of saw grass growing in the shallow bog, making "gator holes," which give it room to maneuver. These patches of open water in the marsh create a better habitat for freshwater fish and for birds that feed on crawfish, snails, and insects. During periods of drought the water-filled gator holes become a refuge for fish, turtles, frogs, and lizards.

The alligator and crocodile are two direct descendants surviving in the United States of the huge crocodilians that roamed the earth during the Age of Reptiles, some 200 million years ago. They are quite distinct in their likes and dislikes: the alligator prefers fresh water, while the crocodile is at home in salt marshes and even swims into the ocean. The crocodile is the more widespread, found in Mexico and Central America; the only other place the alligator survives is in China's Yangtze Delta.

In this country, crocodiles are very few in number; without Everglades National Park, there would be none. Alligators once lived in coastal swamps and rivers from northern North Carolina to the southern tip of Florida and westward into Texas as far as the mouth of the Rio Grande. Because the wetlands environment has been steadily shrinking, gators are actually smaller in size than they were a century ago. Those remaining are subject to intense exploitation. Young gators are taken from native streams and shipped to distant cities, where they are sold as pets—though they are hard to feed and make poor pets. In addition, poachers operating from high-speed boats sell their hides to manufacturers in cities, who make belts, wallets, handbags, and shoes for unthinking customers who probably have no idea that they are helping to hasten the extinction of a creature so essential to the total environment of the swamps.

The life span of all wetlands is limited, as vegetation creeps in from the shore and submerged plants take root, creating a seedbed for the next stage. One set of plants and animals replaces another. The pond becomes shallower and narrower until it eventually dries up completely.

This natural aging process normally takes place over long periods of time. Recently, however, uncontrolled industrial pollution, human wastes, fertilizers, and detergents have accelerated the process.

But good things have happened, too. The state and federal governments have acquired and restored waterfowl areas vital to spring and fall migration. So have organizations of concerned citizen conservationists. New programs are emerging to save remaining wetlands as wild islands in a sea of cultivated farmland, furnishing a welcome habitat for marsh birds, muskrats, and mink, all of which are part of the life-community that offers joy and pleasure.

Forests Across America

Forests even now cover one-third of the land area of the United States. As sources of raw material, they play a significant part in the physical standards of American life. As conservers of soil and water, they are absolutely necessary if we are not willing to have our country become as denuded and flood-swept as the Chinese hillsides and valleys. As environment for the highest type of recreational and esthetic enjoyment, including wilderness vestiges of the original America, they are essential to the happiness of millions of human beings.

The unlimited supply of pure air has always been taken for granted; but the only reason the earth's atmosphere contains oxygen for us to breathe is that oxygen is constantly being given off by green plants. Forests serve as barriers to hot polluted air and restore the atmosphere with volumes of oxygenated air. In urban areas they reduce harsh sounds and the effects of solar radiation and limit the movement of wind, dust, and snow. Economic, physical, and social considerations demand that we maintain a bountiful forest resource. Yet the prolonged failure to protect and enhance these forests has contributed directly to the environmental problems of today.

When the first European settlers arrived, forests of marvelous diversity covered 800 million acres of continental United States. The land was dense and dark with trees. The early forests endured for millions of years, through natural attacks by fire, insects, tornadoes, volcanoes, and hurricanes; the greatest disasters have been caused by man.

To the early pioneers, trees were useful, but barred the way of farms, homes, cities. The more felled, or burned, the better; there would always be more—such was the philosophy from colonial days to the latter part of the 19th century.

The years after the Civil War were marked by wasteful exploitation and devastating fire. In 1871, the nation was shocked by the worst fire in United States history, in which 1,500 persons lost their lives and nearly 1,300,000 acres were burned at Peshtigo, Wisconsin. A few years later, Carl Schurz, the German-born Secretary of the Interior, called for a reversal of public opinion "looking with indifference on this wanton, barbarous, disgraceful vandalism; a spendthrift people recklessly wasting its heritage; a Government careless of its future."

Facing dissolution of the nation's treasures on all fronts, the federal government set aside Yellowstone in 1872 as a public trust. In this manner the foundation was laid not only for additional national parks, but for the Forest Reserve Act of 1891, authorizing the president to withdraw portions of the public domain as "forest reserves." It was the beginning of the National Forest System, which today covers 187 million acres in 41 states and Puerto Rico.

The forest is essentially an association of plants providing food and shelter for a large variety of animal life. Its principal characteristic is the presence of a tree, king of the world of plants, just as man is king of the world of animals. Of all 335,000 known kinds of plants, only this marvelous creature can develop a tall, woody stem and stand erect without support. It is normally at least ten feet high and wears a definite crown. The tree breathes, drinks water, nourishes itself, and transmits qualities of heredity through reproduction.

The forest is a community, or a whole complex of interwoven communities, dynamic and ever changing, in which millions of living creatures struggle for water, sunlight, soil nourishment, and space in which to grow. Some grow because others die, decay, and decompose. The blight of one can be the blessing of another. Others benefit through cooperation or partnership, such as that between the fungus and algae in a lichen, or the tree and fungi in which the fungi's vegetative portion becomes associated with the tree roots. If you study the Indian pipe, the ghostly white plant appearing through moist woodlands, you will learn that its roots have no actual contact with the soil, but it gets food, minerals, and water from fungi attached to them. Insects and animals benefit plants by carrying pollen. Wherever insects are abundant, other insects come to eat them. An abundance of insects means an abundance of birds; the young of insect-eating bird species hatch at the very time when insects are nearing their maximum numbers for the year—such is the marvelous mechanism of the biological clock.

The lowest forest community is composed of the organisms and microorganisms of the soil: earthworms, ants, termites, sowbugs, bacteria, fungi, and simple plant forms which do not contain chlorophyll. An acre of healthy soil is densely populated with millions of insects and tiny animals, diligent architects and engineers that sift air and water and return valuable nutrients to build the soil in support of higher life-forms. Above them are the liverworts, living on soil, rock, decaying wood or the bark of trees, mushrooms, moss, fern, and plants. Then comes the higher level of the plant kingdom, which includes wildflowers and shrubs capable of producing seeds, interplayed with bees, insects, and rodents. Finally there are the trees which furnish cover and feed for the larger animals. In an area of a retreating glacier or recent fire you can witness the process of plant succession and the emergence of a new virgin forest. For instance, at Acadia National Park, Maine, a month-long fire in 1947 destroyed 10,000 acres. When it stopped, a number of species of little plants took hold, building soil texture and nutrients. They were succeeded by blueberries, then by birch, aspen and sumac, pioneering the new forest, and ultimately these will be replaced by spruce and firs.

Though trees make demands on the soil, they also help enrich it. Through weathering and interplay of myriad insects and fungi living on dead material, they decompose into humus. Humus loosens compact soil; it is soil, providing the porous quality that opens the way for air and water, elements vital for plant growth. And it combines with the interlacing roots of trees and other plants to influence the flow of streams—in fact, a healthy forest is by far the best means of flood prevention.

Trees feed on materials from the forest soil and air. Within tiny cells of their leaves the green pigmentation called chlorophyll absorbs the light waves or energy of the sun. Through the magic process of photosynthesis this energy is combined with carbon dioxide breathed from the air and water drawn through the roots to produce nourishment and growth. It manufactures glucose, a simple sugar, and subsequently carbohydrates. These in turn combine with nitrogen to form more complex foods, which are transported throughout the tree. As part of the process, it "exhales" oxygen into the air. How magic a process is photosynthesis! Science, for all its efforts, has yet to understand the exact process, let alone duplicate it, but there is no doubt that green plants are the foundation upon which the rest of life is built, the source of the food we eat and the oxygen we breathe.

Forests have been forming for a long time. The oldest tree family is the conifer, which grew abundantly over the earth in the Jurassic Age, 175 million years ago, and which retains a simple floral structure. More than 100 species of conifer, the needle-leaved cone bearer, also called softwood or evergreen, grow in the United States, including pines, firs, spruces, hemlocks, junipers. The deciduous, also known as hardwood or broadleaf, include the oaks, maples, sycamores, elms—all told about 650 species. Within these two families are rule-breaking exceptions, such as deciduous trees with evergreen leaves (holly, live oak, some magnolias) and conifers which shed their leaves (larch, bald cypress). There are many important forest associations worthy of study and appreciation: hardwood-conifer mixtures of New England; the wonderful cove hardwoods of Appalachia; Southern pines; high alpine forests; white pine of Idaho and the Northwest; and the tallest living things on earth, the redwoods, flourishing in the summer fog belt from San Francisco into southern Oregon.

Providing timber is only one use of the nation's forests. The immediate values of timber yield must be balanced against the needs for long-range environmental protection of soil, water, wildlife, and wilderness, and harvested trees must be replaced by more trees for future timber needs. Protection and perpetuation of "biotic diversity" in the nation's forests deserves the highest priority. The mixed hardwood or hardwood-and-pine forest is a complex, diverse, and relatively stable association of plants. There is plenty of room for timber cutting within this norm. But vast areas that once supported mixed forests are being converted to stands of pine only. Such farm-lot forest management breaks down life-communities and favors the irruption of pests and diseases. Infection can be rapid and direct from tree to tree; if one species is destroyed there is nothing left. This situation creates the need for herbicides and pesticides, which destroy biotic diversity, and for soil nutrients, which lead only to unending applications of chemical poisons and fertilizer and to steadily decreasing productivity. The forest animals become victims and transmitters of poisons. Both indigenous and migratory birds are threatened by the entire milieu of persistent poisons and other chemical agents. The key idea in perpetuating forest wildlife is diversity, yet many desirable plants for animals are being eliminated with conversion of mixed forests into farm-lot stands.

On the other hand, wilderness of the national parks (as well as of other jurisdictions) constitutes a preserve for rare species of plants and animals and for entire endangered life-communities. Innumerable laws of nature can never be thoroughly understood without some access to conditions of the primeval. The preservation of forest plant communities is of the utmost value to scientists and ecologists throughout the world, now and in the future. This is part of the value of the national parks, which contain the last large remnants of the great forests that once covered North America.

National Park System rangers give excellent campfire talks and guided nature walks to explain to visitors how various species of trees and plants follow one another in succeeding life cycles. Western forests may be seen and studied in Grand Canyon (Arizona); Lassen Volcanic, Sequoia, and Yosemite (California); Rocky Mountain (Colorado); Glacier (Montana); Wind Cave (South Dakota); Big Bend and Guadalupe Mountains (Texas); Olympic (Washington); Grand Teton and Yellowstone (Wyoming). In the East are Acadia (Maine), Isle Royale (Michigan), Great Smoky Mountains (North Carolina and Tennessee), and Shenandoah (Virginia).

Grasslands of Prairies and Plains

Before the land was settled, a sea of grass spread between the Western desert and forests of the East. The Great Plains and prairies were the home of the bison, pronghorn, wolf, and the Indian, in competition for survival and yet sustaining one another without disrupting the natural cycle.

Where fragments of the original remain there is still immense variety—in scene, weather, and life. Vegetation stretches as far as the eye can see, green in the rainy season, sprinkled with brightly colored wildflowers, and brown in the dry season. A common morning scene, as described by the pioneer ecologist Victor Shelford, contains a herd of bison or pronghorns in the distance, jackrabbits returning to their forms, a wolf or coyote trotting to its den, several small birds flying overhead and singing, and a prairie dog or ground squirrel sitting upright at its burrow.

Like the forests, these grasslands vary widely. They are flat, or rolling, often broken by wooded drainages, and divided into different types, depending on soil quality and the amount of moisture they receive.

The tall-grass prairie originally extended from Indiana, Wisconsin, and Illinois through Minnesota, Iowa, and Missouri into Manitoba, the eastern Dakotas, Nebraska, Kansas, eastern Oklahoma, and Texas. It was here the early pioneers walked amid grasslands of bluestem and Indian grass that rose above their heads. They found some of the world's most fertile soil, built deep, dark, and rich through patient ages. Rainfall within the prairie ranged from 20 to 40 inches annually, making the area wetter than the Great Plains but drier than the forest. The settlers broke the heavy sod (and sometimes their plows) while converting this region into the corn belt, or "the nation's breadbasket."

To the west lies a belt of mixed-grass prairie, dominated by little bluestem, June grass, wheat grass, and others, not as high or as continuous, allowing space between them for a variety of flowering herbs. Still

farther west are the Great Plains, where the short grasses grow to the base of the Rocky Mountains. In the long course of geologic history the western plains were raised to their present high elevations, 2,500 or more above sea level, while mountain ranges were thrust even higher to intercept most rain and snow. The plains are dry, receiving less than 20 inches of rainfall a year, and the wind blows relentlessly, harder and longer than in any other part of the country. In the native setting the soil was mineral-rich, producing forage for large animals such as buffalo and pronghorn.

The vast open spaces and valuable grasses made the Great Plains valuable to man's economic use. Following the Civil War, the cowman, sheepman, buffalo hunter, and trader in skins marched across the continent. Livestock syndicates based in the East and Europe annihilated buffalo by the millions and replaced them with cows. Herds of bighorn sheep and elk were driven from valleys and lower hills to what appears now to be their final refuge in the mountains. Kit fox, red fox, skunk, eagle, magpie—these and other creatures perished by the tens of thousands. Livestock herds grew larger and larger. Grasses thinned and disappeared. Trampling hooves stripped the protective layer of decaying plant materials from the soil.

Then the farmers came. Few could make a decent living on a 160-acre homestead in the high plains, unsuited for intensive cultivation and with insufficient rainfall. Recurrent drought, excessive grazing, and relentless winds changed sod to dust. In the 1930s two dust storms blew 2,000 miles to pass over the nation's capital, almost blotting out the sun, and then settling on the decks of ships 300 miles offshore in the Atlantic Ocean. To this day, some areas still bear the scars of a thoughtless past, with dust blowing and gullies gnawing at lands on abandoned farms. In place of the sturdy original grassy cover, sage and thistle and scrawny, short-lived "cheat grass" share the landscape.

Important strides have been made in recent decades, through government programs to restore the grassland. Grass is recognized as the key to a whole system of life. Man, his domestic stock, and the animals of the wild all depend on the power of grass, a humble but efficient plant.

There is now a new appreciation of the mechanism of the grassland life-community. The taller plants protect the lower ones from the heat of the sun. The lesser grasses reduce the loss of water from the soil by mulching it with their own prostrate forms. Although the vast bison herds trampled the grass, the droppings of these huge beasts served as natural fertilizers, while gophers and ground squirrels by their burrowing invited penetration of air and moisture. Wolves and coyotes controlled the numbers of prairie herds so the community of plants and animals maintained its balance.

Great armies of rodents helped to build the soil, their numbers kept in check by snakes, coyotes, owls, and hawks.

The swift pronghorn, or antelope, found nowhere in the world outside North America, bespeaks the glory of the grassland community. Subsisting on grasses, forbs, and shrubs, its population has been appreciably restored after reaching near extinction several decades ago. No other region contains such a variety of upland birds as the grasslands. Native sage grouse and quail are common.

One of the most interesting species is the upland plover (a bird that was seemingly headed toward extinction in the early 1900s), a prominent figure in the prairie community from the time it arrives in spring until it departs for South America late in July. Then there is the celebrated prairie chicken, performing its unusual strutting "dance" on the grounds of its ancestors. Waterfowl find the prairie lakes and ponds attractive after their long annual flight from the North; many waterfowl, in fact, are born at waterholes on the prairie.

No longer is the grassland perspective termed "monotonous." To see the ever-changing flower show of the prairie is never to forget it. From the spring freshness of the windflower through the blue of verbena and wild indigo to the autumn yellow of goldenrod and sunflower and the bronze red of the tall grass with its waving seedhead, it is continually splashed with color.

Grassland is now cherished as part of this country's heritage, a priceless treasure. Yet it represents the greatest single gap, and most critical need, in the entire National Park System. The native prairie is nearly gone. Forty years ago there were still virgin grasslands in abundance, even in highly developed Illinois and Wisconsin. Today not many acres of deep-soil prairie remain in the entire "prairie state" of Illinois. Virgin prairie once covered four-fifths of Iowa; now only a few small study areas are left.

Recurrent proposals have been made to establish a major grasslands national park. Dr. Hugh Iltis, distinguished botanist and ecologist of the University of Wisconsin, and others have proposed to establish four big national parks: a tall-grass park in the Flint Hills, near Manhattan, Kansas, an area which probably contains the largest remaining prairie anywhere in the country; a sandhills park in Nebraska; a short-grass park in the Dakotas; and the Llano Estacado park near Lubbock, in the Texas panhandle. In addition, there would be a Prairie Research Institute to train students in the ecology of the prairie and Great Plains, plus a system of school prairie preserves and hiking trails. This latter concept has been gaining increasing support and educators see it as an excellent means of insuring that children may always feel the sense of peace and wonder implicit in the sea of grass.

Mountains and the Human Environment

In less than an hour an entire family can follow a footpath in the Southern Appalachians from a warm, humid valley into an evergreen forest, a wonderland in the clouds. Parents and children pass rhododendron plants as tall as trees but blooming with clusters of purple or white flowers unlike any trees they have seen. Sunlight filters through the leaves, illuminating salamanders, scurrying across the rocks, and wildflowers.

Every mountain offers a different experience, even within its own range. The best way to explore any of them is on foot. By ascending slowly, from one natural environment to another, absorbing en route the details of plant and animal life and rock and water, you cannot help but gain a better understanding of the relationship of mountains to the human environment.

Mountain building has been underway since the world began and still continues as the earth grows and changes in form. Earthquakes are recorded every year. The last series of volcanic eruptions at Mount Lassen, the focus of Lassen National Park, California, began as recently as 1914. In other places, unending changes in the earth's face set up stresses that ultimately yield along the line of a fracture or fault. The San Andreas fault zone, probably the best known in America, is easily observable by air along much of its 600 miles from San Francisco southward. Montana's geology is a history of earthquakes, the most recent occurring just outside of Yellowstone National Park in 1959, following pressures built up over long periods between huge masses of subterranean rocks. When the earthquake hit, it repeated the pattern of history, renewing the environmental lesson to keep human developments away from fault lines.

Mountains vary widely in age. Time has mellowed the eastern mountains so they lack the sharp peaks and sawtooth ridges of the West, though they may once have stood as high as the Rockies. In the ancient Smokies, immense stretches of time and heavy precipitation have rounded off the peaks, washing down rock from the high elevations and filling the slopes with a gentle profile. The mountaintops here are green in contrast to the rock exposure of the New England peaks. This is because the Appalachians were never glaciated by the ice sheets of the Pleistocene age that flowed down over the continent a million years ago. In the Rockies, however, the process is much less advanced, for the mountains are younger, untamed by erosion. Glaciers have been at work so recently that some valleys are still bare of soil and of vegetation.

As you start up the mountain, wherever it may be, observe the interaction of rocks and water. In the unending weathering process, rocks are continually attacked by sun, frost, and rain, then scattered by wind and water. In past ages enormous quantities of rock were ground to dust by moving glaciers and carried many miles before being added to the material of the soil. Even now you can see how wind and flowing water sweep rock fragments from the ridges, drive them against other exposed rocks, grind them into smaller pieces, and reduce them to particles that go into the making of soil. Thus the coves at the base of steep Appalachian slopes, where rushing mountain streams have brought and deposited organic materials, are marked by deep, rich soil with thriving forests of many species.

Most rivers are born in the mountains, often in the form of snow at high elevations; so stable watersheds —the drainage basins of rivers and streams—are the key to protecting the water supplies of towns, cities, and industries. Wherever mountain slopes are abused, whether by farming, mining, livestock grazing, logging, or unrestricted construction, the impact is felt upon community life downstream.

Trees and brush, and in fact nearly all vegetable growth along the trail, have a great power of holding rainwater, retarding its flow until it has time to sink into the earth. Leaves, twigs, and branches intercept raindrops, diminish their force. Roots, fallen leaves, and sticks hold back the water and divide its currents. Humus or soil of forest and brush land has the power of absorption like a sponge. Protected watersheds improve percolation through the soil to produce high-quality water for recreation and industry. In contrast, whenever rain falls on bare ground, it flows overland, picking up undesirable salts, sediment, and other surface pollutants. Accumulating sediment from muddy waters steadily reduces the storage capacity in reservoirs.

The higher you climb, the cooler the air becomes. Because it is thinner it absorbs less radiation, so the temperature drops three degrees per thousand feet. This corresponds to driving north 300 miles at sea level. By climbing some of the mountains of the Southwest, you can travel through most of the North American life zones, passing pinyon-juniper that gives way to ponderosa pine, then finally ending up on a Canadian island of Douglas fir, white fir, and quaking aspen overlooking a sea of desert below.

In the Rockies, Sierra Nevadas, and Cascades are broad sweeping valleys, huge natural amphitheaters gouged by the glaciers from the sides of mountains, and crystal-clear lakes. Near the summit trees become shorter, contorted, struggling to survive against wind and snow. Then you reach the timberline, or tree line, where conditions become too harsh for trees of any sort and they are succeeded by grasses, sedges, and herbs. Timberline varies widely. On exposed, north-facing slopes trees give way much lower than on warm, south-facing slopes and sheltered ravines.

The high meadows support plants in a frigid tundra climate, clustered in low, compact clumps to avoid buffeting by winds, but more luxuriant in crevices and sheltered hollows. As the season advances and snow-banks recede up the slopes, the same species of plants continue to bloom at successively higher elevations in the alpine garden.

In several of the Western parks—Glacier, Grand Teton, Mount Rainier, North Cascades, Olympic, Rocky Mountain, Kings Canyon-Sequoia, Yosemite—glaciers lie at the end of the trail, reminders of the great mile-thick sheets of ice that once swept over much of the continent. About 1,100 glaciers are still found in parts of the West, but these are relatively small compared with those of Alaska, including those of Glacier Bay National Monument and Mount McKinley National Park.

About three-fourths of all the fresh water in the world is stored as glacial ice. In North America, the volume is many times greater than that stored in all of the lakes, ponds, rivers, and reservoirs on the continent. The glaciers work in ways to fill human needs. The water is stored in winter when the need for irrigation and domestic water is least; then it becomes available during the heat of summer when the need is greatest.

In national parks where glaciers still flow, visitors learn that melting depends on the delicate balance of heat at the snow or ice surface, rather than the amounts available or the outside air temperature. This produces a natural regulation of runoff from year to year, with significant economic importance in regions like the Northwest, where glaciers assure hydroelectric power and irrigation water.

Some foreign nations are experimenting with manipulation of melting, to accelerate or slow the rate. But more than nine-tenths of all glaciers in the United States lie in wilderness areas, protected from such manipulation—and this country may be better off for it.

All of America's mountains are rich in wildlife. In canyons from Alaska to Panama, one encounters the chunky, short-tailed, tuneful ouzel, or dipper, flourishing wherever it can find tumbling streams. This fascinating little bird captures the bulk of its food on the stream bottom, plunging in fearlessly, then swimming underwater to forage among rocks and pebbles for water insects and other morsels.

Besides the common varieties, the Western mountains provide sanctuary for rare and vanishing species. Mountain goats pick their way nimbly with padded

hooves along narrow ledges, high above the predators, grazing on tundra plants. Scattered populations of bighorn sheep are found from Alaska to Mexico, but in mere remnants of flocks that once numbered a million or more. The history of this handsome horned animal has been one of gradual retreat. John Muir once pointed out the California bighorn would be extinct, like the elks of the valley and hills, were it not for its requirement of wilderness habitat and the agility to match the environment.

Another highly adapted creature, the golden eagle, raises its young on rocky ledges in the high mountains. Truly a bird of prey, it normally feeds on rodents, squirrels, and rabbits, but occasionally attacks a deer or other large mammal. Because the golden eagle may attack calves or lambs when nothing else is available, it has been ruthlessly trapped, shot, and poisoned. Bounty hunters gunned down thousands of eagles from airplanes until public protest forced Congress to outlaw such slaughter. Eagles that kill livestock can be dealt with individually, without a war of extermination over the mountains.

The Desert... Living Library, and a Quiet One

In ancient times the maximum daily water requirement for all purposes was about three to five gallons a person. Even today primitive people of Asia and Africa scoop up water from shallow pools or streams and carry it home in jars. In some places they store it in the trunks of hollow trees and seal the openings with wet clay to keep it uncontaminated.

But in our civilized way, with running water, flush toilet, lawn sprinkler, and swimming pool, we consume more than sixty gallons per person each day, and waste an appreciable amount of the precious substance in the process.

The desert is a living library in the frugality of water, abundant with plants and animals which through centuries of evolution have adapted themselves to endure where water is scarce and undependable. Think of it, the little kangaroo rat is so admirably fitted to his environment that he can go through his entire life without a drink! The coyote is able to scoop out sand in some favorable dry wash to reach water. Some plants live on dew alone.

Various plants fit themselves into particular conditions of moisture on earth. Deciduous trees like oak and maple require moisture year-round. Conifers like the pine can survive where the moisture supply is concentrated in winter. Chaparral occupies the driest forest environment. Cacti, emblems of the desert, have tissues that enable them to retain water through prolonged drought.

Perhaps 25,000 years ago, the first nomadic hunters ventured into the great desert of the American Southwest. Two thousand years ago the first farmers arrived. The Anasazi—an Indian word meaning "the ancient ones"—built a culture that was successful for a millenium, leaving behind them mesa-top villages of pit houses and a treasure in petroglyphs and pictographs. Their descendants, the Pueblo Indians, still inhabit the Southwest. The Anasazi culture began to decline about the time of the Magna Carta. Perhaps a subtle shift in climate, leading to sustained drought, made it impossible to farm the higher mesas, but by the time of Columbus the watchtowers stood empty, the fields fallow.

There is one lesson to be learned from the partnership between the Anasazi and their land, even though the land finally defeated them. Their methods of working with soil and water were primitive, but they met the desert on its own terms, living for more than ten centuries without altering the balance of nature. In less than four centuries the European and his descendants have disrupted it beyond belief, and much of the land is still deteriorating. At last we have come to realize our deserts are fragile; there is a delicate balance that can be easily upset. Yet the deserts, though steadily shrinking, are primitive, alive, challenging, and inspiring.

The Great Basin Desert covers most of Nevada and some of Utah, with fringes in Oregon, Idaho, Wyoming, and Colorado. This is the "high desert," an arid upland of broad basins and plateaus, shut off from the moist Pacific by the Sierras.

The few trees are mostly pinyon pine and juniper. Vegetation is grayish in tone—the low, clumpy sagebrush, rabbit brush, grass saltbush, and most of the weeds. So are the lizards, rattlesnakes, coyotes, deer, and most birds. But the flowers, including primroses, buttercups, Indian paintbrush, larkspur, phlox, and the beautiful coral mallow, flash in vivid colors during springtime. The Great Basin is marked by the remnants of Pleistocene lakes, like Lake Bonneville, an ancient inland sea in northwest Utah, and Great Salt Lake, the ancestral nesting places of pelicans, cormorants, and terns—birds that are normally seen at the distant seashore.

Approaching the southwestern borders of the Great Basin, the sagebrush bows to the Joshua tree, which characterizes the Mohave Desert of southeastern California and Nevada, one of the driest areas in the world.

Ages ago the Mohave was covered with rivers and lakes and supported a variety of life. As the climate became more arid, the waterways gradually dwindled, and the dependent plants and animals with them. Though it may seem barren, the Mohave is rich in life-forms. Through most of the year plants lie dormant and invisible, but when it rains they burst into bloom and grow. Likewise, during these fleeting periods of moisture, many animals produce their young in response to the biotic timetable.

How much life in the Mohave? A survey in Death Valley National Monument reveals 608 different kinds of plants, growing everywhere except on the salt flats. About 160 species of birds have been recorded in the hottest, driest areas below sea level and 230 species in the entire monument.

The Sonoran desert, extending from southern California across western Arizona into the Mexican state of Sonora, receives only 10 inches of rainfall annually. Spring is the magic time, with short-lived wildflowers bursting into color. These include the sundrop, which opens delicate yellow petals at night and closes soon after sunrise in order to conserve the moisture; the violet-purple curling scorpionweed; the lavish poppy, covering wide sections with a cloth of gold. Above them, the misty green-branched palo verde, the state tree of Arizona, bursts into pale yellow bloom, and the ocotillo, formed of slender, wandlike stems, wears scarlet clusters at its tips. Penstemon, usually on rocky hillsides, flames in various colors from violet to deep red. Here you can learn how many herbs, grasses, and shrubs store water within their stems, leaves, roots; some succulents spread closely meshed root systems like a bowl to trap water.

Along the few stream beds, phreatophytes are found in dense clusters, with roots reaching deeply into the water. Among them, tamarisk, or salt cedar, grows 20 feet tall and stands lush green in contrast to the other gray vegetation. Then there are shrubs like mesquite, greasewood, willow, and baccharis, and trees of the streamside and valley bottom like cottonwood, mountain ash, alder, and sycamore. These have not been popular, since man thinks they utilize water that belongs to him. But phreatophytes help to stabilize the stream banks, and they provide beauty to the landscape and food and cover to many birds and small animals.

The giant saguaro cactuses stand like gnarled, primitive pillars, grotesque but beautiful, bearing creamy white flowers in spring. The saguaro, the largest tree of the American desert, reaches its greatest size and concentration in and around Saguaro National Monument, in southern Arizona. Following soaking rains, a saguaro's widespread root system draws in immense quantities of water—possibly as much as a ton—to store it for long dry spells.

The saguaro is an inseparable part of an entire life-community. The trunk provides shelter for spiders and lizards, home for woodpeckers and flickers, places to lay eggs and rear young. Even now, the Papago and Pima Indians, using a long forked stick, collect the egg-shaped fruits of the saguaro, just as their fathers before them; they either eat them fresh or make preserves and a heady beverage.

Though striking to the eye of the visitor, the saguaro now struggles desperately to survive. Hungry, thirsty rodents, avoiding the spiny armor, chew into the succulent tissues unmolested. Snakes, hawks, and owls

formerly kept the rodent population under control; but now the hunters have become the hunted, vanishing under human pressures. In addition, as a result of chronic overgrazing of livestock, seedlings are deprived of moisture-holding duff, so that only an occasional seed produces a plant. The effect of the saguaro decline will be felt on birds like the flicker, wren, and woodpecker.

The Chihuahuan desert lies mostly south of the border, with prongs into southeastern Arizona, New Mexico, and western Texas. It is nearly as extensive as the Great Basin. Its plant emblems are the narrow-leafed sotol and the lechuguilla, a small plant with yellow flowers. It spreads across ancient lava flows, lost rivers, an ancient inland lake, and dunes of white sand.

It seems impossible that any living thing could survive in the almost pure gypsum of White Sands National Monument in New Mexico, but yucca, the "candle of the gods," and other pioneer plants pin down the dunes with their roots; their decaying parts supply organic matter for other plants fighting the instability of the dunes and the high salt content. The animals of the gypsum dunes have adapted to life in a harsh setting.

These include the coyote, an animal pursued, trapped, shot, and poisoned throughout the desert kingdom, although he really bothers no one.

The great asset of desert is aridity. This is the main reason the Colorado Plateau alone has more than two dozen national parks and monuments, great landmarks of the West with their carved mesas, natural bridges, lava flows, meteor craters, and impressive cliffs. With a humid climate, the spectacular landforms and immensely colorful rocks would be concealed. Though shrinking under human demands, the desert retains much of its wilderness feature, with immeasurable values as a haven for people.

*   *   *   *   *

Desert, seashore, mountains, prairies—no matter where you travel in the nation you can see every aspect of the environment in the parks, monuments, and preserves of the National Park System. Through its enlightened attitude toward conservation of our natural treasures the Park Service will continue to fulfill its original purpose and will hold these precious gifts intact, not only for us but for all the generations to come.